HERITAGE STUDIES 6

Third Edition

bju press®

Greenville, South Carolina

Note: The fact that materials produced by other publishers may be referred to in this volume does not constitute an endorsement of the content or theological position of materials produced by such publishers. Any references and ancillary materials are listed as an aid to the student or the teacher and in an attempt to maintain the accepted academic standards of the publishing industry.

HERITAGE STUDIES 6
Third Edition

Authors
Peggy S. Alier
Marnie Batterman
Eileen M. Berry
James R. Davis
Annittia Jackson
Debra White

Second Edition Authors
Sharon Hambrick
Linda K. Hayner
Kimberly H. Pascoe
Stephanie Ralston
Dawn L. Watkins

Consultants
Dennis Bollinger
Kenneth Matesevac
James J. Swingle
Sherri H. Vick

Project Editors
Maria S. Dixson
Paul Michael Garrison

Bible Integration
Brian C. Collins
Bryan Smith

Page Layout
Bonnijean Marley

Project Managers
Faith Larson
Donald Simmons

Permissions
Sylvia Gass
Brenda Hansen
Joyce Landis

Cover Design
Peter Crane
Cathryn Pratt

Concept Design
Michael Asire
Cathryn Pratt

Page Design
Dan Van Leeuwen

Illustrators
Paula Cheadle
Preston Gravely
Keith Neely
Duane Nichols
Kathy Pflug
Dave Schuppert
Lynda Slattery
Del Thompson

Image credits appear on pages 455–57.

p. 34: Translation of Nabonidus Cylinder, The British Museum (http://www.mesopotamia .co.uk/ziggurats/explore/, Accessed 8/16/10.)

p. 36: Translation of brick of Ur-Nammu, The British Museum (http://www.mesopotamia .co.uk/ziggurats/story/, Accessed 8/16/10.) © Trustees of the British Museum.

p. 297: Diego de Landa, *Yucatan Before and After the Conquest*, trans. William Gates, (Baltimore: The Maya Society, 1937), 82

Produced in cooperation with the Bob Jones University School of Education, Bob Jones Academy, and BJU Press Distance Learning.

© 2012 BJU Press
Greenville, South Carolina 29614
First Edition © 1986 BJU Press
Second Edition © 1998, 2008 BJU Press

ISBN 978-1-59166-565-6

15   14   13   12   11   10   9   8   7   6   5   4   3   2   1

Handcrafted.

BJU Press employs a team of experienced writers and artists whose best work goes into every book we produce. Because of our emphasis on quality, our textbooks are the top choice in Christian education. Each book is designed to give your student a learning experience that is enjoyable, academically excellent, and biblically sound.

Contents

Chapters

Resource Treasury

Index

Chapter 1

In the Beginning

1. What are some of the false ideas about Moses and why he wrote the books of the Law?

2. What do Christians believe about prehistory?

Where Does History Come From?

Have you ever wondered how historians know what happened in the past? Most of the time they look for writings about what happened in the past. Sometimes they look for clues that can be dug out of the earth. By excavating an old city, historians might be able to tell what people used to eat, what kind of jobs they had, what they wore, and more.

But where did the first people come from? What did they do? How did they think? These are questions that many historians think are impossible to answer. No tomb has been discovered with a skeleton identified as "the first man." A writing that tells about the very beginning of history would be a valuable document.

Believe it or not, that document does exist. You might even read from it every day. If you open your Bible, you will see that the first words of the first verse say, "In the beginning." The Bible is the only completely reliable source that reveals how history began.

Of course, the Bible is more than just a historical source. It is the Word of God that tells us what we need to know about every aspect of life. Every word is true, and it stands above anything written by mere men. Some historians think the Bible is just a religious book. They think it might be useful for Christians, but they do not think it contains helpful historical information. Many people fail to see how important the Bible is for history.

Christians know that the Bible is God's Word. Who could be a better source for how history began than the God Who knows and controls all things?

The first book of the Bible was written by **Moses** around 3,500 years ago. As God's prophet, Moses wrote exactly what God wanted him to write.

BIOGRAPHY

Who: Moses

What: leader of the Israelites

Where: Egypt and the wilderness

Moses was born into a Hebrew slave family. The pharaoh's daughter found him in a basket on the Nile River. She raised him as her own son, and Moses grew up with all the benefits of the highest class in Egypt. At one time, Moses witnessed an Egyptian beating a Hebrew. Moses reacted and killed the Egyptian. Afraid because of what he had done, Moses fled to Midian, where he lived with a Midianite family. He became a shepherd and married Zipporah. The Lord spoke to Moses from a burning bush and ordered him back to Egypt to lead God's people from slavery.

Inspiration of the Books of the Law

The Bible tells us that all Scripture was given by **inspiration** of God (2 Tim. 3:16). This means that the Holy Spirit guided the men who wrote the Bible, breathing out God's words through them so that what they wrote is the Word of God.

The first five books of the Bible are known as the books of the Law. Other names for this section of the Bible are the Pentateuch and the Torah. Many verses in the Bible show us that Moses wrote these books. In the New Testament, Jesus Himself referred to Moses as their author when He said,

> These are the words which I spake unto you, while I was yet with you, that all things must be fulfilled, which were written in the law of Moses . . . concerning me (Luke 24:44).

Some people argue that the books are merely Hebrew folklore. Such people reject the biblical accounts that record miracles. But God is not limited to the natural laws of this world. He can cause a rod to become a snake or part the Red Sea.

Some say that Moses wrote the books to control the Hebrews for his own purposes. However, it would not make sense for Moses to include his own sins and shortcomings if this was his goal.

Others argue that Moses learned his religion from the Egyptians. But God's truth existed before the foundations of the world. False religions distort that truth. Moses received the truth from God Himself.

> And it came to pass, when Moses had made an end of writing the words of this law in a book, until they were finished, That Moses commanded the Levites, which bare the ark of the covenant of the Lord, saying, Take this book of the law, and put it in the side of the ark of the covenant of the Lord your God, that it may be there for a witness against thee (Deut. 31: 24–26).

3

PREHISTORY

Most history textbooks begin by talking about how humans evolved. To evolve means to change over time. The period when humans supposedly evolved is called **prehistory**. The term *prehistory* is used because no written records from that time exist. In fact, evolutionists do not believe that mankind had developed the ability to write during that period.

The story, as evolutionists tell it, begins with early human-like creatures that lived in East Africa about 3,500,000 years ago. At this time these creatures learned how to make simple stone tools. Then the creatures evolved to the point where they could stand upright and develop more advanced tools. Supposedly, around 250,000 years ago, these human-like creatures evolved into the earliest humans. The early humans continued to develop. Some began to carefully bury the dead. Evolutionists think this might be the first evidence of religion among humans. Other early humans began to paint the walls of the caves in which they lived.

During all this time the early humans gathered fruits and nuts or hunted for their food.

But around 12,000 years ago, as the evolutionary story goes, humans learned they could plant seeds and grow plants that they could eat. When they discovered this, humans began to settle down and build homes. They also began to tame animals to help them do work. Eventually, around 6,000 years ago, the first cities were developed. Soon humans learned to write. They created written records and history began.

However, there is no "prehistory" because the Bible is a written record that tells the history of the world from the very beginning. The Bible says that people were created directly by God around 6,000 or 7,000 years ago. It also says that humans could speak, and presumably write, from the very beginning. Agriculture and cities did not take thousands of years to develop. They appear in Genesis 4 in the first generations of people.

What skills and tools did Cain and Abel have and use early in the history of the world?

1. Why is history important?

2. What are the three major sources that a historian uses for studying history?

Why Study Ancient History?

History is a big story full of all kinds of smaller stories. Anyone who reads a novel or watches a movie understands the enjoyment of a good story. The study of history holds the same enjoyment with the benefit that the stories of history are based on fact.

The goal of most historians is to tell the true stories of the past. People can use these accounts from history to know how to live in the present and in the future. We can learn from the accomplishments as well as the mistakes of people in the past.

History is important because it teaches us about ourselves. What are people like? The most important way to answer this question is to look in the Bible to see what God says. That is the one sure way to know. Another way to learn about people is studying how they have acted for thousands of years.

History is also important because it provides an opportunity to praise God. Throughout history, God has used people and events to complete His sovereign or supreme plan. Recorded history shows the struggle of man against God. Man,

in his selfishness, continues to strive for power and resist God.

A good example of such a man was King Nebuchadnezzar in the book of Daniel. Nebuchadnezzar was a great and powerful ruler of Babylon. At one time, he even declared himself to be a god and expected everyone to worship him. God taught him some lessons about who is really in control of the world. This king learned that God is the sovereign Ruler over everything. He also learned that no one can question God or stop Him from doing His will both in heaven and on earth. By studying history, we can see the mighty acts of God through events and in the lives of people.

In the 1970s thousands of clay tablets were found at Ebla, an ancient city in what is now Syria. The information written on the tablets show that names of people and places recorded in the Old Testament are genuine. The name *Canaan* was in use in ancient Ebla. Critics had said that the name was used incorrectly in early chapters of the Bible. *Do Christians need such an artifact to know that the Bible is true?*

Modern view of the ruins of ancient Babylon

How Do We Study History?

How do historians learn about the past? The historian first must gather all the facts that he can find. He has three major sources for facts about the past. First, the historian studies *artifacts*, physical man-made objects from the past. These could include ancient pottery or artwork that an archaeologist finds at a site. Historians also study important buildings of the past or the ancient ruins of a city. These are all valuable clues about the past.

A second source for the historian is *tradition*, or the passing of information from generation to generation. In some cultures, people did not preserve memories of the past in writing. Instead they told about the past in stories and songs. These traditions were then passed on to later generations.

A third source for the historian is *written records*. Many people in the past recorded historical events of their time. These writings are primary sources, or firsthand accounts, and are valuable to historians. Other written primary sources that interest historians are private letters, diaries, official records of a kingdom, and records of births and deaths.

Written records are more important than artifacts or traditions. Artifacts need explanations to be understood, and traditions are often changed as they are passed on.

The gathering of information is just the beginning. A historian needs to evaluate the accuracy of the traditions and the written records he has gathered. Some historical accounts may present

St. Luke, Guido Reni, From the Bob Jones University Collection

A painting of Luke receiving inspiration from God to write the book of Luke

only one side of a story. For example, a written record by a Greek about a war with Persia may not accurately tell the Persian side of the story. But if the historian can find some Persian records that confirm the Greek record, then he will have more confidence in the accuracy of both sources.

Research, for the historian, presents challenges. Sometimes historians disagree about how to interpret evidence. These disagreements result from historians' differing worldviews. A person's **worldview** is how he sees and interprets the universe and everything in it. A Christian historian's worldview begins with the Bible. Someone who does not believe in the Bible will view evidence differently. Some non-Christian historians believe that early man was a primitive, ape-like creature. They do not believe that early man was advanced or had much intellect. The Christian historian believes that man was created in God's image and has always been intelligent. Shortly after Creation, people were inventing things such as musical instruments and metal tools (Gen. 4:21–22).

The historian also needs to understand what is important and what is not. If he is telling the story of how empires rose and fell in China, the design of Chinese dishes would probably not be relevant.

As the historian examines his sources, he can begin to see a picture of what happened in the past. He will look at written records and artifacts to explain what life may have been like at that time. He will look at the sequence of events in history to see how some events affected others. He will look for explanations for how and why events happened. Many of a historian's questions may get answered, and many others may not. A Christian historian, however, can remember that God, the Creator, knows and controls all things, including history (Col. 1:16–17).

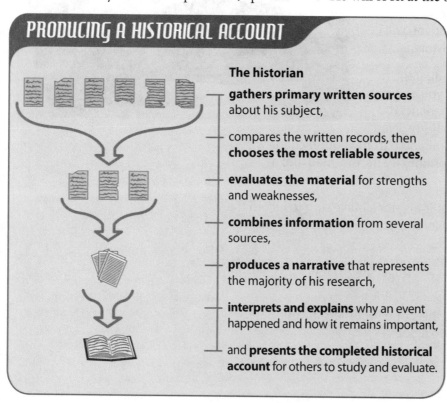

PRODUCING A HISTORICAL ACCOUNT

The historian

gathers primary written sources about his subject,

compares the written records, then **chooses the most reliable sources**,

evaluates the material for strengths and weaknesses,

combines information from several sources,

produces a narrative that represents the majority of his research,

interprets and explains why an event happened and how it remains important,

and **presents the completed historical account** for others to study and evaluate.

Recording History

Society today recognizes the importance of historical records. These records help us remember the peoples and significant events of the past. Many memorials and museums contain these records for visitors to view and experience for themselves.

Some families and communities have created their own recordings and journals of family histories to share with future generations. Your parents, your grandparents, and other adults in your church and community have interesting experiences from their pasts too.

Through this project you will help create a written history.

1. Ask a parent, grandparent, or other adult to tell you about something he experienced earlier in life. Perhaps he lived through a war, immigrated from another country, or saw his small community transformed into a modern city.

2. Take notes as he tells his story. Make sure to record the full name, birth date, and other information about the adult.

3. Type the story. Include photographs and other illustrations if they are available.

4. Add your story to the stories of others in your class. Combine them into a book.

Evaluating Historical Resources

Sources can be classified as primary or secondary. A primary source gives a first-hand, eyewitness account of an event. A secondary source usually contains information taken from a primary source.

Historians use these two kinds of sources to gain insight into the major events in history. Different authors have varying viewpoints of the same events. By gathering multiple sources and combining the information, historians can gain a more accurate picture of what occurred.

Stonehenge is a famous archaeological site in southern England.

1. Examine the sources provided by your teacher. Complete the chart to determine which are primary sources and which are secondary sources.

2. Determine the author's viewpoint or possible bias and record examples in the chart to support your opinion.

3. Discuss the strengths and weaknesses of your sources. Record them in a chart.

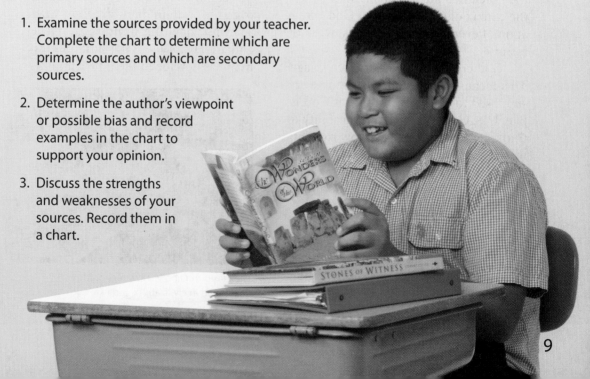

Creation

What happened "in the beginning"? At first there was nothing but God. No people. No animals. No earth. Then "in the beginning God created the heaven and the earth" (Gen. 1:1). In the first week of history, God created light and darkness; sky, sea, and soil; trees and plants; sun, moon, and stars; animals and man.

God created the world by speaking it into existence. There was no pain, suffering, or death. All He created was good. But God saved His masterpiece for last. He took the soil He had already created and with His own hands made man. He then breathed life into man. Man was the climax of God's creation. God's creation of everything was the first week of history.

God created man in His own image. This means that in some way people are supposed to be a picture of what God is like. Like God, people have the ability to think, love, use language, know right and wrong, and enjoy relationships.

God also created people with a job to do. Genesis 1:28 records what God told man and woman to do.

> Be fruitful, and multiply, and replenish the earth, and subdue it: and have dominion over the fish of the sea, and over the fowl of the air, and over every living thing that moveth upon the earth.

George Washington Carver developed over three hundred products from peanuts, such as cheese, dyes, and wood stains.
How did Carver demonstrate dominion over the earth?

History is all about man living out this command. People subdue, or rule over, the earth in many different ways. They use language, technology, science, and art. History tells the story of how man has developed these fields.

The computer shows how technology has developed in civilizations today.

FEATURES OF A CIVILIZATION

The word **civilization** comes from a Latin word that means "citizen of a city." A civilization is a group of people who have established cities, government, social classes, specialized jobs, arts, science, written language, and religion.

❑ **Organized cities and government**—Cities are central locations for government, religion, and culture. An organized government manages resources and provides defense, an economic system, and rules of conduct.

❑ **Social classes**—Within a civilization, there are social classes, or different levels that people are divided into. Each level, or class, of people has a different role.

❑ **Job specialization**—Each person or family focuses on a specific job or trade. They then rely on others to supply the goods and services to meet their other needs.

❑ **Arts, sciences, and written language**—As people work together in a civilization, they communicate through art, music, and written language. They also develop and use sciences, mathematics, and technology.

❑ **Religion**—The original people within a civilization usually share religious beliefs.

Roman theater at Ephesus in modern-day Turkey

As job specialization developed, some people became builders, architects, and musicians.

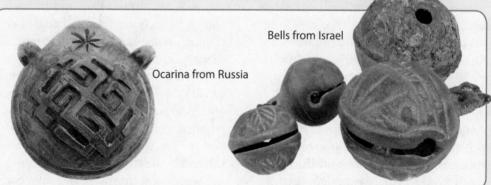

Bells from Israel

Ocarina from Russia

The Fall

Sadly, the story of history is not the story of people providing a beautiful picture of God. People have not used the abilities God gave them to rule wisely over the earth. Instead, our history includes bloody wars, heartless oppression, devastating diseases, and false religions.

Why is the story of history often so sad? The Bible answers this question in the book of Genesis.

The first humans, Adam and Eve, were created in God's image but were not equal to Him. God is the Creator, and Adam and Eve were His creation. Although God gave them **dominion**, or the authority to rule, over all the earth, He was still the King over all things.

One day, Satan, in the form of a serpent, tempted Eve to break the one law God had given to humans. If she and Adam broke that law, Satan told her, they would be like God in a new and special way. Eve and her husband, Adam, tried to become like God. They chose to break God's law.

But they did not become like God. Their disobedience brought sin, suffering, and death into the world. All the people after them were born sinners. People were supposed to picture what God is like, but their sin distorted that picture. The ability God gave man to rule over the earth was twisted for evil purposes. The breaking of God's law by Adam and Eve with the consequence of sin for them and all people is called the **Fall**.

History is now filled with the stories of men who sought to rule over the earth as if they were gods. In fact, some of them claimed to be gods. But their rule was not the good and caring rule that God intended mankind to have over the earth. They ruled harshly and selfishly.

For a civilization to prosper, it needs people who share the same values to work together. People use their different abilities to help the whole civilization succeed. But time and again history has shown how civilizations fall apart because of man's selfishness, pride, and rebellion toward God.

As a consequence of the Fall, God caused the earth to rebel against man's efforts to subdue it, just as people had rebelled against God's authority. Man planted crops to grow food, but the ground made this difficult by growing weeds and thorns. Man built roads and cities, only to have them destroyed

by floods, earthquakes, and volcanoes. Man built great civilizations, but wars, diseases, and plagues killed off the people.

Worst of all, people turned away from loving and worshiping the one true God. They made and worshiped gods in their own image.

RELIGION

Have you ever wondered where religions come from? Every civilization you will study in this book has a religion.

As God's creatures, people have within them the sense that there is a God and that He deserves to be worshiped and obeyed. This explains why religions exist worldwide. Atheism, a belief that there is no God, is something people have to talk themselves into. It is not the natural response of humans.

Even though people have been created with the knowledge that God exists, people cannot know God unless He speaks to them. The speech of God to man is found in the Old and New Testaments of the Bible.

False religions form when people reject God and His Word. These people reject the parts of the Truth they do not like. Then they use the parts they do like to create false religions and gods. Some religions develop from sinful human imaginations. These religions sometimes mix worship with evil practices. The Bible repeatedly tells of false religions and how God desires for people to put away their gods and worship Him alone (Deut. 30:2, 17–18).

Buddha statue in Thailand

Ganesha, a Hindu god, in Indonesia

Moai statues on Easter Island

Examining an Artifact

When studying some ancient civilizations, archaeologists must rely on their interpretation of artifacts to glean information. This is necessary when written records from those civilizations are not available. The main sources of information would have to be the everyday man-made objects, or artifacts, that are dug up. Archaeologists must attempt to understand the use of each artifact by examining its shape and size and the materials that were used to construct it. Studying where an artifact was located is important. Archaeologists also examine designs and decorations to gather information about the culture of the people who created and used them.

1. Examine the coin your teacher gives you. Imagine that you live thousands of years from now and have just uncovered this artifact. Record your observations about both sides of the coin.

2. Look at your list of observations and draw conclusions about the civilization that used this object. Think about the materials used to make the object as well as the symbols and languages on the coin.

3. Make a list of ten items from your house that could be used by a future archaeologist to determine something about you.

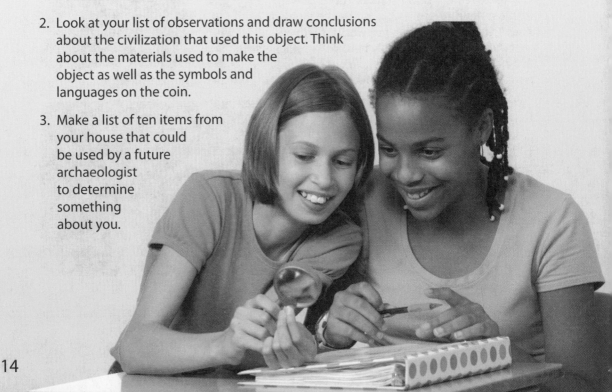

Abel obeyed God and offered a sacrifice that God accepted. Cain's unacceptable sacrifice showed his rebellious attitude toward God.

FOCUS

1. When did the history of redemption begin?

2. How did nations develop?

God's Promise of Redemption

History is not all bad news. Much of the Bible is history, but it is a special kind of history. The Bible traces the history of **redemption**. It tells how God has provided people with salvation from their sins.

The history of redemption began in the Garden of Eden when God told Satan that there would be hatred between Satan and Eve and between Satan's offspring and Eve's offspring. In the future, one of her offspring would defeat Satan entirely. Genesis 3:15 promises that God will provide salvation through a Man (Jesus Christ) Who will defeat Satan. It also outlines history as the struggle between God's people (the seed of the woman) and Satan's people (the seed of the serpent).

A World of Sin

Archaeological remains from before the Flood have not been found. Therefore, there are no historical records about the world before the Flood other than the Bible. Though Genesis does not reveal much about life before the Flood, it does tell us that the descendants of Adam and Eve's son Cain developed a civilization (Gen. 4:17). **Descendants** are generation after generation of people who originated from a certain person or group. Some of Cain's descendants worked in agriculture. Some developed the arts and made musical instruments, and others pioneered a tool-making industry.

Sadly, this first civilization followed Cain's rebellion against God and lived

FIGURATIVE LANGUAGE IN THE BIBLE

Some Bible verses use words as pictures or symbols. This use of words is an example of figurative language (a writing technique that expresses a different meaning from the literal word or phrase). For example, in John 10:9, Jesus says, "I am the door." He did not mean that He is literally a door. Instead He meant that He is the Way to salvation. *What other examples of figurative language from the Bible can you find on this page?*

away "from the presence of the Lord" (Gen. 4:16). As with all people, God had given Cain's descendants the ability to subdue the earth and to develop civilizations. But instead of doing this to please God, they followed the wicked example of their ancestor Cain.

Another son God gave Adam and Eve was named Seth. At first Seth and his descendants worshiped the Lord. But soon most of Seth's descendants also stopped following God, and the whole earth declined deeper into sinfulness.

The Flood

Mankind became so sinful and wicked that God was grieved that He had even made man. So God sent a **universal flood**, a flood that covered the entire earth. All the people died except for one man and his family.

Noah was a man who lived righteously, and God showed grace to him and his family. God gave Noah the task of building an ark that could house Noah's family and many animals. Noah's family included Noah; his wife; their sons, Ham, Shem, and Japheth; and the sons' wives.

After the Flood, Noah and his family saw that all previous civilizations had been washed away. God repeated the command that He had given Adam and Eve. He told Noah and his family to multiply and subdue the earth. Here was a fresh chance for God's people to rule the earth in God's way.

But a problem remained. Water could not wash away the sinfulness of the human heart—not even the water of a worldwide flood. Noah soon stumbled and sinned. And his son Ham was revealed to be a wicked man.

God used Noah to punish **Ham**. Noah prophesied that the descendants of Canaan, one of Ham's sons, would be slaves to the descendants of Shem and Japheth (Gen. 9:25).

At the same time that Canaan received his curse, **Shem** and **Japheth** each received a blessing. Shem's blessing was that his descendants would have a special relationship with God. Japheth's descendants would benefit from this blessing on Shem. In the future Shem's descendants, the nation of Israel, became God's special people. God would bless all other people through them.

BIOGRAPHY

Who: Noah

What: shipbuilder

Where: Israel

Noah was 480 years old when God told him to build the ark. Noah took 120 years to build it. The ark had no navigation system to guide it. All of the ark's movement was in the care of God.

"By faith Noah, being warned of God of things not seen as yet, moved with fear, prepared an ark to the saving of his house; by the which he condemned the world, and became heir of the righteousness which is by faith" (Heb. 11:7).

Rainbows

The spectacular colors of a rainbow are beautiful. It is fun to learn how the rainbow is formed. But it is the significance of God's promise to the world that should make the Christian stare in wonder at the rainbow. God gave the rainbow as a symbol of His promise to all life that He would not allow the earth to flood again (Gen. 9: 11–13). Thankfully, God's promise has nothing to do with man's behavior. It is a covenant of God's own goodness. A rainbow appears brightest when the clouds behind it are darkest. A Christian should be reminded that during life's greatest trials, he can rest assured that God will be true to His promises. And God's promises echo today whenever a rainbow is seen.

Babel and the Rise of Nations

After the Flood, descendants of Noah's sons gathered in the plain of Shinar (SHY nahr). These people began to build the city that would later be called Babel. They planned to build a great tower. Their reasons for doing this are revealed in Genesis 11:4, which says "Go to, let us build us a city and a tower, whose top may reach unto heaven; and let us make us a name, lest we be scattered abroad upon the face of the whole earth."

God decided to stop these people from carrying out their plan. At that time all the people of the world spoke the same language. God caused the people of Babel to speak multiple languages so they could not understand each other. Because they could no longer communicate as one group, they could not work together. The people were forced to abandon the construction of the tower. They formed groups that spoke the same languages, and these groups scattered throughout the earth.

Genesis 10 records the descendants of Noah's sons and where their nations developed. Ham's descendants founded nations in the Far East, in Africa, and along the eastern coast of the **Mediterranean Sea**. Shem's descendants formed nations along the Persian Gulf and in the Middle East. Japheth's descendants

migrated, or moved, to what is now Turkey and eastern Europe.

History is the story of nations rising and falling in accordance with God's sovereign will. Throughout history one nation after another has sought to be the greatest. If a nation conquered and ruled over other nations, another nation would fight for that power. It is God's mercy to man that He directs the fall of great civilizations that do not follow Him. By ending a civilization, God keeps man from much of his destructive sinfulness.

Through the Israelites, God provided for mankind's salvation. The history of Israel shows how God fulfilled His promise to Eve to crush the "head of the serpent." God's own Son, Jesus Christ, provided redemption through His death on the cross.

As you study the different civilizations of the past, you will look at how man's history fits together with redemptive history and how the kingdom of God, Christ's kingdom, will subdue all the kingdoms of man.

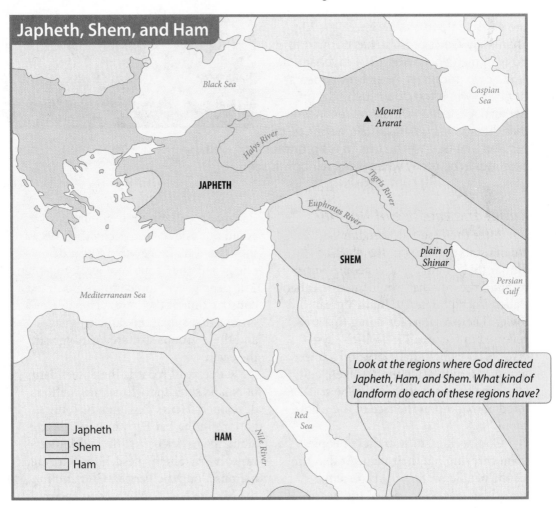

Japheth, Shem, and Ham

Black Sea

Caspian Sea

Mount Ararat

Halys River

JAPHETH

Tigris River

Euphrates River

SHEM

plain of Shinar

Persian Gulf

Mediterranean Sea

Look at the regions where God directed Japheth, Ham, and Shem. What kind of landform do each of these regions have?

Red Sea

Nile River

HAM

☐ Japheth
☐ Shem
☐ Ham

Chapter 2

Mesopotamia

Sumerian Civilization

Geography

The period of history in this chapter begins after God multiplied the languages. Shem's descendants migrated along the **Tigris River** and the **Euphrates** (yoo FRAY teez) **River**. These rivers flowed down from the mountains into a plain that historians call **Mesopotamia** (mes uh puh TAY mee uh). This name comes from a Greek word that means "between the rivers." The region Mesopotamia is considered the cradle of civilization. The earliest evidence of agriculture, written language, and cities was discovered there.

Mesopotamia was part of a larger region that historians call the **Fertile Crescent**. This was a curved area from the Persian Gulf to the Mediterranean Sea. Its fertile land was good for farming.

Over time villages in Mesopotamia expanded into cities. The cities became the civilization that archaeologists and historians call **Sumer** (SOO muhr).

Archaeology

Archaeologists study artifacts to find clues about the Sumerian people. For instance, a woman's jewelry could give clues to whether she was rich and powerful or poor but inventive. Many artifacts are found during a dig, when archaeologists excavate a historic site.

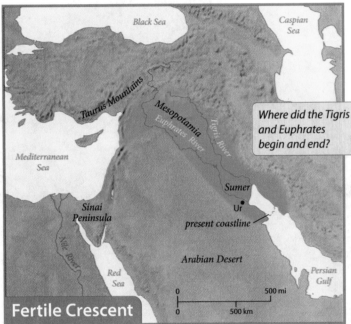

Where did the Tigris and Euphrates begin and end?

Fertile Crescent

Every dig needs experts in history, archaeology, architecture, translation, photography, and drawing. These experts try to interpret and preserve what is found.

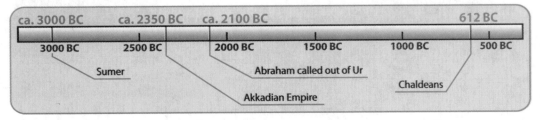

| ca. 3000 BC | ca. 2350 BC | ca. 2100 BC | | | 612 BC |

Sumer

Abraham called out of Ur

Chaldeans

Akkadian Empire

Archaeology and the Old Testament

Many secular archaeologists and historians assume that Sumer was one of the first civilizations. They do not believe the Bible's account of a worldwide flood destroying previous civilizations. Although no artifacts have been found from before the Flood, the Bible informs us that civilizations before the Flood did exist. These early civilizations were quite advanced. Genesis records that the people who lived before Noah built cities. They were skilled musicians and workers in brass and iron. They knew much about agriculture.

Archaeological evidence has proved many skeptical views of the Bible wrong. For example, people believed that the story of Abraham was a myth. The Bible states that Rebekah rode to meet Isaac on a camel. Researchers assumed that camels would not have been used as beasts of burden during Abraham's time, but records from Sumerian tablets show that camels were indeed ridden.

Archaeologists also discovered many skeletons in caves around Ur. The same burial caves were used by Sumerians for generations. This explains the biblical phrase "gathered to his people." Thus, Abraham's sons were following a common custom when they buried him.

Sometimes a dig is chosen by the presence of a tell. A **tell** is a mound made up of layered dirt and the remains of earlier buildings and structures. *Tell* comes from the Arabic word for "high."

Work at a dig begins with surveys of the site. These surveys are done on the ground or from the air. Archaeologists use the information from these surveys to draw a map and section off the area into squares. Today archaeologists often use computers to map the area, make calculations, and keep records. The actual digging is done slowly by hand, a layer at a time. Everyone must work carefully to avoid damaging fragile objects. When an object is found, it is photographed, labeled, and recorded.

In the 1850s British archaeologists discovered Mesopotamian artifacts in

Leonard Woolley's team excavated Pit X during the years 1933–34. Its final depth was about 60 feet (18 m). This site near the Royal Cemetery revealed hundreds of burials (left). A modern archaeological dig (above).

day used canals to irrigate their fields. They grew grain and vegetables and sold wool to other countries. Some people were weavers or metalworkers, and some studied medicine or the stars.

Iraq. Most archaeologists believed that the site where the artifacts were found was the biblical city of Ur. In 1922 a British archaeologist named **Sir Leonard Woolley** began excavating the site. He successfully uncovered many treasures from Ur and from the land of Sumer. Evidence from archaeological digs reveals that Sumer appears to have been one of the earliest civilizations after the Flood.

Objects that were long hidden under the soil tell us about the Sumerians. From them we know that Ur was a grand place surrounded by high walls. It boasted huge palaces and plazas. People of Abraham's

BIOGRAPHY

Who: Sir Leonard Woolley

What: archaeologist

When: Apr. 17, 1880–Feb. 20, 1960

Where: Great Britain

During World War I, British intelligence officer Woolley was a prisoner in Turkey. Being an expert in Mesopotamian studies, he was knighted in 1935 for his contributions to modern archaeology.

1. How did agricultural techniques affect the growth of cities?

2. What was the occupation of most Sumerians?

The Rise of Sumer
Agriculture

Planting

The Tigris and the Euphrates carried a fine, fertile soil called silt down from the mountains. When the rivers flooded, they spread silt across the plains. The fertile soil left behind made the land good for farming.

Early Sumerian farmers used sticks to poke holes in the ground. Then the farmers dropped seeds into each hole. This was hard, slow work. Later the Sumerians developed plows as a better way of preparing the soil for planting. Early plows were pieces of wood that made long, shallow trenches in the soil. It was much easier for farmers to drop seeds into a trench than into individual holes. The plow also loosened the soil so the roots of the crops could grow more easily.

Eventually farmers found that hitching oxen to the plows helped prepare even more land for planting. A pair of oxen was hitched to a plow with a yoke. Use of this tool was first recorded in Sumer. The yoke helped the oxen pull a plow or a heavy wagonload.

Sumerian farmers were also the first known people to use the wheel. Pulling a heavy load on a cart with wheels was much easier than dragging that same load on a cart without wheels.

The Sumerian farmers grew nearly all the barley, wheat, sesame seeds, flax, vegetables, and dates that the Sumerian people needed. The farmers who owned their own land sold their harvests in the city market. Many farmers did not own their own land but worked on land owned by the temple or by wealthy individuals. These farmers received part of the harvest to use or sell.

Flood Control

Outside the great city of Ur, farmers worked hard in the fields. Farming was not always easy. Mesopotamia had fertile soil, but the crops also needed water.

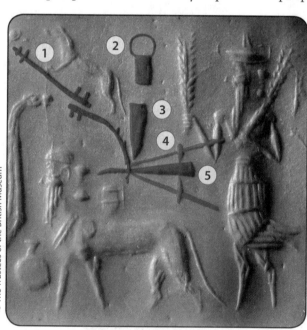

Agricultural tools on a detail of a cylinder seal from Mesopotamia: (1) yoke, (2) seed bag, (3) seed funnel, (4) handle, and (5) plow share

RIVER CIVILIZATIONS

Early people settled in river valleys for several reasons. The lands close to the rivers were flat, making it easier for farmers to plant crops. The rivers nourished the soil and made it fertile. The rivers also provided fish to eat and fresh water to drink. The rivers served as highways on which people could travel from one place to another, exchanging goods and ideas.

Some years the right amount of rain fell. But more often, the region received either so little rain that the crops withered from the heat or so much rain that the crops were destroyed from flooding. Sometimes floods killed livestock and washed away homes.

To help control the destruction of floods, the Sumerians built levees. These were raised areas of earth that held back the flood waters. The levees protected the Sumerian homes as well as their crops.

Irrigation

Most of the area beyond the rivers was desert. During the summer, the ground became dry and hard under the hot sun. With no rain for months, plants died and winds from the mountains blew the sand.

To help solve this problem, the Sumerians developed **irrigation** (ihr uh GAY shuhn) as a way of supplying water to an area of land or crops. They built storage basins to hold water supplies. Then they dug canals, or man-made waterways, to carry water from the river. The canals allowed the farmers to plant crops in locations that were far from the river. With irrigation a farmer could keep his crops alive throughout the dry summer. The Sumerians had few natural

© Werner Forman/Art Resource

This ancient impression from a Sumerian cylinder seal shows a man leading animals from a gate.

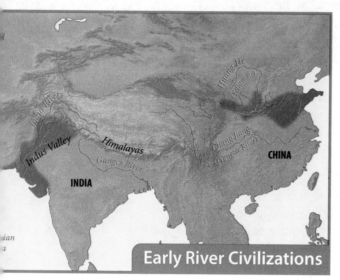

Early River Civilizations

kept order. Craftsmen made goods. Job specialization allowed people to develop new skills. These skills helped to create and maintain the civilization.

Some farm settlements grew into villages, and villages grew into cities. Although most people worked on farms, cities became important places. Each Sumerian city developed into a **city-state**. A city-state was made up of the city and the surrounding land and villages that it controlled. It had its own government and laws. Its people worshiped gods that were special to that city.

Some city-states wanted more power. They fought other city-states for more farmland and water. Because of these battles, the city-states formed strong armies. The people built thick walls around their cities for protection. During Abraham's lifetime, **Ur** was a powerful Sumerian city-state.

resources, so they made good use of the crucial resource of water.

Farmers were also able to use irrigation to water their animals. Cattle and sheep grazed in the fields. Donkeys and oxen worked in the fields and transported heavy loads. Goats, pigs, and sheep supplied meat as well as hides and wool.

Irrigation is still an essential part of farming. Modern farmers use different methods to water their crops. Some farmers use canals to direct water to their fields. Others, like some farmers in the United States, use sprinkler irrigation. This method is similar to watering your lawn with a sprinkler.

Sumerian City-States

The development of the plow and of irrigation helped to increase the amount of food the farmers could grow. They produced a food **surplus**, or more than what was needed. Because of the surplus, fewer people needed to farm. New occupations developed as people began working at specialized jobs and trades.

Priests performed religious activities. Rulers governed the people. Soldiers

An oil painting by Maurice Bardin of Babylon
What characteristics of a civilization do you see pictured?

Making a Book Jacket

When you buy a new hardback book, it may come with a paper book jacket. The jacket helps spark interest in reading the book . The front cover includes the book's title, the names of the author and the illustrator, and often an illustration or a photograph. A brief summary of the book's contents is on the back cover or on the inside flaps. Sometimes the cover includes reviews of the book. These reviews are usually positive comments from writers or critics who have read the book. The flaps may also contain information about the author and the illustrator of the book.

1. Work with a partner to choose a Mesopotamian invention or achievement that had an impact on history. Your choice may come from the chapter or from research.

2. Imagine that the invention or achievement you chose is the subject of a book. Design a book jacket for that book.

3. Write a rough draft of the summary and other information for the back cover and the flaps.

4. Make a neat copy of the summary and information. Add the summary and information to the book jacket.

5. Add an illustration and title to the front of the book jacket. Include your names as the authors.

6. Share or display the completed book jacket.

Date palms commonly grew in large groves, similar to those seen here. Remains of dates were found in the excavation at Ur. This fruit was often featured in the art of Mesopotamia.

FOCUS

1. Which social class was the largest in Sumerian society?

2. What kinds of artisans were in Sumer?

Society

One feature of early civilizations was the development of social classes. **Social classes** are different levels of a culture into which people are divided. The Sumerian civilization had three classes. Each class had a different role. The upper class consisted of the ruler, governmental officials, and priests. These people had the most power. The middle class was the largest class. It consisted of farmers, fishermen, merchants, traders, and skilled workers.

Slaves were in the lowest class. They were common in Sumer. Slaves were forced to serve others and were thought of as property. Some slaves were prisoners of war; others were criminals. Some people became slaves to pay off their debts. Despite being under the rule of masters, slaves had certain privileges. Slaves could hold property or go into business. Sumerian slaves could eventually purchase their own freedom.

27

This boat model, made of a mixture of soil and bitumen (a kind of tar), came from a grave in an Ur cemetery. Model boats have been found in other graves. Compare this model with the modern boats being used in the photo on page 27.

Fishermen, Merchants, and Traders

The Sumerians were among the first people to use sails for harnessing the wind to move boats. Many boats sailed on the Euphrates River. Some were trading ships that had come from faraway places. Others were fishing boats owned by local fishermen. Every day that fishermen went to the river, they returned home to sell their catches at the city market. Fish and bread were important foods in the Sumerians' diet.

At the edge of the city of Ur, on the Euphrates River, stood the docks where trading ships and fishing boats were anchored. Dockworkers, merchants, traders, and sailors conducted their business there. Ships brought goods from as far away as India in the east and Egypt in the west. The ships were loaded with gems, wood, stone, and metal—goods for the workshops of Ur. Why do you think Sumer imported these goods? Because it had none of them as natural resources.

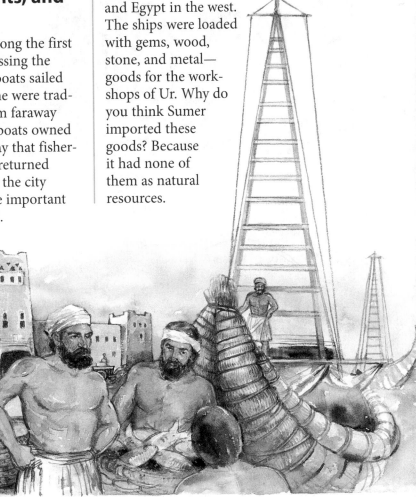

Cylinder seal (above) and impressions from seal (left)

Early trade in Sumer was conducted by barter. Barter is a trading system in which people exchange goods without money. A merchant might trade his grain for another item, such as lumber or copper. Often a food surplus in one city-state was traded for a different kind of good in another city-state. Trade helped city-states grow in wealth and power.

Trading with other countries was essential to the growth of a civilization. Besides the people of Sumer, other groups of people in the world were organizing into civilizations. These groups of people traded with Sumer.

The Sumerians kept careful records of all their business dealings. People who recorded information in writing were called **scribes**. Using a reed stylus, a pointed writing tool, scribes wrote down sales on soft clay tablets. After a scribe recorded a sale, he allowed the tablet to dry. Then he wrapped it in another piece of clay that served as an envelope. The tablet was stored in the temple with other legal records. From these careful records archaeologists have learned much about Sumerian economics.

When two merchants finished a business deal and the scribe put his last marks on the tablet, each man had to sign it. They did not use the scribe's stylus to write their names. Rather they used clay seals shaped like cylinders. This kind of **cylinder seal** was small, only about one to two inches long and about a half-inch in diameter. It had carvings that identified the owner. The carvings could include plants, animals, gods, and wedge-shaped symbols. Each man rolled his seal across the wet clay tablet to approve the sale. The cylinder seal was a fast, simple way to sign one's name. The mark of a cylinder seal stood either for approval, as on a legal document, or for ownership, as on goods ready to be shipped.

Artisans and Buyers

Unloaded goods did not stay long at the docks. Workers gathered them up and took them into the city.

In the center of Ur, **artisans**, or skilled craftsmen, turned raw materials into finished goods. These products made up most of Sumer's exports. Archaeologists have found records and remains of jewelry, pottery, clothing, and other objects made in the artisans' shops.

Many of the workshops in Ur produced goods for everyday use. Some of

Over the centuries the ancient method of making pottery has not changed much. The designs of pitchers, bowls, cups, and plates are also much the same. In this region potters still work at their wheels. Today tourists can buy the beautiful pottery as souvenirs. Ships transport these lovely works of art to countries that did not even exist when Abraham left Ur.

The city of Ur also had shops that made luxury goods. The artisans trained for many years to learn the skills for making beautiful objects. They made jewelry and fine dishes from the copper, silver, gold, and precious jewels imported into Sumer. The finished pieces, intricately and beautifully designed, were either sold in Ur or shipped to other cities and lands.

A special craft in Ur was shell inlay. An artisan used white shells from the river and arranged them into a design. He made sure the pieces fit together,

the busiest shops in the city were those that sold cloth. The cloth makers employed many women to spin thread from flax or wool and then weave it into cloth. The people of Ur bought their cloth at one shop, had it dyed at another, and then took it home to make clothing.

After leaving a cloth maker's shop, a shopper in Ur might have stopped at a pottery workshop. Clay was one of the few raw materials that was plentiful in the river valley. The potters busily threw clay onto their wheels and formed pots. Sumerians were possibly the first people to use the wheel to make clay pots. Before that time, pots were either molded or coiled by hand. The potter's wheel allowed a potter to produce pots of uniform size and shape faster than before. Potters in Ur made all sorts of containers for storing and serving food. The potters added carvings and decorations to make the pots attractive as well as useful.

A modern Iranian potter shapes a vase as it rotates on his potter's wheel. This trade has been in his family for generations.

What was the economy like in Sumer? Farming was the main economic source. Farmers grew everything they needed and then sold their food surpluses. Many people worked for owners of farms. Trade was very important. Skilled artisans turned raw materials from foreign countries into finished goods. These goods were exported to other countries.

When the United States was being settled, it had an economy similar to Sumer's. Colonists were sent to the Americas to provide raw materials for countries in Europe. The Sumerians had turned raw materials into finished goods themselves. But the colonists shipped raw materials abroad, where they were made into goods. The goods were then shipped back to the Americas to be sold.

The American people eventually began to cultivate wheat, corn, tobacco, indigo, and rice. These crops became the people's exports. Because America had many natural resources and hard-working people, the country became the wealthiest nation in the world.

almost like pieces of a puzzle. Once satisfied with his design, he pressed the pieces into softened tar on another surface, such as metal. After the main design was finished, he may have surrounded it with a bright blue stone called lapis lazuli (LAHP-is LAZ-uh-lee). A shell inlay artisan had to be patient and careful. Some works of sparkling white shells and lapis lazuli inlay still exist and show the high quality of Sumerian workmanship.

The Granger Collection, New York

Sumerian necklaces of carnelian, lapis lazuli, and gold

Echoes from the Past

The Standard of Ur

Detail from "War" panel
What advancement in technology helped the army in war?

Leonard Woolley excavated at the Tell el-Muqayyar, also known as the ancient city of Ur. In one of the largest graves in the Royal Cemetery, Woolley uncovered a wooden box. The weight of the soil had crushed the sides of the box together. The box was later restored to what was possibly its original appearance. Today it is on display in the British Museum. Although the box's original purpose is unknown, Woolley thought the box may have been carried on a pole as a standard, or a flag. That is why today the box is called the Standard of Ur.

The artisan who made the box used shell inlay with red limestone and lapis lazuli to create the scenes on the sides, or panels, of the box. The two larger panels are known as "War" and "Peace." The "War" panel shows a Sumerian army with cloaked infantry carrying spears and chariots being pulled by donkeys. This piece is one of the earliest representations of a Sumerian army. The "Peace" panel shows a banquet scene with a procession of people bringing animals and goods.

The shell inlay work of the Sumerian artisans is "echoed" in modern-day products such as guitars, jewelry boxes, hair combs, and furniture.

"Peace" panel

FOCUS

1. Where was the center of religion in a Sumerian city-state?

2. Who ruled the city-states?

Priests and Religion

Religion played a role in almost every aspect of Mesopotamian life. The Mesopotamians worshiped their gods by praying to them, giving them gifts, and performing rituals. They believed that if the gods were pleased, the people would prosper. If the gods were not pleased, disaster would strike. Religious rituals and prayers accompanied all the Mesopotamians' activities, no matter how ordinary.

The Mesopotamian religion was a clear rejection of the one true God. The Mesopotamians practiced **polytheism**, the worship of many gods. The gods they worshiped were made up by men. The people believed that the gods ate, slept, and married just like people. Unlike people, the gods supposedly lived forever.

In the center of Ur stood an impressive pyramid-like structure called a **ziggurat** (ZIG uh rat). This temple could be seen by people approaching the city while they were still a long distance away.

A ziggurat usually had three to seven terraced levels with a shrine or a tiny temple on top. A couch or bed was placed in the shrine for the god to rest on. Gardens were planted on each terrace. The bricks were often covered with tiles or painted to make the levels different colors. In an area beside the ziggurat, there were homes for the high priest and the priestess, a storehouse, and additional chambers.

The ziggurat at Ur was originally built by a king named Ur-Nammu (uhr NAHM oo). He built the ziggurat in honor of the moon god. A later king, Nabonidus, rebuilt the ziggurat and made some changes. How do you think archaeologists later knew about these architects? In 1864 the archaeologist J. E. Taylor began an excavation at the temple site. He found four cylinders, one at each corner of the ziggurat. The text on one of these

Today the reconstructed ziggurat in Ur can be seen from a great distance.
What does the size of the ziggurat say about the importance of religion to the people?

One of the four cylinders found at the corner of the ziggurat at Ur

cylinders was a record of the ziggurat's architects.

> I am Nabonidus, king of Babylon, patron of Esagila and Ezida, devotee [follower] of the great gods. . . . Now that ziggurat had become old, and I undertook the construction of that ziggurat on the foundations which Ur-Nammu and his son Shulgi built following the original plan with bitumen and baked brick.

The Mesopotamians worshiped hundreds of gods. Each god had a name and a responsibility. Every city-state had its own god or goddess. In Ur one god the

MESOPOTAMIAN BELIEFS

Mesopotamians practiced polytheism. Their many gods were invented by man and were false. The Bible teaches that there is only one true God.

Mesopotamians believed that the earth was born of a sea that surrounded it on all sides. The Bible teaches that God created the heavens and the earth in six days.

Mesopotamians believed that man was created to serve the gods and provide them with food, clothing, and shelter. The Bible teaches that man was created in God's image to have dominion over the earth and to glorify and serve God alone.

Mesopotamians generally believed that a person's fate was decay and dust. The Bible teaches that those who trust Christ to save them from their sins will spend eternity with Him. All others will be judged eternally for their sins.

people worshiped was the moon god Nanna. His statue was kept in the ziggurat's shrine, and food was offered to him

Some of Mesopotamia's Gods				
	Sumerian name	Akkadian name	City	Responsibility
Morning and evening star goddess	Inanna	Ishtar	Uruk	goddess of love and war
Sun god	Utu	Shamash	Larsa and Sippar	lord of truth and justice
Freshwater god	Enki	Ea	Eridu	lord of wisdom, magic, and arts and crafts
Storm god	Ishkur	Adad	several cities	lord of thunder and rain

A people called the Akkadians later conquered Sumer. They worshiped many of the same gods as the Sumerians but called the gods by different names.

Historians call this statue worshiper the "Little Priest." His shaved head and beardless face are typical of Mesopotamian priests. He stands in a worshiping position, with his arms folded in front of him and his eyes wide open in awe.

daily. The priests and priestesses who lived at the temple sacrificed animals and followed rituals, believing this would keep the god happy.

The people believed that several gods controlled parts of the universe, such as the sky, the sun, and the air. They were considered the main gods.

People relied on the priests to help gain the favor of the gods. The priests also interpreted the wishes of the gods. The people were taught that only priests could communicate with the gods. This made the priests powerful people in Mesopotamian society. The priests and priestesses controlled much of the land.

The hundreds of Mesopotamian gods required constant worship. Archaeologists think that the people may have placed statues of worshipers in temples. These statues would have stood in continuous prayer while their owners went about their daily lives. Placing the statues in the temple was a convenient way for the people to provide constant worship.

Kings and Government

A civilization needs a well-organized government to manage its resources. When the Mesopotamians began to live in cities, a large portion of the population stopped growing its own food. The people who continued to farm needed to grow enough food to trade with those who did not farm. This required a manager to make sure everyone was able to get food.

Sumer was made up of several city-states that often fought each other for more land and power. At first the priest of a city-state tried to pick the best military leader to defend that city-state in battle. After the fighting was over, the leader was expected to return to normal life. Some of these leaders held on to their positions and became rulers. This was the beginning of kings.

Eventually every city-state had its own king. The king was considered a god's highest representative on earth. The Sumerians believed that a god selected the king, giving him rightful authority. To stay in power the king needed the approval of the priest. A king respected the priest, and the priest acknowledged

that king as the god's choice to rule the city-state.

The temple was important not only as the center of religion but also as the seat of the Sumerian government. The king took over some of the jobs once done by the priests. He directed the building of new canals, temples, and roads. Each king served as the chief lawmaker and judge. Some kings wrote down laws and ruled by them. In Ur a lawbreaker often had to pay fines as a punishment. For example, if a man cut off another man's foot or nose, he paid the injured man a certain amount of silver.

Legal records were required for all business transactions, contracts, marriages, adoptions, and wills. Archaeologists have found many of Sumer's records, still in their clay envelopes, filed in the temples.

Archaeologists often identify a building by reading stamped bricks. The brick can provide information about the type of building, the name of the city, which god was worshiped, and who was king. This brick of Ur-Nammu reads, "For his lady Inanna, Ur-Nammu, the mighty man, the king of Ur, the king of Sumer and Akkad, built her temple."
What information do we learn from this brick?

This bronze and copper statue of King Ur-Nammu was found in a box buried beneath the temple of Enlil. Small pieces of gold, carnelian, and lapis lazuli were also found in the box. In the basket the king carries the clay for the first brick of the temple.

Ruins of the temple complex in Ur

Advances and Inventions

Sumerians had many advances in technology. The people of Sumer developed many things that still affect our lives today. You have already read about the plow, the wheel, irrigation, the potter's wheel, and the sail.

Writing

As you may recall, written language is one important feature of a civilization. Sumerians developed one of the earliest writing systems.

Early writing in Sumer used picture symbols or signs that were drawn on clay tablets. As time passed, the picture symbols were gradually replaced with wedge-shaped characters. This wedge-shaped writing was later known as **cuneiform** (kyoo NEE uh form). *Cuneiform* comes from the Latin words for "wedge-shaped."

Over the centuries the placement of written symbols also changed. They were written in boxes, rows, or columns. Evidence shows that a symbol could represent an entire word or only a syllable. Scribes combined symbols to express more complex ideas. For example, the Sumerian word for barley was *she*. The symbol for barley could then represent the sound "she" in any word. In the Sumerian word for fig cake, *she-er-ku*, the barley symbol represented the word's first syllable.

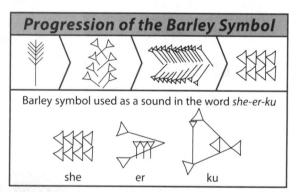

Progression of the Barley Symbol

Barley symbol used as a sound in the word *she-er-ku*

she   er   ku

Different peoples used the cuneiform script to record information. Cuneiform was used in the Sumerian, Akkadian, Hittite, and Urartian languages.

Cylinder seals were rolled across both the clay tablet and the envelope of this legal document. *Why do you think the tablet and the envelope were both impressed with seals?*

Discovering How

Writing Cuneiform and Making a Cylinder Seal

Scribes were important people. In addition to keeping track of items for merchants, they kept records for the temple and the government. From these careful records we have learned much about Sumerian life.

A scribe would record transactions on a clay tablet in cuneiform and place it in a clay envelope. The envelope was marked with a cylinder seal for security so that the information inside could not be changed. When the tablet dried, it was stored in the temple with other legal records.

Part 1: Writing Cuneiform

1. Get a styling tool, clay, and the page from your teacher.

2. Form the clay into a flat square about 1/2 inch thick.

3. Find the letters of your initials on the chart. Press the wedge-shaped marks that represent your initials on your clay tablet. Allow it to dry.

Part 2: Making a Cylinder Seal

1. Create a design for a cylinder seal on your page. Keep in mind that small details will not show up very well.

2. Shape your clay into a cylinder about 2 inches long and 1 inch wide. With your styling tool, press the reverse of your design around the clay cylinder. Remember that the indentations you make will produce raised areas when the hardened cylinder is used on soft clay. Let the cylinder harden.

3. On another day make small tablets with soft clay. Roll your cylinder seal over a clay tablet to imprint your design.

FOCUS

1. What similar legends do most ancient civilizations have?

2. Why did Mesopotamian houses have thick walls?

Math and Sciences

The different civilizations of Mesopotamia developed mathematical ideas still used today. These people were the first to recognize the concept of zero and to give a number a place value. They developed a number system based on the number 60. They gave us our 60-minute hour, 60-second minute, and 360° circle. They also used geometry to measure fields and to build temples.

Mesopotamians studied the sciences as well. They made important contributions to the field of astronomy, the study of stars and heavenly bodies. However, they did not recognize the true God to Whom the heavens declare glory. Instead they tried to interpret human events by the position of the stars and the planets. Interpreting events in this way is called astrology. The position of the stars does not determine what will happen. God determines what will happen.

The Mesopotamians divided the year into two seasons—summer and winter. Using the cycles of the moon, they developed a twelve-month calendar. They also made advances in medicine, such as making a list of symptoms with a diagnosis for each of those symptoms.

WHEELS

The Sumerians used wheeled vehicles such as carts and wagons. They used the potter's wheel to spin clay into bowls, pots, and vases. Try to imagine life without the wheel. How would you get to church, school, or the library? The ancient achievement of the wheel affects our lives today. Wheelchairs, inline skates, tractors, bicycles, and airplanes all depend on the wheel.

Ancient pull toy

39

Arts and Architecture

Music

The Mesopotamians enjoyed music. Musicians played drums, tambourines, reed pipes, and stringed instruments called lyres. Kings hired musicians to play at special occasions. Music was important to religious rituals and daily work. People sang to the gods and to the kings. Music provided entertainment in the homes and the marketplaces.

Literature

Cuneiform helped the Sumerians record stories, proverbs, and poems about their gods and military victories. A well-known Mesopotamian poem is the *Epic of Gilgamesh* (GIL guh MESH). An **epic** is a long poem that tells the story of a hero. This epic describes the adventures of the legendary hero Gilgamesh and his search for eternal life.

In one part of the epic, Gilgamesh meets Utnapishtim (OOT nah PEESH teem). Utnapishtim tells Gilgamesh about how the god Enlil had been angry and had decided to cover the earth with water. Another god, Ea, had helped Utnapishtim by delivering him and his family from the universal flood. Ea had given him these instructions:

Tear down (this) house, build a ship!
Give up possessions, seek thou life.
Despise property and keep the soul alive!
Aboard the ship take thou the seed of all
living things.

Utnapishtim tells how he had built a ship and had gathered aboard his family, the craftsmen who had helped him, and the animals of the field. The rains and the

A bull-headed lyre
What instrument is the lyre similar to?

flood had raged for six days and nights and had stopped on the seventh day.

Most ancient civilizations had similar stories. In all these stories a great flood nearly destroys the human race, but it is saved by a person similar to Noah. For the Christian, these similarities support the truth of the biblical account of Noah and the universal Flood. These similarities reveal that various civilizations remembered Noah and the Flood. God ensured that this event was recorded accurately in Genesis 6–8. As other civilizations abandoned God, their records of the Flood mixed with their own myths, creating the different accounts.

Arts

The Mesopotamians were wonderful artisans. They created statues of gods for their temples. You have already seen several examples of their statues in earlier

Some archaeologists attribute the invention of glass-making to the Mesopotamians.

photographs. Because the Mesopotamians did not have the natural resource of stone, they did not have large stone sculptures. They made beautiful things with the materials they did have. They made jewelry of gold and lapis lazuli. They created colorful mosaics in beautiful patterns using little pieces of painted clay. Archaeologists have found remains of mosaics, helmets, lyres, jewelry, and decorated tablets. Perhaps the Mesopotamians' most famous works of art are the cylinder seals.

Architecture

The climate and natural resources available determined what types of buildings were constructed in Mesopotamia. Wood was in short supply and stone was not available, so buildings were constructed with bricks made of mud. Over the centuries rains and shifting sands destroyed much of Mesopotamia's mud-brick architecture. Archaeologists have not found as many buildings in Mesopotamia as in other ancient civilizations.

The *arch* and the *column* were developed by the Mesopotamians. They were some of the first people to use domes. These elegant architectural features were found in temples and wealthy homes.

Mesopotamians built thick walls around their cities for defense. The walls had turrets and gates. Temples and palaces were located inside the walls. Houses were located both inside and outside the walls. If an enemy attacked, everyone moved inside the walls for protection.

Mesopotamia

Location—Modern-day Iraq contains much of what is recognized as ancient Mesopotamia. Iraq is located in the Middle East at the head of the Persian Gulf. The following countries border Iraq: Turkey in the north, Kuwait and Saudi Arabia in the south, Jordan and Syria in the west, and Iran in the east.

Climate—Summers are usually hot and dry in the central or southern regions. Temperatures can reach as high as 118°F (48°C) in July and August. Temperatures are cooler in northern Iraq, where the land is mountainous. The mountains receive more precipitation and colder winters than the lowlands. Rainfall in Iraq usually occurs between December and April, averaging about 4–7 inches (10–18 cm) of rain annually.

Topography—Southern Iraq is a low floodplain between the southern part of the Tigris and the Euphrates. Northern Iraq has rolling hills and fertile soil. Mountains rise in the northeast, and desert spans the west.

Natural Resources—The region's natural resources include oil, natural gas, phosphates, and sulfur. The Tigris and the Euphrates provide water for irrigation.

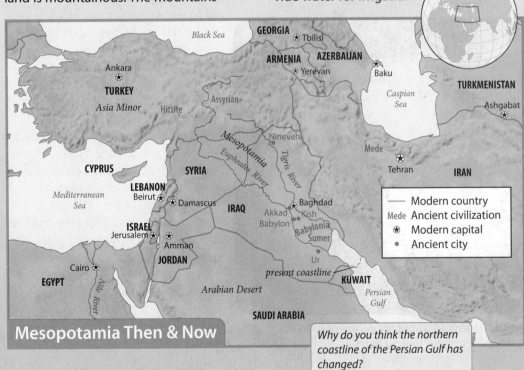

Mesopotamia Then & Now

Why do you think the northern coastline of the Persian Gulf has changed?

Mesopotamian kings lived in palaces. Wealthy upper-class families lived in two-story houses. Each house had a large central open courtyard. The family cooked, rested, and worked as much in the courtyard as in the rest of the house. There was a special area for the family's statue of their personal god. Most common middle-class families lived in smaller, one-story houses that crowded the narrow, winding streets and alleys. These houses usually had one outside door and no windows.

The thick mud-brick walls kept the houses cool in the hot Mesopotamian climate. Often a family slept or entertained guests outdoors on their home's flat roof, where the air was cooler in the evenings. The basic style of homes in the Near East today is similar to that of ancient Mesopotamian homes.

Daily Life

School and Family

Education for the youth is an important part of a civilization. Sumerian schools, called tablet-houses, were attached to the temple. The "school father," or chief teacher, gave students lessons to practice. School fathers were very strict. The school also had a teacher called "the man in charge of the whip." He helped maintain school discipline. Usually only boys from wealthy families attended school. The instruction the boys received helped them learn to become scribes, who were highly respected in Sumer. From sunrise to sunset, the students wrote lists on clay tablets, did mathematical problems, and learned grammar.

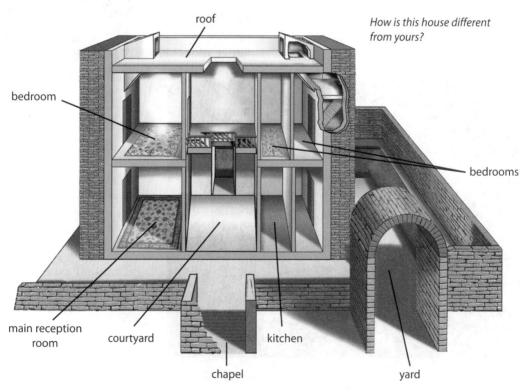

roof

How is this house different from yours?

bedroom

bedrooms

main reception room

courtyard

kitchen

chapel

yard

Parents in Sumer believed in strong discipline. They taught their children obedience and respect. A child who disobeyed might even be disowned or sold into slavery. When children reached marrying age, the parents arranged marriages for them. Women were not considered equal to men, but they did have some rights. For example, women had the right to conduct business and own property.

Clothing

The Sumerians made their clothing from wool or flax, natural resources that were available to them. Men wore skirt-like garments or robes pinned at the right shoulder. Women wore similar robes or dresses but pinned their garments at the left shoulder. Fringe was a decorative adornment added to the clothing of both men and women. Both men and women wore jewelry, including bracelets, necklaces, and earrings. Hairstyles changed over time in Mesopotamia just as they do in the modern world.

The headdress for the queen Puabi was found in the Royal Cemetery of Ur.

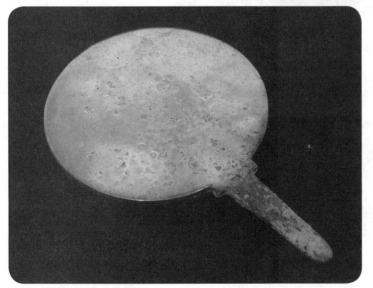

This polished bronze mirror is an example of the types of personal grooming tools that were found in ancient homes. *What does the use of mirrors tell you about the ancient Mesopotamians?*

Making a Cone Mosaic

Thousands of painted cones cover these ancient pillars.

Since houses and temples in Mesopotamia were made out of dried mud bricks, the buildings were dull in appearance. Mesopotamians developed a decorative technique to enhance these plain mud walls. Cones were formed out of clay, and their flat surfaces were painted. The pointed ends of the cones were pushed into a mud wall. The painted flat surfaces of the cones formed a mosaic. Beautiful patterns have been found on walls and pillars of important buildings.

1. Get a container, a pattern, beads, and glue.

2. Plan the number of beads you will need to cover your container with a mosaic design.

3. Plan and color your design within the spaces you have marked on your pattern.

4. Following your pattern, glue the beads one row at a time starting at the bottom of the container.

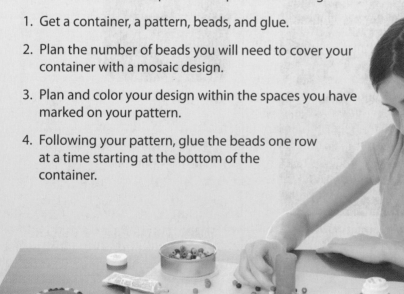

Later Mesopotamian Civilizations

The Sumerian civilization began about 3000 BC. One of the reasons Sumer maintained its power was its military knowledge and might. The Sumerians fought with a variety of weapons, including spears, axes, clubs, bows, and chariots. Soldiers wore copper helmets and leather cloaks dotted with metal disks. For additional protection, the solders carried rectangular shields. The soldiers marched as a phalanx (FAY langks), a group of warriors who stood close together in a square.

Model of a driver in a wooden chariot drawn by four donkeys
What animal do you usually think of as pulling a chariot in battle?

Despite Sumer's many accomplishments, the civilization remained alienated from God. Other countries began to win their battles against Sumer. These countries eventually came to power in Mesopotamia.

Akkadian Empire

Around 2270 BC the ruler **Sargon I** (SAHR gahn) came to power in the Sumerian city-state of Kish. Sargon conquered other city-states as well. He built the city of Akkad and made it his capital. He established the first **empire**, which is a group of lands under one government. The Akkadian (uh KAY dee un) Empire stretched from the Persian Gulf to northern Mesopotamia. The Akkadians borrowed many ideas from the Sumerians. They adopted their cuneiform writing, farming techniques, and religion.

BIOGRAPHY

Who: Sargon I

What: emperor of Akkadian Empire

When: ruled ca. 2270–2215 BC

Where: Mesopotamia

Sargon I was the first ruler to unite the city-states of Mesopotamia into one empire. He also helped the Sumerian and the Akkadian peoples learn from each other.

Numbering the Years

Nearly 1,500 years ago people stopped using the Roman system for numbering years. Instead European scholars decided to number years from the birth of Jesus Christ.

The years prior to Christ's birth are labeled **BC**. BC stands for "before Christ" and is written after the year. For example, if talking about a time three thousand years before Christ, you would write "3000 BC." Historical dates become smaller as they approach the year 1.

The years following Christ's birth are labeled **AD**. AD stands for "anno Domini," which is Latin for "in the year of the Lord." In this case the letters are written before the year. Usually AD is not written unless there would be confusion without it. For example, if someone lived from 43 BC until AD 25, AD is included with the year 25. Otherwise it may be misunderstood that he died in 25 BC.

Several centuries after the labels BC and AD became popular, a new movement developed. Some scientists, historians, and religious leaders called the time after Christ's birth the Vulgar Era. At that time vulgar meant common. These scholars decided to label dates as CE or BCE. BCE stands for "before the common era" and CE stands for "common era." Both abbreviations go after the year. BCE and CE are often preferred by those who seek to remove Christ from history.

If the date of an event is not known with certainty, the term circa is used. Circa is Latin for "around." It can be abbreviated **ca.** or c. Either circa or one of its abbreviations is written before the date.

Even in the various labels used to number years, the truth that Jesus Christ came to earth remains. Any reference to a date will always echo one of the most important events in history.

Ways to write dates

Sumer
   3000 BC
   3000 BCE

destruction of Jerusalem
   AD 70
   70 CE
   70

King Tut
   ca. 1358 BC
   c. 1358 BC

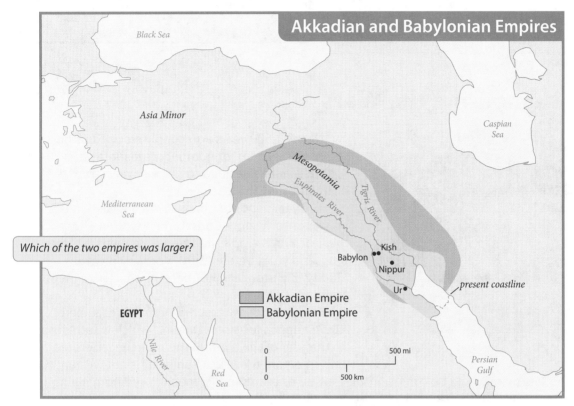

Akkadian and Babylonian Empires

Which of the two empires was larger?

Akkadian Empire
Babylonian Empire

About one hundred years after the death of Sargon I, the city-state of Ur grew in importance. This may have been the same Ur that is mentioned in Genesis 11:31 as the birthplace of Abraham. We do know that Abraham was born into a world under the control of polytheism and idolatry. God revealed Himself to Abraham around 2100 BC. When God called Abraham to leave Ur, God was not simply telling Abraham to leave home but also telling him to leave a way of life.

The End of Sumer

After the death of Sargon I, the Akkadian Empire began to weaken. Sumer was again united. Around 2050 BC, Ur-Nammu ruled over the Sumerian civilization. But after his death, Sumer weakened from a series of wars with its neighbors. In the same way God had ended previous civilizations, God decided to end the Sumerian civilization. Invaders began to battle to gain control of Mesopotamia, and by 2000 BC the Sumerian civilization fell.

Amorite Civilization (Babylonian Empire)

The Sumerian civilization fell to a people called the Amorites. The Amorites established the Babylonian Empire. The empire's capital was the city of **Babylon** (BAB uh lawn), one of the greatest cities of the ancient world. Babylon was located on the Euphrates River near what is modern-day Baghdad, Iraq. Babylon quickly became a center of trade.

The city of Babylon began shortly after the Flood. Nimrod, the great-grandson of Noah, established a kingdom that included Babylon (Gen. 10:10). It was probably in or near this city that the tower of Babel was built.

Hammurabi (HAH moo RAH bee), king of the Amorites, united the land of Mesopotamia. He was a successful military leader. Under his rule, city walls and new canals were built and maintained. He sent out governors, tax collectors, and judges to the city-states.

Hammurabi is best remembered for his code or collection of laws. He did not create these laws, but he gathered, organized, and simplified existing laws. There were laws on almost every aspect of daily life, including marriage, trade, theft, and murder. **Hammurabi's Code** contained some ideas that are still found in laws today. This inscription introduced the 282 laws in his code:

> To cause justice to prevail in the land, to destroy the wicked and the evil, that the strong might not oppress the weak.

Hammurabi's Code was one of retaliation. Specific crimes brought specific penalties. However, the penalty for breaking Hammurabi's laws varied according to the social class of the offender. For example, if a wealthy man broke a bone of a member of his own social class, his own bone was to be broken. If a wealthy man broke the bone of a commoner, he had only to pay a fine. Hammurabi had the code engraved on stone pillars. They were placed throughout the kingdom so that everyone would know the law.

BIOGRAPHY

Who: Hammurabi

What: king of the Amorites

When: ca. 1795–1750 BC

Where: Mesopotamia

Hammurabi succeeded his father to the throne. He fought against his enemies to control the Euphrates River. He used the river against them by damming it and withholding water. Then he would release the water, causing a flood.

This stele, or pillar, is decorated with a bas-relief of Hammurabi being commissioned by the sun god Shamash to inscribe the laws. The laws are written in cuneiform. *How does this method of communication compare with how laws are recorded and displayed today?*

49

FOCUS

1. How does Hammurabi's Code compare to God's law?

2. How did God judge Nebuchadnezzar for his pride?

Hittite Empire

The Hittites were descendants of Heth, the grandson of Ham and great-grandson of Noah (Gen. 10:15). For a time, historians did not think they existed. The Old Testament was the only source of information about these people until archaeological discoveries in the early 1900s confirmed their existence.

The Hittites began to settle in Asia Minor about 2000 BC. **Asia Minor** is the peninsula between the Black Sea and the Mediterranean Sea in what is now Turkey. The Hittites were not ruled by priests or gods like the Sumerians. The Hittites had a king who was the commander of the army. His power depended upon the chief warriors. The Hittites excelled in the production of iron. They made the strongest weapons of the time and skillfully used horse-drawn chariots.

GOD'S LAW

The law given from God through Moses is known as the Mosaic law. Some people claim that Moses copied Israel's law from Hammurabi. There are several places in which Hammurabi's Code is similar to the Mosaic law. But there are enough differences between Hammurabi's Code and the Mosaic law to make this claim unlikely. The Bible tells us that Moses received the law directly from God.

How do we explain the similarities? The Babylonians and Israelites had similar living conditions at that time. Also all people have a basic sense of what is just and unjust because of the law of God written on their hearts (Rom. 2:14–15).

The differences between the codes are more significant. The Mosaic law contains large sections about how to worship God. There are no religious sections in Hammurabi's Code. Unlike Hammurabi's Code, the Mosaic law forbids giving special treatment to wealthy people.

Most importantly, the Mosaic law is God-centered. Crime is not merely doing wrong to another person. It is a sin against God. God's concern is that people think, act, and feel rightly toward Him and others in their hearts. This concern with the heart sets God's law apart from every other code of law.

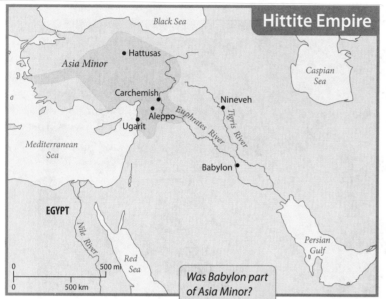

Hittite Empire

Was Babylon part of Asia Minor?

The Assyrians adopted their gods, language, art, architecture, sciences, and literature mostly from the Sumerian and Amorite civilizations. The Assyrians spread these accomplishments throughout the ancient world by their military invasions. One of the first libraries was in Nineveh. Modern historians have learned much about ancient civilizations from this library.

The Assyrian military was well organized. It included foot soldiers, spearmen, archers, and a cavalry. The Assyrians learned how to make iron weapons from the Hittites. They were also skilled with war chariots.

The Assyrians earned a reputation for fierceness. They terrorized the nations

The Hittites extended their empire throughout Asia Minor, the Fertile Crescent region, and into Mesopotamia. Soon after they took control of the Amorite capital of Babylon, other countries invaded Hittite territory and the rule of the Hittites ended.

Assyrian Empire

The Assyrians (uh SIHR ee uhns) created the largest empire the world had seen up to that point. For centuries they lived in northern Mesopotamia along the Tigris River. By around 750 BC they had built an empire that included the Fertile Crescent, Egypt, and part of Asia Minor. **Nineveh** (NIN uh vuh), the city built earlier by Nimrod, became the capital city of the empire.

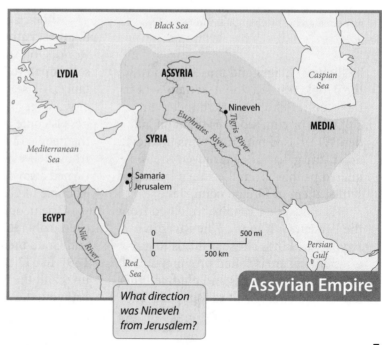

Assyrian Empire

What direction was Nineveh from Jerusalem?

51

A local worker poses with a relief panel that was found during the1933–34 excavation of Gate A in the citadel of King Sargon II. This excavation was directed by the Oriental Institute in Chicago.

by looting villages and burning crops. If the people resisted, the Assyrians sent in their forces. The soldiers tunneled under city walls or climbed over them on ladders. They used battering rams to knock down city gates. They removed the conquered peoples from their own lands and settled them in foreign countries.

The Assyrian Empire stretched from the Persian Gulf to the Nile River in Egypt. The kings chose officials to govern political areas called provinces. Each official collected taxes and enforced the laws. Roads were built to join parts of the empire. Along the way soldiers were posted to protect travelers from thieves.

Although the Assyrians were among the most ruthless people of the ancient world, God showed mercy on them. He sent **Jonah** to Nineveh to preach repentance. "Arise, go to Nineveh, that great city, and cry against it; for their wickedness is come up before me" (Jon. 1:2). As the people of this heathen city "turned from their evil way" (Jon. 3:10), God turned away His wrath. This was a great example of God's mercy.

The people of Nineveh, however, eventually returned to their wicked ways, and God's mercy turned to wrath (Nah. 1–3). In 612 BC the Chaldeans (kal DEE unz) and the Medes destroyed Nineveh, bringing the Assyrian Empire to an end.

Chaldean Empire

Shortly before 1000 BC, the Chaldeans began to settle around Babylon. They were constantly overrun by the Assyrian kings. In 612 BC the Chaldeans joined with the Medes and helped destroy Nineveh. Babylon became the capital city of the Chaldean Empire, so sometimes this empire is called the New Babylonian Empire.

During the reign of **Nebuchadnezzar** (NEB uh kud NEZ er), the empire reached its height. The ancient world was amazed at the Chaldeans' sudden rise to power. The Lord explained Nebuchadnezzar's success:

> I [the Lord God] have made the earth, the man and the beast that are upon the ground, by my great power and by my outstretched arm, and have given it unto whom it seemed meet unto me. And now have I given all these lands into the hand of Nebuchadnezzar the king of Babylon, my servant. . . . And all nations shall serve him. (Jer. 27:5–7)

Nebuchadnezzar is remembered not only for his military accomplishments but also for building up Babylon as "the glory of kingdoms, the beauty of the Chaldees' excellency" (Isa. 13:19). The ancient Greek historian Herodotus said of Babylon, "In magnificence there is no other city that approaches it." Babylon was surrounded by a brick wall. The wall was so wide that two chariots could pass on the road on top of it. A moat surrounding the wall also protected the city.

The Hanging Gardens of Babylon were one of the wonders of the ancient world. The gardens were probably built by Nebuchadnezzar for his wife, who missed the plants of her mountain homeland. The terraced gardens contained tropical palms, trees, and flowers. From the ground the gardens seemed to hang in the air. The Euphrates River ran under the wall and through the middle of the city. It watered the gardens and provided a water supply for the city.

From the book of Daniel, we learn that "wise men," or astrologers, had an important position in the Chaldean Empire. They were called upon to advise the king. Although they claimed power to interpret dreams, these wise men were false prophets. Time and again they proved themselves unable to interpret the king's dreams (Dan. 2:10–11; 4:7).

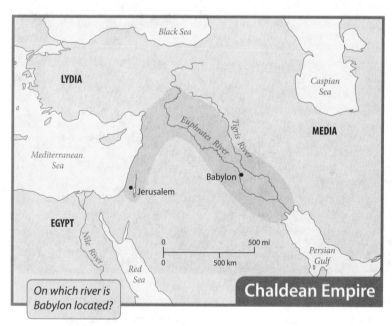

On which river is Babylon located?

Chaldean Empire

Despite the glories of the Chaldean Empire, it did not last even one hundred years. Daniel had shown Nebuchadnezzar God's power. But Nebuchadnezzar viewed his own accomplishments with a heart of pride. He said, "Is not this great Babylon, that I have built for the house of the kingdom by the might of my power, and for the honour of my majesty?" (Dan. 4:30). God's judgment fell upon Nebuchadnezzar. The king lost his throne and he became like a beast of the field. When Nebuchadnezzar recognized the foolishness of his pride and God's greatness, God restored him as king (Dan. 4:31–37). Several years later, under the rule of Belshazzar, the Medes and Persians conquered the Chaldeans. The Chaldean Empire was no more.

Here we pause the story of Mesopotamia. It will begin again when you read about the ancient civilization of Persia.

The cylinder displayed here is an official document inscribed in cuneiform. It records the efforts of King Nebuchadnezzar as he built his empire. The translation reads

I am Nebuchadnezzar, King of Babylon, lawful son of Napolassar. I the king of righteousness, the interpreter, the spoiler, filled with the fear of the gods and loving justice, have placed in the hearts of my people the spirit of reverence and have rebuilt their temples. My great god, Lord Merodach singled me out as the restorer of the city and the rebuilder of its temples, and made my name illustrious. I built temples, I rebuilt temples. The god hearkened to no king before me, so I built his temples. Let me state myself with glory, let me be an everlasting ruler.

Babylonian Pottery Cuneiform Cylinder, Bowen Collection of Antiquities, Bob Jones University Museum & Gallery (photo and translation)

The cuneiform inscription on this Babylonian cylinder supports the biblical account of Nebuchadnezzar found in Daniel 4:29–30.

Chapter 3

Ancient Egypt

The Egyptian Civilization

At the time the Sumerian civilization was developing in Mesopotamia, other civilizations were growing in Europe, Asia, and Africa. A group of people settled in northeastern Africa in a land called **Egypt**. These people were the descendants of Mizraim, a son of Ham and a grandson of Noah. In the Bible the land is called Mizraim, but it is usually translated "Egypt." Several Old Testament accounts took place in Egypt.

The Nile

If you were to fly over Egypt, you would see a thin ribbon of green cutting a desert into two parts. Running through that green ribbon, you would see a long blue thread, the Nile River.

The **Nile River** is the longest river in the world. It begins in central Africa and runs four thousand miles north to the Mediterranean Sea.

Imagine how the descendants of Mizraim felt when they saw the mighty Nile River for the first time. Egypt has been called "the Gift of the Nile." Without the Nile River, Egypt as we know it would have not existed. The Nile was a necessary part of ancient Egyptian life.

Aerial view of the Nile River

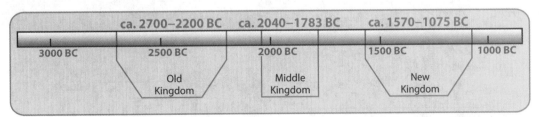

The Nile River continues to provide water and transportation today.

we are familiar with flow from north to south. The Nile, however, flows from south to north. The current floated boats northward. Winds blowing from the north moved boats with sails southward against the current.

Egyptians throughout history honored and gave thanks to the Nile. They gave it the nickname *Hapi*, which means "well fed" or "fat." They worshiped the Nile as a god rather than acknowledging God, Who created the Nile. The following lines are from the Egyptian "Hymn to the Nile":

The geography of Egypt protected the people from most outside invasions. The vast and treacherous desert, the Sahara, provided protection from enemies in the east and the west. As the Nile flows through the Sahara, sections of the river become very shallow and rocky, causing dangerous rapids. These areas are called cataracts. Six cataracts appear along the path of the Nile. The cataracts slowed the advancement of invaders using the river to attack from the south.

The Nile River provided other benefits for the people. The Egyptians depended on the Nile for food and water. Wherever the Nile flowed, plants grew nearby. However, where there was no water, all was desert. At the edge of some Egyptian farms, a person could stand with one foot in green grass and the other foot in yellow desert sand.

The Nile River became a useful highway for transportation. Travelers and traders navigated the river. Trade settlements developed near the cataracts, where river traffic slowed. Most major rivers

> Hail to thee, O Nile! Who manifests thyself over this land, and comes to give life to Egypt! . . . Lord of the fish, during inundation [flood], no bird alights on the crops. You create the grain, you bring forth the barley, assuring perpetuity [eternity] to the temples. If you cease your toil and your work, then all that exists is in anguish. . . . O Nile, come (and) prosper, come O Nile, come (and) prosper!

Silt from the Nile River provides rich farmland. Farmland touches the desert sand.

The Region Today

Egypt

Location—The Arab Republic of Egypt is located in northeastern Africa. Ancient Egypt was the land along the Nile River. Egypt is bordered by Libya to the west, Sudan to the south, the Red Sea to the east, and the Mediterranean Sea to the north.

Climate—Egypt has hot, dry summers and moderate winters. Temperatures range from 107°F (42°C) in the summer to 55°F (13°C) in the winter.

Topography—The land is dominated by the Nile River and its valley. Desert lies to the east and west of the Nile. The Sinai Peninsula is in eastern Egypt.

Natural Resources—Egypt's greatest natural resource is water from the Nile River. Other natural resources include iron ore, petroleum, natural gas, phosphate, limestone, manganese, talc, zinc, asbestos, gypsum, and lead.

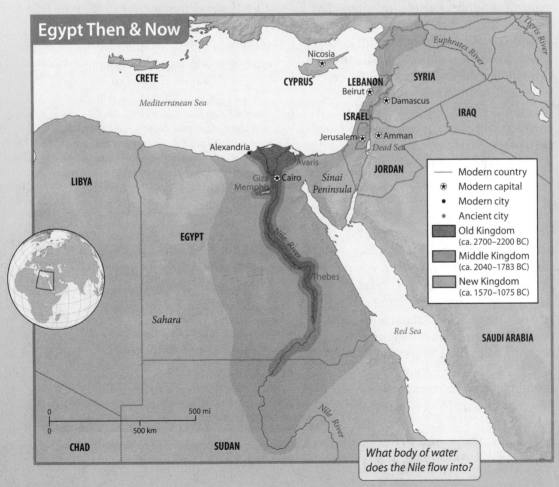

Egypt Then & Now

Legend:
— Modern country
⊛ Modern capital
• Modern city
• Ancient city
■ Old Kingdom (ca. 2700–2200 BC)
■ Middle Kingdom (ca. 2040–1783 BC)
■ New Kingdom (ca. 1570–1075 BC)

What body of water does the Nile flow into?

1. What were some of the tools early Egyptians used for irrigation?

2. How many seasons did Egypt have?

Flooding of the Nile

Each summer in ancient Egypt, the Nile overflowed its banks. Melting snows in African mountains and heavy spring rains far to the south caused the river to rise dramatically. The water would rush down the mountains and across the flat land of Egypt. Soon everything except the tallest palm trees was under water. The flood typically lasted for four months. During those months the water soaked into the land. Silt would settle from the water. This silt became the life-sustaining feature of the flood. Without the annual fertilizing quality of the silt, the crops would not have thrived.

Farming Along the Nile

When the land was nearly dry from the flood, Egyptian farmers went to work in their fields. Because the soil was still soft, plowing was not necessary. The farmers simply scattered their seeds onto the damp ground. After that, they walked their farm animals back and forth across the field. The animals' hooves pushed the seeds into the soil.

Once the planting was done, the next task was to keep the crops watered. To plant crops farther away from the river, the Egyptians dug irrigation canals.

Many farmers used a **shadoof**, a long pole with a bucket on one end and a weight on the other. The farmers dipped the bucket into the Nile River, pulled the bucket up, and emptied it into an irrigation canal. It was hard, daily work for the farmers until the crops were ready to harvest.

Some farmers used a water wheel that raised water to the fields. A donkey or an ox could be used to help turn the wheel. Few farmers could afford such luxuries. Most fathers relied on help from their sons.

Shadoofs are still used in some areas today.
What do you think were the benefits and disadvantages of using a shadoof?

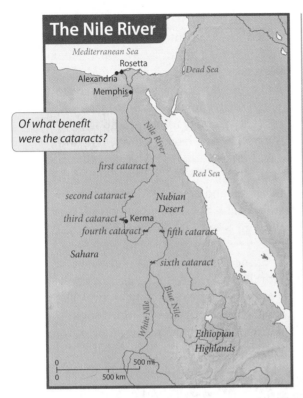

The Nile River

Mediterranean Sea
Rosetta
Alexandria
Memphis
Dead Sea
Nile River
first cataract
Red Sea
second cataract
Nubian
Desert
third cataract Kerma
fourth cataract   fifth cataract
Sahara
sixth cataract
White Nile
Blue Nile
Ethiopian
Highlands
0   500 mi
0   500 km

Of what benefit were the cataracts?

many kinds of fish and waterfowl. People also raised animals, but usually only the wealthy had them for meat.

Because Egypt's land was fertile and watered by the Nile, much food was produced. Egypt became the storehouse of the ancient world. Large harvests allowed Egyptians to store food for times of famine when the Nile River did not rise. Because of their careful planning, the Egyptians usually had more than enough to eat.

cucumbers

Other civilizations knew of Egypt's bounty. Many traveled to Egypt when they were in need of food. God used Egypt as a temporary place of safety for His chosen people during a famine that lasted seven years.

figs

garlic

The strip of fertile land along the Nile River is only about ten miles wide. However, it stretches the whole length of the river. As the river empties into the Mediterranean Sea, the Nile widens into a fan shape called a **delta**. A delta gets its name because it resembles the Greek letter delta (Δ). Early settlers found the Nile delta an ideal location to grow crops. They did not have to worry about having a water resource because the land was low and well watered.

When everything went well, the people ate very well. They grew wheat and barley, melons and cucumbers, onions and garlic, and dates and figs. The river supplied

pomegranate

onions

dates

Kunsthistoriches Museum, Vienna

The colorfully dressed people in the middle band of this Egyptian wall painting may be the Israelites being presented by Joseph to the pharaoh.

Joseph

During a period known as the Middle Kingdom, a young Hebrew named Joseph was taken from Canaan to Egypt after his brothers sold him to some traveling merchants. Joseph had already made up his mind to serve God no matter where he was. Potiphar, the captain of the pharaoh's guard, bought Joseph as a slave. While serving in Potiphar's house, Joseph was falsely accused by Potiphar's wife and sent to prison.

God blessed Joseph for his faithfulness. Soon Joseph was placed in charge of the other prisoners. During his time there, Joseph interpreted the dreams of some of the pharaoh's imprisoned workers. One day Joseph was taken to see the pharaoh. The pharaoh had been having dreams that his magicians and wise men could not interpret. God helped Joseph interpret the pharaoh's dreams about withered grain and starving cattle. Joseph explained that the dreams were God's message about a famine that would come. However, God would allow Egypt to have seven years of good harvest before the famine. Joseph advised the pharaoh to have Egypt save food and prepare.

The pharaoh was grateful and chose Joseph to manage the harvests and plan for the famine. When the famine years came, people went to Joseph to buy food. The famine had also devastated the region beyond Egypt. But Joseph's wise planning gave Egypt the ability to provide for both its people as well as others in the region.

Joseph's family was among those who came for food. He invited them to live in Egypt. Over time, they grew into the nation of Israel (Exod. 12:40–41). Joseph's life is an example of how God blesses those who honor Him.

61

Nilometers on Elephantine Island near the first cataract

Taxes and Time

All Egypt depended on the Nile River. Governmental officials kept detailed records of when the river flooded and how high the water rose. The Egyptians used a **nilometer** (NY lahm uh tur) to measure the Nile's water levels. The measurements affected how much the people owed in taxes. The amount of taxes changed each year depending on how good the crops were. The more the Nile River flooded, the more fertile farmland there was to produce crops.

Because of the importance of the Nile's floods, the Egyptians developed a calendar that told the exact days on which the Nile was expected to flood. This calendar had three seasons: Flood (Akhit), Planting (Perit), and Harvest (Shemu).

The Egyptian calendar was based on the phases of the moon. There were four months in each season. Each month had three weeks with ten days each. Since this calendar was five days short of a full year, the Egyptians added five more days to the calendar. They used these days to celebrate the birthdays of the gods.

The Egyptians also used two types of twenty-four-hour clocks—the water clock and the sundial. Both kept time, but each had a disadvantage. The water clock had to be refilled often. The sundial could only be used during the daytime. Ancient Egyptians used the stars to determine the time at night.

Comparison of Seasons and Calendars		
	Egypt	United States
Seasons in a year	3	4
Months in a season	4	3
Days in a month	30	28–31
Weeks in a month	3	4–5
Days in a week	10	7

FOCUS

1. How were early pyramids different from later pyramids in the Old Kingdom?

2. Why are there more artifacts in Egypt than in other civilizations?

A Unified Egypt

The Egyptians began settling in two areas along the Nile River. The plain around the Nile delta was called Lower Egypt. The area along the river to the south was Upper Egypt. Around 3000 BC, Lower and Upper Egypt were unified under a leader named Menes (MEE neez).

Menes began the first dynasty of Egypt. A **dynasty** is a line of kings or rulers who belong to the same family. At the time people still identified Lower Egypt and Upper Egypt as two separate geographic regions, even though they were one kingdom.

Old Kingdom
(ca. 2700–2200 BC)

Pharaohs

Most of Egyptian history is divided into three kingdoms. The first kingdom is known as the Old Kingdom. It started with Egypt's Third Dynasty. During this time the rulers of Egypt, known as **pharaohs**, had great power. The Egyptians began to believe that the pharaohs were gods.

Probably the most spectacular accomplishment of the pharaohs was the building of large tombs called **pyramids**. Each pyramid showed the power and wealth that the pharaoh had gained during his reign.

Archaeologists have found evidence of at least eighty pyramids. Most of them were built during the Old Kingdom. Another name for the Old Kingdom is "the Age of Pyramids."

Pyramids

Today, people are amazed that the pyramids were built without modern technology. Each pyramid was constructed on a rectangular base with four sloping triangular sides. The earliest pyramids were step pyramids made of mud bricks. The outer bricks were arranged like stairsteps. The Egyptians believed that the pharaoh would climb the steps to reach the afterlife.

The Great Sphinx was built near the Great Pyramid during the Old Kingdom.

63

The design of pyramids changed over time. Later pyramids were made of large cut stones. The large building blocks were carefully cut to fit snugly together. These pyramids had smooth sides made of polished limestone.

INSIDE THE GREAT PYRAMID

1. **entrance**

2. **underground chamber**—possibly the pharaoh's original burial chamber or designed as a fake chamber to fool robbers

3. **Grand Gallery**—a large passageway that leads upward to the pharaoh's burial chamber

4. **queen's burial chamber**—possibly the location where the pharaoh's possessions were placed for the afterlife; the queen was actually buried in a smaller pyramid nearby.

5. **pharaoh's burial chamber**—the location of the pharaoh's sarcophagus

6. **air shafts**—thought to provide ventilation for the workers

Each pyramid contained more than just the buried body of a pharaoh. Food, clothing, furniture, and even games and toys were placed in the pyramid's burial chamber. The pharaohs thought these things would bring them pleasure and ease in the next life. Small statues were also placed in the tombs. These were thought to act as servants to the pharaoh in the afterlife. Detailed scenes of daily life were painted on the walls to make the pharaoh feel at home. Pyramids were usually built for royalty, but some other Egyptians were able to afford such tombs as well.

The three pyramids in the valley of Giza are the most well-known. The largest of these is the **Great Pyramid**, which was built for the pharaoh Khufu (KOO foo). Khufu ruled during the Fourth Dynasty. His magnificent pyramid covers thirteen acres and can be visited today.

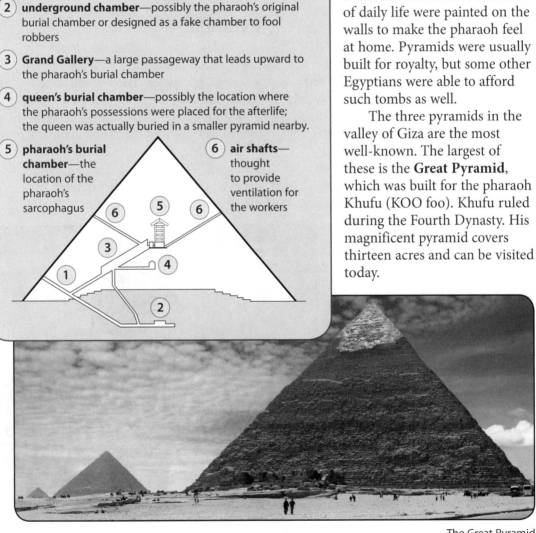

The Great Pyramid

The Rosetta Stone

Ancient Egyptian writing is called **hieroglyphics** (hy er uh GLIHF iks) or picture writing. People drew pictures of the ideas they wanted to express. This kind of writing was used from about 3000 BC to AD 1100—longer than any other form of writing used.

For many centuries after the Egyptian civilization declined, no one was able to read hieroglyphics. In 1799 a large black stone was found in the town of modern-day Rosetta, near the Mediterranean Sea. The stone was the lower part of an upright monument called a stele (STEE lee). This stele had been engraved to record a decree of the pharaoh Ptolemy (TOL uh mee). The inscription was written in Egyptian hieroglyphics, common Egyptian, and Greek.

The **Rosetta stone** became the key to unlocking the Egyptian language. Since Greek was a known language, it was used to translate the Egyptian symbols and words. However, it was not until 1822 that **Jean-François Champollion** (zhahn frahn-SWA shahn-po-LYON) successfully translated several of the hieroglyphics on the stone. Historians and archaeologists can now read Egyptian hieroglyphics for themselves.

The Rosetta stone was the key for unlocking the Egyptian language.

Artifacts

As with most civilizations, our knowledge about the Old Kingdom comes from its artifacts. Because the Egyptians were so careful to preserve things for the afterlife, a large number of objects survived. Egypt's hot, dry climate was also important in preserving artifacts. If artifacts were from regions with high humidity, they decayed more quickly. In Egypt, however, ancient food items, clothing, and some colored paintings have survived. As a result, more has been learned about the ancient Egyptian civilization than any other.

Who: Jean-François Champollion

What: Egyptologist

When: 1790–1832

Where: France

By the age of nineteen, Champollion had received his Doctor of Letters. By age twenty he had mastered thirteen languages. He was appointed conservator of the Egyptian Museum at the Louvre in Paris. Champollion was the first to translate a portion of the hieroglyphics on the Rosetta stone. He died of a stroke at the age of forty-one.

The largest artifacts in Egypt are structures such as the great pyramids and the Sphinx. The colorful paintings inside the pyramids tell us a great deal about the daily life of the Egyptians. In addition to pyramids, the pharaohs erected storehouses, beautiful palaces, and temples to their gods. Most of these buildings are located in the cities of Memphis and Thebes.

Historians have learned much about Egypt from records written on papyrus. **Papyrus** (puh PY ruhs) is the name given to the paper made from the pith (the soft sponge-like center of a stem) of the papyrus plant. Our word *paper* comes from the word *papyrus*. Papyrus was readily available since it grew along the banks of the Nile. Papyrus was light and thin and could be stored easily. Egyptian scribes and priests used it for thousands of years to keep records, write letters, and tell stories. This natural plant resource was also used to make baskets, boats, and rope. People in Europe also used papyrus. They used it until the Middle Ages.

Papyrus growing along the Nile River. Papyrus stems are cut into sections, peeled, and thinly sliced. The slices are soaked, layered, and pounded. The finished paper is then dried before use.

FOCUS

1. Why did Egyptians make mummies?

2. What was the significance of the way the embalmer dressed?

Mummies

You have no doubt heard about Egyptian mummies. A **mummy** is a dead body that has been preserved from decaying. The study of mummies has given archaeologists a significant amount of insight about the ancient Egyptians. Studying mummies has revealed what the people of Egypt actually looked like. Because of their religious beliefs, the Egyptians carefully preserved the bodies of their dead. Some civilizations buried or burned their dead, leaving nothing for archaeologists to study.

As you can see from how Egyptians provided for a pharaoh's afterlife, they did not believe in the true God. They believed that without a body, a person could not exist in the next world. After a person died, his family paid a person called an *embalmer* to preserve the body.

The embalmer dressed in the jackal-headed costume of the embalming god, Anubis. First, the embalmer cleaned out the body's skull. Then he cleaned the abdominal cavities and dried the liver, stomach, lungs, and intestines. The embalmer placed each of these organs in special containers called **canopic jars**. He then filled the body with spices. The body was soaked for seventy days in a salt solution called *natron*. Once removed from the natron, the body was washed and wrapped in linen strips.

The embalmer returned the preserved mummy to the family for burial. Wealthy families purchased several coffins that fit one inside another. The coffins were made of metal, wood, or stone. This type of stone coffin is called a **sarcophagus** (sahr KOF uh guhs). Some coffins were

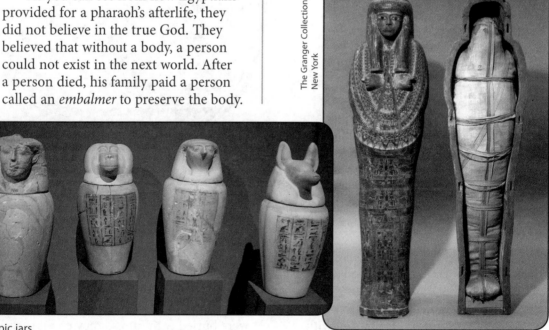

The Granger Collection, New York

Nina Aldin Thune/Wikimedia Commons/ Creative Commons Attribution-Share Alike 2.5 Generic license

Canopic jars
Which four organs were placed in canopic jars?

An Egyptian mummy

The Cartouche

A pharaoh often had the hieroglyphs of his name written inside an oval shape called a *shenu*. The word *shenu* came from the Egyptian word for "encircle." The Egyptians believed that the person whose name was encircled with a shenu would be protected.

A shenu served as a nameplate. Archaeologists have found shenus on monuments, tombs, amulets, and papyri. These shenus contained hieroglyphs that represented a pharaoh's birth name, throne name, and sometimes other information.

The shenu shape became very important to the Egyptians. The use of the shape extended beyond nameplates. Many sarcophaguses, burial chambers, and other structures were made in this long oval shape.

In the 1800s Napoleon Bonaparte invaded Egypt. His French soldiers saw shenus on buildings and artifacts. They thought the shape of a shenu resembled the shape of their gun cartridges. Since the French word for "cartridge" is *cartouche*, the soldiers gave the name **cartouche** (kar TOOSH) to the shenu symbols. Today archaeologists and historians continue to call them cartouches.

This artifact shows Rameses II with a bow and arrow next to a cartouche.

richly decorated. The mummy of a wealthy person was also buried with many items to be used in the afterlife.

Sometimes the deceased person's servants were buried with him so they could serve him in the afterlife.

Deciphering Hieroglyphics

Have you ever seen a message written in code and wondered what it meant? To decipher a coded message, you need a key. Champollion used Greek as a key to interpret the hieroglyphics on the Rosetta stone. In this activity, you will use a key containing a hieroglyphic alphabet to decipher and write hieroglyphic words.

1. Get your Activity Manual.

2. Match the words and hieroglyphic spellings in Section A.

3. Answer the questions in Section B using words spelled in hieroglyphics.

4. Write your name in hieroglyphics in the blank cartouche in Section C.

A modern restorer works to repair and preserve hieroglyphics in the tomb of Queen Nefertari, wife of Rameses II.

vulture A	foot B	hand D	reed E (I)	horned viper F (V)	pot stand G
house H	cobra J (G)	basket K (C)	lion L	owl M	water N
lasso O	stool P	hillside Q	open mouth R	folded cloth S (C)	bread loaf T
quail chick U (W)	two reeds Y	doorbolt Z	hobble rope CH	lake SH	cow's belly TH

FOCUS

1. How did the construction of pyramids differ between the Old Kingdom and the Middle Kingdom?

2. Who was the first female ruler in Egypt?

Middle Kingdom
(ca. 2040–1783 BC)

The Old Kingdom thrived for over five hundred years. However, the later pharaohs were weak rulers, and their reigns resulted in disorder and war. More than a century of fighting took place in the land. Then a new dynasty came into power. Egypt was united once again.

A new period began, called the Middle Kingdom. During this time the Egyptians experienced peace and stability. The pharaohs showed greater care for the people of the land. Under their leadership, larger canals and ponds were made to store the Nile's floodwaters for later use during the dry season.

Egypt restored trade with its neighbors. The Egyptians built forts along the Nile River between the river's first and second cataracts. The presence of these forts helped control the trade routes. It was during this kingdom that the biblical account of Joseph took place.

Temples, pyramids, palaces, and other buildings were also constructed during the Middle Kingdom. The people decorated these buildings with sculptures and paintings, much like those of the Old Kingdom. However, the pyramids built during the Middle Kingdom were smaller and less grand than those of the Old Kingdom. Less care was used in their construction. Instead of using stone, builders used mud bricks. Since the bricks were less durable, not many of the Middle Kingdom's pyramids survived.

The Black Pyramid at Dahshur was built during the Middle Kingdom. *How is this pyramid different from the one pictured on page 64?*

The Hyksos considered the hippopotamus to be sacred.

New Kingdom
(ca. 1570–1075 BC)

The peace of the Middle Kingdom did not always remain. The pharaohs neglected the security of the borders and failed to keep their forts in good repair. A people called the **Hyksos** (HIK sohs) took advantage of the defenseless situation and swept into Egypt. The word *Hyksos* means "foreign rulers." Historians are not certain who these foreigners were, but evidence shows that the Hyksos brutally attacked and seized whatever they wanted. The Hyksos ruled for about 150 years. From these people the Egyptians learned to use weapons made of bronze and iron, as well as the horse-drawn chariot with two wheels.

An Egyptian prince named Ahmose eventually drove out the invaders. He created a protective buffer south of the Upper Kingdom to prevent further invasions. He also expanded the kingdom farther east. This set the stage for what is called the New Kingdom.

The New Kingdom was the greatest period in Egyptian history. Ahmose made Egypt mightier than it had ever been. Eventually Egypt became a regional power. The pharaohs of the New Kingdom were warrior kings. They expanded Egypt's borders by conquering neighboring peoples. They also gained wealth by trading with other civilizations to obtain gold and ivory.

Queen Hatshepsut (hat SHEP soot) was one of the early rulers during the New Kingdom. She ruled with her husband until his death and then ruled with her young nephew. She decided to make herself pharaoh. Hatshepsut was the first woman to be a ruler in Egypt.

Moses

During the first part of the New Kingdom period, the Egyptians kept the Israelites enslaved. God used Moses to free His people from slavery.

Moses was an Israelite who was brought up in the pharaoh's household. There Moses probably learned to read and write, as well as studied history, arithmetic, and science.

After he committed a murder, Moses fled from Egypt. He lived in Midian as a shepherd. There God spoke to him from a burning bush. God told Moses to return to Egypt and lead the Israelites to freedom. Moses went before the pharaoh to ask him to free the slaves. When the pharaoh refused, God sent a series of ten plagues on the Egyptians. During the last plague, all the firstborn sons of the Egyptians died. The pharaoh finally agreed to let the Israelites go.

After the Israelites left, the pharaoh changed his mind. He chased them with an army and six hundred chariots. But the Lord protected the Israelites. He destroyed all of the pharaoh's army in the waters of the Red Sea.

Thutmose III (thoot MO suh) was the next pharaoh. He was the greatest Egyptian warrior king. He used the chariot to invade Palestine and Syria. During his reign, the Egyptian empire stretched to the Euphrates River in the northeast.

Not all pharaohs began ruling as adults. Try to imagine being the ruler of a powerful civilization at your age. **Tutankhamen** (TOOT ahng KAH muhn), also called King Tut, was only nine years old when he became pharaoh of Egypt. He died when he was about nineteen and was buried at Thebes in the Valley of the Kings. He did nothing of great importance during his short reign. However, King Tut is famous for his tomb. It is described as one of the greatest discoveries of all time.

The British archaeologist Howard Carter discovered the tomb in 1922. The tomb was found in very good condition.

It contained thousands of objects and much wealth. Carter took over eight years cataloging all the statues, furniture, toys, pottery, and precious objects he found. Because of King Tut's tomb, historians now have extensive information about how the pharaohs of the New Kingdom lived and died.

Golden funerary mask of Tutankhamen

Howard Carter near Tutankhamen's golden sarcophagus

Rameses II is also known as Rameses the Great. He had a reputation for being a wise and good pharaoh and was kind to his subjects. When he died, he was buried in a beautiful tomb. Although grave robbers broke into his tomb, his mummy was not destroyed. Today the mummy is in the Egyptian Museum in Cairo.

Egypt grew weaker after the death of Rameses II. The pharaohs were no longer able to protect the empire from invaders. Two hundred years after the death of Rameses, people from the west invaded Egypt. From then on Egyptians were ruled by foreigners until the 1900s, when the modern state of Egypt was formed.

Statue of Rameses II at the Karnak temple in Luxor, Egypt

Rameses II (RAM ih seez) was one of the last pharaohs who kept the empire strong. He defeated the Hittites, who were the greatest enemy of Egypt at the time. Later he signed a lasting peace treaty with a new Hittite king. Rameses also built some of the greatest temples in Egypt. The temple at Karnak is the most famous. Rameses also had many colossal statues made of himself.

Close-up view of one of the colossal statues of Rameses II guarding the Abu Simbel temple

1. What was the social structure of Egypt shaped like?

2. What did Egyptians wear to protect themselves from evil spirits?

Culture of Egypt

Social Classes

The social structure of ancient Egypt can be arranged in a triangle-shaped diagram called a **social pyramid**. An Egyptian's social class depended on his wealth or power. At the bottom of the social pyramid are the farmers, merchants, servants, and slaves. They represent the largest social class. On the next pyramid level are the priests, soldiers, scribes, and artisans. The next level includes the nobles and the pharaoh's generals and viziers. Viziers were the highest-ranking officials under the pharaoh. At the top of the pyramid is the pharaoh and the royal family. They make up the smallest social class.

Anyone from a lower class could rise to a higher class if he gained the pharaoh's favor. Even a foreign slave could rise to a higher class. This happened to Joseph, a Hebrew slave who became the second-most-powerful man in Egypt.

Unlike in most ancient civilizations, some women in Egypt held important roles. Women were able to buy and sell property. Many worked as farmers or merchants and at other jobs usually held by men. Some even served in the temples as priestesses.

Music

The ancient Egyptians loved music. It was part of their everyday life rather than just for celebrations. Farmers sang while they worked in the fields. Children sang as they played. Raftsmen and traders lifted their voices in song as they worked in their shops or sailed up and down the Nile. Slaves made their chores less tedious by blending their voices in song. The pharaoh and the nobles often had musicians to entertain them.

Religious ceremonies used many songs, both of praise and prayer to the gods. One of the main themes in Egyptian music was the Nile. The people sang thankful praises to the great river.

Daily Life

Egyptians were known for their cleanliness. Each day they wore fresh clothing made of linen, cotton, or wool. Ancient washrooms have been found in some of the ruins. With this in mind, you can imagine the terrible trial the plagues of frogs, lice, and flies sent by God were for the Egyptians.

Both men and women wore wigs made from human hair and beeswax. Women usually wore their hair long, while men were bald or cropped their hair just above their shoulders.

Men and women also wore cosmetics. They used black cosmetic powder called kohl (KOL) to make their eyes look bigger. The kohl also protected their eyes from the glare of the sun. Egyptians loved strong-scented perfumes. On special occasions a woman might wear on her wig a cone made of scented animal fat. As the fat melted, the perfume was released.

Egyptians ate mainly bread made from either wheat or barley. They also ate melons, cucumbers, onions, dates, and figs. The river supplied them with many kinds of fish and waterfowl. They also raised animals for meat.

The Egyptians weaved flax, a kind of plant, into cloth to make their clothes. Men wore skirts that wrapped around their waists. This type of skirt was tied with a belt. Women wore long sleeveless dresses. Young children did not wear any clothes until they were old enough for school. Then they dressed as the adults.

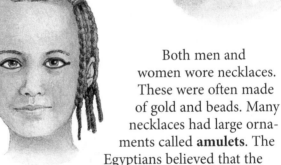

Female hairstyle with perfume cone, male hairstyle, child's hairstyle

Both men and women wore necklaces. These were often made of gold and beads. Many necklaces had large ornaments called **amulets**. The Egyptians believed that the amulet protected its wearer from evil spirits.

Egyptians believed that after they died they would be rewarded according to the good things they had done. The people put much time and effort into preparing for death and the afterlife.

Scarab amulet

Boys of upper-class families started school at age four or five. Boys of the middle-class and lower-class families did not attend school. They learned the same trades as their fathers. Girls from all classes were trained by their mothers to run a household. Many girls were married about age thirteen.

Everyone worked for the pharaoh. People were paid with food and clothing rather than with money. Most of the people were farmers or other laborers.

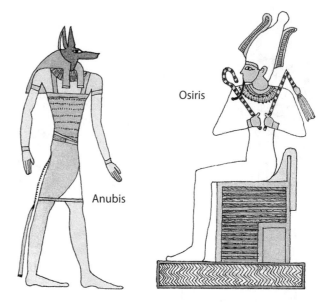

Osiris

Anubis

Religion

Although the people of Egypt had seen the power of the one true God, they refused to believe in Him. They continued to worship their own false gods. The Egyptians were polytheistic. They had hundreds of gods—one god for each village and city. There were gods of the land and of the heavenly bodies, such as the sun, moon, and stars. There were gods who provided protection. There were even gods who represented daily activities. Families built altars in their houses to worship their favorite gods.

Egyptians believed that Ra, the sun god, created and ruled the world. During the Middle Kingdom, the priests of Thebes joined their god, Amen, to Ra. They called the new god Amen-Ra. They also told everyone how to worship the new god. This made the priests very powerful.

Osiris, the god of the underworld, was a favorite of the Egyptians. They believed that after burial, a dead person traveled by boat to the Hall of Judgment, where Osiris presided. Anubis, the jackal-headed god, weighed the dead person's heart against the feather of justice, order, and truth. A papyrus copy of the *Book of the Dead* was buried with the person. This scroll provided the person with instructions of what to do and say in the afterlife. The following translation is a portion of text from the book. It tells the person what to chant to declare his innocence during judgment.

> I have not committed sins against men. . . . I have not made any man to weep. I have not committed murder. I have not given the order for murder to be committed. I have not caused calamities to befall men and women. . . . I have not carried away the milk from the mouths of children. I have not driven the cattle away from their pastures. I have not snared the geese in the goose-pens of the gods. . . . I have not stopped water when it should flow. I have not made a cutting in a canal of running water. . . . I am pure. I am pure. I am pure.

Isis

Horus

The Egyptians taught that Isis, the wife of Osiris, protected children. Their son, Horus, had the body of a man and the head of a falcon or a hawk. These three gods formed the model family that Egyptians tried to follow. There were also gods of medicine, education, music, and even love. Hathor, the goddess of love, had the body of a woman and the head of a cow.

Egyptians believed that the pharaoh was the son of Horus. This made the pharaoh a god and the high priest of Egypt. Every morning, after washing and dressing, the pharaoh went to the temple to "awaken" the idol of Horus. He washed and clothed the idol, gave it food, and put makeup on it. After that the people believed the day could proceed with the god's blessing.

Temple of Horus in Edfu, Egypt

Relief carving showing Akhenaton and his family making an offering to the sun god Aton

One pharaoh of the New Kingdom tried to change the Egyptian beliefs. His name was Amenhotep IV. He believed there was only one great god, called Aton. The pharaoh even changed his own name to **Akhenaton** (AH kuh NAHT n) to show that he worshiped the god Aton.

The priests of the old gods did not like losing their influence. The Egyptian people did not want to give up the old gods either. After the death of Akhenaton, his successor, Tutankhamen, returned to the old religion.

EGYPTIAN BELIEFS

The Egyptians were polytheistic. Their gods were false and were invented by man. The Bible teaches that there is only one true God.

The Egyptians believed that, after death, they would be judged according to their works. If their works were good enough, they would spend the afterlife in a place of peace—fishing, hunting, and relaxing. The Bible teaches that where man will spend eternity depends on his relationship with Jesus Christ.

The Egyptians believed that they could preserve their souls and provide for them in the afterlife. The burial practices were based on this belief. They believed it was important to preserve the deceased body to preserve that person's soul. But they did not believe that body would ever live again. The Bible teaches differently. The resurrection of Jesus from the dead guarantees that all who put their trust in Him will also one day be raised bodily from the dead (1 Cor. 15:20).

Ancient Egypt was a great civilization for many centuries, but its greatness could not last forever. God allowed Egypt to fall to several other peoples, including the Kushites, the Assyrians, the Persians, the Greeks, and the Romans.

God tells us in Ezekiel 29:3–4 that He judged the Egyptians for their worship of false gods and their pride. Yet one day God will show mercy to Egypt. In Isaiah 19:21–22 the prophet Isaiah tells of a time when Egypt will turn to the Lord and He will heal them.

Making an Egyptian Wig

1. Gather the following materials: glue, a stapler, a tape measure, colored construction paper, 5–6 yards of black yarn, and a 9-inch circle of black felt.

2. Get a class member to measure the circumference of your head about an inch above your eyebrows.

3. Connect 2-inch-wide strips of construction paper to form a head-band 1 inch longer than the circumference of your head.

4. Cut the black yarn into 8-inch lengths. Lay the headband out flat. Glue the yarn strands side by side along the length of the head-band. Leave a 6-inch gap for your face in the center and 1 inch at one end for stapling.

5. Staple the ends of the headband together. Staple or glue the circle of black felt to the inside of the headband to form the top of the wig.

Comparing and Contrasting Egypt with Mesopotamia

Comparing and contrasting two things can help you learn more about them. When you compare and contrast, you are finding similarities and differences between things. The similarities and differences can be written in a chart or a Venn diagram.

Writers often use clue words to show similarities. Clue words that show similarities include *similar to, like,* or *resembling.* Clue words that show differences include *different from, but, unlike,* or *however.*

When you compare and contrast different civilizations, begin by looking for similarities. Some characteristics to look for are geography, climate, government, social structure, occupations, religion, and the advances each civilization has made.

1. Work with a partner to compare and contrast ancient Egypt with Mesopotamia. Use your Student Text and other resources.

2. Complete your diagram with the information that compares and contrasts these two civilizations.

3. Share your information.

Kush

Along the Nile River to the south of Egypt was a land called **Kush**. The kingdom of Kush extended from the first cataract of the Nile to Khartoum in present-day Sudan. Just as the Nile was vital to Egypt's survival, it was also very important to the survival of Kush. Many of the Kushite villages depended on the Nile for food, water, transportation, and trade.

Kushite Culture

The Kushites lived in farming villages where they were either farmers or animal herders. Like the Egyptians, they used an irrigation system to be able to farm more land. In the southern part of Kush, the villagers raised cattle on the savanna, or grassy plain.

The people of Kush had an abundance of natural resources, including gold, copper, stone, fertile soil, ebony (dark, hard wood), and ivory. The Kushites' diet was more limited than the Egyptians' diet because Kush had less ground that was good for farming. The Kushites grew wheat, barley, and a variety of vegetables. They ate fish, cattle, and birds. Hippopotamus, ostrich, and turtle were delicacies that the people enjoyed on special occasions.

The Kushites used palm wood and bricks for building. They fashioned pottery out of clay. They were also skilled hunters. They used the bow and arrow to hunt elephants, lions, leopards, and panthers. Elephants were tamed and used as work animals. Sometimes the Kushites traded animals with other civilizations.

© James Morris/Art Resource, NY

Tomb painting showing Kushites leading a giraffe and other animals

Pyramids in Kush
How do these pyramids compare with the Egyptian pyramids?

Like women in the Egyptian civilization, women in Kush held a variety of roles. There were female warriors as well as queens and priestesses. But women were still the primary caregivers of the children and maintained the households.

The people of Kush developed two systems of written language. One system was a form of hieroglyphics similar to the Egyptian hieroglyphics. The other system was a form of script, or handwriting, with symbols that looked more like letters. This script used a limited number of symbols to form words. The script language was later called **Meroitic** (mehr oh EE tick). It was named after the people of Meroë (MEHR oh EE), the ancient city where the language was first used. Scholars have been able to decipher only a little of the Meroitic language.

The Kushites, like the Egyptians, were polytheistic in their religion. They pictured their primary god, Amun, with a head like a sheep's. The architecture of their pyramids and temples was also similar to that found in Egypt.

History of Kush

You have read how an ancient civilization sometimes begins as a strong village. This village then becomes wealthy and powerful and conquers smaller villages around it. Kush was one such strong village. As it gradually extended its power, Kush developed into a civilization. The people of Kush established Kerma as a capital city. Kerma began trading goods with Egypt.

As the Kushites became wealthier and more numerous, the Egyptians began to fear their growing power. During Egypt's Middle Kingdom the pharaoh led his army to invade Kush. The Egyptians completely destroyed Kerma and conquered Kush. Over time, Kush adopted the Egyptian culture. The Kushites dressed like the Egyptians, worshiped Egyptian gods, and changed the Egyptian hieroglyphics to fit their own language.

Egypt dominated the Kushites for about five hundred years. But toward the end of Egypt's New Kingdom, Kush became stronger. Egypt eventually lost control, and the Kushites established their independence. The Kushite king became known as a pharaoh, and Napata became the capital. Under the rule of Piye (PY), Kush eventually conquered Egypt. Kush ruled Egypt for only about forty years.

In the mid-600s BC, the Assyrians invaded Egypt during the Kushite rule. The Assyrians had the advantage of iron weapons, and the Kushites were unable to defend Egypt. The Assyrians drove out the Kushites, who returned to their homeland.

The Kushites established a new capital at Meroë. In the surrounding areas, they discovered iron ore deposits. Iron became a valuable item for trade with other civilizations. Kush also exported gold, pottery, tools, ivory, leopard skins, ostrich feathers, and elephants. Slaves were also exported. The Kushites imported jewelry and other goods.

After a period of about four hundred years, the Kushite civilization began to decline. They had used nearly all their natural resources. Most of the trees had been burned as fuel. The savannas were overgrazed and the cattle herds had diminished. Trade began to wane.

To the southeast of Kush, in what is Ethiopia today, the Aksum civilization had developed. Eventually the Aksum people destroyed Meroë and took over the land of Kush in AD 330. The Kushite kingdom had existed for more than one thousand years.

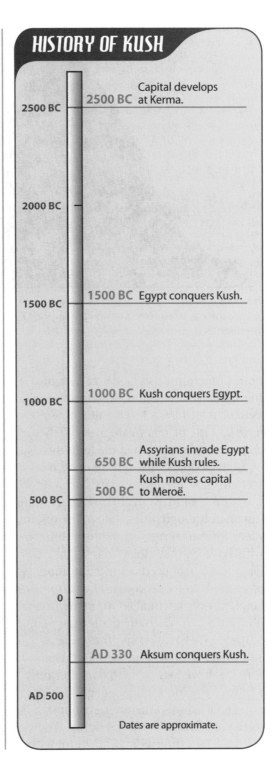

HISTORY OF KUSH

2500 BC — 2500 BC Capital develops at Kerma.

2000 BC

1500 BC — 1500 BC Egypt conquers Kush.

1000 BC — 1000 BC Kush conquers Egypt.

650 BC Assyrians invade Egypt while Kush rules.

500 BC — 500 BC Kush moves capital to Meroë.

0

AD 330 Aksum conquers Kush.

AD 500

Dates are approximate.

Sudan

Location—Ancient Kush was located in northeastern Africa along the Nile River in northern Sudan. Sudan is bordered by Egypt to the north; the Central African Republic, the Democratic Republic of the Congo, Uganda, and Kenya to the south; the Red Sea, Eritrea, and Ethiopia to the east; and Libya and Chad to the west.

Climate—Sudan has hot, dry summers with moderate winters. Temperatures range from 100°F (38°C) in the summer to 55°F (13°C) in the winter. The northern part of the land has little or no rainfall, while the southern part has a rainy season.

Topography—The land is dominated by the Nile River and five of its six cataracts. To the east and west of the Nile is desert. The southern region is savanna.

Natural Resources—The land's greatest natural resource is water from the Nile River. Other resources include gold, ivory, ebony, and iron ore.

What helped sustain life in both Kush and Egypt?

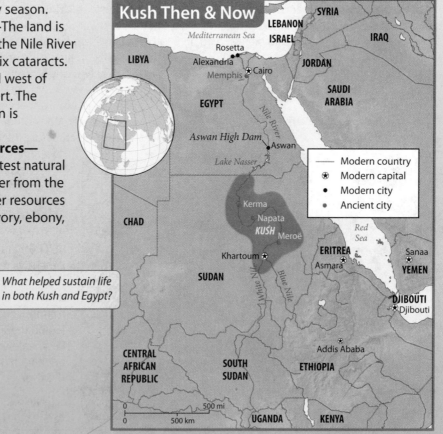

Kush Then & Now

Modern country
Modern capital
Modern city
Ancient city

THE ASWAN HIGH DAM

Floods and droughts have been a part of Egypt's history since Bible times (Gen. 41:35–36). Many years the Nile River flooded, destroying the land and the crops. Throughout history Egyptians desired to control the water of the annual floods. In the late 1890s, while Egypt was under British rule, construction on a dam began. This dam was completed in 1902. It was located near the border of Egypt and Sudan. The dam helped control the annual flooding and held water in a reservoir for later release.

The Great Temple at Abu Simbel
What in the photograph lets you know that the statues are very tall?

Over the next thirty years, the height of the dam was raised and hydroelectric generators were added. By the 1940s the height of the dam needed to be raised again. Instead the decision was made to build a second dam further upstream. After ten years of construction, the **Aswan High Dam** was completed in 1970. The first dam, known as the Old Aswan Dam, remains but has limited function.

The Aswan High Dam formed a large man-made lake, **Lake Nasser**. The water in this reservoir began covering many of the temples, tombs, and villages of ancient Kush. Archaeologists from other countries helped save as many artifacts as they could before the area was completely flooded. The Temples at Abu Simbel were moved to higher ground. Many other monuments were documented before the lake waters covered them.

Not everyone approves of the dam. Silt gets caught behind the dam, so the area below the dam no longer receives rich nutrients for farming. Expensive fertilizers have to be used instead. The dam has also affected fishing, since some fish fed on the silt in the water. People downstream depended on fishing from the river.

Satellite picture of the Aswan High Dam

Chapter 4

Ancient Israel

FOCUS

1. How is the history of Israel different from the history of other nations?

2. From where did the nation of Israel get its name?

Israel's Beginning

The nation of Israel began like no other nation in the world. And its history is unlike the history of any other nation. Much of Israel's history was recorded in the Bible by prophets. God used them not only to tell what happened but often to reveal why those things happened. God's purposes and actions in history are revealed more clearly in Israel's history than in that of any other nation.

Around 2091 BC God revealed Himself to a man named Abram. Abram

Today in the Middle East, Bedouins dwell in tents just as Abraham did.

lived in Ur of the Chaldeans. Ur was a developed city-state. The people there worshiped many gods and idols. Abram believed in the same gods as those people. But God chose to reveal Himself to Abram. God told Abram to leave Ur and to travel to wherever God showed him. Abram then believed in the one true God.

God gave Abram many promises and changed his name to **Abraham**. These promises are called the **Abrahamic Covenant**. In this *covenant*, or binding agreement, God promised Abraham that his descendants would become a great nation. God promised to bless Abraham. God told him that all the nations of the world would be blessed through him.

ABRAHAMIC COVENANT

Genesis 12:1–7

God promised Abraham that his offspring would become a great nation. They would live in the land that God gave them. Through Abraham God would bring a great blessing to all the families of the earth. Jesus, a descendant of Abraham, fulfilled this last promise.

Abraham showed that he believed God by doing what God said. He moved his family to Canaan, the land where God told him to go. Because Abraham believed God, God considered this former idolater to be a righteous man.

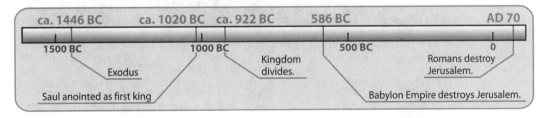

ca. 1446 BC   ca. 1020 BC   ca. 922 BC   586 BC   AD 70

1500 BC   1000 BC   500 BC   0

Exodus

Kingdom divides.

Romans destroy Jerusalem.

Saul anointed as first king

Babylon Empire destroys Jerusalem.

Abraham and His Sons

The nation of Israel came into being because of God's promises. But it did not happen right away. The Abrahamic Covenant was not given to all of Abraham's descendants. God chose only Isaac among Abraham's sons, and among Isaac's sons, only Jacob was chosen. But God chose all of Jacob's twelve sons to inherit the promises. The twelve tribes of the nation of Israel would come from them. The nation would be called **Israel** because that was a special name that God had given Jacob.

The Israelites in Egypt

During Jacob's lifetime a great famine struck the entire ancient Near East. God had providentially moved Jacob's son, Joseph, to Egypt years before the famine. God enabled Joseph to interpret the pharaoh's dream, which predicted the famine. Joseph was then made a ruler in Egypt. He was the second-highest ruler of the land. Joseph oversaw the building of storehouses to prepare for the famine.

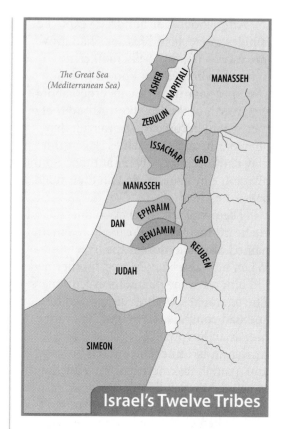

The Great Sea (Mediterranean Sea)

ASHER NAPHTALI MANASSEH ZEBULUN ISSACHAR GAD MANASSEH EPHRAIM DAN BENJAMIN REUBEN JUDAH SIMEON

Israel's Twelve Tribes

When the famine struck, people from many nations went to Egypt for food. In this way Joseph was a blessing to many nations. Joseph's father and brothers and their families also came to Egypt. Joseph made sure that they were given a portion of good land to live in.

Joseph Sold into Bondage by His Brethren, Giovanni Battista Carlone, from the Bob Jones University Collection
Look at the men's clothing. Which are probably the wealthy men from the caravan, and which are the sons of Jacob?

After about four hundred years, the families of Jacob and his sons had grown into a large nation. A pharaoh came to power who had not known Joseph. The Egyptians became concerned about the growth of the Israelites. Afraid that they would become too powerful, the pharaoh made the Israelites slaves. But they continued to grow in number. So the pharaoh commanded that all their male babies be killed.

The people of Israel cried out to God. He heard their cry and called on a man named **Moses** to deliver the Israelites. When he was a baby, Moses' mother had hid him from the pharaoh's executioners. The pharaoh's daughter discovered him and had compassion on him. She raised him as an Egyptian, but Moses knew he was an Israelite. Once when he saw an Egyptian taskmaster beating a fellow Israelite, Moses killed the taskmaster. Because of this, Moses fled from Egypt. Later, when God called him to return and lead the Israelites out of slavery, Moses made many excuses. He did not feel qualified. God made it clear to Moses that He would deliver His people and that He would use Moses to do it.

Moses returned to Egypt and told the pharaoh to let God's people go. But the pharaoh's heart was hardened, and he did not let them go. Because of the pharaoh's stubbornness, God unleashed ten plagues on Egypt. God wanted the Israelites, the Egyptians, and all people to know that He is the true God. The ten plagues ended with a final judgment on Egypt in which all the firstborn males in the land were killed. God had instructed the Israelites to spread the blood of a sacrificed lamb on each doorpost and lintel (the beam

above the door). This protected the Israelites from death when God judged Egypt. The Jews still remember this event during their holiday called **Passover**.

After the death of the pharaoh's firstborn, the ruler agreed to let the Israelites leave Egypt. This event in Israel's history is known as the **Exodus**. The Exodus took place about 1446 BC.

Moses, following God's direction, led the nation of Israel into the Sinai wilderness. The nation gathered at the base of Mount Sinai, and God declared that Israel was to be a nation set apart from all other nations. Israel was to point these nations to the true God. In this way Israel would be a blessing to them.

The Mosaic Covenant

At Mount Sinai God gave the nation of Israel His law through Moses. This law is known as the Mosaic law. God commanded the Israelites to obey His law. If they obeyed, God promised to bless Israel. All the other nations would know how good God is. But if the Israelites chose to disobey, God promised to punish the nation of Israel with famine, military defeat, and exile. These promises are called the **Mosaic Covenant**.

MOSAIC COVENANT

Exodus 19:3–6

God gave Israel laws that told the people how to live to please Him. If they obeyed these laws, the nations around Israel would see the great and true God, and He promised to bless Israel. If the Israelites disobeyed, God promised to punish them. Israel's history under the Mosaic Covenant shows that it is impossible to please God with one's own efforts.

TEN COMMANDMENTS

In most ancient civilizations the king or the ruler made the laws. In ancient Israel God made the laws. The most well-known laws that God gave Israel are the Ten Commandments. They are recorded in Exodus 20. These laws have made a great impact not only on Israel but also on other lands.

The United States is one such land. Though many of the Founding Fathers of the United States were not Christians, the society in which they lived was heavily influenced by the Bible. As a result the law of God had a profound influence on the shaping of the United States. The U.S. Supreme Court building has several images of Moses and the stone tablets. Many American laws are based on the Ten Commandments.

In Deuteronomy 4 God told the Israelites that one of the reasons He gave them the law was so other nations could see the wisdom and righteousness of God. This purpose has been fulfilled as other nations have recognized the wisdom in the laws God gave Israel.

Moses (center) on the east pediment of the Supreme Court building

91

Worship in the Wilderness

God told the Israelites to build a place for worship called the **tabernacle**. The tabernacle was a symbol of God's presence with His people. When Adam and Eve first sinned, God withdrew His presence. The Garden of Eden, a place of fellowship with God, was no longer accessible to people. By giving Israel a special symbol of His presence, God was giving them a very special gift.

Because the Israelites were still sinners, the priests sacrificed animals daily on the altar in the tabernacle to atone for their sins. Once each year, the high priest entered the most holy place to sprinkle blood on the ark of the covenant.

God Himself gave Moses the instructions for the materials, the size, and the placement of each part of the tabernacle. The workers took special care to follow God's plan as they built. The materials and the furnishings of the tabernacle symbolized God's holiness, justice, and other attributes. The tabernacle reminded the Israelites that God was providing a way for them to have a relationship with the one true God.

High priest offering incense in the Holy Place

Tabernacle

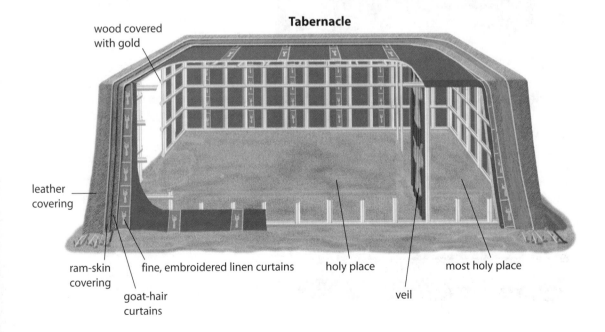

wood covered with gold

leather covering

ram-skin covering

fine, embroidered linen curtains

goat-hair curtains

holy place

veil

most holy place

Working with a Research Team

A research team works together to find information about a topic. Their work often includes writing reports and making models to present their findings. In this activity you will work in a research team to write about one of the tabernacle furnishings. Then you will make a model of it. The Bible provides many details about the structure and furnishings of the tabernacle. The Bible is the best source to start with as you research.

1. You and your research team will need a Bible, a pencil, a ruler, paper, and materials to make your model.

2. Choose one of the tabernacle furnishings with your team.

3. Each person on the team should read the Bible passage about the furnishing. While reading, write down the details of the item's appearance, dimensions, purpose, and location in the tabernacle.

4. Compare notes with other team members and make a drawing of the furnishing based on the biblical description.

5. Work together to write the report and make the model.

6. Present the report and the model.

Religion

The defining characteristic of the Israelite religion as revealed by God is monotheism. **Monotheism** is the belief in one god. The Hebrew name for the one true God is **Yahweh**. The Bible is clear about there being only one God. The key text for this truth is Deuteronomy 6:4, which says, "Hear O Israel: the Lord our God is one Lord." Jews call this important verse the Shema.

God's covenants with His people were very important to the Israelite religion. The Abrahamic Covenant provided the basis for Israel as a special, chosen nation. The Mosaic Covenant provided the guidelines for national life. Later the Davidic Covenant and the New Covenant promised a future for Israel despite her disobedience.

The tabernacle, and afterward the temple, was the center of Israelite worship. Three times a year all the men of Israel traveled to the capital city of **Jerusalem** for the Feast of Unleavened Bread (Passover), the Feast of Weeks, and the Feast of Tabernacles (Exod. 23:14–19). The Day of Atonement was another important time of worship for the Israelites. **Atonement** means the restoration of the broken relationship between God and man. The Day of Atonement was the one day every year that the high priest could enter the most sacred room in the temple, the holy of holies. He would sprinkle blood on top of the ark of the covenant. This act was a symbol of atonement for the people's sins. True atonement was made possible by Christ's sacrificial death on the cross.

Although many religious celebrations and ceremonies took place during the Old Testament period, most Israelites did not worship God as He commanded. The Israelites often abandoned the worship of Yahweh for the worship of the gods of other nations.

Hebrew Months			
Number	Name	Days	Equivalent
1	Nisan	30	Mar.–Apr.
2	Iyar	29	Apr.–May
3	Sivan	30	May–June
4	Tammuz	29	June–July
5	Av	30	July–Aug.
6	Elul	29	Aug.–Sept.
7	Tishri	30	Sept.–Oct.
8	Heshvan	29 or 30	Oct.–Nov.
9	Kislev	29 or 30	Nov.–Dec.
10	Tevet	29	Dec.–Jan.
11	Shevat	30	Jan.–Feb.
12	Adar	29 or 30	Feb.–Mar.

The Hebrew religious calendar is a lunar calendar. *How do the number of days compare to the calendar you use?*

Passover

In Exodus 12:24–27 God commanded the Israelites to commemorate their deliverance from the death of the firstborn and from slavery in Egypt. Today the Jews still celebrate Passover each year to remember what God did for them.

Passover occurs in March or April. Leviticus 23:5 tells us that Passover is celebrated "in the fourteenth day of the first month." The first month of the Jewish calendar is Nisan. It occurs at a different time of year than our first month of January.

All four Gospels record that Jesus celebrated Passover with His disciples in an upper room. As part of that Passover, Jesus broke bread and said, "This is my body." And He took a cup of wine and said, "This is my blood." With these words, Jesus established the Lord's Supper that is observed by Christians. Christians recognize that Jesus is the fulfillment of the Passover lamb (1 Cor. 5:7). The shedding of His blood makes salvation possible for those who come to Him by faith. Like the Passover, the Lord's Supper is an event that "echoes" God's deliverance of His people.

The Passover feast is called the *seder* (SAY duhr). Each item of food has a symbolic meaning related to the first Passover in Egypt.

1. What happened when the Israelites did not trust God to help them take the land of Canaan?

2. What additional promises did God make to Israel's second king?

Dwelling in Canaan

God led the Israelites from Sinai to the edge of the land of Canaan. Along the way the people complained about God's care of them. They lacked faith, forgetting the mighty acts God had done in leading them out of Egypt. They did not believe God's promise to help them take the land from the Canaanites. Because they did not trust God, they wandered for forty years in the desert before entering the Promised Land.

Entering the Promised Land

Once in the Promised Land, the Israelites were to do what Adam had failed to do—exercise good and wise dominion over the land. But before the Israelites could live in the land, they had to conquer it. Because the people of Canaan were very wicked, God commanded the Israelites to purge them from the land.

Moses' successor, Joshua, led the Israelites to obey God and conquer Canaan. God showed the people that when they obeyed Him, He would bless them and do miraculous works on their behalf. When the people disobeyed God, He punished them with defeat.

God helped the Israelites by parting the **Jordan River**. He also caused the walls of Jericho to fall. Under Joshua's leadership, the people of Israel conquered the land.

Priests leading the people around Jericho, one of the Canaanite cities Israel defeated

Israel

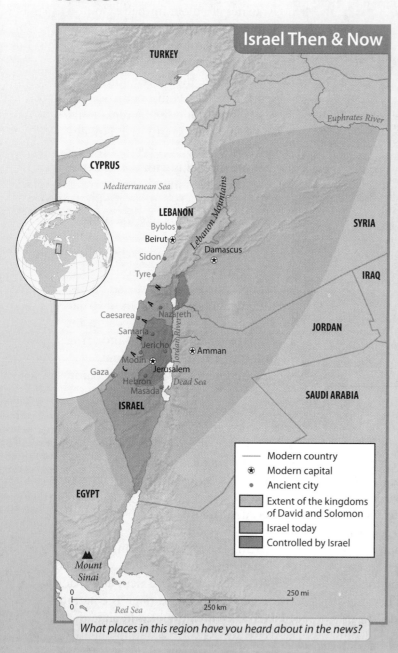

Israel Then & Now

TURKEY

Euphrates River

CYPRUS

Mediterranean Sea

LEBANON

Byblos
Beirut
Damascus
Sidon
Tyre

SYRIA

IRAQ

Lebanon Mountains

Caesarea
Nazareth
Samaria
Jericho
Modin
Gaza
Hebron
Masada

Amman

JORDAN

Jordan River

Jerusalem
Dead Sea

SAUDI ARABIA

ISRAEL

EGYPT

— Modern country
⊛ Modern capital
• Ancient city
  Extent of the kingdoms of David and Solomon
  Israel today
  Controlled by Israel

Mount Sinai

0   250 mi
0   250 km
Red Sea

What places in this region have you heard about in the news?

Location—Israel is located in the Middle East on the eastern shore of the Mediterranean Sea. The ancient territory of Canaan is now Israel, Lebanon, Jordan, and Syria.

Climate—The climate is temperate with mild winters and warm summers. Temperatures range from 48°F (9°C) in the winter to 90°F (32°C) in the summer. In the northern mountains annual precipitation may reach 40 inches (102 cm). In the southern deserts little or no rain falls.

Topography—Five major land regions run north to south. The lowland coastal plain lies along the Mediterranean Sea. Rolling hills and valleys lead to the Lebanon Mountains in the northeast. The valley of the Jordan River lies to the east of these hills, and farther east is a large plateau. The desert lies in the southeast.

Natural Resources—Modern Israel has few natural resources. Petroleum and natural gas are available. Salt is mined near the Dead Sea.

Samuel anointing David as king

Judges and Kings

Although God enabled the Israelites to conquer the land of Canaan, the Israelites failed to obey. They allowed some of the people who lived there to remain. Furthermore, the Israelites did not exercise wise dominion over the land. They did not show the nations the greatness of their God by living according to His laws. Instead the Israelites became more and more like the wicked nations around them. They began to worship the same gods and practice the same sins. In keeping with the Mosaic Covenant, God punished them by sending other nations to rule over parts of Israel. When the Israelites cried out for help, God sent deliverers. But each time the Israelites went back to doing evil and suffered defeat from their enemies.

For more than three hundred years, a pattern of disobedience and punishment followed by repentance and deliverance continued. Finally, the people of Israel began to believe that the problems with their enemies could be solved in only one way. They asked the last judge, **Samuel**, to give them a king like the other nations.

God warned the Israelites that a king would take their sons for his armies. The king would also take their daughters to work in his palace. He would take the people's land and crops to feed his servants and armies. Still the people wanted a king.

About 1020 BC God told Samuel to anoint **Saul** as Israel's first king. At first it seemed that Saul would defeat Israel's worst enemies, the Philistines. But Saul refused to obey God. Although Saul was king for many more years, he never led the Israelites to victory as the people had hoped.

Because Saul disobeyed God, **David** was chosen by God to replace Saul. Under King David the Philistine armies were finally defeated. David also captured the Canaanite city of Jerusalem and made it the capital. During his reign the nation of Israel more than doubled in size.

Canaan contained several different civilizations. One was the Phoenicians. They were prosperous traders, craftsmen, and businessmen. Traders from other civilizations went to Phoenicia for one of its special products—a purple dye made from shellfish. People used this dye to color cloth. This purple cloth was very popular. It was worn only by royal or wealthy people.

The hills of Phoenicia were covered with forests. Many of the trees in these forests were the famous cedars of Lebanon. David used wood from these forests when he built his palace. Solomon also included Lebanon cedar in the construction of the temple in Jerusalem.

The Phoenicians' greatest achievement was the development of one of the first alphabets. In fact, our modern English alphabet can be traced back to the Phoenician alphabet.

The leading city-state of Phoenicia was Tyre. It was located along the eastern coast of the Mediterranean Sea both on the mainland and on an island. Tyre grew wealthy and prosperous through trade. However, the prophet Ezekiel warned that Tyre would be destroyed. Nebuchadnezzar, the Babylonian king, destroyed the mainland section of Tyre in 571 BC. Years later the city's rubble was thrown into the sea to expand a causeway, or land bridge, to the remaining island city of Tyre. After this time it was never again a powerful city.

The ruins of Tyre
How were many of the stones used after Tyre was destroyed?

David was the king of God's special choosing. He would serve as a model for all the kings who followed him. David was not a perfect king. He did some very bad things. But when confronted with his wrongdoing, David confessed his sin and repented. Most importantly, David led the nation in worshiping the true God.

Just as God had made special covenants with Abraham and with the Israelites, God made a covenant with David. In the **Davidic Covenant**, God promised that David would have a great name. David's dynasty would last forever, and God would be a father to the Davidic kings. If David's descendants disobeyed God, they would be punished. But God promised that He would fulfill all the promises of the Davidic Covenant in the end.

At David's death in 961 BC, his son Solomon became king. God gave Solomon wisdom and understanding that no other man has ever known. Solomon built forts, palaces, and storehouses throughout Israel. His most impressive project was the temple in Jerusalem. It was built from huge stones and cedar timbers from the Lebanon Mountains. The temple's decorations were made from gold, ivory, and precious stones.

During Solomon's reign, the people of Israel had peace. Yet Solomon disobeyed God and married the daughters of foreign kings to make treaties, or peace agreements, with their countries.

Solomon had seven hundred wives. They included Ammonite, Phoenician, and Egyptian princesses. Each wife brought with her the false gods of her people. Even though Solomon worshiped the true God, he began to worship these false gods as well.

Although the kingdom was at peace, the people became discontent. They did not like the heavy burden laid on them by Solomon's building projects. God sent a prophet to tell Solomon of the future. He told Solomon that the peace in the kingdom would not last. The prophet said that after Solomon died, Israel would split into two kingdoms. However, God would keep His promise and permit David's dynasty to continue.

An artist's idea of how Solomon's temple may have looked

Identifying Costs and Benefits

Throughout history, man has made decisions. Each decision involves choosing between at least two things. As a decision is made aspects of each choice must be considered. We may call these rewards and consequences, pros and cons, or benefits and costs.

As a person makes a decision, he must look at the choices or options available. Looking at the costs and benefits of each option can help you better understand history. You can also relate the decisions to choices you have to make.

In this activity you and a partner will look at a decision that was made in the history of Israel. Together you will list costs and benefits of that decision. Then you will write about the decision and make a personal application.

1. Get your Bible and the Activity Manual page.

2. With your partner, choose a Bible account on the Activity Manual page.

3. Read the Bible passages. Identify the people involved and the choice that was made. List the options with their costs and benefits on the T-chart.

4. Write a paragraph summarizing the decision that was made. Include an application to your own life.

1. What names were given to the two kingdoms?

2. What does it mean to be assimilated into another culture?

FOCUS

Kingdom Divided

At Solomon's death in 922 BC, the twelve tribes of Israel gathered and asked Solomon's son *Rehoboam* if he would rule them more gently than his father. He denied their request. Rehoboam said that he would rule them more severely. This caused the kingdom to split. The ten northern tribes followed *Jeroboam*, one of Solomon's officials. They formed the Northern Kingdom. The two southern tribes, Judah and Benjamin, remained under Rehoboam's rule. They formed the Southern Kingdom.

The northern tribes kept the name *Israel*. Jeroboam established his capital at Samaria. To keep his people from returning to Jerusalem to worship, he made two golden calves and proclaimed them the gods of Israel. The Northern Kingdom of Israel experienced some times of great prosperity. But over the next two hundred years, none of its nineteen kings served the Lord. God continually sent prophets to bring messages of warning and judgment to the people. In 722 BC the judgment came. Israel was conquered by the Assyrian Empire and the people were carried away as captives.

The tribes of the Southern Kingdom took the name *Judah.* They kept the capital at Jerusalem. Judah's kings were all descendants of King David. A few of Judah's rulers lived righteously before God, but many were wicked. God sent prophets to warn Judah of coming judgment.

Divided Kingdom

Map showing the Divided Kingdom with locations including:
Tyre, Dan, SYRIA (ARAM), Kedesh, PHOENICIA, Hazor, The Great Sea (Mediterranean Sea), Sea of Galilee, Bashan, Megiddo, Jezreel, Dothan, Jabesh-gilead, ISRAEL, Jordan River, Succoth, Shechem, Samaria, Joppa, Shiloh, AMMON, Bethel, Gilgal, Jericho, Ashdod, Jerusalem, Heshbon, Ashkelon, Bethlehem, PHILISTIA, Hebron, Gaza, En-gedi, Dead Sea, JUDAH, Beersheba, MOAB, EDOM

Legend:
Northern Kingdom
Southern Kingdom

0   50 mi
0   50 km

In **586 BC** King Nebuchadnezzar of the Chaldean (New Babylonian) Empire conquered Judah. He destroyed Jerusalem, including the temple. He also took over ten thousand people away to exile in Babylon. This time for the Israelites is known as the Babylonian captivity.

Many of those who were left behind fled to Egypt, Moab, or other countries. This scattering of the Israelites into many other nations is known as the Dispersion, or the **Diaspora** (dye AS pur uh). About this time the Israelites became known as the *Jews*.

God had told the Israelites that if they did not keep the Mosaic Covenant, they would be scattered among other nations. The prophets had warned the people that God would be true to His word. But the prophets also had good news. God would make a **New Covenant** with His people. He would restore the Israelites to their land and change their hearts so they would love and obey Him.

NEW COVENANT

Jeremiah 31:31–40; 1 Corinthians 11:25

God made the New Covenant with Israel and Judah. He later included the Gentiles in its most important promises. God promised to restore Israel and Judah from exile. He also promised Jews and Gentiles alike that those who are part of this covenant would receive the Holy Spirit. The Spirit would change their hearts from hard hearts to hearts that loved and wanted to obey God. God also promised that He would forgive His people of all their sins. Jesus enacted this covenant in His death and resurrection. A Christian remembers this covenant when he partakes of the Lord's Supper.

Daniel was one of the Jewish exiles in Babylon under the Persian Empire. He chose to obey God rather than man's law and spent a night in the den of lions.

God's People in Exile

When an empire made war and conquered a nation, it often forced the ruling class and the wealthy to relocate. This was a way of controlling the captives. Generally the commoners left in the land would not rebel without their leaders. Both the Assyrians and the Chaldeans often relocated captives.

Life in the Assyrian Empire

The Assyrians relocated the wealthy and important people from the northern tribes of Israel to the eastern part of Assyria. These Israelites were **assimilated**, or absorbed, into the Assyrian culture. The Assyrians moved people from other conquered nations into the Northern Kingdom's region. Israelites who remained in the region eventually intermarried with these people. Their descendants were called **Samaritans**, after the former capital city of Samaria.

Life in the New Babylonian Empire

King Nebuchadnezzar relocated the southern tribes of Judah to Babylon. The Jews were allowed to retain their religion and cultural traditions. Some of the most important Jewish men were trained to serve in the government.

Life in the Persian Empire

In 539 BC the Persian army, under the leadership of Cyrus the Great, conquered Babylon. Cyrus allowed the Jews to return to Judea. Judea was the name given to the former Southern Kingdom of Judah. Some Jews returned, but many chose to stay in Babylon, where they had already made their homes.

The Babylonian Chronicles are a series of clay tablets. They contain important events in Babylonian history. Each entry begins with the year and the name of the reigning king. This tablet describes the events in the reign of Nabonidus, who ruled Babylon when it was conquered by Cyrus the Great.

Later, King Xerxes (also known as Ahasuerus) ruled Persia. During his reign a palace official named Haman grew angry with one of the Jews named Mordecai. Haman decided to take revenge on Mordecai by plotting to kill all the Jews of Babylon. **Queen Esther**, who also was a Jew, heard about Haman's plan. She risked her life and went to the king. Queen Esther pleaded with him to save her people from destruction. King Xerxes gave the Jews permission to defend themselves from anyone who would try to hurt or kill them. He also ordered the execution of Haman.

After Haman's death the Jews held a great feast. They sent each other presents and gave gifts to the poor. This celebration became the holiday *Purim*. Purim is still celebrated today by Jews around the world.

This is thought to be the tomb of King Xerxes. The relief at the top (see detail above) shows Xerxes before the altar of his god.

1. How did Antiochus IV respond to the rebellion in Jerusalem?

2. Why is Hanukkah celebrated?

Return from Exile

The Jews returned from captivity in Babylon in waves. One group led by Zerubbabel rebuilt the temple. Ezra, a priest, returned to Judea with another wave of Jews. He taught the people the Law and worked to uproot sinful practices among the people. Nehemiah returned with another wave of returning Jews, and he led the rebuilding of the walls of Jerusalem. These three leaders, along with the prophets Haggai, Zechariah, and Malachi, helped the Jews become re-established in their land.

Life in the Greek Empire

As the Persian Empire continued to expand, it tried to conquer the Greeks. But the Greeks repeatedly defeated the Persians. Under the leadership of Alexander the Great, the Greeks conquered the Persians. The land of Judea became part of the Greek Empire.

After Alexander died, his kingdom was divided and distributed among his generals. Egypt was ruled by the Ptolemies (TOL uh mees), and Syria was ruled by the Seleucids (sih LOO sids). Judea lay on the border between the two kingdoms. As Egypt and Syria fought each other, Judea was often under the rule of one or the other.

While Judea was being ruled by the Ptolemies, a large number of Jews were relocated to Alexandria, Egypt. This created a thriving Jewish community in Alexandria.

By this time Greek had become a common language. It had spread under Alexander's leadership. Eventually the Old Testament Scriptures were translated into Greek. The Greek translation is called the **Septuagint** (SEP too uh jint). This was an important accomplishment. The Scriptures were now available to scattered Jews who had lost their Hebrew language and to the Gentiles. **Gentiles** was the name given to the Greeks and to other people who were not Jews. The New Testament writers often quoted from the Septuagint in their writings. Most of the Gentile Christians in the early church used the Septuagint.

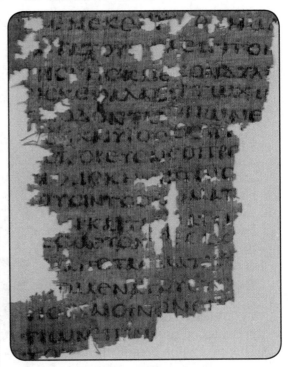

A portion of Amos 2, from the Septuagint, on papyrus

Many of the Jews living under Greek rule began to adopt the customs and the lifestyle of the Greeks. The high priests, who were appointed by the Greek rulers, often promoted the sinful lifestyle of the Greeks more than the true worship of God. Some of the Jews were concerned about this. They began to insist on a strict, careful observance of the law in all its details.

In 176 BC the Seleucid king **Antiochus IV** (an TYE uh kus) became ruler of Judea. During his reign he personally entered the temple in Jerusalem and seized its treasures and sacred vessels. This was a great offense to the Jews.

Later, while Antiochus was fighting in Egypt, the Jews attempted to overthrow his appointed leaders. When Antiochus returned from Egypt, he found Jerusalem at war.

Antiochus responded to this rebellion by tearing down the city's walls. He also placed idols in the temple and sacrificed pigs on the altar of God. He placed altars to false gods in many Jewish cities. Jews were put to death for keeping the Sabbath or owning a copy of the Torah. Antiochus thought that if the Jewish religion were destroyed, the Jews would become like Greeks and not revolt anymore.

Coin of Antiochus IV

An ancient Torah scroll *What did Antiochus think of the Jews and the Torah?*

Each relief on the Knesset Menorah in Jerusalem depicts a scene from Jewish history (left). The second scene (right) is of the Maccabean Revolt.

The Maccabean Revolt

The Jews who strictly followed the books of the Law were not about to accept the destruction of their religion by Antiochus. Some Jews fled to the desert. In the small Judean town of Modin, some Jews began to rebel. A Jewish priest named Mattathias refused to worship the Greek idol that was placed in his town. He resisted by killing an official and destroying the altar.

Mattathias raised an army and began a revolt. But he soon died of old age. His son, Judah, took leadership of the revolt. He was also called **Judas Maccabeus**, or Judah the Hammer. He led surprise attacks throughout the countryside. Though the Seleucids had superior forces, Judas defeated them several times.

After securing his victory, Judas led his army to Jerusalem. They cleansed and rededicated the temple 2,300 days after the first pagan sacrifice was offered, just as the prophet Daniel prophesied (Dan. 8:11–14). The rededication of the temple was celebrated for eight days. Judas Maccabeus declared that this festival, **Hanukkah**, should be celebrated every year with gladness and joy.

The temple was now cleansed. But Judas wanted the Jews to be completely independent of the Seleucids. Judas continued the war against them. After he died, his brothers and their sons continued the fight. The Seleucid Empire became weak. It was not able to keep the Jews under its rule. The Jews were able to set up their own kingdom once again.

The descendants of Judas's brother, Simon, created a dynasty. But it did not last long. Its kings proved to be both ruthless and highly influenced by Greek culture. During this time two groups became important in Judea. They were the Pharisees and the Sadducees. The *Pharisees* were Jews who continued to stress purity of life and obedience to the Torah. They opposed the current rulers. The *Sadducees* were also Jews, but they supported the current rulers. The Sadducees were more influential among the priests and the rulers of Judea.

HANUKKAH

Hanukkah (or Chanukah) is an eight-day holiday that appears on most calendars. It is also referred to as the Festival of Lights. This holiday commemorates the cleansing and rededication of the temple in Jerusalem by Judas Maccabeus and his army.

The most familiar symbol of this holiday is the menorah. The menorah is lit on each night of the festival. According to Jewish tradition, when the menorah was lit at the temple's rededication, there was only enough oil for the lamp to burn for one night. However, the lamp stayed lit for eight nights!

Some menorahs use oil, while others use candles.

One of the activities during Hanukkah includes spinning a top called a dreidel (DRAYD il). Each of the four sides of the top has a Hebrew letter. They are the first letters of the Hebrew words for a "great miracle happened there."

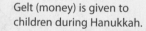

Gelt (money) is given to children during Hanukkah.

Roman Rule

By 200 BC the Roman Republic was the dominant power of the Italian peninsula and the western Mediterranean region. The republic continued to push eastward. It conquered what remained of the Seleucid Empire. Eventually the Roman Republic was ruled by the dictator Julius Caesar. Under his rule the Romans took control of Judea. In 63 BC Caesar made Herod king over Judea. The Jews did not like Herod. He was a ruthless king. Herod continually worried about the security of his throne, so he was willing to kill anyone he thought was a threat to him. The Romans liked Herod because he was a faithful ally of the Roman Republic. They could depend on him to keep Judea under control. Eventually the Romans took over direct rule of Judea.

The Life of Jesus Christ

The Jews believed that the Messiah would be a descendant of David who would come to right all the wrongs they had suffered. During Herod's reign **Jesus** was born. He was a descendant of David and thus of the rightful royal line. The angels who announced His birth identified Him as the King of the Jews. Jesus identified Himself as the **Messiah**, or the *Christ*, Who was anointed to save His people.

Jesus performed many miracles and preached to the people that the kingdom of God was near. He taught that He was a man, yet also God. The followers of Jesus later examined the Hebrew Scriptures. They saw how the prophecies about God's delivering His people through a Messiah were fulfilled in the person of Jesus Christ.

Bethlehem, the city where Jesus was born

Old Jerusalem surrounded by modern Jerusalem

The message of Jesus included an important element. He preached about the need of repentance. Like the ancient prophets, Jesus told the people that the root of all their problems was their sin. If they were to be included in the kingdom of God, they had to repent of their sins.

But the Jews did not recognize Jesus as their Messiah. Instead they rejected Him. The Pharisees and the Sadducees were rivals in Judea. But they conspired together to have Jesus executed for claiming to be the king of the Jews. They accused Jesus of being against Caesar. Jesus was brought before the Romans and crucified.

Those who followed Jesus grieved at His death. But three days later a great miracle happened. Jesus rose from the grave and appeared before His followers alive. All that happened was part of God's sovereign plan. Jesus' death was the payment before God the Father for

the sins of the world. Jesus had taken the penalty for sin that was deserved by all mankind. His death and resurrection made possible the salvation of all people who repent and trust Him for eternal life.

After Jesus ascended back into heaven, His followers continued to spread His message of salvation. They preached the gospel to the people of Israel and to people all over the world. In this way the Jews proved to be a blessing to all the nations, just as God promised Abraham.

One day Jesus will return to earth to rule from Jerusalem. This will be the final fulfillment of the Davidic Covenant. When He rules from earth, He will set all things right. Those who refuse to repent and submit to His lordship will be judged for all eternity. But those who have entered into His kingdom by faith will rule with Him for all eternity.

Ancient synagogue ruins in Bar'am, Israel

Religion After Exile

The punishment of the exile to Babylon cured the Jews from the sin of idolatry for good. To this day the Jewish religion of **Judaism** is a monotheistic religion. The loss of both the temple in Jerusalem and the ability to offer sacrifices there brought changes in Judaism. During the exile, when the Israelites had no temple, the synagogue became the center of Jewish worship instead. The **synagogue** was a place where the Jews could gather for prayer and Scripture reading.

When the Jews returned to Jerusalem after their exile in Babylon, they rebuilt the temple. It became known as the second temple. The Jews could offer sacrifices once again. The synagogue still remained a part of Jewish worship. Jesus taught in synagogues during His earthly ministry.

Later, after the Romans destroyed the second temple, Judaism underwent a further change. The Sadducees lost influence. However, the influence of the Pharisees became strong. The Pharisees practiced what is called rabbinic Judaism. In rabbinic Judaism, the focus is no longer on sacrifices to atone for one's sin. The focus is on careful obedience to the law so that one lives a life that is as pleasing to God as possible.

However, God's purpose for the law is to cause people to turn to the Messiah for salvation. Paul described the problem in the book of Romans. He said that Israel had tried to keep the law but had been unsuccessful. The Jews were so focused on keeping the law to be acceptable to God that they had not recognized Jesus as the Messiah (Rom. 9:31–33).

THE TALMUD

Under rabbinic Judaism, the focus on the law resulted in the production of religious writings. In the first and second centuries AD, the **rabbis** (Jewish religious teachers) wrote down the interpretations of the Law. This writing is called the Mishnah. Later more traditions and stories about how the Law had been applied were recorded in the Gemara. Together, the Mishnah and the Gemara are called the Talmud. The Talmud was completed by the fifth century AD.

Caesarea (SEE zuh REE uh) Maritima was a port city located approximately sixty miles northwest of Jerusalem. King Herod employed Roman engineers to build the city and the harbor. The harbor had loading docks, storage areas, an inner harbor, and an outer harbor with a lighthouse. Caesarea Maritima became a main port for trade.

The harbor had been constructed over a geological fault line that runs along the coast of Israel. Seismic action and the sandy ocean floor caused the foundation to be unstable. There is also evidence that a tsunami struck the area sometime between the first and second centuries AD. Whether this tsunami only damaged the harbor or brought about its complete destruction is unknown. By the sixth century AD, the harbor lay in ruins below the ocean waves.

In June of 1961, Italian archaeologists led by Dr. Antonio Frova uncovered a limestone block at Caesarea Maritima. The block had an inscription that was part of a dedication to Tiberius Caesar from "Pontius Pilate, Prefect [governor] of Judea." The original artifact is now in Jerusalem in the Israel Museum.

The Bible says that, at the time of Jesus Christ, Pilate was the Roman governor of Judea. The limestone is one of the first artifacts discovered that states Pontius Pilate's actual name. It is also the first artifact to identify him as the Roman prefect who made his official residence in Caesarea.

The inscription of this limestone reads:

TIBERIEUM
(PON) TIUS PILATUS
(PRAEF) ECTUS JUDA (EAE)

FOCUS

1. What historian told about the destruction of the second temple?

2. How did the Romans get into Masada?

Destruction of Jerusalem

During the time of Jesus, the rule of Israel began to shift from the Herodian dynasty to Roman rule. Eventually Roman governors ruled the entire region. The governors enriched themselves by taking money from the people. This extortion, combined with the brutality of the Romans, made the Jews yearn for freedom.

Some Jews, known as *Zealots*, were already plotting the overthrow of Rome by military action. But the rest of the people were not ready for such drastic action. That changed, however, when the Roman governor, Florus, took money from the temple treasury for himself. Two Jews responded by mocking the governor as a penniless beggar who needed to steal to get money. Florus responded by having his troops beat, rob, and even crucify Jews. The city erupted and Florus had a full-scale rebellion on his hands. He asked help from his superior and received an entire legion. A **legion** consisted of three to six thousand men. But a legion was not enough. The Romans were ambushed and suffered defeat.

Roman triumphal arch panel showing spoils from the Jerusalem temple

Josephus's Account of the Burning of the Temple

Translated by William Whiston

While the holy house was on fire, every thing was plundered that came to hand, and ten thousand of those that were caught were slain . . . but children, and old men . . . and priests were all slain in the same manner . . . and as well those that made supplication for their lives, as those that defended themselves by fighting. The flame was also carried a long way, and made an echo, together with the groans of those that were slain. . . .

And now the Romans, judging that it was in vain to spare what was round about the holy house, burnt all those places, as also the remains of the cloisters and the gates. . . .

. . . And now all the soldiers had such vast quantities of the spoils which they had gotten by plunder, that in Syria a pound weight of gold was sold for half its former value.

The Roman emperor at the time was Nero. He called on Vespasian, a successful veteran commander, to go to Judea. Vespasian took with him over three legions. Within a year Vespasian had conquered the surrounding country and was preparing to take Jerusalem. At this point, in AD 68, the Roman Empire plunged into civil war. This delayed Vespasian's assault on Jerusalem.

The Jews thought that God had intervened on their behalf. They thought that the Roman Empire would shatter and that Jerusalem and the Jews would be freed once again. But Jesus had already predicted what would happen. He said that when armies surrounded Jerusalem, the people should know that its destruction was about to happen. God would pour out His wrath on His people. Many would be killed and those who remained would be scattered among the nations. Jerusalem itself would be "trodden down of the Gentiles, until the times of the Gentiles be fulfilled" (Luke 21:20–24).

Vespasian received word that an army won for him the position of emperor. He returned to Rome, leaving his son, Titus, in command of the Roman army in Judea.

In **AD 70**, Titus and the Roman army surrounded Jerusalem. For months they stayed in their camps and waited. The people of Jerusalem could not leave their city. No one could enter. The Romans continued to wait until the city suffered from famine. Then the Romans broke down the walls and marched through Jerusalem. After about two months of difficult fighting, the city was firmly in the hands of the Romans.

During the destruction of Jerusalem, the second temple was set on fire and was completely destroyed. The Jewish historian **Josephus**, who was on the side of the Romans in this war, claimed that the destruction of the temple was an accident. Another Roman account says that Titus had ordered the temple's destruction in an effort to destroy the troublesome Jewish religion. In any event the prophecy of judgment recorded in Matthew 24:2 came true. Jesus said of the temple, "There shall not be left here one stone upon another, that shall not be thrown down."

top prevented the attacking army from reaching them.

But the Romans did not give up. For three years they worked to move tons of earth to build a huge ramp. The ramp reached to the top of one of the walls of Masada. When the Jews inside saw that the Romans would break through, they committed mass suicide.

Masada

After the destruction of Jerusalem, three Jewish strongholds remained. The first two fell to the Romans by AD 72. The third stronghold, a mountaintop fortress called Masada, seemed impossible to capture. The Zealot Jews who had taken refuge there had plenty of food and water, and the winding narrow path to the

Israel ceased to exist as a nation in AD 70. However, throughout the centuries, the Jews maintained their identity as a people. In 1948 the nation of Israel was reborn. Although the Jewish people had rejected God's Messiah, God remained faithful to them. The apostle Paul, looking to the future, said, "And so all Israel shall be saved: as it is written, There shall come out of Sion the Deliverer, and shall turn away ungodliness from Jacob: For this is my covenant unto them, when I shall take away their sins" (Rom. 11:26–27).

Masada
What characteristics made Masada a strong fortress?

Chapter 5

Ancient India

FOCUS

1. What two ancient cities were unearthed in India in the 1920s?

2. How do historians know that the people of the Harappan civilization were intelligent and advanced?

A Mystery Unfolds

The sun is starting to rise over a distant sandy hill. Dark-skinned men in flowing robes murmur in the hush of the early morning as they swing shovels rhythmically into the earth. Suddenly, like a rush of wind, the murmur rises to an excited buzz. The men have found something!

The supervisor walks slowly to the spot where the helpers have dug. He cannot get too excited—it could be a false alarm. He kneels beside the hard brick that one of the men has uncovered. The supervisor removes a small, delicate brush from the satchel slung over his shoulder. He gently sweeps the brick. Terra cotta! He leans closer, using his magnifying glass to examine the terra-cotta piece.

Slowly, the supervisor's eyes look upward. He stares at the distant hill, the air now blurring with the sun's bright heat. "It is Mohenjo-Daro," he whispers. "We have found the Indus civilization."

Uncovering the Harappan Civilization

Throughout history, many great civilizations have come and gone. Some of them have left behind a wealth of information. Other civilizations, however, remain a mystery. For a long time, historians did not know much about the ancient civilizations of India. But that all changed after a major discovery.

During the 1920s **Sir John Marshall** and his team of archaeologists discovered the ancient city of **Harappa** (huh RAP uh) and its sister city, **Mohenjo-Daro** (mo-HEN-joh DAR-oh). These cities were located in the Indus Valley in what is now Pakistan. They have been dated at approximately **2300 BC**, and they existed at the same time as Mesopotamia and ancient Egypt.

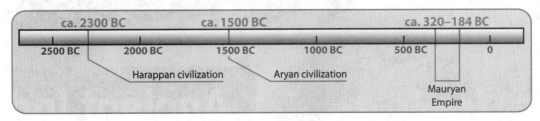

ca. 2300 BC		ca. 1500 BC			ca. 320–184 BC	
2500 BC	2000 BC	1500 BC	1000 BC	500 BC		0
	Harappan civilization		Aryan civilization			
					Mauryan Empire	

In this view of Mohenjo-Daro, the large area at the center is called the Great Bath.
What do some historians believe the Great Bath was used for?

Harappa and Mohenjo-Daro

Archaeological digs do not always uncover secrets from the past. Archaeologists may spend years studying and searching for ancient civilizations. They may excavate site after site, only to end up empty-handed. However, John Marshall and his archaeologists were not disappointed. The discovery of Harappa and Mohenjo-Daro opened the door to a long-forgotten world. Archaeologists and historians could finally begin unraveling the mystery of India's past.

Locate Harappa and Mohenjo-Daro on the map on page 120. Although these cities were far apart, historians believe that both were part of the same civilization. Excavations have uncovered similar artifacts, street plans, and architecture in both cities.

The people from these cities are called the **Harappan civilization**. For about eight hundred years, these ancient Indians flourished in the fertile Indus Valley. Because of the valley's closeness to the river, the land was good for farming and raising animals.

Around 2300 BC some of the first communities in ancient India formed in the Indus Valley. The people of the Harappan civilization were highly sophisticated. Archaeologists have found their cities well-organized. Each city had two-story houses, indoor bathrooms, and a drainage system that ran throughout the entire city. Mohenjo-Daro had a large public pool made of tightly fitted bricks layered with a kind of tar called bitumen. Archaeologists call this structure the Great Bath. Many historians believe that it was used for religious ceremonies.

More artifacts, such as gold ornaments, bronze utensils, and bronze pots, showed archaeologists that the Indus people were artistic and skilled craftsmen. Many of these artifacts contain pictographs, or pictures that represent words or ideas. These ancient writings remain an unsolved mystery even today.

Harappan jar

India

Location—India is a large peninsula in southern Asia, jutting out into the Indian Ocean above the equator. India is bordered by Pakistan to the northwest. China, Nepal, Bhutan, Myanmar, and Bangladesh are on the northeastern and eastern borders. The ancient Harappans lived in what is now Pakistan.

Climate—India's climate varies and can range from dry to tropical. The country is affected by yearly monsoons. Temperatures are above 70°F (21°C) most of the year, except in the north. Annual precipitation ranges from 0 to over 400 inches (1016 cm), depending on the region and the season.

Topography—India contains three major regions. The Himalaya Mountains stretch across northeastern India, forming a natural barrier that separates India and some neighboring countries from the rest of the continent. For this reason, India is often called the **Indian subcontinent**. To the south of the mountains is the northern plain, watered by three rivers: the Indus, the Ganges, and the Brahmaputra. Southern India is a large plateau called the Deccan.

Natural Resources—Natural resources include large deposits of iron ore and some coal. India also has small amounts of other minerals, such as gold, silver, uranium, diamonds, and emeralds. There is also much fertile land.

What geographic feature are both Harappa and Mohenjo-Daro located near?

India Then & Now

Map legend:
- Modern country
- Modern India
- ✴ Modern capital
- • Modern city
- • Ancient city
- – – Harappan civilization

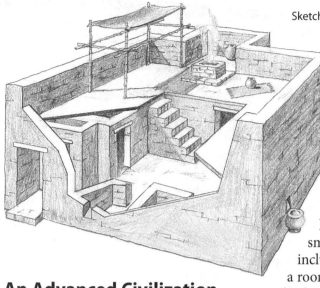

A typical middle-class house had a floor made of red brick. Archaeologists believe the second story may have been made of wood. They found charred bits of wood along the top of some brick walls. Each house had an open courtyard to let in light. Evidence shows that small rooms around the courtyard included a bathroom, a kitchen, and a room for the water well. The house also had rooms that may have been used for hosting guests. The family's sleeping quarters were located in the back area and on the second floor of the house.

The archaeologists found some interesting artifacts in the houses. Weights, jewelry, seals, pottery, utensils made of shells, small clay balls and toys, and statues were common finds. Historians are not certain whether the statues were used as idols or as pieces of art.

An Advanced Civilization

The houses unearthed at Mohenjo-Daro show some interesting details about the Harappan way of life. Mohenjo-Daro appeared to have had two main streets. Many of the buildings along these streets seemed to be middle-class houses, probably owned by merchants and craftsmen.

INDOOR PLUMBING

People today tend to think of ancient peoples as primitive. But in reality, some of them were quite advanced. The Harappans developed technology that allowed them to have running water and indoor plumbing. In the United States, people did not have indoor plumbing until the 1800s. The Harappans also had an advanced sewage system. Homes were equipped with indoor bathrooms and drains that carried the waste to pools. Eventually waste was conveyed to a river or out to the surrounding fields where it could fertilize the crops.

Harappan artifact

Secular historians were surprised to learn how advanced the Harappans were. The Harappan civilization is proof that ancient minds were not inferior to the modern minds of today.

Cataloging an Artifact

When archaeologists work on an excavation site, they must be very careful to keep accurate records of the artifacts they find. Each artifact must first be photographed where it was found and then labeled and removed.

Once the artifact is removed, it is cataloged. When an archaeologist catalogs an artifact, he records certain details about the object and the location where he found it.

1. Work with a partner or a group. Get the following supplies: your Activity Manual, a dig site pan, tape, string, a permanent marker, a spoon, a toothpick, a watercolor paintbrush, a scale, resealable plastic bags, and self-adhesive labels.

2. Use string and tape to divide the pan into four sections. Label each section to match the site map page.

3. Use the spoon, the toothpick, and the paintbrush to carefully work your dig site. Slowly uncover an artifact. Observe its physical appearance. Before removing it, sketch it on the site map page.

4. Carefully lift the artifact and brush away any soil.

5. Examine the artifact and complete the catalog page.

6. Label and package each artifact separately for safe storage.

1. Why is the Harappan language difficult to decipher?

2. What group of people took control of the Indus Valley after the Harappans disappeared?

The Harappan Language

Ever since the excavation of India's ancient cities began, scholars have tried to decipher the writing on the Harappan artifacts. Many of the seals, pottery, and other artifacts display a language written in pictographs. Unfortunately, **linguists**, scholars who study languages, have been unable to decipher the script. Jean-François Champollion deciphered Egyptian hieroglyphs by comparing them with a translation in a known language on the Rosetta stone. Since no such artifact with a translation of Harappan writing exists, it is very difficult for anyone to crack the code.

Without knowing the Harappan people's language, historians have been unable to unravel much of the mystery surrounding their culture. Historians can make guesses about the Harappans' religious beliefs and customs by looking at the pictographs, but they cannot conclude anything definite.

The Disappearance of the Harappan Civilization

The mystery that surrounded the ancient Harappan people deepened as archaeologists uncovered more and more artifacts. One interesting discovery was a group of fourteen skeletons found in one room. Although the room may have been a burial place, it was more likely the scene of a tragedy. The Harappans may have been invaded by another people. Evidence suggests that the civilization came to a sudden halt between 1700 and 1500 BC. There could be a variety of reasons for its disappearance. If not an invasion, a flood or a famine could have driven the inhabitants of Harappa and Mohenjo-Daro from their homes.

Monkey statue

Indus seals were made from clay or stone. *What are the markings along the top of these seals called?*

123

Modern Indian farmers grow much of the world's rice.
What provides much of the water for growing rice?

The Aryan Civilization

One possible cause for the disappearance of the Harappans may have been an invasion by another people from the north. A group of nomads moved into the Indus Valley after **1500 BC**. These nomads called themselves *Arya,* meaning "noble." The **Aryans** began a new period of civilization in the history of India.

The Aryans were warlike people. They came into India with horses, chariots, and weapons. They spread across northern India and settled into villages.

The Aryans also took control over the non-Aryan people of northwestern India. The Aryan way of life became the characteristic culture of ancient and modern India.

Because the Aryans had a written language, much more is known about them than about the Harappans. The written language of the Aryans is called **Sanskrit**. Unlike the Harappan pictographs, Sanskrit has been translated.

The Aryans in India did not form a strong central government but allowed each village to function independently. Each village was governed by a council of leading men and a headman. The headman was the most important man in the village.

Every village had farmers and craftsmen. The craftsmen made tools and household items for the villagers. They also produced artwork. Much of their art reflected their religious beliefs. Sculptures of gods and goddesses were very common and were probably used in worship.

Other villagers farmed for a living. Their success depended upon the annual rains of the wet season. In India the rains come during the summer monsoon season. A **monsoon** is a wind that reverses direction with the change of season. India's summer winds blow from the southwest and bring moisture off the Indian Ocean. Once over land, the water vapor in the air condenses and falls as rain. If the rains are light or late, drought and famine may occur.

Aryans Throughout History

The term *Aryan* has echoed throughout history with different meanings. The original Aryans were the nomadic warriors who invaded India from the north. Some of the Aryans migrated to the area that is now Iran. The name Iran means "land of the Aryans." Thousands of years later, in the twentieth century, *Aryan* was used to describe the people of Hitler's Germany.

The German dictator Adolf Hitler borrowed a false idea from a French philosopher. This idea was that one "master race" was superior to all other races. Hitler believed that the northern European people were the most important race. He called them Aryans. He believed that other races, particularly the Jews, did not deserve to live, so he started executing them. His monstrous crimes against the Jews finally ended with his defeat in World War II. Today the term *Aryan* is often associated with Hitler and the racist ideas he represented.

The swastika prominently displayed at one of Hitler's Nazi rallies

The Aryan name was not all that Hitler borrowed from the Aryans. He also borrowed one of their symbols, the swastika. This symbol has been found on ancient buildings and artifacts from India, Turkey, and Egypt. The term *swastika* in the Sanskrit language means "a sign of good luck." In modern times the swastika and the term *Aryan* have gained a negative tone because of their association with Hitler.

This seal (right) and its imprint (left) have a swastika design.

1. What religion did the Aryans develop?

2. How does Hinduism influence family and social life in India?

Religions of Ancient India

Hinduism

While the nomadic Aryans traveled, they likely encountered different peoples and cultures. As the Aryans settled in India, they adopted many beliefs and customs from other people groups. The Aryans developed a religion called **Hinduism** (HIHN doo IHZ uhm). Hinduism spread across India and still exists today. This religion was not fully formed until after the time of Christ. However, its beliefs and practices quickly grew to influence the Indians' entire way of life.

Beliefs and Practices

Like many other ancient religions, Hinduism is polytheistic. Hindus worship thousands of gods, but they consider three gods to be the most important. These three gods are *Brahma*, the Creator; *Shiva* (SHEE vuh), the Destroyer; and *Vishnu* (VISH noo), the Preserver.

> Thou shalt have no other gods before me. Thou shalt not make unto thee any graven image, or any likeness of any thing that is in heaven above, or that is in the earth beneath, or that is in the water under the earth: Thou shalt not bow down thyself to them, nor serve them.
>
> **Exodus 20:3–5**

Hindus believe that these three gods, as well as thousands of other gods, are different forms of the great god **Brahman**. He is not a personal being, so he is often called the great soul, or world soul. Hindus believe that everything in the world, including plants, animals, and gods, is part of Brahman. This belief is **pantheism**, the idea that everything in the universe is part of a supreme being.

Vishnu
What is unusual about Vishnu's arms?

HINDUISM

Hinduism teaches that there are many gods. It also teaches that the universe is part of the great god or world soul. The Bible clearly tells us that the one true God is the Creator and Lord over all things.

Hinduism teaches that, to have a better state in the next life, people should obey the Hindu rules and do good works. The Bible teaches that Jesus Christ is the Savior of the world and that salvation does not depend on good works.

Hindus believe that a person might live many different lives through reincarnation. The Bible teaches that it is appointed to each person to die once, and after this, he must face judgment (Heb. 9:27).

Hindus believe that each person eventually becomes part of a world soul called Brahman. The Bible teaches that a person will spend eternity with Jesus Christ if he has confessed his sinfulness and asked the crucified and risen Son of God to save him.

Hindus are very concerned about doing their duty. Their duty, or **dharma**, requires them to always behave in a certain way to be part of Brahman. Most Hindus follow their religious practices diligently. They pray, perform rituals, worship at Hindu temples and shrines, and bring sacrifices and money to the priests. Some Hindus try to become holier by disciplining their bodies. They seclude, starve, and inflict pain on themselves in an attempt to make their souls purer for Brahman. By following these practices, the Hindus hope to be good enough to eventually become a part of him.

Another part of Hinduism is **reincarnation**, the belief that a person lives more than once in different bodies—even in animals. A person's state in reincarnation depends on the karma he has built up in his present state. **Karma** is the result of one's good or bad deeds. A person who does good deeds will build good karma. Someone who has done evil or failed to do his duty builds bad karma. Because of their belief in reincarnation, many Hindus seek to increase their good karma through good works.

This tower, called a gopura, marks the entrance to the Hindu temple in Mysore, India.

In this Indian illustration, Brahma (lower left) is holding the Vedas. *What language is written along the top of the picture?*

वाता वसाता शरद अश्रु श्रीविचित्रेवेदिपरिकर्मसम्काः कुंदावदाता चतु: नस्या घभावती लध्वविचित्रसेवाा दी ।

The Written Legacy

How do we know so much about early Hinduism? The ancient Hindus left a written legacy called the **Vedas**, the sacred books of Hinduism. These books were written in Sanskrit. The Sanskrit word *veda* means "knowledge."

The Rig-Veda is the oldest Veda. It has been dated at around 1500 BC and is one of the earliest known books in the world.

PASSAGE FROM THE RIG-VEDA

Here is the English translation of a passage from the Rig-Veda. It is taken from a hymn addressed to Ushas, the Hindu goddess of dawn. When you first read it, it might seem similar to a psalm in the Bible. But when you take a closer look, you will see important differences. *What false ideas are promoted in this Hindu hymn?*

Dawn on us with prosperity, O [Ushas], Daughter of the Sky,
Dawn with great glory, Goddess,
Lady of the Light, dawn thou with riches, Bounteous One....
For in thee is each living creature's breath and life.

(tr. by Ralph T. H. Griffith, "Dawn," Hymn XLVIII)

The Rig-Veda is a collection of hymns, prayers, and poems. It tells of the rituals and the philosophy of ancient Hinduism and shows that the ancient Indians enjoyed beauty and artistry.

A later book, the Upanishads, describes the Hindu teachings in more detail.

These Indians and their livestock have gathered for the Pushkar Fair, a religious occasion.

Families and Castes

In Hinduism man's relationship to the gods is very important, but his relationship to other people is important as well. Because Hinduism teaches that everything is a part of Brahman, it emphasizes the group above the individual. Social relationships in Hinduism center on the group. The two basic groups in India since the rise of Hinduism have been the family and the **caste** (KAST), or social class.

The core of ancient Indian life was the family. When the Aryans settled in India, they encouraged large families. Families included more than just parents and their children. Grandparents, parents, sons, daughters-in-law, unmarried daughters, and grandchildren lived together in compounds made up of several huts or houses.

The oldest man in the family had complete authority over the other members. Everyone had to follow his orders. Hinduism teaches that obedience in the family is an important duty for becoming part of Brahman.

The second important social group that every Indian belonged to was the caste. Castes were the classes of Indian society. Every person was born into a caste, which he would stay in for the rest of his life. Hindus believe that the higher a person is in the caste system, the closer he is to reuniting with Brahman. Every Hindu hopes that when he is reincarnated, he will be reborn into a higher caste.

A Hindu wedding
How does this bride and groom differ from ones you have seen?

There were four main caste divisions in Indian society. The highest was the priestly caste. The priests held a great deal of power over the people. Hindus believed that when a member of the priestly caste died, he reunited immediately with the Brahman world spirit.

The next caste was made up of warriors and rulers. The caste below that was made up of farmers, traders, and artisans. Finally laborers and servants belonged to the lowest caste. Within the four main castes, there were hundreds of subcastes.

Some Indians were outside the caste system. They were called **untouchables** or outcastes. Untouchables included any non-Hindu, anyone who worked with meat, and anyone who had been expelled from his own caste. The English word *outcast* and its meaning come from the Hindu caste system.

Each caste had rules for its members. The caste rules dictated whom one married, one's occupation, and one's clothing. Caste rules even determined whom a caste member could eat with. Part of dharma was keeping the rules of one's caste and being content to stay in it. In this way, an Indian would gain good karma and have an opportunity to be reborn into a higher caste. A Hindu who did more or less than what his caste demanded was unlikely to be reborn on a higher level. The caste system made Indian society very rigid. Today the caste system still exists in India although it is not as rigid as it once was.

Modern Indian people whose lives are similar to the untouchables of the past

FOCUS

1. Who developed the religion of Buddhism?

2. Why did Buddhism appeal to Indians who were not satisfied with Hinduism?

Life Under the Caste System

If you had lived in ancient India, how do you think you would have felt about the caste system? It would probably depend on which caste you had been born into.

People who were part of the higher castes were proud of their status in life. People in the highest caste had all their needs met by people in the lower castes. The lower castes grew food for them to eat, made clothes for them to wear, made furnishings for their homes, and defended them against their enemies.

A modern Hindu priest

The Caste System	
Caste	**Occupations**
Brahmans	priests
Kshatriyas	warriors rulers
Vaisyas	farmers traders artisans/craftspeople
Sudras	laborers servants
Outcastes (untouchables)	non-Hindus unclean laborers expelled caste members

Some people in the lower castes enjoyed their work. They were content with their place in society and did not want to change. However, others may have wished for better or different jobs. Some people may have wished to marry someone in a higher or lower caste. These people either had to accept their place in life and keep the rules or be expelled from their caste.

Many people were satisfied with the Hindu caste system. They believed that it kept order and peace in Indian society. Others suffered because of the strict caste rules. The untouchables were rejected by others and excluded from normal life. Their only hope was to do their duty, die, and have a better life in a reincarnated state.

131

Siddhartha Gautama

Siddhartha Gautama was born into a ruling family as a member of the warrior caste. His family was wealthy and his early life was comfortable. He grew up and married, and he and his wife had a son. Although Gautama had many of the luxuries this world could offer, he was not happy. The poverty and pain he saw in the world bothered him. At age twenty-nine, he left his home to find a remedy for his own unhappiness and that of the world.

Sadly, Gautama did not search for truth from the right source. For six years he lived in seclusion and nearly starved himself to death by fasting. But he found no answers that satisfied him. Then, according to legend, one day while meditating beneath a tree, Gautama became **enlightened**, or gained understanding, about the meaning of life. After this he changed his name to Buddha.

Buddha thought that he had discovered the truth. He believed that he had found the solution to the problem of suffering in the world. He devoted the rest of his life to telling people what he believed to be the truth. He traveled around India teaching and gaining many followers for his new religion.

Gautama teaching followers
What kind of feeling does the picture portray?

Buddhism

Around 500 BC, one man began to question the teachings of Hinduism. His questions eventually led him to develop a new religion. His name was **Siddhartha Gautama** (si-DAHR-tuh GOU-tuh-muh). Siddhartha Gautama became dissatisfied with Hindu beliefs. He disliked the caste system and the priests who ruled the people. The Hindus believed that only members of the priestly caste were ready to reunite with the Brahman. But Gautama could not accept that. He decided that he was going to change his beliefs.

Siddhartha Gautama changed his name to **Buddha**, meaning "Enlightened One." He introduced what he called the Four Noble Truths. In these writings he proposed that suffering can be overcome if a person does good works and ignores his desires. His religion became known as **Buddhism**.

The Eightfold Path was Buddha's list of good works. According to Buddhism, doing the things on the list is supposed to help a person achieve happiness and peace.

In Buddhism a person's ultimate goal or salvation is to reach **nirvana** (nir VAH nuh), a state of complete enlightenment, with peace and freedom from desires and wants. Only in this way will a person stop suffering. Like Hindus, Buddha believed in reincarnation. He believed that people would have another chance to reach nirvana if they did not achieve it in the present life.

THE FOUR NOBLE TRUTHS

1. All people experience suffering.
2. Suffering is caused by desires for pleasures or things that a person cannot have.
3. A person can end suffering only by getting rid of all his desires.
4. A person can free himself from desires and end suffering by following the Eightfold Path.

THE EIGHTFOLD PATH

1. Know and believe the Four Noble Truths.
2. Be good and kind to others.
3. Be truthful and refrain from gossip.
4. Live a moral life, avoiding evil actions, like stealing and harming others.
5. Work in a job where you can help, not hurt, others.
6. Do good and oppose evil.
7. Think positive, healthy thoughts.
8. Practice meditation.

The sleeping Buddha

133

BUDDHISM

Buddhism teaches that a person's salvation, or enlightenment, depends on his good works and right thinking. The Bible teaches that salvation from sin comes only through Jesus Christ and His payment of sin's penalty on the cross.

Buddhism teaches that suffering can be overcome by getting rid of desires and wants. The Bible teaches that suffering is the result of man's sin. Christ suffered in man's place on the cross to take away sin. Christians can view suffering as an opportunity to see God's faithfulness. Someday God will end suffering for believers forever when He makes a new heaven and a new earth.

Buddhism requires its followers to meditate on riddles or pleasant thoughts to find peace. The Bible instructs Christians to meditate on God's Word to experience God's blessings.

Buddhism gained popularity in India. Which classes of Indian society do you think Buddhism appealed to the most? It was especially attractive to the untouchables and to the members of the lower castes. Buddhism was not based on a caste system. Buddhism gave everyone an equal opportunity to be enlightened. It gave the lower classes hope that they could change their circumstances. Some people in the higher classes also appreciated Buddha's ideas.

Buddhism spread to other parts of the world besides India. It gained many followers in other parts of Asia. Later in this chapter you will learn how it became so widespread.

Key Gompa, built in the early eleventh century, is still an active Buddhist monastery in the Himalaya Mountains of India. *Locate the Himalaya Mountains on the map on page 120.*

Recognizing Sanskrit's Influence on English

Linguists are interested in how languages influence each other. When two different language groups frequently have contact with each other, both languages change. Each people group tends to adopt words and phrases from the other. The spellings or meanings of borrowed words can change slightly in the new language. Over time the borrowed words may become so common that no one thinks about their being from another language.

English has been influenced by many other languages. One of those languages is Sanskrit, the ancient language of the Aryans. English is a much newer language than Sanskrit, so you might be surprised to discover how many commonly used English words have been borrowed from Sanskrit.

MMMM SANSKRIT, SANSKRIT, SANSKRIT MMMM

1. Look up the following words in a dictionary.

   bandanna   loot   shawl
   guru   mantra   sugar
   jungle   orange   yoga

2. Examine the etymology of each word. The etymology is the word's origin or history, including what language the word came from. It is usually found in brackets at the beginning or the end of the dictionary entry. You will find that some Sanskrit words are related to Indian religions. Others are taken from daily Indian life and culture.

3. Write out the Sanskrit word that each English word on the list comes from. If the meaning of the original Sanskrit word is given, write down that meaning as well. Compare the Sanskrit meaning with the English meaning.

4. Write a paragraph about your findings. Which Sanskrit words are related to Indian religions? How have the meanings of these words changed in English? What can you learn about daily life and culture in ancient India from the meanings of these words?

Identifying Cause and Effect

As we study history, we can learn from the accomplishments and the mistakes of people in the past. Often we can see how one event affected another. Looking for causes and effects in history can help us avoid repeating the mistakes of the past.

A *cause* is an event or circumstance that makes something else happen. An *effect* is the result of a cause. Recognizing these relationships can help you gain a better understanding of historical events.

1. Get your Student Text and Activity Manual page.

2. With your partner, read a section in this chapter to find an important event or circumstance.

3. Decide whether the event represents a cause or an effect. Record this event in the correct column on your chart. If this event is a cause, go to step 4. If it is an effect, skip to step 5.

4. If the event is a cause, identify one of its effects. As you look for the effect, think through the following questions: *What did this event lead to? What was the result?* Record the effect in the appropriate space on the chart.

5. If the event is an effect, identify the event or circumstance that caused it. As you look for the cause, think through the following questions: *Why did this happen? What led to this?* Record the cause in the appropriate space on the chart.

6. Continue reading other sections in the chapter. Record six cause-and-effect relationships.

FOCUS

1. What did Asoka do to encourage the spread of Buddhism in Asia?

2. What are some of John Marshall's contributions to our knowledge of ancient India?

The Mauryan Empire

Chandragupta

In 326 BC the army of the Greek leader Alexander the Great conquered portions of northwestern India. According to legend, while Alexander was in India, he met a young Indian warrior named **Chandragupta Maurya** (CHUHN-druh-GOOP-tuh MAH-ur-yuh). Like Alexander, Chandragupta decided to train a large army of his own.

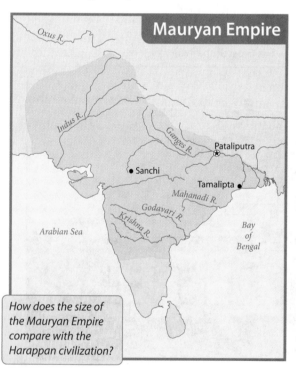

Mauryan Empire

Oxus R.

Indus R.

Ganges R.

Pataliputra

Sanchi

Tamalipta

Mahanadi R.

Godavari R.

Krishna R.

Arabian Sea

Bay of Bengal

How does the size of the Mauryan Empire compare with the Harappan civilization?

Chandragupta conquered most of the Ganges River Valley. After Alexander died, Chandragupta and his army conquered the portion of India that Alexander had taken. Chandragupta added these small kingdoms to his empire and became the first ruler in the Mauryan dynasty. Almost all northern India was under his rule.

Chandragupta made many decisions that strengthened India as an empire. He chose **Pataliputra** (POT uh lih POO truh) as his capital city and established a centralized government there. He maintained a strong army of six hundred thousand soldiers. His military also included elephants and chariots. However, Chandragupta did not trust his subjects. He set up a network of spies throughout the empire to inform him of any rebellion.

137

Asoka

Asoka (uh SOH kuh), a grandson of Chandragupta, came to the throne in 273 BC. Asoka was one of the greatest rulers of the Mauryan Empire. He united most of the Indian subcontinent under his leadership.

However, after years of great military successes, Asoka began to hate warfare. He saw the bloodshed that resulted when he subdued other cities, and he lost his desire to conquer. Instead, he devoted himself to Buddhism and its teachings.

TWO TYPES OF BUDDHISM

As Buddhism spread to other countries, it developed into two different branches: Theravada Buddhism and Mahayana Buddhism. Theravada Buddhism is practiced mainly in southern Asia. It is the stricter of the two branches and sticks very closely to Siddhartha Gautauma's teachings. Mahayana Buddhism interprets Buddha's teachings more freely. Mahayana Buddhists do not believe it is as difficult to reach enlightenment as Theravada Buddhists do. Mahayana Buddhism is the larger of the two branches.

Asoka worked diligently to promote Buddhism in his empire. He built thousands of dome-shaped shrines called **stupas** (STOO puz). His most well-known structure is the Great Stupa.

Since Buddhism emphasizes doing good works and relieving suffering, Asoka also made many improvements to give his people better lives. He dug wells, planted trees, and constructed hospitals throughout his realm. Asoka did much good, but in his spiritual blindness, he led his people away from the true God.

Asoka had a major part in spreading Buddhism to other countries. His zeal led him to send Buddhist missionaries into areas outside his own borders. Many other Asian countries adopted Buddhism. Even today it is a popular religion in countries such as Myanmar, Thailand, Cambodia, Sri Lanka, China, Korea, Japan, and Tibet.

The Great Stupa in Sanchi, India

Sir John Hubert Marshall

John Marshall was a British archaeologist who became famous for his work in India in the early 1900s. He was born in 1876 in Chester, England. Marshall received his college education at King's College, Cambridge. While still in his early twenties, he took part in excavations on the Greek island of Crete.

In 1902 Marshall was named Director General of Archaeology in India. He excavated sections of the cities of Harappa and Mohenjo-Daro. He also helped uncover the ruins of the Mauryan Empire.

John Marshall helped restore the Great Stupa. The structure is shaped like the top half of an egg. It was originally surrounded by four gateways that were decorated with ornately carved reliefs. The reliefs included various Buddhist symbols, such as wheels, footprints, and trees. The Great Stupa was damaged after the fall of the Mauryan Empire. Marshall rebuilt the damaged section and added a railing around the walkway that encircled the stupa. He also helped restore several of the smaller stupas in the same location. Students of art and architecture still study the Great Stupa today for its fascinating design.

John Marshall was a careful and tireless leader of the archaeological work in India. He organized excavations, recorded data, and established museums. He also recruited and trained Indian nationals to help him. Marshall was knighted in 1914 and received numerous other awards for his work.

Most people living in modern India, however, claim Hinduism as their religion. Ancient Hindu priests saw Buddhism as a threat to India's caste system, but during his reign, Asoka tolerated those who opposed Buddhism and allowed them to practice other religions. Perhaps this is one reason that Buddhism is not a major force in India today.

Asoka is believed by many to have been the greatest of the Mauryan kings. He died in 233 BC, and his sons struggled for power. As the empire weakened, invaders were able to overcome the last Mauryan king in 184 BC.

Nearly six hundred years later, around AD 400, a great empire called the Gupta was established in India. This empire began a period called the Golden Age of India.

Only in the last century has the mystery surrounding the ancient civilizations of India begun to unravel. As time goes on, more facts may be discovered. Perhaps one day we will even be able to read the Harappan language.

Sadly, much of India's history is shadowed by the false religions that its people created. Yet God has not forgotten India. One day people of every language and nation will worship Christ as the Lamb. Jesus Christ shed His blood to redeem them to God (Rev. 5:9–10). Many of India's people will be among them.

The gospel being preached in modern Mumbai, India

Chapter 6

Ancient China

Geography

In the eastern part of the world, a civilization quietly grew and thrived. Ancient China was hidden from the rest of the world by mountains, jungles, a desert, and an ocean. These natural boundaries protected the Chinese people from foreign invaders for many centuries.

This isolation did not keep China's culture from flourishing. The Chinese were not behind for their time. In fact, they were an advanced people—more skilled than many other peoples of their day. The advanced skills of the Chinese support the fact that man, created in God's image, has always been intelligent.

When the early Chinese migrated to East Asia, they settled near rivers. These rivers flooded and left fertile silt behind, making the land suitable for farming. Along these rivers the Chinese built villages that eventually grew into a civilization. They named their land the **Middle Kingdom**, because they thought it was in the center of the earth. The Chinese flourished as an advanced civilization.

What was one of the geographic features that protected China from its enemies?

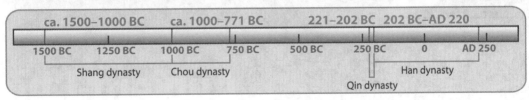

ca. 1500–1000 BC		ca. 1000–771 BC			221–202 BC	202 BC–AD 220	
1500 BC	1250 BC	1000 BC	750 BC	500 BC	250 BC	0	AD 250
	Shang dynasty		Chou dynasty			Han dynasty	
					Qin dynasty		

China

Location—China is the third-largest country in the world. It is located in East Asia, also known as the Far East. China shares its borders with fourteen countries: North Korea to the east; Russia and Mongolia to the north; Kazakhstan, Kyrgyzstan, Tajikistan, Afghanistan, and Pakistan to the west; and India, Nepal, Bhutan, Myanmar, Laos, and Vietnam to the south.

Climate—Most of China has a temperate climate similar to that of the United States. Both countries are close to the same lines of latitude. China's temperature varies from region to region. The climate is affected by yearly monsoons. Annual precipitation ranges from less than 1 inch to more than 80 inches (about 2–203 cm). The northern regions are snowy in the winter, and the southeastern coast is rainy in the summer and autumn.

Topography—The eastern region is the lowlands, where the Huang He and the Yangtze River flow to the ocean. In central China the land becomes rolling hills. The western part of China is hilly and mountainous. Tibet, in southwest China, has some of the highest mountain peaks in the world.

Natural Resources—China is one of the world's largest producers of iron ore. Large amounts of coal and oil exist there, but the industry for these resources needs further development. Other natural resources include deposits of tungsten, bauxite, aluminum, zinc, uranium, iron ore, tin, lead, and mercury. The land has been heavily farmed, and many of the original forests have been destroyed.

China Then & Now

Modern country
Modern China
Modern capital
Shang dynasty

RUSSIA
MONGOLIA
KAZAKHSTAN
KYRGYZSTAN
TAJIKISTAN
AFGHANISTAN
Gobi Desert
Beijing
NORTH KOREA
SOUTH KOREA
CHINA
Huang He
JAPAN
TIBET
Himalaya Mountains
Yangtze R.
PAKISTAN
NEPAL
BHUTAN
INDIA
PACIFIC OCEAN
MYANMAR
LAOS
BANGLADESH
THAILAND
VIETNAM
INDIAN OCEAN

0   500   1,000 mi
0   1000 km

What ocean borders China?

143

The Huang He, or Yellow River, was important to the Shang civilization. The silt in the river gives it a yellow color.

The Shang

China was ruled by several dynasties. One of the earliest was the **Shang**. This dynasty started ruling about 1500 BC. The Shang settled along the **Huang He**, or Yellow River, in northern China. Most of the common people during the Shang dynasty were farmers. They grew vegetables and grains, especially rice, for food. The Huang He was often called "China's Sorrow" because its many floods killed thousands of people and ruined many harvests.

Religion

The Shang people, particularly the royal family, practiced a religion that involved **ancestor worship**. An ancestor is anyone from whom a person is descended. The Shang believed that the spirits of their departed ancestors lived on in the afterworld. They thought the ancestors had magical powers that allowed them to punish or help the Shang people. When the weather was good, the Shang believed that their ancestors were pleased. If drought or famine came to the land, the Shang thought they had angered their ancestors in some way.

To please their ancestors, the people used ornate bronze vessels, called **tings** (or dings), to cook meat for a sacrifice. Royal families had special ceremonies for preparing and serving their sacrifices. These sacrifices were offered as food to the ancestors.

Shang dynasty bronze ting
How was a ting used in worship?

144

Oracle bone
What did priests write on oracle bones?

rains flood the land?" Then the priest heated the bone with a hot metal rod. The heat caused the bone to crack. These cracks were believed to be the "answers" from the gods and the ancestors. The priest interpreted these cracks and reported to the king. The king could then make his decisions based on these answers. Kings consulted priests and oracle bones before making decisions about planting, fighting, and building.

The priests were also governmental officials. They kept a close watch on political and economic affairs. Most of the priests' interpretations of oracle bones were based on current events. Because the king and the people believed that the priests could interpret oracle bones, the priests had great power in the Shang dynasty.

ANCESTOR WORSHIP

The Chinese believed that their ancestors had the power to influence the affairs of the living. The Bible teaches that only God has control over all things (Dan. 4:34–35).

Many Chinese still believe that descendants must perform proper rites to give their ancestors the proper afterlife. This duty makes it very difficult for many Chinese to become Christians. They know that if a person becomes a Christian, he will not offer sacrifices to his ancestors. He might be told that he is not honoring the family. The Bible teaches that children should honor their parents (Exod. 20:12). However, Jesus said in Luke 14:26 that honoring parents cannot be placed above honoring God.

In addition to ancestor worship, the Shang practiced polytheism. They worshiped a supreme god who was over lesser gods.

The Shang religion centered on rituals and superstition. Besides using tings in ancestor worship, the Shang also used oracle bones. **Oracle bones** were animal bones or turtle shells used to predict the future. The king had a priest write a question on the bone, such as "Will we win the battle?" or "Will the

Making a Raised Relief Map

The China Then & Now map on page 143 is a physical map of modern China. It is a flat representation that shows physical features, such as mountains, rivers, and valleys. In this activity, you will be making a kind of physical map, but your map will be a three-dimensional model. This kind of map is called a raised relief map. On it you will show details of land features, such as the heights of mountains, the depths of valleys, and the paths of rivers cutting through the surrounding land.

1. Gather the following materials: the instruction page, a map pattern, cardboard, salt dough, a paintbrush, and paint.

2. Trace the outline of the map onto the cardboard.

3. Fill in the outline of your map pattern with the dough. Shape mountains, valleys, rivers, and other land features.

4. Let the dough dry.

5. Paint and label your map. Include a key.

6. Display your map.

FOCUS

1. What three metals were used to make bronze?

2. What did the Chou leaders use to justify their rebellion against the Shang dynasty?

Arts

The ancient Chinese were skilled artists. One area of their skill was in metalworking. Their special techniques in making bronze have not been equaled, even today. For centuries the Chinese kept their metalworking knowledge from other countries.

The Shang used bronze to make ornaments, statues, and vessels, such as tings. They developed a difficult process of bronze casting that no other ancient people used. First, metalworkers made a mold in the shape of the object to be cast. The mold was made of several pieces of clay that fit tightly together. The detailed designs of the object were carved into the clay. After the mold was made, the metalworker poured the molten bronze, consisting of copper, tin, and lead, into the mold. When the bronze cooled and hardened, the mold was carefully removed and saved for reuse. Once polished, the bronze object was ready to use.

Mineral Resources of Modern China

Legend:
- ✚ Antimony
- ✩ Bauxite
- ■ Coal
- ▢ Copper
- ▨ Gold
- ● Graphite
- ○ Iron
- ▲ Lead
- ✳ Mangnesite
- ● Mercury
- ▣ Petroleum
- ○ Phosphates
- ◆ Tin
- ⬟ Tungsten
- ✘ Zinc

In what part of China are the metals found to make bronze?

Although the Shang are best known for their works of bronze, they made advances in other arts as well. Farmers produced silk, which weavers made into colorful clothes. Artisans made vases and dishes from fine white clay. The Shang also carved statues from a green stone called jade. The use of chopsticks dates back to the Shang dynasty.

Royal palaces and walled cities were part of the Shang heritage in architecture. The ruler's palace was at the center of the capital city. The houses of the artisans surrounded the palace. These houses were rectangular and built on flattened earthen platforms.

Shang Tombs

Toward the end of their rule, the Shang moved their capital near the present-day city of Anyang (AHN YAHNG). Much of what is known about the Shang dynasty comes from the royal tombs discovered in Anyang. The Shang buried their rulers with their valuables and pottery. Bronze cups, chariots, and oracle bones have been discovered in the tombs. The oracle bones show that the Shang had a system of writing.

The Shang buried their dead in deep, cross-shaped pits. Each pit was covered with a wooden roof. Slanted ramps leading from the center of each grave allowed the body and burial offerings to be carried to the bottom. Some tombs contained the remains of human and animal sacrifices.

Government

In many ancient dynasties, the rule of the throne passed from the father to the son. However, in the Shang dynasty, the rule passed from the eldest brother to the youngest brother.

The Shang dynasty lasted for about six hundred years. It eventually weakened and was conquered. This sequence of events became a pattern throughout Chinese history. Each dynasty prospered for a period, but then it declined and was overthrown.

Ancient chariots

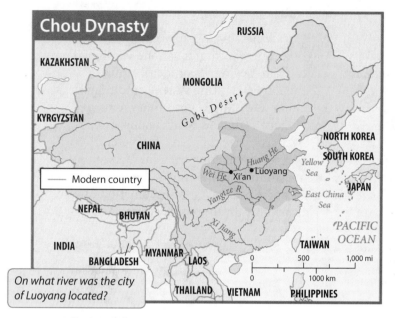

Chou Dynasty

On what river was the city of Luoyang located?

The Chou

About 1000 BC the **Chou** (JO) invaded the Shang from the west and overthrew their dynasty. The Chou rule lasted longer than any other dynasty in Chinese history. There were thirty-seven kings in eight hundred years.

The period in which the Chou dynasty ruled is called China's classical age. Much of China's culture was established during this time. A **classical age** is a time in a civilization's history that is thought to be its high point of cultural development and achievement.

Government

The Chou believed that heaven, the supreme force of nature, gave the king his right to rule. This belief was called the **Mandate of Heaven**. According to the mandate, a king should be righteous and kind. If a king failed to act properly, he lost his right to rule. The mandate allowed the people to seize control from the king by force if needed. If the new king they placed on the throne was successful, the people viewed his success as proof of heaven's support for his rule. The king was called the Son of Heaven. The Mandate of Heaven became a tradition of Chinese government. The Chou leaders used this belief to justify their rebellion against the Shang.

The king was the highest authority in the Chou dynasty. Beneath him were the nobles, and under them were the peasant farmers. The king gave his nobles land in exchange for their loyalty. Nobles also paid taxes and provided soldiers for the king's use. Nobles governed over the land that they owned. They gave plots of land to the peasant families to farm in return for a portion of the crops and goods produced.

King Wu of the Chou fulfilled the wish of his dying father by defeating the Shang dynasty.

The Family

China developed and preserved its culture throughout history. Its culture was built around strong family ties.

The traditional family in China included many generations. A family usually occupied the same house or houses around a common courtyard. The members of the family that lived together included children, parents, grandparents, aunts, uncles, and cousins. Older family members had more power and privileges than younger ones. Men were considered more important than women. Fathers were respected and obeyed by their wives and children.

The Writing System

The Chinese firmly established their writing system during the Chou dynasty. Like the writing of many other ancient peoples, early Chinese writing consisted of pictographs. The Chinese used brushes to make fine strokes when writing. This way of writing became a form of art.

Chinese pictographs changed over time. Some pictographs were combined to form new words or ideas. Unlike the English writing system, traditional Chinese writing is not based on a simple alphabet. Chinese writing consists of over sixty-five thousand characters that represent complete ideas, objects, and sounds. For example, the character for the word *good* is a combination of characters for the words *girl* and *boy*.

女　子　好

girl　　　boy　　　good

People learn to read Chinese by memorizing each of the characters. Those who master the written language have always had a place of distinction in Chinese society. Most Chinese people today know only about four thousand characters.

Chinese characters are made with a brush.

1. On what occasions was music played during the Chou dynasty?

2. What did Confucius believe was needed to keep harmony and order in a society?

Classical Art

Artisans of the Chou dynasty worked with bronze as the Shang had done. But the Chou craftsmen developed a simpler method of making bronze. Many of their fine works still exist today. Artisans covered many of the bronze items with Chinese writing and intricate carvings of both real and imaginary animals.

The Chou, like the Shang, used their bronze works mainly in religious ceremonies. The ceremonies often included placing the vessels in the tombs of ancestors. The Chou also carved pieces of jade to create decorative pieces of art.

Jade art

Music was important to the ancient Chinese. It was played during times of worship, work, and pleasure. Beautiful music and an elaborate ceremony often accompanied archery tournaments attended by Chou nobles.

Sets of bronze bells played an important part in many social activities and political state ceremonies. Most Chou bells did not have a clapper. The bells were struck with metal objects such as hammers.

Classical Education

Education was important during the Chou period. A good education was highly prized by Chinese philosophers such as **Confucius** (kuhn FYOO shuhs). A **philosopher** is a scholar who dedicates himself to the pursuit of earthly wisdom. Confucius was also a teacher. His ideas greatly influenced China's classical age.

Confucius wrote many proverbs about everyday life. A **proverb** is a wise saying that expresses a simple truth. One of his proverbs was "Learning without thought is a snare; thought without learning is a danger." Confucius made education available to students from all social classes. A person from even the poorest background could have a good future if he had a good education.

In China education began at an early age and demanded total dedication of time and energy. Students spent many years learning the difficult Chinese language. They also memorized classical Chinese literature.

In most ancient civilizations, soldiers, priests, and merchants held important positions among the people. Through

Confucius was a teacher during the Chou dynasty. *What are some differences between this scene and your school?*

much of Chinese history, however, no one exceeded the influence of the scholars.

Scholars during the Chou dynasty wrote many books. These books are considered the classics of Chinese literature. Poetry, history, rituals, conduct, and music are some of the subjects of the books from that period. One had to have a thorough knowledge of these books to be considered a true scholar in China. Many ancient Chinese books were based on the teachings of Confucius.

The Influence of Confucius

Confucius was born into a poor but respected family. He lived during a time of social and political unrest. Confucius believed that through proper behavior man could solve the problems of society. He taught his students that proper behavior would also allow man to live in complete happiness. Confucius especially tried to convince the rulers of his ideas.

One part of his teaching was the belief in five basic human relationships. In these relationships a person's duty is to obey the elder person or the ruler. And

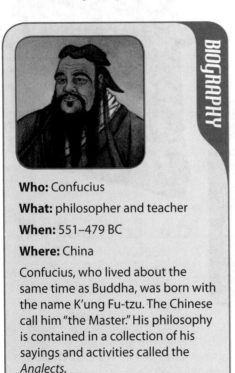

BIOGRAPHY

Who: Confucius

What: philosopher and teacher

When: 551–479 BC

Where: China

Confucius, who lived about the same time as Buddha, was born with the name K'ung Fu-tzu. The Chinese call him "the Master." His philosophy is contained in a collection of his sayings and activities called the *Analects*.

the elder person or the ruler must set a good example for those under him.

Confucius believed that if proper relationships in these five areas were kept, society would have harmony and order. Confucius expressed his belief about human relationships in the proverb "What you do not want done to yourself, do not do to others."

Five Basic Relationships

Duty: to set a good example of proper behavior	Duty: to show respect and obedience
father	son
elder brother	younger brother
husband	wife
elder friend	younger friend
ruler	subject

CONFUCIANISM

Confucianism identifies five basic human relationships, but it leaves out the most important relationship of all—man and God. Jesus said that the greatest commandment of all is to love God with all of one's heart, soul, and mind (Matt. 22:37).

Confucianism teaches that people simply need to choose to act rightly in every relationship. It assumes that people are basically good. The Bible teaches that since unsaved people are slaves to sin, they are unable to simply choose to do right (Rom. 6:17; 8:7–8).

Confucianism is man-centered and relies on man's effort to achieve human goals. It does not teach that there is a divine being. Christians know that God exists. They know that sinful man has to depend on God's grace for salvation (Eph. 2:8–10).

Confucianism teaches that children must fulfill their parents' wishes, even if any of those wishes are wrong. Christ said that loyalty to Him may demand sacrificing loyalty to family (Matt. 10:37–38).

Temple of Confucius in Beijing

Illustrating a Proverb

A proverb is a wise saying that gives a bit of wisdom in a short, easy-to-remember form. Sometimes a proverb offers common sense observations on life. A proverb may also contrast two types of behavior. Many cultures have proverbs. Usually a person understands proverbs from his own culture better.

The Chinese people used proverbs to teach children good manners. They also used proverbs to encourage others to think about things the right way.

1. Get drawing materials and a list of proverbs from your teacher.

2. Choose a proverb.

3. Make a picture that illustrates your proverb. Then write a sentence that gives the proverb's meaning.

4. Present the proverb and the illustration.

Chinese proverb: A dog in a kennel barks at his fleas; a dog hunting does not notice them.

FOCUS

1. What did the Taoists believe men were to be in harmony with?

2. What changes did Qin Shi Huang Ti make to help to unify China?

The Influence of Lao Tzu

Lao Tzu (LOU DZUH) was another influential teacher in China. His teaching, called **Taoism** (DOU IZ um), rose to second in importance to the teachings of Confucius. Taoism takes its name from the word *tao*, meaning "the way." Lao Tzu taught that tao was the guiding force in nature. He encouraged men to find peace and happiness by living in harmony with nature. Men should not seek power, wealth, or learning. They should be content with a simple lifestyle. Everyone should live together in love and peace.

Followers of Taoism did not like the differences that Confucianism made between the social classes. Because man was a part of nature, Taoists believed that man was not better than any other thing. Taoists had little use for government. Instead they felt that the government should leave the people alone to follow their own nature. According to Taoism, men could accomplish great things by being passive and obedient. Men should be like water and simply let things flow in a natural way.

Confucianism guided the thinking of China's educational, social, and political systems. Taoism became the basis of magical and superstitious elements in Chinese culture. In many ways, Confucianism and Taoism are opposites.

Comparison of beliefs

Confucianism	Taoism
active lifestyle	passive lifestyle
fulfillment of social obligations	freedom from responsibility
improvement of government, laws, and education	minimizing of government authority and involvement in society
focus on the human world	focus on the natural world

TAOISM

Taoism (also spelled Daoism) teaches that people should not try to make things better for themselves. Neither should they allow themselves to be motivated by desires. Taoists believe that by getting rid of desires, a person can achieve balance and serenity. The Bible teaches that Christians should have right desires. They should love God and other people (Matt. 22:36–40). They should also do their best to improve the world around them for God's glory and for other people's good (Gal. 6:10).

Taoism teaches that people should not plan but simply accept what happens in any situation. While Christians believe that God is in control of all that happens, they also know that God gives them commands that they must obey. Christians trust God to direct their lives as they live in obedience to Him (Prov. 3:6).

Taoism encourages man to be in harmony with nature. A Christian believes that man is created in God's image. God commands man to have dominion over creation and be a good steward of it (Gen. 1:28).

155

Legalism

One group of thinkers in China did not believe that religion could solve society's problems. They believed that people were evil by nature and needed to be controlled by strict laws. This Chinese philosophy was known as **Legalism**. Legalists felt that those who disobeyed the law should be punished harshly. They thought a strong ruler was needed to maintain order. Confucianism, Taoism, and Legalism all became popular, but the Legalists were the first to put their ideas into practice throughout China.

Unrest in Government

As the nobles passed their power to their sons, loyalty to the king became less important. A time came when the king could no longer control the nobles. Many people refused to defend themselves and their king against invasions. In 771 BC invaders reached the capital. China endured an extended period of unrest. Instead of having a strong central government, powerful families struggled to govern. When a family became weak, a more powerful family seized control.

The Qin

The **Qin** (or Ch'in) dynasty began to rule about 221 BC. It was founded by the fierce emperor **Qin Shi Huang Ti** (CHIN SHEE HWAHNG DEE). His name means "First Emperor." Under his rule China experienced many changes and became more unified.

Government

Qin Shi Huang Ti established a Legalist government and set up a

BIOGRAPHY

Who: Qin Shi Huang Ti

What: emperor during the Qin dynasty

When: ruled 221–210 BC

Where: China

Qin Shi Huang Ti began his reign at the age of thirteen. He conquered his six rival states and united them by making changes in the government. He brought order and protection to China through harsh and ruthless measures.

bureaucracy. A **bureaucracy** (byoo ROK ruh see) is the managing of government through bureaus, or departments, with appointed officials. The emperor divided his empire into thirty-six districts. He appointed a governor in charge of each district. Qin Shi Huang Ti said, "I have brought order to the mass of beings."

Changes in China

The government put in place by Qin Shi Huang Ti gave him great power. His power allowed him to make changes to unify China. But his methods to implement the changes were often cruel and harsh. He took land from the nobles to limit their authority. Those who did not agree with him faced severe punishment that included hard labor or death.

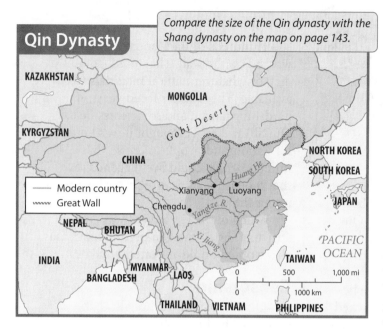

Qin Dynasty

Compare the size of the Qin dynasty with the Shang dynasty on the map on page 143.

KAZAKHSTAN

MONGOLIA

Gobi Desert

KYRGYZSTAN

CHINA

NORTH KOREA

SOUTH KOREA

Huang He

Xianyang   Luoyang

JAPAN

Chengdu

—— Modern country
～～～ Great Wall

Yangtze R.

NEPAL
BHUTAN

Xi Jiang

PACIFIC
OCEAN

INDIA

MYANMAR
BANGLADESH   LAOS

TAIWAN

0   500   1,000 mi

0   1000 km

THAILAND   VIETNAM

PHILIPPINES

The emperor's building projects also helped to unify China. The Chinese built a network of roads. Each road was built to a standard width. The roads made traveling easier for the people. The roads also allowed the Chinese army to move quickly to put down revolts. Workers built canals to connect the rivers and improve transportation throughout the country. The rivers and canals made it easier to ship goods from the north to the south. To help protect the country, the Chinese built a wall in the north. They also built an irrigation system to make more land available for farming.

China became more unified as Qin Shi Huang Ti established the same laws and taxes for everyone. He standardized weights, measurements, and the money system. All Chinese people were required to use the same writing system.

The Dujiangyan irrigation system built during the Qin dynasty is still in use today.

157

FOCUS

1. What were two ways the Great Wall benefited the Qin people?

2. What was the purpose of the civil service system?

The Great Wall

The **Great Wall** is one of the best-remembered accomplishments of Qin Shi Huang Ti. He ordered the wall to be built by linking a series of existing fortifications. The wall was actually designed as two walls with a space between them. Soil was piled and packed between the walls to form a road on top. The wall kept out invaders from the north, and the construction work kept discontented citizens busy.

Hundreds of thousands of men worked on the wall. They used stone, dirt, or whatever natural materials were available. The workers faced years of hardship, danger, and sometimes death. Qin Shi Huang Ti thought it was better for a thousand people to die so that a million people could live. Legends say that thousands of dead laborers lie buried under the wall.

Much of the Great Wall was constructed during the Qin period, but it was also worked on during later dynasties.

Censorship

Qin Shi Huang Ti thought that scholars who knew philosophy and wrote books wanted to break up his empire. So he censored them, or used the government to control their influence. He persecuted scholars and destroyed books. Over four hundred scholars who refused to turn in their books were either buried alive or sent to work on the wall. The emperor did not believe in education for the common man. He thought that the common man was wasting time if he was not growing food. He ordered all written documents that contradicted his way of thinking to be destroyed. Qin Shi Huang Ti especially disliked the teachings of Confucius and had all the books about his teachings burned.

The people did not like the emperor's harsh punishments. Neither did they care for the way he spent large amounts of money on himself. He built magnificent palaces and a tomb that covered twenty square miles.

The Great Wall of China

A Terra-Cotta Army

Like other ancient peoples, the ancient Chinese commonly buried their dead with supplies, such as food, weapons, and money. The Chinese believed in life after death, but not as the Bible teaches. Like the Egyptians, they thought that their dead ancestors would live on into the next world and needed supplies to survive.

In 1974 some Chinese farmers were digging for a well when they made an incredible discovery—a giant under-ground room filled with an entire army of statues. The army was keeping a silent guard at the tomb of Qin Shi Huang Ti. Each life-sized statue was made of hard, waterproof clay called terra cotta. The statues were uniquely carved with great detail. The terra-cotta army included over six thousand soldiers with weapons, horses, and chariots. Historians believe that this army was built to protect the emperor as he lived on in the next world. Artifacts like the terra-cotta army provide information about the way people in the ancient world lived and died.

A portion of the thousands of life-sized clay soldiers
Why was this terra-cotta army made?

The powerful Qin dynasty lasted less than thirty years, yet it left a lasting monument—the name China comes from the name Qin.

Currency

Imagine what the world would be like without coins and paper money. Before money was used, many civilizations bartered or traded. It was often difficult to know the worth of items and services.

Ancient cowry-shell currency

Currency, or money, is any material of value that is exchanged for goods or services. Seashells, beans, and pieces of iron, gold, silver, and bronze have all been used as money. These items were not always easy to carry in a pocket.

Cowry shells were the earliest known form of currency used in China. These shells were easy to carry and count. During the Chou dynasty, coins, small knives, and spades were used as currency. These were all made from metal.

Knife

Spade

During the Qin dynasty Emperor Qin Shi Huang Ti standardized the currency used in China. The emperor minted coins that were round and flat with a square hole in the middle. The hole allowed people to carry the coins on a string. Coins continued to be used during the Han dynasty. They were imprinted with the image of the emperor.

Eventually the Chinese made paper money. The money we use today echoes back to the ancient Chinese use of money.

Coin

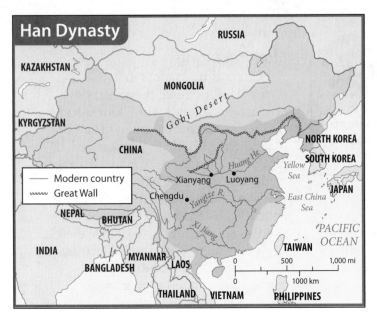

Han Dynasty

RUSSIA
KAZAKHSTAN
MONGOLIA
Gobi Desert
KYRGYZSTAN
NORTH KOREA
CHINA
SOUTH KOREA
Huang He
Yellow Sea
Xianyang Luoyang
Chengdu
East China Sea
JAPAN
Yangtze R.
NEPAL
BHUTAN
Xi Jiang
PACIFIC OCEAN
INDIA
TAIWAN
MYANMAR
BANGLADESH
LAOS
0   500   1,000 mi
0   1000 km
THAILAND VIETNAM
PHILIPPINES

— Modern country
〰 Great Wall

The Han

The **Han** dynasty rose to power around 202 BC. Emperor **Wu Ti** (WOO DEE) extended China to include present-day North Korea and parts of central Asia. Unlike the Qin dynasty, Wu Ti provided a strong and fair central government. However, like some of the rulers before him, Wu Ti took land from the nobles, raised taxes, and placed the supply of grain under governmental control. Confucianism became the Chinese government's official philosophy. The philosophy was promoted through a university that Wu Ti began. The Han dynasty was so popular with the people that to this day some Chinese call themselves the "sons of Han."

Government

The Han rulers needed well-trained officials to help run the country, so they developed a civil service system. This system trained people for governmental service. A person interested in becoming an official first needed a recommendation. Then he studied for many years. After his studies he took three public exams. The first exam covered history and the principles of government. The second exam was on the teachings of Confucius. Palace guards supervised the first two exams. The emperor himself directly supervised the third, which was on poetry and political essays. Those who attained this level were given positions in the government.

Governmental officials were not just scholars. They had a vital role in government. They supervised activities such as the building of roads, the dealings of merchants, and the collecting of taxes.

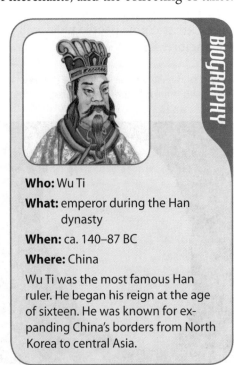

BIOGRAPHY

Who: Wu Ti

What: emperor during the Han dynasty

When: ca. 140–87 BC

Where: China

Wu Ti was the most famous Han ruler. He began his reign at the age of sixteen. He was known for expanding China's borders from North Korea to central Asia.

1. What were some of the achievements of the Han dynasty?

2. What did the Chinese keep written records on before the invention of paper?

Achievements

The era of the Han was a glorious period in Chinese history. The Chinese made achievements in medicine, manufacturing, science, and literature.

Medicine

The Han used special herbs as medicine. They also developed the use of **acupuncture** (AK yoo PUNGK chur). This procedure is done by poking needles through the skin at specific points on the body. The purpose is to relieve pain or cure sickness. Some people today still use acupuncture.

A model of the ear with acupuncture points labeled and three different sizes of acupuncture needles

Manufacturing

China also advanced in manufacturing. This increased the country's production of goods. The Chinese had become master metalworkers. The iron plow and the wheelbarrow increased production on farms. Swords and armor made the army more powerful.

The Chinese began using the rudder, a vertical blade attached to a ship. The rudder could be turned to change the ship's direction. Ships traveled farther, allowing China to establish trade connections with other countries.

For centuries the Chinese had known the procedures for making silk. The Chinese raised silkworms and unwound the threads from the worms' cocoons. The threads were dyed and woven into beautiful fabrics. The Chinese kept these procedures secret. Revealing the secret was punishable by death. During the Han dynasty weavers used foot-powered looms to weave the silk threads into fabric. Clothing made from silk was very expensive. It was originally reserved for the emperor and other important leaders.

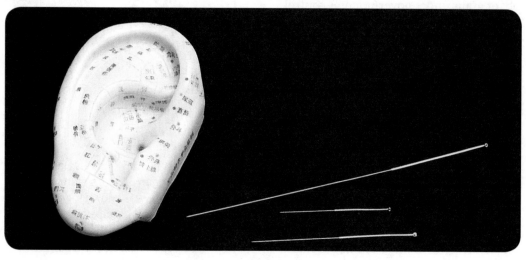

Science

A man named **Chang Heng** invented an important scientific instrument called the **seismoscope** (SIZE muh SKOPE). It was used to detect earthquakes. The Chinese called it an "earthquake weather-clock." Chinese seismoscopes were bronze jars decorated on the outside with eight dragon heads. Each dragon held a small ball in its mouth and pointed in one of eight different directions. Under each dragon sat an open-mouthed frog.

Inside the bronze jar was a pendulum. Whenever the earth moved, the pendulum would move, causing one of the balls to drop from the dragon's mouth into the frog's mouth. The Chinese determined the direction of the earthquake by which frog the ball fell in.

Earthquakes caused damage to buildings and land. After an earthquake struck, the Chinese leaders used the seismoscope to determine the earthquake's location. Then the leaders sent troops out to that area. The troops carried food and supplies to help people, particularly the farmers, whose work supported the entire country.

Literature

During the Han dynasty, poets created long works of literature that combined poetry and prose. Another poetry style featured short lines of verse that could be sung. Poets were hired for the beauty of their verses.

Han writers also created important works of history. Sima Qian (SIH-mah CHYEN) wrote a complete history of all the Chinese dynasties through the early Han. His writings were important, especially since Qin Shi Huang Ti had destroyed many works during the Qin dynasty. Sima Qian's work was called the *Shiji* (*Records of the Grand Historian*). His style and format became the model for later historical writings.

A Chinese seismoscope
How did the development of this invention help the Chinese?

Echoes from the Past

Paper

How many times a day do you use paper? Paper has become a part of everyday life. Newspapers, textbooks, labels, and money are just a few things that are made from paper.

People did not always have paper to write on. Before paper was invented, the ancient Chinese used silk, bone, turtle shell, and other materials to keep written records.

The Chinese invented paper during the Han dynasty. They took hemp (plant fiber) or tree bark and pounded it to a pulp. The pulp was mixed with water. Then the mixture was spread into a thin layer. The dried pulp formed a coarse sheet of paper. Unlike today's paper, this early paper was difficult to write on. The paper also had other uses. It was used as wrapping for clothing or other items. It was also used in making lightweight armor. Arrows could not penetrate through the armor's many layers of paper.

Making handmade paper

Chinese papermakers later used fibers from rags, rope, or fishing nets to make a smoother pulp. The Chinese continued to use paper for writing and eventually for making money. This page you are reading is an echo of the ancient Chinese invention of paper.

Making Paper

Like the ancient Chinese, you can make paper too.

1. Gather the following materials: a jar, water, clean tissue, 2 pieces of screen, a dish pan, towels, and 2 pieces of smooth cloth.

2. Fill your jar 3/4 full with water. Tear the tissue into small pieces and drop it into the jar. Seal the jar tightly. Shake it until no pieces of tissue can be seen. This is your paper pulp.

3. Place one piece of screen in the dish pan. Pour the pulp onto the screen. Lift the screen and place it on a towel. Place the second screen on top of the first and cover it with a second towel. Firmly press to remove excess water from the pulp.

4. Remove the screens from the towels. Carefully lift off the top screen and peel the layer of damp paper from the bottom screen.

5. Place the damp paper between the pieces of cloth. Firmly press again.

6. Remove the paper and place on a flat surface to dry.

FOCUS

1. By what means did Buddhism enter China?

2. Why were boys valued more than girls?

Trade Routes

Emperor Wu Ti sent his general, Zhang Qian (JAHNG CHYEN), to explore regions to the west of China. Wu Ti wanted him to find allies to help defend China from its enemies, especially the ones from the north.

Zhang Qian was unable to find allies for China. But he brought back information from his travels. He had discovered a breed of horse that would be useful in battle. These horses were larger and more powerful than the horses in China. Wu Ti encouraged trade with a foreign king to get these horses for China's cavalry.

Trade routes formed as the Chinese began trading with other regions. The main trade route was called the **Silk Road**. It stretched about 4,000 miles (6440 km) from China to lands in the west. The Silk Road was named after the most famous item that was carried on it for trade—silk.

Traveling on the Silk Road was difficult and dangerous. Merchants traveled together in groups for protection. They

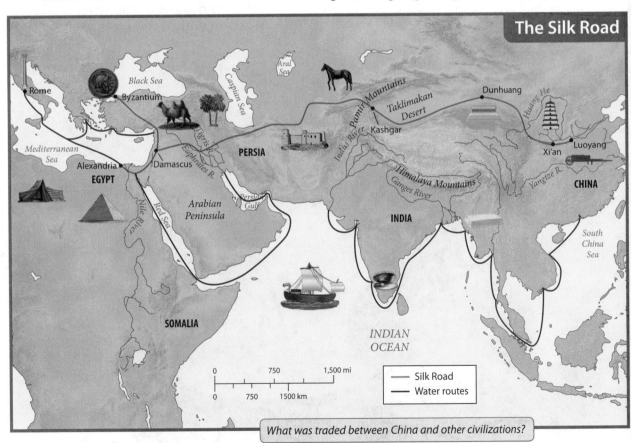

The Silk Road

Silk Road
Water routes

What was traded between China and other civilizations?

166

According to tradition, the White Horse Temple in Luoyang was the first Buddhist temple in China.

hired armed guards to protect them from bandits who stole goods and water. Traders used the Bactrian camel to transport goods. This two-humped camel endured the extreme heat of the desert and the freezing cold of the mountains.

Silk and fine pottery from China were highly valued by people in other lands. Chinese merchants traded with those people and brought home horses and new products, such as fruits and cotton. Other civilizations eventually exchanged ideas and inventions with China.

Buddhism Comes to China

The Silk Road and other trade routes brought products and ideas from other lands. This included religion. Merchants and teachers from India brought Buddhism to China in the second century AD.

As Buddhism spread from India to other countries, it developed into Theravada Buddhism and Mahayana Buddhism. **Mahayana Buddhism** was the branch that spread to China.

Unlike the Theravada Buddhists, Mahayana Buddhists believe it is a duty to help others reach nirvana, the state of peace or bliss. A Mahayana Buddhist hopes to become a bodhisattva (BOH dih SUHT vuh). A **bodhisattva** is a person who has reached enlightenment but delays nirvana to help others reach enlightenment.

MAHAYANA BUDDHISM

Mahayana Buddhism teaches that everything that people see is an illusion. The Bible teaches that God's creation is very good but cursed as a result of the Fall (Gen. 3:17–19). One day creation will be restored (Rom. 8:20–25).

Buddhism teaches that the ultimate goal for people is the state of nirvana, a state of freedom from suffering and desires. The Bible teaches that people will not be completely delivered from sin and suffering until they are reunited with Christ. The Christian looks forward to a glorified body and a new creation (1 Cor. 15; Rev. 21–22).

Society

During the Han dynasty there was a time of social change. Social classes became more rigid. Confucianism divided people into four social classes. The upper class was made up of the emperor, his court, and scholars who held governmental positions. The second class, which was the largest, was the peasants, and the third class was the artisans. Merchants made up the lowest class because they did not produce goods for society.

A person's class had nothing to do with wealth or power. The peasants were poor yet made up the second-highest class. Merchants were often very wealthy but ranked as the lowest class. The lifestyles of the people, however, did vary according to their wealth.

The emperor and his court lived in a large palace. Many of the wealthy families lived on large estates. They filled their homes and their tombs with expensive and beautiful things. They hired laborers to farm their land and private armies to defend it.

Most people were poor and lived in the countryside. They wore plain clothes and lived a simple life. The peasants worked long days farming. In the winter they were forced to work on governmental building projects.

The Han believed that the family should be strong. Children were taught to respect their elders. Disobeying parents was a crime. Children also honored dead parents with offerings and ceremonies. Boys were valued more than girls because sons carried on the family line and were responsible for the care of elderly parents.

Artifact from the Han Dynasty

End of the Han Dynasty

By AD 220 the last of the Han rulers had been overthrown. For the next four hundred years, China suffered from internal wars and invasions. But it would unify and flourish once again during a period known as China's golden age.

The influence of ancient China has continued across the centuries. Chinese inventions, such as paper and the seismoscope, made life more convenient. The Chinese laid the foundation for many advances that would later follow. Today many of the things we enjoy come from the ancient Chinese and their culture.

Chapter 7

Ancient Persia

1. Who were the first people the Persians conquered under Cyrus II's rule?

2. How is the Cyrus Cylinder related to Israel's history in the Bible?

An Empire Is Born

Great empires often have humble beginnings. While dynasties flourished in China and pyramids towered in Egypt, two tribes of nomads—the Medes and the Persians—moved into southwest Asia. They settled south of the Caspian Sea in the area that is now Iran.

For a time the Medes were stronger, but then a leader named **Cyrus II** rose to power among the Persians. Cyrus led a rebellion against the Medes and defeated them.

With Persia in control, the two nations combined armies and advanced westward into Asia Minor. As the Medo-Persian army neared Lydia, Croesus (KREE sus), Lydia's king, came out to fight them. The kingdom of Lydia was wealthy because of its mineral resources, especially its gold. Cyrus and his army defeated Croesus and captured Lydia's capital city, Sardis. Now the Persian Empire extended west to the Aegean Sea.

Next Cyrus led his army against the Chaldean Empire, which ruled the lands

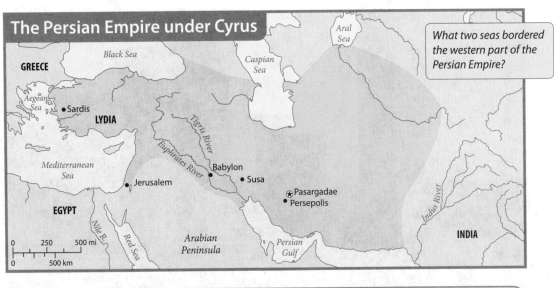

The Persian Empire under Cyrus

What two seas bordered the western part of the Persian Empire?

GREECE · Black Sea · Aral Sea · Caspian Sea · Aegean Sea · Sardis · LYDIA · Tigris River · Euphrates River · Babylon · Susa · Mediterranean Sea · Jerusalem · Pasargadae · Persepolis · Indus River · EGYPT · Nile R. · Red Sea · Arabian Peninsula · Persian Gulf · INDIA

0   250   500 mi
0   500 km

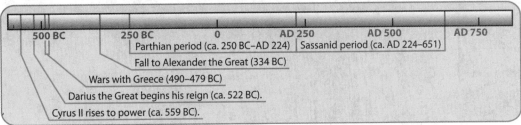

500 BC   250 BC   0   AD 250   AD 500   AD 750

Parthian period (ca. 250 BC–AD 224) | Sassanid period (ca. AD 224–651)

Fall to Alexander the Great (334 BC)

Wars with Greece (490–479 BC)

Darius the Great begins his reign (ca. 522 BC).

Cyrus II rises to power (ca. 559 BC).

The Fall of the Chaldean Empire

God used Daniel, a Jewish exile, to warn Belshazzar, the last Chaldean ruler, that his kingdom would soon fall to the Medo-Persian army. One evening Belshazzar held a feast for a thousand of his nobles. He commanded that the gold vessels from the Jewish temple be brought out. As this pagan ruler and his friends drank from God's holy vessels, a hand appeared and wrote a message on the palace wall. The king's face paled in alarm. He called Daniel, who was known for his great wisdom, to interpret the message for them.

"Mene, mene, tekel, upharsin," Daniel read. The words meant that God had numbered the days left in the Chaldean kingdom and it had come to an end. It was as if God had weighed the king's life and it was not as it should have been. As a result, the kingdom would be divided and given to the Medes and Persians. That very night Belshazzar lost his life in the Medo-Persian invasion.

Daniel 5 records the account of how Daniel interpreted the writing for Belshazzar.

BIOGRAPHY

Who: Cyrus II (the Great)

What: founder of the Persian Empire

When: ruled 559–530 BC

Where: ancient Persia

Cyrus II was a tolerant ruler. He allowed his defeated enemies some self-rule and freedom of religion. God used him to free the Israelites from Babylon, restore them to the land of Israel, and let them rebuild their temple.

to the south. Cyrus conquered the Chaldeans in 539 BC. It was, for the most part, a peaceful conquest. Cyrus added the new land to his spreading empire.

Cyrus II was a wise ruler. He treated his defeated enemies well. He let them help make their own laws, speak their own languages, and keep their customs and religious beliefs. Many believe that the empire was strengthened because of this tolerance.

ARCHAEOLOGY: THE CYRUS CYLINDER

The prophet Isaiah mentioned Cyrus by name 150 years before Cyrus's birth. Isaiah called Cyrus "the Lord's anointed." Why was this title given to a king who did not even worship God? Isaiah foretold that God would use Cyrus to free the Israelites from slavery in Babylon and let them rebuild their temple (Isa. 44:28–45:6).

Like the Mesopotamians, the Persians used cylinder seals. One famous Persian cylinder seal can be found in the British Museum. This artifact, known as the **Cyrus Cylinder**, tells more about Cyrus's tolerant attitude toward his subjects.

In 1879 a scholar named Hormuzd Rasam found the cylinder seal at the site of the ancient Babylonian temple. The cylinder seal contained a message about Cyrus's respect for Marduk, Babylon's god. It also told how Cyrus freed some of his conquered peoples. He let them return to their homelands and make sanctuaries for their gods.

The Cyrus Cylinder does not mention Israel by name, but the book of Ezra tells that Cyrus allowed the Israelites to return to Judah and rebuild God's house in Jerusalem. Cyrus also returned the temple treasures that the Chaldeans had taken from the Israelites. When God allowed the Cyrus Cylinder to be found, it became an important testimony to the truth of His Word.

From the Cyrus Cylinder:

I am Cyrus, king of the universe, the great king, the powerful king, king of Babylon, king of Sumer and Akkad, king of the four quarters of the world. . . . I sought the safety of the city of Babylon and all its sanctuaries. As for the population of Babylon, . . . I soothed their weariness; I freed them from their bonds. Marduk, the great lord, rejoiced at [my good] deeds, and he pronounced a sweet blessing over me. . . . I collected together all of their people and returned them to their settlements.

Translated from Persian by Irving Finkel, Assistant Keeper, Department of the Middle East, British Museum. ©Trustees of the British Museum.

Cyrus Cylinder

Iran

Climate—The climate is mostly arid or semiarid. Cooler temperatures are found in the north with heavy snowfall in winter, especially in the mountains. Summers are hot and dry with temperatures exceeding 100°F (38°C) daily. Most of Iran's rainfall occurs along the coast of the Caspian Sea.

Topography—The Zagros Mountains cut diagonally across the country from the northwest to the southeast. The Elburz Mountains line the Caspian Sea. In the central region is a desert plateau. A coastal plain runs along the Caspian Sea. Another marshy plain lies in the southwest.

Natural Resources—The country's natural resources include petroleum, natural gas, coal, chromium, copper, iron ore, lead, manganese, zinc, and sulfur.

Geography and Culture—Persia's mountainous terrain encouraged the Persians to develop a strong cavalry for warfare. The Persian road system allowed the East and the West to be in contact as never before.

Location—Ancient Persia was located in the Middle East in what is now Iran. At the height of Persia's power under Darius I, the Persian Empire extended from the Mediterranean and Aegean seas in the west to the Indus River in the east.

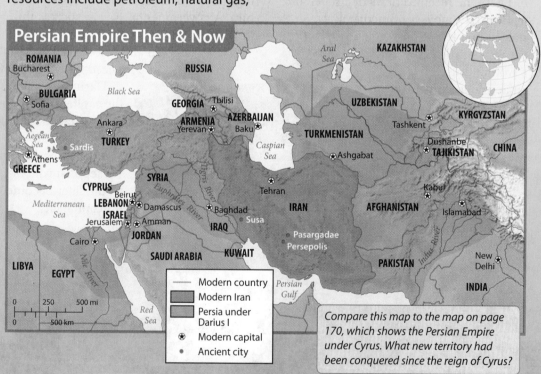

Persian Empire Then & Now

Legend:
- Modern country
- Modern Iran
- Persia under Darius I
- ✴ Modern capital
- • Ancient city

0   250   500 mi
0   500 km

Compare this map to the map on page 170, which shows the Persian Empire under Cyrus. What new territory had been conquered since the reign of Cyrus?

173

1. Under which king did the Persian Empire reach its greatest size and power?

2. How did Darius keep the empire organized and protected?

The Empire Grows

The dynasty that Cyrus began is known as the **Achaemenid** (uh KEE muh nid) period of Persia. Cyrus ruled the Persian Empire until his death in 530 BC. He was buried in a grand royal tomb in his capital city, **Pasargadae** (puh SAHR guh DEE). His son Cambyses took the throne after him.

Cambyses continued to extend Persia's empire. His most important success was conquering Egypt. But while in Egypt, he received news of a rebellion in Persia. Cambyses immediately started home. But on the way, he died of a wound caused by an accident with his own sword. It was not clear who was next in line for the throne.

Darius (duh RYE us) and some other nobles put down the rebellion, and Darius became the next king. He was known as **Darius the Great** because of his long and successful reign.

Under Darius, the Persian Empire reached its greatest size and power. Less than thirty years had passed since Cyrus rose to power among the nomads. Now Persia had become a world superpower. People from many different lands were paying tribute to Darius. He needed a strategy for keeping his large empire organized.

Central Government

Darius formed a plan for governing the empire. He set up a place for government in one central city. Then he divided the conquered lands of his empire into twenty provinces. Each province was known as a **satrapy**. A governor, or a **satrap**, was assigned to each satrapy. The satrap's responsibilities included collecting tribute for Darius and reporting to him. A governmental system such as this in which local governments are subject to a main authority is called a *centralized government*.

Darius moved the capital from Pasargadae to the city of **Susa**. He also began building **Persepolis**, which would later become his capital city.

Cyrus's tomb at Pasargadae

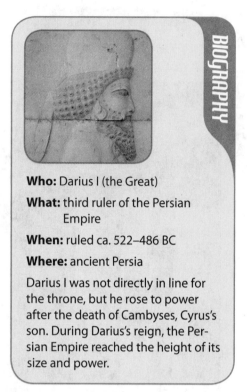

Who: Darius I (the Great)

What: third ruler of the Persian Empire

When: ruled ca. 522–486 BC

Where: ancient Persia

Darius I was not directly in line for the throne, but he rose to power after the death of Cambyses, Cyrus's son. During Darius's reign, the Persian Empire reached the height of its size and power.

The Road System

Darius faced another challenge as the ruler of a large empire. How would he communicate important messages to different parts of his kingdom? How would he receive news and collect wealth from distant areas? To keep his empire connected, Darius built and maintained a good road system. This system was a network of about 8,000 miles of stone roads that connected the entire empire. The longest road, called the **Royal Road**, stretched over 1,600 miles from Susa to Sardis.

Darius had royal messengers stationed along this road to carry messages in relay style. **Herodotus** (hih ROD uh tus), a famous historian from Greece, describes the Royal Road and the king's messengers who traveled it.

Nothing mortal travels so fast as these Persian messengers. . . . Along the whole line of road there are men, they say, stationed with horses, in number equal to the number of days which the journey takes, allowing a man and a horse to each day; and these men will not be hindered from accomplishing at their best speed the distance which they have to go, either by snow, or rain, or heat, or by the darkness of night. The first rider delivers his despatch to the second, and the second passes it to the third; and so it is borne from hand to hand along the whole line, like the light in the torch-race. (George Rawlinson, trans. *The History of Herodotus*, Book VIII, ed. Manuel Komroff [NY: Tudor, 1928], 461)

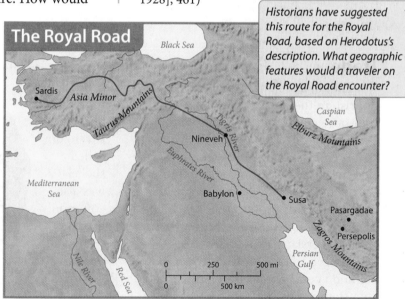

The Royal Road

Historians have suggested this route for the Royal Road, based on Herodotus's description. What geographic features would a traveler on the Royal Road encounter?

Black Sea

Sardis

Asia Minor

Taurus Mountains

Tigris River

Caspian Sea

Elburz Mountains

Nineveh

Euphrates River

Mediterranean Sea

Babylon

Susa

Pasargadae

Zagros Mountains

Persepolis

Nile River

Red Sea

Persian Gulf

0   250   500 mi

0   500 km

Echoes from the Past

Persia's Royal Road

If you were to visit the James A. Farley Building in New York City, you would see a quotation engraved on the outside of the building. "Neither snow nor rain nor heat nor gloom of night stays these couriers from the swift completion of their appointed rounds." Does that saying sound familiar? It is an "echo" of Herodotus's description of the messengers on Persia's Royal Road. After an architect added the quotation to this post office building in New York, people used it to describe the United States Postal Service.

Front of the James A. Farley Building

Trade

The road system helped trade to flourish in the Persian Empire. People transported all kinds of goods on the Persian roads. About once a year, ambassadors from all parts of the empire traveled the roads carrying goods to present as tribute to Darius. As people saw the variety of goods produced in other lands, the demand for those goods grew.

The Persians' coin system also encouraged trade. Darius introduced a common currency for his empire. A gold coin stamped with his image was called a **daric**. This coin could be used throughout his lands. A silver coin called a shekel was also commonly used.

Ancient Persian coin

176

Persian soldiers on a relief

A Strong Military

Darius needed military strength to keep his empire under control. Persia had a strong force of paid soldiers who were professionally trained. Ten thousand of these soldiers were the king's own special force, called the **Immortals**. When one of the Immortals died, he was immediately replaced. Darius himself had been one of the Immortals during the reign of Cambyses.

Persia also had a well-trained cavalry. Horses helped the soldiers travel more quickly over Persia's mountainous terrain. When fighting an enemy, the Persian cavalry usually attacked first, followed by foot soldiers.

The Persian military was well organized and loyal. Herodotus described them as the most valiant of all the armies he had seen. Darius used his army to end several rebellions during his reign. He also needed the army to expand his empire. In the east he conquered territory as far as the Indus River. In the west he conquered a number of Greek city-states around the Aegean Sea. He never gained control over all of them.

Herodotus

The Greek scholar Herodotus has become known as the Father of History. He lived during the fifth century BC. Born in Asia Minor, he grew up as a subject of the Persian Empire. From his writings we know that he was well educated and traveled widely.

Wherever he went, Herodotus listened and watched. He talked to people who remembered the past. He wrote down the interesting stories he heard. Over the years, he recorded the major events of his time in a lengthy work called *The Histories.* Herodotus spent most of his adult life working on this project. Much of what we know about ancient Persia comes from his writings. He describes the rise and fall of each of the Persian rulers. He also gives detailed accounts of the wars between Persia and Greece. Herodotus even records backgrounds and customs of other peoples he came in contact with during his travels.

Scholars today disagree on how accurate Herodotus was in his historical accounts. Some say that he did not always give objective details, especially when he recounted stories he had heard from others. Yet most scholars agree that in the *The Histories*, he demonstrates some of the best qualities of a historian. Herodotus gathered information diligently. He paid attention to details and tried to bring people and places to life. He seems to have tried to present his material honestly and fairly.

Herodotus was also an excellent writer. He had studied the classic works of Greek literature—prose, drama, and poetry. His reading had taught him to use language in a beautiful way. Many scholars compare *The Histories* to a work of poetry because of its graceful style.

Herodotus wrote in Greek. Scholars have translated his work into English. Now we can read and enjoy it. Herodotus's work has also been translated into Latin, French, German, Italian, and Swedish.

FOCUS

1. What does the art of Darius's time tell about the Persians?

2. What made the Persian religion different from most of the others in the ancient world?

Culture in Ancient Persia

Language

If you had traveled through ancient Persia, you probably would have heard many different languages spoken. However, a language called Aramaic became the common tongue of the empire. Parts of the Old Testament are written in this language rather than Hebrew.

The kings of the Persian Empire wrote and spoke in a language that became known as Old Persian. Old Persian was written in cuneiform, a wedge-shaped script that looked similar to the one used by the ancient Sumerians. Each symbol stood for a syllable.

Art

Darius built the city of Persepolis on a terrace with a huge stairway leading up to it. The city had splendid palaces, a royal treasury, and the Hall of a Hundred Columns for important gatherings. Parts of these buildings are still standing today.

Darius filled the city with glorious works of art. On the steps, entrances, and walls of buildings were ornate carvings. Columns adorned the halls. Doors and furnishings were decorated with gold, silver, and bronze. Floors were often paved with brick or stone and covered with carpets.

The Persians had great wealth and they loved beautiful things. Archaeologists have found many Persian carvings showing people wearing bracelets, necklaces, earrings, and elaborate headdresses. Bowls carved with intricate patterns have been found. Jars, jugs, utensils, and drinking vessels called **rhytons** (RY tons) often have animal-shaped handles. Tombs of Persian kings and nobles reveal that these wealthy people were buried with their jewelry and other valuables.

Ibex head bracelet found in Pasargadae

Gold lion-shaped rhyton

CARVINGS ON A CLIFF

On a cliff face near the town of Behistun (BAY his TOON), Darius had an inscription, or rock carving, made. The inscription told about his rise to power and was made up of both pictures and cuneiform symbols. The symbols were carved in three languages—Old Persian, Babylonian, and Elamite. After Darius's scribes finished carving the inscription, they removed the rock ledge they had been standing on.

Can you locate the inscription on the cliff?

For centuries, no one could read the Behistun inscription. It was too high on the cliff face to be read. In 1836 a British diplomat and scholar named Henry Rawlinson began studying the Behistun inscription. He risked his life to climb the cliffs and copy the cuneiform script. Then he worked on deciphering the three languages.

The Behistun carving was just one of the sources used to decipher Persian cuneiform. Rawlinson and other scholars worked for years to solve the mystery of the wedge-shaped symbols. Their work resulted in a great breakthrough in understanding ancient civilizations. Many other cuneiform scripts were finally able to be read.

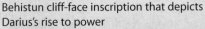

Behistun cliff-face inscription that depicts Darius's rise to power

Who: Zoroaster

What: founder of Zoroastrianism

When: sixth century BC

Where: ancient Persia

Zoroaster claimed that there was one god, Ahura Mazda, who had shown him visions about what to teach. Based on these visions, he developed the Zoroastrian religion.

ZOROASTRIANISM

Zoroastrianism recognizes only one god, but not the God of the Bible.

Zoroastrianism's god is equal with the evil being he battles against. The true God rules over all. Satan is a rebellious angel who can do nothing unless God permits it.

Zoroastrianism teaches that what man does in this life determines what his eternity will be like. The Bible teaches that where man spends eternity depends on his relationship to Jesus Christ.

Zoroastrianism teaches that a battle rages between good and evil. People must choose which side they are on. The Bible teaches that all people are born sinful and need God to save them from their sins. Salvation is only through Jesus Christ, Who paid the penalty for sin through His death and resurrection.

Religion

Zoroaster (ZOR oh AS ter) was a man who lived during the sixth century BC. He founded the main religion of ancient Persia, **Zoroastrianism** (ZOR oh AS tree uh NIZ um). Through this religion, Zoroaster tried to explain the existence of good and evil. He taught that a good god, Ahura Mazda, struggled with an equally powerful evil being, Ahriman. Ahura Mazda was believed to be the creator and the only god. Monotheism made Zoroaster's religion different from most of the other religions in the ancient world.

Zoroastrianism contained many false beliefs. Zoroaster claimed that he had seen visions sent from Ahura Mazda. Zoroaster taught that each person must choose between good and evil. He also taught that man could have eternal happiness if he did more good than evil in this life. The holy writings of Zoroastrianism are called the **Avesta**. The Avesta is made up of myths, rules, and hymns.

Sculpture of Zoroaster on the Appellate Court Building in New York City

181

In the Bible

Darius's Order About the Temple

Cyrus had allowed the Israelites to return to Judah to rebuild the temple. The Israelites did so, but their work was stopped many times. Other people often tried to discourage them. Ezra 5 tells us that an official named Tatnai questioned the Jews' right to rebuild the temple. He wrote to King Darius to find out whether their rebuilding of the temple should be allowed to continue.

Darius searched for and found Cyrus's decree. He wrote a letter back to Tatnai, telling him to leave the work on the house of God alone. He also ordered that Tatnai help the Israelites with their expenses. Darius included a threat of death for anyone who tried to change his orders.

Once again, God used a king who did not worship Him as part of His plan. God used Darius's order to clear the way for God's people to continue their work on His house.

> "And the God that hath caused his name to dwell there destroy all kings and people, that shall put to their hand to alter and to destroy this house of God which is at Jerusalem. I Darius have made a decree: let it be done with speed."
>
> **Ezra 6:12**

The Zoroastrians believed that Ahura Mazda was represented by fire. Their priests kept fires burning continually on altars in their temples. The priests in the Persian Empire were called **magi**. We get our word *magic* from their name. History is not clear on whether all the magi followed Zoroastrianism. Some sources suggest that kings relied on the magi to interpret dreams and tell the future by the stars. Some people in modern Iran and India still follow Zoroastrianism. They call themselves *Parsis* (PAR sees), another word for Persians.

Zoroastrianism was the official religion of Persia. But like Cyrus, Darius tolerated other religions in his empire. He respected the God of the Israelites and played an important role in the rebuilding of the Jewish temple.

Piecing Artifacts Together

Pottery is one of the objects commonly found at an archaeological site. But much of the pottery that archaeologists find is broken. The pieces of one broken artifact may even be scattered over a large area. If an archaeologist can put the broken shards, or pieces, of an artifact together, he can tell more about it. Pottery from different periods sometimes looks different. Depending on the era, a pot might have been made with a certain shape, texture, color, or style. The more complete an artifact is, the more an archaeologist can make reasonable guesses about its date and the people who made it.

1. You will need a bag of pottery shards, masking tape, and craft glue.

2. Lay the shards out on the floor or a table and study them closely. Carefully put the pot back together. Use tape or glue to hold the pieces in place.

3. Write a detailed description of the pot, using precise words. Describe the pot's color, shape, texture, and what you think it was used for.

War with Greece

The Battle of Marathon

In 499 BC the Greek city-states in Asia Minor rebelled against the Persians. Athens and a few other city-states on the mainland of Greece sent an army to help the Greeks in Asia Minor. Persia put down the rebellion. But Darius was angry with the Greeks for banding together to rebel. In 490 BC Darius and his army sailed to the plain of **Marathon** near Athens.

The mighty Persian army of about twenty thousand soldiers spread out on the plain. The Athenian army had only about ten thousand men. The Athenians stayed hidden and planned their strategy. They would wait in the hills and attack the Persians the next day.

The next morning, one of the Athenian generals ordered his men to attack the Persians. He placed the army in a long line and had them run full

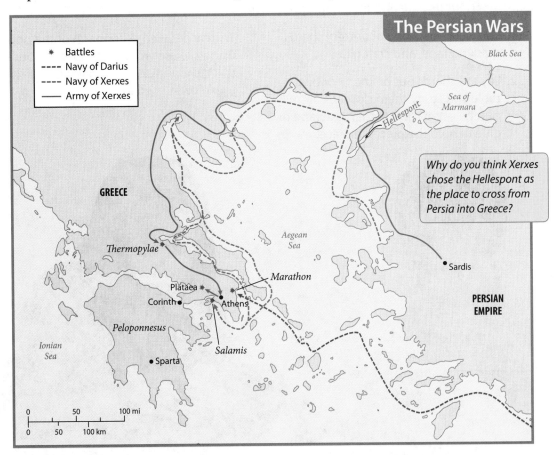

The Persian Wars

- ✳ Battles
- ---- Navy of Darius
- ---- Navy of Xerxes
- —— Army of Xerxes

Black Sea

Sea of Marmara

Hellespont

GREECE

Why do you think Xerxes chose the Hellespont as the place to cross from Persia into Greece?

Aegean Sea

Thermopylae ✳

• Sardis

Plataea ✳
Corinth •   ✳
      Athens   ✳ Marathon

PERSIAN EMPIRE

Peloponnesus

Ionian Sea

Salamis

• Sparta

0   50   100 mi
0   50   100 km

Soldiers beating the waters of the Hellespont

speed toward the Persians. It looked like a foolish plan to the Persians, but it worked.

The Persians forced back the center of the Athenian line. But the soldiers who were out on the wings of the line were stronger. They attacked both sides of the Persian army, trapping them and then drawing together like giant pincers. The Persians lost the battle of Marathon and suffered heavy losses.

According to Greek legend a runner named Pheidippides ran back to Athens, a distance of more than 25 miles, to report the good news. When he got there, he could breathe out only one word, "Victory." Then he collapsed and died. The name for our modern **marathon**, a race of 26.2 miles, comes from this story.

The Battle of Thermopylae

Darius died before he could take revenge on the Greeks. His son **Xerxes** (ZURK seez) became king in his place. Xerxes decided to continue his father's war with Greece.

In 480 BC the Persian army attacked Greece again. They crossed from Asia Minor to Greece through a strait called the **Hellespont**. Xerxes had his men build bridges across the Hellespont. They laid planks across two long lines of Persian ships to make the bridges. But a storm destroyed the bridges before they could be completed. Xerxes was so angry that he executed the engineers who had designed the bridges. He also ordered his soldiers to beat the waters of the Hellespont with three hundred lashes. When his anger subsided, Xerxes ordered that the bridges be rebuilt. Finally his army was able to march across to the coast of Greece.

Sparta, another Greek city-state, joined with Athens in fighting the Persians. Sparta had a strong army. The Greeks decided to position their forces at **Thermopylae** (ther MOP uh lee), a mountain pass only about fifty feet wide. At first it looked like they would be able to defend the pass and hold the Persian army back. But then a Greek traitor showed the Persians another path through the mountains.

Before long, the Greek army was surrounded. They fought to the end but lost. The Persians marched on to Athens and burned down the entire city.

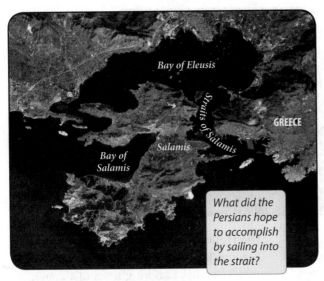

Bay of Eleusis

Straits of Salamis

GREECE

Salamis

Bay of Salamis

What did the Persians hope to accomplish by sailing into the strait?

The Battle of Salamis

The Persians had won the battle of Thermopylae. But the Greeks were not ready to give up. An Athenian general named Themistocles (thuh MIS tuh KLEEZ) had a plan to help the Greeks win the war with Persia.

Themistocles knew that the Greek ships were smaller and faster than the Persian ships. If the Greeks could trap the Persian ships in a tight space, the Greeks could win.

The strait between the island of **Salamis** and the mainland of Greece was where Themistocles decided to fight the Persians. The Greeks lured the Persians into the strait with a false report that the Greek ships were trying to flee. The battle began in the morning, the time when sea breezes created strong waves in the strait. Once the Persian fleet had entered the strait, the sailors had a difficult time steering their large ships against the waves. Meanwhile, the Greeks launched their ships from the beach of Salamis. The small, lightweight Greek ships rammed and sank many of the Persian ships. The Greeks won the battle.

During the next year, the Greeks fought one more battle with the Persians in the city of Plataea. Many Persian soldiers were killed, and in the end Persia had to admit defeat. Xerxes pulled the last of the Persian troops out of Greece and went home.

The wars between the Persians and the Greeks are known as the **Persian Wars**. Although Persia lost the wars, it still remained a powerful empire for more than a century.

Greek ships ramming and sinking Persian ships

Making an Annotated Map

Have you ever been to a museum or a historical park? There you will often see large colorful maps on display. These maps often include additional information about the places they show. Visitors can use these maps not only to locate places but also to read notes about those places.

These kinds of maps are *annotated*, a term which means "with notes added." An annotated map contains notes that describe places, events, or other important features. Often an arrow connects a note to the appropriate place on the map.

In this activity you will work together to create an annotated map of a Persian battle.

1. Choose a battle from one of the Persian wars.

2. Research the battle.

3. Create a flat map that shows the land features, especially the ones that may have affected the outcome of the battle.

4. Display information about the military that fought on each side. Include the numbers and kinds of soldiers, their locations, and their movements.

5. Add notes of other historical information you gathered from primary and secondary sources.

6. Display and present your completed map.

Xerxes and Esther

The Persian king Xerxes is called **Ahasuerus** (uh HAZ yoo EER uhs) in the book of Esther. *Ahasuerus* is the Hebrew form of *Xerxes*. When Ahasuerus's queen, Vashti, refused to obey his summons at a royal feast, he became angry and removed her from being queen. He then ordered that all the beautiful, young, unmarried women of his kingdom be brought to the palace. He would choose a new queen from among them.

Esther was one of the women chosen to come to the king. She was an Israelite whose parents had died. Her cousin Mordecai was bringing her up as his own daughter. Her Hebrew name was Hadassah.

Mordecai's great-grandfather had been brought to Babylon as a captive when Nebuchadnezzar invaded Jerusalem. Several generations later, Mordecai was living far from home in a land that was now part of the Persian Empire. He and Esther lived in the city of Susa, one of the capital cities of the Empire. The palace at Susa was Xerxes' main residence during the winter.

Xerxes chose Esther to be his queen. God placed Esther in this important position for a special purpose. Haman, one of the king's officials, plotted to destroy all the Jews. Following Mordecai's guidance, Esther used her influence with King Xerxes to plead for the lives of her people.

As shown during the crossing of the Hellespont, Xerxes sometimes gave way to unreasonable anger. The historian Josephus claimed that men with axes guarded the king's throne from anyone who approached it without a summons from the king. It took great courage for Esther to go before Xerxes without being summoned. But God gave her favor with the king. Through Esther, God brought about deliverance for His people.

An artist's **rendering**, or interpretation, of how Esther may have looked

Creating an Artist's Rendering

Artists play an important role in the study of the past. It is sometimes hard to imagine how things looked in ancient times. No one had cameras to take pictures, and sometimes artwork from the past does not give the details we would like. Using sources from a particular time, an artist can fill in details with his imagination to create a rendering of a place or an object from history. Although a rendering may not represent exactly what a historical place or object looked like, it helps us form a picture in our minds. Some artists draw or paint renderings on paper. Others use computers to create renderings.

One of the most detailed descriptions of a room in an ancient Persian palace is found in Esther 1:5–6. The description includes the room's colors, fabrics, furniture, and the materials used in the mosaic floor.

1. You will need your Bible, paper, and materials for drawing and coloring or painting.

2. Read the description of the banquet hall in the court of the palace at Susa. Research to find examples of the kinds of materials and furnishings used during that time.

3. Create an artist's rendering of the banquet room based on the description. You may choose to enhance your drawing with color, fabric scraps, glitter, or other materials.

4. Compare your completed rendering with those of other students. How are the drawings alike? How are they different? How do the drawings help you interpret the description in the Bible?

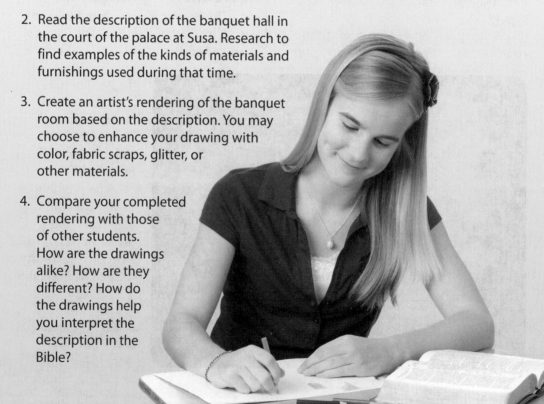

FOCUS

1. How did Artaxerxes I help the Israelites?

2. What are some of the reasons for the decline of the Persian Empire?

The Empire Declines

After twenty years as king, Xerxes was assassinated. A power struggle followed. Finally Xerxes' son Artaxerxes (AHR tuh ZURK seez) became king.

The Reign of Artaxerxes I

Artaxerxes I was the last of the strong Achaemenid kings. He continued the building projects his ancestors had started. He also dealt with a major Egyptian revolt and more skirmishes with the Greeks.

Artaxerxes showed kindness to the Israelites, as several other Persian kings had before him. He is mentioned in the Bible. It was during his reign that Ezra and Nehemiah returned to Jerusalem. Ezra, an Israelite scribe, traveled to Jerusalem to teach the people after the temple was rebuilt. Artaxerxes paid Ezra's expenses for the journey. Nehemiah, the king's cupbearer, later returned to lead the Israelites in rebuilding the wall around Jerusalem. Artaxerxes supplied the wood that Nehemiah needed to build the city gates. The king also sent letters to guarantee Nehemiah's safety in his travels.

Artaxerxes was one of the few Persian kings to die a natural death. Among the sons of royal families, there were often plots to seize the throne by violence. Many of the Achaemenid rulers after Darius I were assassinated.

A Weakening Kingdom

The Persian Empire had weakened since the days of Darius I. The wars with Greece had been costly and had resulted in great losses. Yet the Persian royalty continued their luxurious lifestyle. They placed heavier and heavier taxes on the people.

The people were discontent with the high taxes and with their rulers. As time went on, the loyalty of the people decreased.

Cup with a frieze of gazelles. 1st millennium BC, early, Iran, Caspian region. Gold, H. 2½ in. (6.5 cm). Rogers Fund, 1962 (62.84). © The Metropolitan Museum of Art/Art Resource, NY

Gold cup decorated with gazelles

Alexander the Great battling Persians

Alexander's Conquest

A young man of twenty named Alexander had taken the throne in Macedonia, north of Greece, after his father, Philip II, was killed. Most of Greece was already under Alexander's control when he became king. He was to conquer many more lands during his short life. He would become known as **Alexander the Great**.

In 334 BC Alexander invaded the Persian Empire. Although the Persian army was larger than Alexander's, he defeated them. In only four years' time, Alexander ruled all the lands that had once made up the Persian Empire.

Alexander destroyed many of the beautiful structures and works of art when he burned the city of Persepolis.

Yet Alexander admired many things about the Persian Empire. He continued the Persian form of centralized government. He placed the Persian cavalry in his own army. He married several Persian princesses. He also kept some of the Persian customs and blended them with influences from Greek culture.

Rule by the Seleucids

But Alexander's reign over Persia was short. He died in his early thirties. After his death his empire did not last. The lands he had conquered were divided and given to four different generals. Persia came under the control of a family called the Seleucids. Hellenistic culture continued to spread throughout Asia, including Persia. **Hellenistic** is a term used to describe Greek culture as it made its way into other lands after Alexander's conquests.

Weaving Carpets

Have you ever seen a Persian carpet in someone's home? A Persian carpet usually has a colorful design in an intricately woven pattern. Many historians believe that the art of weaving rugs from animal wool first prospered during the Parthian period. Even today Parthia is the name for a popular style of Persian rug.

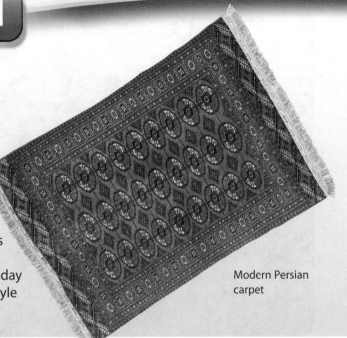

Modern Persian carpet

Persian Rule Revived

The Parthians

It was only a little more than a century before Persians controlled the Persian territory again. Parthia was a province in northeast Persia near the Caspian Sea. A tribe of nomads called the Parni moved down from central Asia, fought the Seleucid king, and took over Parthia. Beginning around 171 BC, the **Parthians** slowly began to extend their control. Toward the end of the second century BC, they had recovered nearly all the eastern part of the former Persian Empire.

The Parthians ruled for about four centuries. The art that survives from their culture reflects their close contact with the Greeks. The coins minted in their empire have Greek writing on them. Parthians also had contact with the Asian peoples farther east. The Silk Road from China ran through their empire. For a while the Parthians controlled the road and collected a toll from those traveling on it.

The Parthians lacked a strong central government like the one Darius I had established. They were further weakened by war with the Romans. In the second century AD they were defeated by the Sassanids.

Parthian coin
The Granger Collection, NYC (front and back)

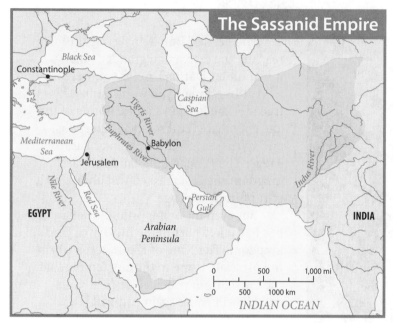

The Sassanid Empire

The Sassanids

The Sassanian dynasty, or **Sassanids**, came from the area around Persepolis. They ruled from AD 224 to 651. The first Sassanid king, Ardeshir, defeated the last Parthian king and established himself as Persia's ruler. The Sassanid kings wanted to bring back all that was truly Persian and rid the culture of Greek influences.

Each Sassanid ruler called himself a "king of kings." These rulers conducted their empire much the same as the Achaemenid kings had. They strengthened the central government again. They revived Zoroastrianism as the state religion. And under their rule there was a strict system of social classes. The highest classes were the powerful priestly class and a network of noblemen who ruled the provinces and collected taxes. Other classes included the military and the peasants.

Persia achieved its greatest wealth during this period. Tribute money and trade from the Silk Road allowed Persia's economy to thrive. Persian arts and crafts flowered again. Some of the Sassanid kings built new cities, buildings, and canals. They improved irrigation and industry.

But the Sassanids also fought with the Romans and later with the Byzantines. The Sassanids' losses from warfare brought about decline, and the power of their ruling class waned.

The end of the Sassanid period brought an end to Persian culture in its purest form. The last Sassanid king was conquered by Arab invaders, who introduced the religion of Islam to Persia.

Relief showing Sassanid king Shapur I victorious over Roman emperor Valerian

A modern Zoroastrian fire temple

The Persian Empire never again reached the extent and grandeur that it had under Darius I. Yet if you were to visit Iran today, you would still see traces of the Persian Empire. Ruins of the ancient palaces still stand at Persepolis, and Cyrus's tomb can be seen at Pasargadae. The Persian kings and the vast kingdom they established will always be a part of Iran's heritage.

But even more importantly, Persia has had a key part in the history of God's kingdom. The King of Kings, Jesus Christ the Messiah, came to the city temple that the Persian rulers helped restore. One day He will come again and will reign on this earth.

Of the increase of his government and peace there shall be no end, upon the throne of David, and upon his kingdom, to order it, and to establish it with judgment and with justice from henceforth even for ever. The zeal of the Lord of hosts will perform this. (Isa. 9:7)

The ruins of Apadana, an ancient royal reception hall at Persepolis

Chapter 8

Ancient Greece

1. What period in Greece was a peak of human achievement?

2. How were the earliest civilizations that settled in Greece different from each other?

FOCUS

The poet Edgar Allan Poe once wrote of "the glory that was Greece." What do you think he meant? Was he describing the land of Greece itself—its steep white rocks towering above a sapphire blue sea? Was he thinking of Greek architecture—magnificent marble buildings, columned porches, and statues? Or was he speaking of the Greek people draped in flowing robes or clad in bronze armor—accomplished warriors, philosophers, mathematicians, poets, and artists?

A view of the modern seacoast of Syme, Greece

Poe was referring to the classical age of Greece, a period that began about **500 BC**. The classical age is often described as glorious. During this time the Greeks reached a peak of human achievement. Their great accomplishments were known throughout most of the ancient world. Greek culture made a lasting impact especially on the Western world. Over the centuries people have looked back to the classical Greeks for patterns to follow in government, philosophy, and the arts.

The Land of Greece

The ancient Greeks lived in what is still known as Greece today. Greece is a land of mountains, valleys, natural harbors, and hundreds of tiny islands. Greece is a peninsula bordered by three seas: the Ionian, the Mediterranean, and the Aegean. The southern portion of this peninsula is called the **Peloponnesus**.

Greece's mild climate, rugged coastline, and island-strewn seas led its people to become fishermen, seafarers, and traders. It was often easier to travel on the sea than on the mountainous land.

Some Greeks were farmers. The rocky soil in Greece made farming difficult. Farmers still managed to grow crops such as barley, wheat, olives, and grapes.

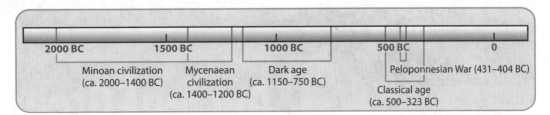

| 2000 BC | 1500 BC | 1000 BC | 500 BC | 0 |

Minoan civilization (ca. 2000–1400 BC)

Mycenaean civilization (ca. 1400–1200 BC)

Dark age (ca. 1150–750 BC)

Classical age (ca. 500–323 BC)

Peloponnesian War (431–404 BC)

The palace at Knossos on the island of Crete
What made this palace unusually luxurious for its time?

Early Civilizations

The Minoans

The Bible says that, after the Flood, the sons of Javan journeyed westward from Mesopotamia and settled in the "isles of the Gentiles" (Gen. 10:4–5). These islands could very well be the area that is known as Greece. The earliest known civilization from the land of Greece is the **Minoan** (mih NO uhn) **civilization**. The Minoans lived on the island of **Crete**. Their civilization existed at the same time as the Shang dynasty in China and as the New Kingdom in Egypt.

By 2000 BC the Minoans had settled in Crete and had built a large, beautiful palace in the city of Knossos (NOS uhs). The palace had hundreds of rooms and even some unusual luxuries for its time, such as bathtubs and piped water. Archaeologists have found pottery, carvings, and wall paintings in the palace that reflect a wealthy and artistic people. The Minoans gained their wealth through trading with other peoples from lands as far away as Egypt.

Ancient container

The Minoan people also traveled to other parts of the Mediterranean region and formed colonies. Some scholars believe that the Philistines, enemies of ancient Israel, were colonists of the Minoan civilization.

By 1400 BC the Minoan civilization had come to an end. The reason for this is not known. It is believed that a volcanic eruption or an invasion took place.

Ancient jars in the palace at Knossos

197

Lion Gate at Mycenae
How do this gate and these walls reflect the warlike nature of the Mycenaeans?

The Mycenaeans

Another civilization that had been growing on the mainland of Greece was the **Mycenaean** (MY suh NEE uhn) **civilization**. Possibly these people were the invaders who brought about the fall of the Minoans in Crete.

The Mycenaean civilization was made up of many cities. Each city had its own king. Like the Minoans, the Mycenaeans built large palaces. But these palaces were not as richly adorned. Instead they were heavily fortified with thick walls and built on high hills. The Mycenaeans designed their buildings more for military strength than for artistry.

The Mycenaeans were often at war. Instead of trading peacefully, they frequently attacked other cities or pirated ships. Many scholars believe that the Mycenaeans attacked the city of Troy and started the **Trojan War**. According to legend, this war lasted ten years. The Trojan War became a popular subject in Greek literature.

The Mycenaean civilization lasted until about 1200 BC. Around this time, invaders from the north attacked and conquered many of the Mycenaean fortresses. A time that historians call the dark age of Greece followed.

UNCOVERING MYCENAE

The gold mask found at Mycenae

In the late 1800s a German archaeologist named Heinrich Schliemann excavated the city of Mycenae. The Mycenaeans are named after this city. At its entrance stands a massive stone gate decorated with two carved lions. The city's central building is a great palace with walls more than fifteen feet thick. Many bronze weapons as well as a burial ground were found in Mycenae. One of the many artifacts found in the graves was a gold mask. Schliemann believed it belonged to Agamemnon, the legendary king of Mycenae who led the war against Troy. However, modern research shows that the mask is too old to be from Agamemnon's time. It is still likely the mask of an honored warrior.

Greece

Location—Greece is located in southeastern Europe. The country sits on the southern end of the Balkan Peninsula. Three seas surround Greece—the Ionian, the Mediterranean, and the Aegean.

Climate—The climate of Greece is typical for the Mediterranean region. Summers are long, and winters are mild and rainy. Temperatures range from 80°F (27°C) in the summer to 48°F (9°C) in the winter.

Topography—Greece is mountainous and has a narrow coastal plain. The country includes over 6,000 islands. Crete is the largest of the 227 islands that are inhabited.

Natural Resources—Greece's natural resources include bauxite, iron ore, and small quantities of coal and oil.

Which Greek city-state was located on the Peloponnesus—Athens or Sparta?

Greece Then & Now

Legend	
——	Modern country
——	Modern Greece
▨	Ancient Greece ca. 550 BC
✪	Modern capital
•	Ancient city

1. How did the governments of Sparta and Athens change after the dark age?

2. How was life different for people in Athens compared with those in Sparta?

FOCUS

Athens and Sparta

The Dark Age of Greece

Few records exist to tell us what life was like during the dark age of Greece. Most of our knowledge of this time comes from Greek literature. Stories about life in ancient Greece were passed down from parents to their children by word of mouth. After the Greeks had developed an alphabet, these stories were written down. You will learn more about these stories in a later section of this chapter.

The Rise of City-States

During the dark age the Greeks were made up of many separate groups. Mountains and valleys divided the land, so the people lived in independent societies scattered throughout Greece. These societies were called city-states. The people in a city-state were like a large family. They claimed common ancestors, practiced the same customs, and spoke the same dialect. At the time Greece did not have one central government. Instead each city-state had its own government. A city-state was sometimes ruled by a king. This type of government is called a **monarchy**, which comes from the Greek word for "rule by one."

An artist's rendering of ancient Sparta *Why do you think the Greeks chose to have separate, self-governing city-states rather than one central government?*

200

A meeting of the Assembly
What skills and strengths do you think made certain men rise to power in Athens?

Government in Athens and Sparta

The two most famous city-states were **Athens** and **Sparta**. By the end of the dark age, both city-states had adopted another type of government. This new government was called an oligarchy. By now you might have guessed that the suffix *-archy* means "rule." The prefix *olig-* means "few." An **oligarchy** is a "rule by the few." Usually the few who rule are of the rich upper class. Both Athens and Sparta were ruled by small groups of nobles who owned their own land.

Athens

Although Athens and Sparta were once similar to one another, they ended up being very different.

After the dark age, many city-states branched out and formed colonies along the Mediterranean Sea. People who had gained wealth and power from trading grew discontent with having an oligarchy ruling over them. Soon some city-states began to form new ideas about what type of government was best. Athens was one of these. One Athenian nobleman named Solon wrote new laws that allowed men of the lower classes to participate in government.

Individual men rose to power in Athens, supported by discontented people. These men who ruled with absolute authority were called **tyrants**. Some of them ruled well. Others ruled poorly. Many of them followed Solon's example in trying to give the lower classes better living conditions and more say in government.

One tyrant who brought improvements was Cleisthenes (KLAHYS thuh NEEZ). Under his leadership all male citizens over eighteen years old in Athens could attend meetings of the Assembly. The **Assembly** was a group of citizens who met together to make laws. In these meetings, the citizens could speak out on issues and vote, regardless of their place in society. Women in Greece were not allowed to vote or participate in governmental meetings.

The Agora

The Assembly met in the **agora** (AH guh ruh), a busy marketplace in the center of Athens. The agora was made up of open-air buildings called porches. Citizens gathered there every day to buy and sell. They could buy fresh food that had been brought to the agora from local farms. Since there was not enough good farmland around Athens to produce food for all the people, some foods, such as meats and cheeses, were imported. Shoppers in the agora could also find materials such as iron, copper, timber, ivory, animal hides, wool, and papyrus as well as furniture and textiles.

The agora was more than a marketplace. Schools, governmental buildings, courts, and private businesses were located there. Sometimes people just gathered there to meet friends and talk. They would discuss politics, philosophy, and the latest news.

Olives for sale in a modern market

By 500 BC new laws had greatly changed the government in Athens. Athens became a **democracy**. The word *democracy* comes from the Greek words that mean "rule by the people." The Athenian democracy became the most successful one in the ancient world. Democratic countries today look back to Athens as a model in some ways for a government by the people.

A Spartan warrior

Sparta

Unlike Athens, Sparta kept its oligarchy. The oligarchy had one aim—to have a strong army. For centuries, Sparta made no advances in art or literature as Athens and other city-states did.

Life in Sparta was much more rigid than life in Athens. When a baby boy was born in Sparta, his parents presented him to the rulers of the city. If the rulers thought he was strong, they allowed

him to live. If not, they left him in the countryside to die. The Spartans did not want any weaklings in their army. A boy who was not put to death stayed at home until he was seven years old. Then the army took him and trained him to be a soldier. During most of his young adult life, a Spartan boy lived in army barracks with a group of other boys. Everything about life in the barracks was designed to prepare them for warfare. The boys had little to eat. They were expected to steal food from farms, but if they were caught, they were punished. They were taught to live by their wits so that they would be prepared to survive during wartime. Every year some of the boys were beaten in public as part of a ceremony to the gods. The beatings were meant to help the boys learn to endure pain.

At age twenty, a Spartan man could marry. But he could not live at home with his wife. He had to live with the other men, training to be a soldier, for ten more years. The training a man received in the Spartan army was harsh and disciplined. The Spartans felt that learning to suffer pain and hardship would make a man a good soldier.

Women in Athens and Sparta

Athenian women led sheltered lives. An upper-class woman went out of the house only to festivals and plays, accompanied by her servants. Her slaves did the daily shopping and errands. Even lower-class women who did not have slaves rarely shopped or worked outside the home. They kept their households supplied with meals and clothing. Athenian women were skilled at spinning and weaving. A few women from wealthy families learned to read and write at home.

In Sparta women also managed their households. But since the men were often away from home with the army, the women also tended to jobs the men would have done. Spartan women went out in public more than Athenian women. Some even owned property. Like the men, Spartan women received physical training. This training was designed to make them strong mothers. Mothers taught their children to be brave and loyal to Sparta. Wives sent their husbands and sons into battle with the cry, "Return with your shield or on it!" They meant that the soldier should return as a living conqueror or a dead hero. The Spartan army had no room for cowards or quitters.

A woman spinning thread
How was a Spartan woman's life different from an Athenian woman's?

Voting in the Athenian Democracy

In ancient Athens, only adult male citizens were allowed to participate in politics. They had to meet certain requirements before they could vote. Women, children, and slaves were never allowed to vote.

The Athenians voted on many kinds of issues. They voted on whether to go to war. They voted for leaders. They voted on new laws and who could become a citizen. Once a year, if there was someone who needed to be punished, they voted on whether to banish him from Athens for ten years. This punishment was called *ostracism*.

Most voting was done by a show of hands. However, it could also be done using pebbles or potsherds (pieces of broken pottery). Sometimes, during a trial, voters would place black or white pebbles in an urn to express their belief in a person's guilt or innocence. In a decision for ostracism, voters would write on a potsherd the name of the person they thought should be sent away. Many of these potsherds from the fifth century BC have been found in Athens.

1. You will need a black pebble, a white pebble, a potsherd, and chalk. Pretend that you and your classmates are part of the Assembly in ancient Athens.

2. Participate in voting on three issues as directed by your teacher. The first vote will be done by a show of hands, the second with pebbles, and the third with potsherds.

3. Record the results of each vote on the Activity Manual page.

4. Complete the Activity Manual page.

FOCUS

1. How did Greece put into action the new confidence they had gained in defeating the Persians?

2. What were the consequences of the Peloponnesian War for Greece?

War and Restoration

The Persian Wars

In an earlier chapter, you learned that the Greeks clashed with the mighty Persian Empire in the fifth century BC. The Persians were angered by the growth of the Greek city-states. They wanted to conquer Greece and make it part of the Persian Empire. But they soon found that defeating the Greeks would not be easy. For over ten years the Greeks fought the Persians and won many battles.

After the Athenian army won the battle of Marathon, Sparta joined forces with Athens to fight the Persians in later battles. In the battle of Thermopylae, the Greeks suffered a defeat. They had to watch the beautiful city of Athens go up in flames.

But the Greek spirit was not defeated. One of the most decisive battles was the Battle of Salamis, which took place in 480 BC. The battle took place at sea when the Greeks met the forces of the Persian king Xerxes. The Greeks lost about forty ships but burned at least two hundred of the Persian ships. Following this defeat, the Persians tried only one more time to conquer the Greeks—but without success. Greece was victorious.

Have you ever been a member of a team that beat a stronger rival? If you have, you can probably understand how the Greeks felt after their victory over the Persians. They felt as if they could accomplish anything.

However, war had taken its toll on Greece. Many buildings and temples lay in ruins. One of the first ways the Greeks put their new confidence to work was in restoring their cities.

Battle of Salamis

Greek ships
Persian ships

Bay of Eleusis

Attica

Psyttaleia

Salamis

Byzantium

Aegean Sea

PERSIAN EMPIRE

Corinth
Athens
Sparta

Salamis

The huge fleet of Persian ships could not maneuver well in the narrow waterways around Salamis. The Greeks pretended to retreat in order to coax the Persians farther into the strait before attacking them.

205

Pericles

The most famous leader of the democracy in Athens was **Pericles** (PEHR ih KLEEZ). Pericles is considered one of the greatest public speakers, or *orators*, of all time. The Greeks made him their leader because they respected his wisdom and his ability to reason.

Pericles encouraged as many people as possible to take part in the Athenian government. He even paid people to be officers in the Assembly and to serve on juries. In his speeches Pericles helped define the democracy of Athens.

The Erechtheum, one of the buildings on the Acropolis
How did the rebuilding projects of Pericles improve life in Athens?

Not only was Pericles a powerful speaker and politician, but he loved the city of Athens as well. He had grown up in Athens, and he wanted it always to be a city that others would admire and love as much as he did. After the Persian Wars, he wanted to repair the damages caused when Xerxes burned the city. Pericles helped restore to Athens all of its former beauty and more.

The **Acropolis**, a hill overlooking the city, was the center of religious life in Athens. Pericles encouraged the Athenians to rebuild the ruined temple and construct other sacred buildings on that hill. He hired talented architects, sculptors, and artists. Under his leadership, the architecture of the classical age took shape—the columns, the sculptures, and the great Entrance Gate.

Pericles also supported the growth of manufacturing and trade and helped build up the army. Because of his influence in Athens during the fifth century BC, the period is often called the *Age of Pericles*.

Close-up of one of the statues

The Peloponnesian War

Growing Tension

After the Persian Wars, Athens took steps to protect itself and its trading practices. Athens had a strong navy, but the Athenians knew they were not strong enough by themselves. They wanted to be able to defend their city-state against other world powers like Persia. Athens believed that if the Greek city-states worked together, they would be stronger. Athens formed an alliance with many city-states. The alliance was called the Delian League. The city-states agreed to pay money into the league's treasury to help protect each other. They also contributed troops and ships.

The dominant power of the league was Athens. It had the most control over the Aegean Sea, where the Greeks traded.

Taxes were paid to Athens to maintain its navy. Later, Athens also received payments for guarding the league's treasury. As a result, the city-state grew wealthier and more powerful. Sometimes Athens pressured other city-states to join or stay in the league. Many Greeks sensed that Athens wanted to build an empire and control the rest of Greece.

Sparta did not join the Delian League. Athens and Sparta disagreed on many things, including their forms of government. Sparta felt that Athens was using the Delian League to gain power. Tension grew between the two city-states. Some city-states took sides with Sparta and formed a different alliance—the Peloponnesian League.

Finally, in 431 BC, Athens and Sparta went to war with each other. Their allies joined the fighting. Because most of the fighting took place on the Peloponnesus, the war is called the **Peloponnesian War**. It lasted more than twenty-seven years.

A ship used for trading
How do you think the Delian League helped protect trading vessels from enemies?

The Siege of Athens

The Spartan army marched to Athens and surrounded the city. The Spartans settled in for a siege, hoping that the Athenians would eventually begin to starve. There would be nothing for the Athenians to do except surrender. But even inside its city walls, Athens was not cut off from its seaport. The Athenian navy supplied the city with food and other needed items by way of the sea.

The siege lasted until a plague broke out in Athens. Many Athenians died, including Pericles. The Spartans left because they did not want to get the disease themselves.

Battle by Land and Sea

The Athenian navy continued the war by attacking Sparta's allies on the coast. Both sides won some battles and lost others. Neither Athens nor Sparta could gain the advantage. Finally both agreed to a truce.

The Defeat of Athens

The truce lasted only a few years. Athens broke it by attacking Sicily, one of Sparta's allies. Sicily defeated the powerful Athenian fleet. Then Sparta joined forces with the Greeks' old enemy, the Persians. Persia began giving money to Sparta, and Sparta was able to build a navy of its own. The Spartan navy took control of the Hellespont, blocking Athenian ships from bringing any more food and supplies into Athens. In 404 BC, Athens was forced to surrender. Sparta had won the war.

Consequences of the War

Sparta took control of Greece for about thirty years. But neither Sparta nor Athens ever fully recovered from the effects of the war. Both city-states had been weakened by their losses. Many people had died. Buildings lay in ruins. Farmland had been ravaged. Athens lost its democracy, and the Spartan oligarchy was unpopular with the other city-states. The "glory that was Greece" would never return.

A trireme, a type of Greek warship

208

Thucydides

Much of what we know of the Peloponnesian War comes from a historian named **Thucydides** (thoo SID uh DEEZ). As an Athenian who lived through the war, he was an eyewitness to the sights and sounds of the time. For a while he was a general in the Athenian army. Thucydides wrote from firsthand knowledge and careful research. He tried to verify each fact he wrote down. We have him to thank for recording one of Pericles' most famous speeches during the war. The speech was given at a funeral for Athenian soldiers who had died in battle.

Thucydides lived at the same time as the historian Herodotus did. Most scholars feel that of the two historians, Thucydides was the more accurate recorder of events. Unlike Herodotus, he tried not to include any information that sounded biased or far-fetched.

Thucydides' history of the Peloponnesian War was divided into eight books. In the following quotation from Book I, Thucydides describes his research process and his goal in writing a history of the war.

> Of the events of the war I have not ventured to speak from any chance information, nor according to any notion of my own; I have described nothing but what I either saw myself, or learned from others of whom I made the most careful and particular enquiry. . . . If he who desires to have before his eyes a true picture of the events which have happened . . . shall pronounce what I have written to be useful, then I shall be satisfied. My history is an everlasting possession, not a prize composition which is heard and forgotten. (*Thucydides,* trans. Benjamin Jowett. [Oxford: Clarendon Press, 1900], 15)

Thucydides wanted his work to endure for many years to come, not just to create a momentary sensation.

1. What did the myths tell about the gods?

2. How did the beliefs of Greek religion differ from those of Greek philosophy?

Religion in Greece

The Greeks believed that there were many different gods. They believed that these gods lived on **Mount Olympus**, the highest mountain in Greece. Although these gods had supernatural powers, the Greeks did not believe that the gods were much different from humans. Drawings and sculptures depicted the gods as having human bodies. In their characters, too, the gods were like humans—jealous, vengeful, immoral, and often childish.

The Greeks made up fanciful stories about their gods and goddesses. These stories are called **myths**. They told how the actions of the gods affected events in nature or in the lives of humans. There were myths to explain sunrise and sunset, thunder and lightning, changing seasons, and constellations.

The names of many of the Greek gods and goddesses are well-known. Stories about them became so widely read that people named many things after them. The city of Athens was named after the Greek goddess Athena. The American space program that sent men to the moon was named after the god Apollo. Athletic shoes have been named after Nike, the goddess of victory. Books of maps are named after Atlas, who is often pictured carrying the world on his shoulders.

How do these illustrations reflect the roles of these gods?

Greek Gods and Goddesses

Although there were many gods and goddesses, some were more important than others. The gods and goddesses listed below were thought to be the greatest deities. They play major roles in many of the Greek myths.

Zeus	king of the gods and god of the sky	Apollo	god of the sun, music, and poetry
Hera	queen of the gods and goddess of marriage	Artemis	goddess of hunting
		Athena	goddess of wisdom and war
Poseidon	god of the sea	Ares	god of war
Hades	god of the underworld	Aphrodite	goddess of love and beauty
Hestia	goddess of hearth and home	Hephaestus	god of fire and metalworking
Demeter	goddess of harvest	Hermes	messenger god

Zeus
Hera
Athena
Hephaestus
Hestia
Hermes
Aphrodite
Poseidon

Who: Socrates

What: philosopher and teacher

When: ca. 470–399 BC

Where: Athens, Greece

Socrates taught by asking questions. He encouraged his students to seek truth by using human reason. He was sentenced to death for misleading young people and rejecting the gods of Athens. His teachings paved the way for many other philosophers who came after him.

Philosophy in Greece

The democratic government of Athens during the classical age encouraged free thinking and new ideas. Many scholars lived in Athens during this time. Some of these men did not accept the religious beliefs of the city. They wanted to explain life by their own wisdom, not by the actions of gods. These men were called philosophers. The word *philosopher* comes from the Greek word *philosophos,* which means "lover of wisdom."

Socrates (SAHK ruh TEEZ) taught by asking his students thought-provoking questions. "What is the meaning of life?" he would ask. "What is a good man?" The questions made his students think about what they really believed. Socrates was also a firm believer in democracy. He wanted to make the government a perfect one and believed that right thinking would lead to right actions.

Socrates was eventually sentenced to death for his teachings. His ideas were too different, and they led the young men of Athens to question their beliefs about the gods. The city leaders gave Socrates poison to drink, and he calmly drank it and died.

GREEK PHILOSOPHY

Greek philosophers believed that they could use their own reason and clear thinking to arrive at true wisdom. The Bible says that "the fear of the Lord is the beginning of wisdom" (Prov. 9:10). A proper view of God and ourselves is necessary to be truly wise. The Bible also teaches that we are not to be proud of our wisdom or glory in it. We are to glory only in knowing and understanding God (Jer. 9:24).

The Greek philosophers emphasized many of the same virtues that the Bible does, such as truth, love, wisdom, and discipline. But the Bible teaches that these virtues are granted only through a true knowledge of Christ (2 Pet. 1:3–8). It is impossible to live a godly life without the power of the Holy Spirit. For example, the philosopher Aristotle taught that reason controls behavior. But the apostle Paul tells us that there are times when we know what is right but still choose to do wrong (Rom. 7:15). More is needed than reason. The Bible says that our minds need to be renewed by the Spirit of God (Rom. 8:5–14).

Raphael's famous painting, *School of Athens*, depicts Plato and Aristotle (center back) with other Greek scientists and philosophers around them.

What does this painting show about art and architecture in Greece at that time?

Plato was one of Socrates' students. Plato wrote books in the form of conversations. In these books, called *dialogues*, he said that the ideal government was ruled by a few of the most intelligent men. He also taught that there was a spiritual world—a world of the mind and of ideas—that was superior to the physical world.

Aristotle (AR ih STOT ul), Plato's pupil, was a third great Greek philosopher. To Aristotle, science was the most important academic subject. He introduced the *scientific method*, a method of study requiring careful observation and record keeping. He also taught that reason controls behavior.

Both religion and philosophy in Greece were expressions of the human need to worship. The Greek religion encouraged the worship of imagined gods and goddesses. Greek philosophers worshiped wisdom, reason, and man's ability to think for himself. However, neither Greece's religion nor its philosophy was the answer to the greatest human need, redemption through Jesus Christ.

GREEK BELIEFS

The Greeks worshiped gods and goddesses who were very much like humans. They were just as sinful as humans are, and sometimes even worse. The true God of the Bible is perfectly holy (Isa. 6:3). Humans may have sinful desires and do sinful things, but God never sins. Because God is holy, He will judge sinful people (Rom. 2:12).

The Greeks believed that they needed the favor of the gods to accomplish the various tasks of life. To win the favor of the gods, the Greeks offered them sacrifices. These sacrifices were different from those offered by the Israelites to the true God. In the Old Testament, God required people to make sacrifices to Him as a symbol of mankind's greatest need. Mankind needed a perfect sacrifice to pay for their sins. Since God cannot accept sin, He cannot accept mankind in their sinful condition. When Jesus died on the cross, He paid the sacrifice for all people (Heb. 10:4–14). God provided the perfect sacrifice so that we can be acceptable in His sight.

FOCUS

1. Why are the epics the *Iliad* and the *Odyssey* important in understanding ancient Greece?

2. What other works of literature had an important influence on Greek culture?

Learning and the Arts

Education

Would you like to go to school with a servant who was there just to make sure you behaved? Wealthy boys in Greece had to do this. The servants who accompanied them were called pedagogues. Boys began school at age six and continued to at least age fourteen. At school they studied reading, writing, arithmetic, grammar, music, and sports. Boys from poorer families could not afford to go to school, and girls were not allowed to go at all.

Reading and writing in ancient Greece were much different from how they are at your school. The Greeks had an alphabet with twenty-four letters. Some letters were the same as the English alphabet, and some were different. The Greeks used no punctuation or spacing between words. Greek students wrote on wax-coated tablets with a stylus. The

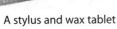

A stylus and wax tablet

stylus was pointed on one end to scratch letters into the wax and blunt on the other end to rub out mistakes.

Literature

Literature in ancient Greece took many forms. Some were records of history or writings on philosophy. Some were speeches. Stories were often presented in poetry and drama. Many of these written works have been preserved and are still studied today.

BIOGRAPHY

Who: Homer

What: poet and storyteller

When: ca. 1200 BC (dark age)

Where: Greece

According to legend, Homer was a blind poet who lived during the dark age of Greece. His epic poems, the *Iliad* and the *Odyssey*, were handed down through centuries of oral storytelling. The *Iliad* tells the story of the Trojan War, and the *Odyssey* recounts the adventures of the Greek hero Odysseus.

Epics

Every Greek schoolboy had to study two long poems called the *Iliad* and the *Odyssey*. These poems were passed down orally from a Greek poet named **Homer**.

The *Iliad* and the *Odyssey* are epics, lengthy poems about the actions of heroes. Students of literature and history still study these two epics today. The poems provide glimpses of life and culture in ancient Greece during the dark age. They also emphasize values every good hero should have, such as dignity, strength, valor, generosity, and wisdom.

Fables

Another type of story that was passed down from the ancient Greeks by word of mouth was the fable. A **fable** is a story designed to teach a lesson. Fables did not usually involve the gods. Often the main characters in fables were animals that talked and acted in many ways as humans do. A fable usually stated its point in a brief closing statement called the moral. **Aesop**, a Greek slave about whom we know very little, was the author of many of these fables.

Plays

The Greeks developed another literary art form as well—the art of drama. Crowds would gather in huge outdoor theaters called **amphitheaters**. There the people watched actors perform plays as part of religious festivals.

Most Greek plays were about the gods and heroes. There were two types of Greek drama—*comedy* and *tragedy*.

Ancient Greek dramatic masks

Comedies mocked certain people or types of people and were meant to entertain the audience and make them laugh. The only ancient Greek comedies that have survived are by the playwright Aristophanes (AR ih STOF uh neez). Tragedies left audiences feeling solemn. These plays usually ended with the downfall of the hero because of a character flaw, such as pride or jealousy. Sophocles (SOF uh KLEEZ) was a popular writer of Greek tragedies. Because Greek plays shed light on human nature, many are still performed today.

Imagine that you are in a large amphitheater in ancient Greece. You are sitting on a cool stone bench that is far away from the stage. How would you see the expressions on the actors' faces and hear their voices? You would probably have little trouble. The actors wore exaggerated costumes and large masks that allowed the audience to tell them apart. Some actors exchanged their masks for different ones to express the characters' feelings. The masks showed whether the characters felt happy, sad, or angry. The funnel-shaped mouthpieces inside the masks acted as megaphones that made the actors' voices carry to everyone in the crowd.

Myths

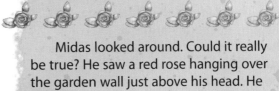

During the dark age, the Greeks developed their myths. We have already learned that the Greek myths tell stories about gods and goddesses. Some myths were also about human heroes. You are probably familiar with some of these myths.

As the myths were passed down from storyteller to storyteller, they sometimes changed. There might be several different versions of one myth, depending on how many of these changes were remembered. Here is one version of the story of Midas.

Midas, the King with the Golden Touch— a Greek Myth

Midas, the king of Phrygia, had a lovely palace and a beautiful rose garden. He also had a little daughter whom he loved very much. But sometimes Midas wished that he could have more.

One day Midas was granted a wish by Dionysus, the god of wine. Dionysus told Midas that he could have any gift he desired.

Midas thought for a moment. "I wish that everything I touch would turn to gold," he told the god. "Then I would have enough gold to buy anything I ever wanted."

Dionysus raised his eyebrows. "Consider carefully, King Midas," he said. "Are you certain this is the wish you desire?"

"This is my wish," said Midas.

"Very well. Your wish is granted," said Dionysus. He said goodbye with a sad expression in his eyes, and he left.

Midas looked around. Could it really be true? He saw a red rose hanging over the garden wall just above his head. He reached up and touched it, holding his breath.

The rose turned into solid gold before his eyes! Midas looked up at the sky and laughed out loud. "It's true!" he cried. "My wish has come true! Thank you, Dionysus. You have made me the wealthiest man in the world!"

Midas leaped and danced around the palace grounds, touching trees, fountains, and benches and watching them turn to gold. Looking down, he saw that he was leaving gold footprints in the grass with every step. He hurried to the palace and entered the front hall.

"Bring me a feast to celebrate!" he called to the servants. "Bring my daughter to eat with me. I have been granted the golden touch by the gods!"

The servants bustled around, preparing a meal, and they summoned the princess to the feast.

"Watch, my dear," said King Midas. He raised his crystal goblet, and it turned to gold in his hands. Midas laughed with delight and started to drink. But as the first sip touched his lips, the liquid turned into a lump of gold. He choked and spat the lump back into the cup.

The princess watched with frightened eyes. Midas too, began to feel worried. "I will try eating meat," he said.

His heart pounded as he speared a piece of meat with his golden fork and raised it to his lips. Before he could even

216

taste the savory beef, it turned to cold, hard metal in his mouth. Midas cried out in alarm and spat out the golden meat.

The princess was watching Midas with huge, fear-filled eyes. "Father," she said, "I fear you will starve. You cannot eat if all your food turns to gold before you can even swallow it."

Without thinking, Midas reached out and patted her hand to comfort her. The moment he touched her fingers, she froze into a solid gold statue.

"No!" shrieked the king. He jumped up and raced outside. Tears streamed down his face, leaving trails of liquid gold on his cheeks. "Dionysus!" he shouted. "Please, have pity on me! I have been greedy and unwise. Please take the gift back!"

Dionysus appeared beside him. "I pity you, my friend," he said. "You have learned a hard lesson today. If you will go and wash in the river Pactolus, you will lose your golden touch. You will return, and all will be as before."

Murmuring his thanks, Midas ran to the river and leaped into it. As he bathed, streams of gold appeared in the water, and flecks of gold sparkled in the sands. But when Midas stepped out, his golden touch was gone.

To this day, the river Pactolus gleams with the last traces of King Midas's golden touch.

Discovering How

Making a Greek Mask

Each mask used by Greek performers showed a different emotion. The expressions on the masks helped the audience better understand the play.

Each person in your group will make a mask that shows the emotion of his character in your play. After designing and making your mask, you will act out your play.

1. Get a mirror, a copy of a play from your teacher, construction paper, markers, and scissors.

2. Practice several emotions as you hold a mirror in front of your face. Note the facial distinctions for each emotion.

3. Read the play your teacher gives your group. Decide which character and which emotion each of you will represent with your mask.

4. Draw a face on construction paper with a pencil, showing the trait or emotion you chose in step 3. Trace the features with a marker.

5. Cut out holes for the eyes.

6. Hold your mask in front of your face and allow the other students to guess what emotion you are illustrating.

7. Act out the play with your group using the masks.

FOCUS

1. What accomplishments were made in the areas of math and science in ancient Greece?

2. What is unusual about the architecture of the Parthenon?

Math and Science

When you study math and certain types of science, you rely upon the discoveries of several Greek scholars. **Archimedes** (AHR kuh MEE deez) was a mathematician who advanced the lever and compound pulleys, machines that make the moving of objects easier. **Euclid** (YOO klid) wrote the first geometry book. The entire study of geometry was built around his teachings. Pythagoras (pih THAG uhr us), another mathematician, studied geometry and came up with an important **theorem**, or a carefully tested idea, about the area of triangles.

In school the Greeks used a special instrument called an abacus to teach math. An **abacus** is a wooden frame with rows of movable beads on it.

Look at a map of the world. A Greek named Eratosthenes (ehr uh TOS thuh NEEZ) was the first to draw latitude and longitude lines on a map. He also calculated the circumference of the earth with reasonable accuracy.

An astronomer named Aristarchus (AR ih STAHR kus) was the first to suggest that the sun was at the center of the universe. Most people in those days believed that the earth was at the center of the universe.

Hippocrates (hih POK ruh TEEZ) is famous today for his contribution to the study of medicine. Hippocrates did not agree with the popular idea of relying on magic to treat patients. He examined them carefully and prescribed treatments. Hippocrates is called the Father of Medicine. Doctors today still take the Hippocratic Oath in honor of his wisdom and principles in the medical profession.

Pythagoras

Hippocrates

Athletics

The Greeks believed that developing the body was as important as developing the mind. Our English word *athlete* comes from the Greek language. Schoolboys spent hours in the gymnasium running, jumping, wrestling, boxing, and throwing the javelin and the discus.

The ancient Greeks were the first to hold the **Olympic Games**. These were special festivals held at the city of Olympia in honor of the gods. Athletes from all over Greece would travel to the city to compete in various events. These athletes competed in many of the same events as Olympic athletes today do—sprints, long jumps, wrestling, and discus and javelin throwing. The ancient Greeks also had chariot races and events for younger boys. The winners were given garlands of laurel leaves to wear on their heads as crowns.

Music

The Greeks regarded music as one of the greatest of all the arts. Their god Apollo was believed to be the god of music. Greek art often pictures Apollo entertaining the other gods with a lyre, a type of small harp. The Greeks also believed that a group of nine goddesses called the **Muses** presided over the arts. Each goddess had a particular specialty, such as epic poetry or religious music. Our word *music* comes from their name.

During the classical age, wealthy boys were required to study music. They learned to play the lyre and the *aulos* (AW los), a type of flute. Singing was also an important part of musical training. Students memorized the *Iliad* and the *Odyssey*, put the words to music, and sang them. Some boys continued their studies with training in public speaking, hoping to become leaders in the democracy.

A Greek schoolboy playing the aulos
Why do you think Homer's epics were learned and sung as part of a boy's musical training?

Vase for a grave

Art and Architecture

Greek artists wanted their work to be perfect. They strove to create the ideal representation of an object or a person. Important qualities of Greek art were balance, harmony, simplicity, beauty, and completeness. Their work has influenced many areas of art and architecture today.

Much of what is known about how the Greeks lived and dressed comes from their art. The work of painters adorned plates, jugs, pots, jars, cups, bowls, and perfume bottles. Craftsmen of metal decorated gold and silver cups and fashioned delicate jewelry. Sculptors created marble statues and designed coins. Greek art also flourished in wall murals, floor mosaics, and embroidery. Many artists portrayed human beings or gods and goddesses. Others depicted mythological creatures such as Pegasus, the winged horse, or animals and birds, such as goats, deer, bulls, lions, dolphins, and cranes.

Greek architecture, too, expressed the Greek love of beauty and harmony. The Greeks perfected the construction of columns to hold up buildings. There were three main styles of columns. The columns differed in the way their tops were carved. Some were plain and others were decorated with scrolls or elaborate leafy patterns.

Ionic, Doric, and Corinthian columns (left to right)

221

The Parthenon

On the Acropolis in Athens stands the **Parthenon**, an enormous temple of white marble. The temple originally had forty-six columns. It was dedicated to Athena, the goddess of wisdom, for whom the city of Athens was named. A huge statue of her once stood in the Parthenon. The statue contained so much ivory, gold, and precious stones that it was worth more than the temple that housed it. Around AD 400, the statue was captured by the Romans and taken to Constantinople. Soon afterward it mysteriously disappeared.

The Parthenon is the ultimate example of Greek architecture. Several optical illusions were included in its design. An optical illusion occurs when an object appears to take a shape it does not really have. The architects of the Parthenon created some clever illusions. They distorted their work on purpose to correct appearance problems. The steps leading up to the temple are humped in the center, but they appear perfectly level from a distance. The columns lean slightly inward and are thicker in the middle than at the top and the base. But to the eye they appear straight and tall.

Each year thousands of tourists travel to Athens to visit and admire the Parthenon. Although the building today is only an empty shell, what remains still echoes the beauty and the intricacy of its original architecture.

The Parthenon as it looks today

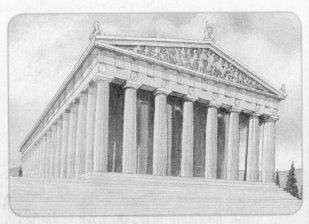
An artist's rendering of the ancient Parthenon
How can an artist get ideas of how something looked in ancient times?

Making a Greek Column

The Greeks decorated their buildings with ornate designs. Skilled craftsmen carefully chiseled each design into stone. Many designs included carvings of animals and Greek gods.

Greek columns had beautiful patterns on them. Several of these patterns are used in modern architecture today. They include the simple *Doric style*, the *Ionic style* (a scroll pattern), and the *Corinthian style* (a leafy pattern).

Imagine you are a craftsman from ancient Greece. You will design and carve your own column.

1. You will need the following materials: an empty paper towel tube, foil, masking tape, plaster of Paris (see package directions for necessary materials), a carving tool (such as a nail, wooden skewer, or plastic knife), and markers.

2. Cover one end of the paper towel tube with foil and tape securely in place. Reinforce the tube with additional foil and tape.

3. Mix the plaster of Paris according to package directions and fill the tube about 3/4 of the way up. Stand upright and allow the plaster to harden.

4. Peel away the tube from the plaster.

5. Draw the design of your choice on the column with a pencil. Use a carving tool to carve the design.

6. Outline your carved design with markers.

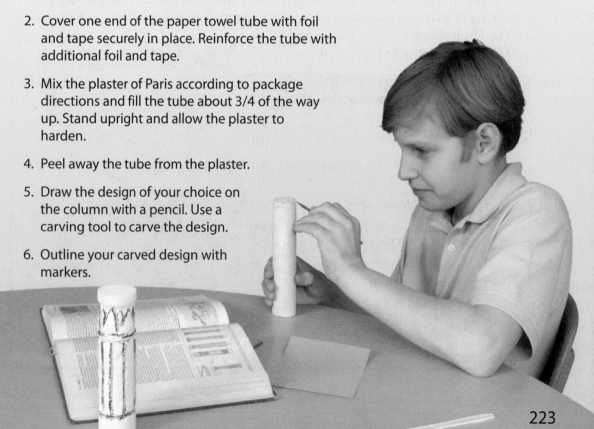

1. What caused Greek culture to spread throughout the Western world?

2. How was the Greek language important in the spread of the gospel?

The Spread of Greek Culture

After the Peloponnesian War, many quarrels broke out between the Greek city-states. The weakened condition of Greece allowed King Philip II of Macedonia to take control of its government in 338 BC.

Philip died two years later, and his twenty-year-old son, Alexander, took the throne of Macedonia. Alexander, who had been tutored by Aristotle, loved the Greek philosophy and way of life.

He took control of the Greek army and began to pursue his dream of uniting the entire world under one empire. Alexander extended his rule eastward as far as India, spreading the Greek culture through much of the world. His military genius and unconquerable spirit earned him the title **Alexander the Great**.

After Alexander's death, his empire was divided into four parts. Most of this empire would later be conquered by Rome.

Meanwhile people all over the Western world were becoming Hellenistic, or "like the Greeks." They adopted the ideas of Greek philosophers. They used Greek inventions and learned the teachings of Greek scholars. The works of Greek artists appeared in all parts of the empire. Most importantly, the spread of Greek culture brought a common language to the Western world.

What were some advantages of having a common language throughout Alexander's empire?

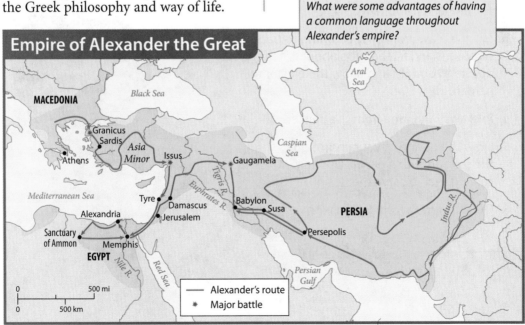

Empire of Alexander the Great

— Alexander's route
* Major battle

Paul's Sermon on Mars' Hill

The ancient Greeks were some of the most well-educated, artistic, and talented people of all time. In the eyes of most of the world, the Greeks had everything. They were a successful people. But the most important thing of all was missing from their lives. Although the Greeks possessed knowledge of many subjects, they had no knowledge of God.

Mars' Hill

The missionary Paul ministered not only to the Jews but also to the Greeks. During his travels, Paul spent time in the city of Athens. Acts 17 tells how Paul noticed widespread idolatry in the city. As he walked through the city, he found an altar with an inscription carved on it—"To the Unknown God."

Paul preached to the Athenians on Mars' Hill. He told them how the one true God is not a statue made of gold or silver or a name carved in stone. Paul shared with them that God, the Creator and Lord, is real, and that He wants people everywhere to repent and seek Him.

Many people made fun of Paul's message. Some left thoughtfully, wanting to hear more. But a few men and women grasped the truth of Paul's words and believed with all their hearts. Paul's mission trip to Athens had not been in vain. Paul said,

> For the Jews require a sign, and the Greeks seek after wisdom: but we preach Christ crucified, unto the Jews a stumblingblock, and unto the Greeks foolishness; but unto them which are called, both Jews and Greeks, Christ the power of God, and the wisdom of God. (1 Cor. 1:22–24)

225

Greek was the language of almost all scholarly writing during the first century AD. As Alexander the Great built his empire, he made Greek the standard language of commerce and government. People still spoke their own languages but had to learn Greek as a second language to do business with other countries. By the first century AD, Greek had become a world language. People spoke it and understood it nearly everywhere.

The Greek language made communication throughout the empire much easier. People could travel for miles and still meet others who spoke their language. Greek writing could be read and understood throughout the region.

In a few centuries there would be a very important message to carry to the world—the message of Jesus. The spread of the Greek language paved the way for the gospel to go into all the world.

The influence of the ancient Greeks touches our lives even today. Every time you see a column, you are seeing an example of Greek architecture. Every time you watch a play, you are enjoying the contributions the Greeks made to drama. Every time you admire a sculpture or read a lovely poem, you are appreciating the very arts that the Greeks mastered. And when you study literature, science, math, and history, you are reaping the benefits of Greek discoveries in those areas.

Each time you open your Bible to the New Testament, you can thank God for allowing the Greeks to develop their alphabet and writing skills. The richness of their language has given us a detailed history of the Lord Jesus Christ, pointing the way to heaven.

THE GREEK NEW TESTAMENT

God chose the Greek language for the New Testament writers to use when He breathed out His Word. Greek was a common language at the time the New Testament was written. For this reason many people were able to read and understand God's Word. The Greek New Testament was eventually translated into over 2,300 languages. The Bible that you read in English is one of those translations. God said that He would preserve His Word, and He has kept that promise.

The Greek Alphabet (letters, name, and English equivalent)

Αα	alpha	Aa	Ιι	iota	Ii	Ρρ	rho	Rr
Ββ	beta	Bb	Κκ	kappa	Kk	Σσς	sigma	Ss
Γγ	gamma	Gg	Λλ	lambda	Ll	Ττ	tau	Tt
Δδ	delta	Dd	Μμ	mu	Mm	Υϑ	upsilon	Uu
Εε	epsilon	Ee	Νν	nu	Nn	Φφ	phi	Ff
Ζζ	zeta	Zz	Ξξ	xi	Xx	Χχ	chi	ch
Ηη	eta	ee	Οο	omicron	Oo	Ψψ	psi	ps
Θθ	theta	th	Ππ	pi	Pp	Ωω	omega	ô

Chapter 9

Ancient Rome

FOCUS

1. Who were the earliest people of the Roman civilization?

2. What are some of the ways the Etruscans improved the Roman way of life?

In the ancient world, it could be said that "all roads lead to Rome." The influence of Rome spread to other parts of the world by means of the roads the Romans built. Modern Spain, France, Great Britain, Italy, Greece, Asia Minor, Palestine, Egypt, and North Africa all show the influence of the Romans from over two thousand years ago.

Ruins on Palatine, the hill where Romulus supposedly built Rome

Early Rome

The earliest inhabitants of Italy were a group of settlers from central Europe. They were called the **Latins**. These settlers were searching for fertile soil and a climate that was more suitable for farming. They migrated south from across the Alps and traveled to the **Italian Peninsula**, known as Italy today. The early Latins settled in a region near the Tiber River. From this region arose the Roman civilization.

The Founding of Rome

As time passed, the Romans told legends about the founding of their civilization. A **legend** is a story that has been passed down for generations. Legends are stories about historical events that are often told as truth. However, they have not been proven and are likely untrue.

According to one legend, Rome was founded in 753 BC by twin brothers. The brothers were born in the land we now call Italy. Abandoned by their mother, they were left floating in a basket on the Tiber River. A wolf spied the basket from the shore and swam out into the river to see it. Tiny cries came from inside the basket. The wolf rescued the babies and cared for them. Soon a shepherd wandered by and found the two babies crying in the basket. "What is this?" he asked himself. "Orphans, no doubt. I will take them home with me." The shepherd and his

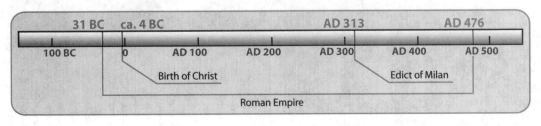

| 31 BC | ca. 4 BC | | AD 313 | | AD 476 |

| 100 BC | 0 | AD 100 | AD 200 | AD 300 | AD 400 | AD 500 |

Birth of Christ

Edict of Milan

Roman Empire

The Seven Hills of Rome

Tiber River

Quirinal Hill

Viminal Hill

Capitoline Hill

Esquiline Hill

Palatine Hill

Caelian Hill

Aventine Hill

wife named the twin brothers Romulus and Remus.

When the brothers were grown, they decided to build a city near the Tiber River so that they would remember the place of their rescue. However, they could not agree on where to build it. After a quarrel, Romulus got angry with Remus and killed him. Romulus built the city and named it Rome, after himself.

This account is only a legend. But historians do believe that Rome began near the Tiber River. They believe the Latins founded a village on the western side of the Italian Peninsula. This village was located on Palatine Hill, one of seven hills near the Tiber River. These hills were natural defenses that helped protect the people from enemies. Soon other villages sprang up on the surrounding hills. Eventually the villages developed into the city of **Rome**.

Phoenicians, Greeks, and Etruscans also inhabited the Italian Peninsula. The Phoenicians and the Greeks were known for their sea trade and colonization. The **Etruscans** were an advanced civilization with a Hellenistic culture.

Bagnoregio, an Etruscan city south of Rome

Ancient restroom

The Roman people were grouped into two social classes. The **patricians** (puh TRISH uhns) made up the ruling class. They were the wealthy landowners and nobles. The **plebeians** (plih BEE uhns) made up the working class. They were the common people, such as farmers, traders, and craftsmen. Most people were plebeians.

Both classes were hard-working people. They valued freedom and desired to have a part in governing themselves.

The Latins had been living in Rome for over one hundred years when the Etruscans from the north conquered Rome. During the rule of powerful Etruscan kings, Rome became the most powerful and respected city in the region. The Etruscans introduced a writing system based on the Greek alphabet. They made many improvements to the city by paving roads, building arches, draining marshes, and constructing a sewage system. But the Latins did not like having the Etruscan kings ruling over them.

Society

A Roman family included all the relatives who lived in the household. The father had sole authority over the life and death of each family member. He expected the family to show loyalty, self-control, and respect.

Early Alphabet			
Phoenician	Early Greek	Etruscan	Early Latin
∃	⊟	⊟	H
⼂	⼂	⼂	K
⼂	⼂	⼂	⼂
⼂	⼂	⼂	⼂
⼂	⼂	⼂	R
⊗	X	T	T

Which ancient letters do you think some of our English letters came from?

Italy

Location—Italy is a boot-shaped peninsula that extends into the Mediterranean Sea in southern Europe. Italy includes the islands of Sardinia, Sicily, and a number of other smaller islands. Northern Italy borders the countries of France, Switzerland, and Austria. To the west of Italy is the Tyrrhenian Sea, and to the east is the Adriatic Sea.

Climate—Italy's climate is mostly temperate. Temperatures in the north are cooler than in the south. Average temperatures range from 33°F (0.56°C) to 70°F (21°C).

Topography—The Italian Peninsula is mountainous and includes the Apennine mountain range and sections of the Alps. Italy also has broad plains. Most of Italy's islands are mountainous.

Natural Resources—Italy's resources include water, natural gas, hydroelectric power, mercury, coal, zinc, potash, marble, barite, asbestos, pumice, fluorite, feldspar, pyrite (sulfur), crude oil reserves, fish, and land that is suitable for farming.

Italy Then & Now

What shape does the Italian Peninsula look like?

231

1. What new form of government did the Romans establish after they drove out the Etruscan king?

2. What were the concessions that the patricians gave to the plebeians?

FOCUS

Early Government

According to legend, seven kings were said to have ruled Rome before the Etruscans invaded. Historians do know that the early government of Rome was a monarchy. The king was also the chief priest, the commander of the army, and the administrator of justice. A group of governmental leaders advised the king on official matters. The fasces (FAS eez), a bundle of rods bound around an axe, was used as a symbol of the king's power. When the Etruscans conquered Rome, they placed an Etruscan king on the throne.

Today the fasces is still used to symbolize power.

Roman Republic
(509–31 BC)

The Etruscan kings ruled Rome for over a century. During that time the Latin people did not like the policies and harsh treatment of the kings. In 509 BC, the people grew powerful enough to drive the king and the Etruscans from the city. In place of the monarchy, the Latins established a new form of government called a republic. A **republic** is a government ruled by laws and representatives chosen by the people. The word *republic* comes from the Latin phrase *res publica*, which means "a public thing." In a republic, citizens can vote and control the power of government through officials they elect under law. The Latins, now called Romans, believed that a republic would best protect the interests of the people.

An Etruscan bronze sculpture of a warrior

232

The artist Maccari showed the Roman Senate as it might have looked in ancient times. *What can you learn about the Roman Senate from this painting?*

A New Government

The newly established Roman Republic was divided into three governing branches—the consuls, the Senate, and the Assembly.

Two patricians were elected as **consuls** in place of a king. It was their responsibility to manage the affairs of the government, command the Roman army, and serve as supreme judges. Their terms lasted for one year. Both men had equal authority.

The **Senate** was the most powerful branch. All of its three hundred members were patricians. Senators served for life. The Senate controlled the finances, passed laws, and oversaw foreign affairs.

Several groups called assemblies existed in the early republic. The most powerful group was made up of patricians and was called the **Assembly of Centuries**. It voted on new laws, made declarations of war, and elected the consuls.

The Struggle

The consuls, the Senate, and the Assembly of Centuries were made up only of patricians. The plebeians did not have the privilege of voting. They had few social privileges and were not allowed to hold a public office. Marriage was forbidden between patricians and plebeians. Over time, more and more Romans became dissatisfied with the inequality between the two groups.

For over two hundred years, the plebeians struggled to gain political and social equality. Rome was constantly waging war against its neighbors. Plebeians served as soldiers of the army. Since they shared in the dangers of fighting, they wanted to be represented in government. Many threatened to leave the army. The patricians gradually began to concede, or grant, the plebeians rights.

The Roman Forum
What took place in the Forum?

The Concessions

The plebeians were finally allowed to have their own assembly. It was known as the **Tribal Assembly**. Its members elected ten leaders, called **tribunes**. The tribunes protected the rights and the interests of the common people.

At the time Roman laws were mostly ancient customs that were not written. The patricians often took advantage of the plebeians who were not familiar with the details of the laws. Without written laws, it was difficult to win court battles.

Eventually the plebeians pressured the Senate to write down the law. Around 450 BC, the Roman law was engraved on twelve bronze tablets. They were called the **Law of the Twelve Tables**. These laws became the foundation of Roman civil law. The tablets were displayed in the **Roman Forum**, a public meeting place.

The law could now be understood by all and equally applied to all.

The plebeians were also given veto power. The Latin word *veto* means "I forbid." Tribunes stood in the Senate doorway during its meetings. The tribunes could stop the Senate's actions at any time by shouting, "Veto!"

Gradually, the plebeians gained more rights. They were allowed to marry patricians. They could be elected as consuls. At last, the Tribal Assembly was permitted to make laws that were just as official as those the Senate made. The plebeians and the patricians now had equal say in the government of Rome.

The republic worked very well for several hundred years. Most people in Rome worked hard and respected the law. Most lawmakers wanted to help and protect the citizens of Rome.

Making a Law in the Roman Republic

A republic allows voting citizens to influence the government by electing officials. The Romans thought that a republic would be best to protect the interests of all the people. They valued a limited government that would keep any one man or group of men from obtaining absolute power.

You will be a member of the Senate or of the Assembly, and you will help make a new law (rule).

1. Find out from your teacher whether you are a member of the Senate or the Assembly.

2. Arrange yourselves so the members of each group are sitting together. Proceed with a meeting to choose a new rule.

3. Evaluate how the meeting proceeded. Did you feel as if your opinion was important? Was your decision respected by the other group? How effective do you think this method is for making laws?

Senate

Assembly

Tribune

1. What were the three major wars between Rome and Carthage called?

2. In which war did the Roman army face Hannibal's army?

Growth of Rome

In the early years of the republic, Rome worked to conquer the entire Italian Peninsula. First, Rome defeated other Latin cities and secured the central part of the peninsula. Then, Rome eventually conquered the Etruscans in the north and the Greeks in the south. By 265 BC all the peninsula was under Roman control.

Unlike other conquering people, the Romans extended mercy to those they conquered. Rome offered Roman citizenship to the Greeks, the Latins, and the Etruscans as long as they did not rebel.

Rome also turned its attention to regions in the west. Over the next 125 years, Rome battled the North African city of **Carthage** for control of the Mediterranean Sea and the lands along its coast. The three major wars between Rome and Carthage

Roman centurion

are called the **Punic Wars**. (*Punici* was the Roman word for Phoenicians, the people of Carthage.) The Greek historian Polybius described the differences between Carthage and Rome as follows:

> With respect to military science . . . the Carthaginians . . . are more skillful than the Romans. . . . The Romans, on the other hand, are far superior in all things that belong to the establishment and discipline of armies. . . . The Carthaginians employ foreign mercenaries; . . . the Roman armies are composed of citizens, and of the people of the country. . . . The Romans place all their confidence in their own bravery, and in the assistance of their allies. From hence it happens that the Romans, although at first defeated, are always able to renew the war; and that the Carthaginian armies never are repaired without great difficulty. Add to this that the Romans, fighting for their country and their children, never suffer their ardor to be slackened; but persist with the same steady spirit till they become superior to their enemies. . . . Even in actions upon the sea, the Romans, though inferior to the Carthaginians, . . . in naval knowledge and experience, very frequently obtain success through the mere bravery of their forces. . . . The valor of the troops that are engaged is no less effectual to draw the victory to their side.
>
> (Oliver J. Thatcher, ed., *The Library of Original Sources*, vol. III, *The Roman World* [Milwaukee: University Research Extension Co., 1907], 187)

The First Punic War (264–241 BC)

Both Rome and Carthage wanted control of **Sicily**, the largest island in the Mediterranean Sea. Sicily's central location, warm climate, fertile land, and fresh water made the island compelling to both cities. Carthage had already colonized Sicily. The Romans feared that the Carthaginians would become stronger and hinder Roman trade in the Mediterranean Sea. The Romans also feared that the Carthaginians might attack the southern region of the Italian Peninsula.

To gain control of Sicily, the Romans needed a way to defeat the powerful Carthaginian navy. Up to that time, naval battles were won by ramming and sinking enemy ships. The Romans developed an effective strategy. They designed a ship that dropped a plank with a spiked tip. The plank could attach to an enemy ship, allowing Roman soldiers to board and capture the enemy. With these newly designed ships, Rome was victorious over

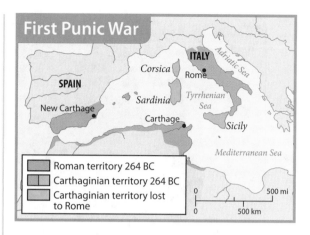

First Punic War

- Roman territory 264 BC
- Carthaginian territory 264 BC
- Carthaginian territory lost to Rome

the Carthaginian navy. The two sides finally formed a peace settlement. Rome gained control of Sicily, and Carthage was forced to pay for Roman losses.

The Second Punic War (218–201 BC)

The Second Punic War began when Carthage violated its treaty with Rome. While extending its borders in Spain, Carthage attacked a Spanish town that was a Roman ally.

The Second Punic War is the most famous of the three wars because of a man named **Hannibal**. He was a brilliant general of the Carthaginian army. He decided that, to defeat Rome, he would first invade regions of the peninsula outside Rome. In this way he would win the support of the people against the Romans. He gathered his army in Spain. To avoid having the Romans see him, he planned to march his soldiers across the rugged, snow-covered Alps. He hoped to surprise the Romans.

ROMAN LEGIONS

Rome's strength came from its military forces. Its soldiers were disciplined and well trained. The infantry was divided into legions. The soldiers in these units were called legionaries.

You have probably seen pictures of Roman legionaries pictured with Bible stories. These soldiers wore short wool tunics under leather jackets. The leather was covered with metal strips. The soldiers also wore bronze helmets with openings for their faces and ears. To be seen easily, centurions and other officers wore tall crests on top of their helmets. Each legionary carried a short sword and a six-foot javelin that weighed about ten pounds.

Hannibal and his war elephants crossing the Alps

often attacked Hannibal's army. Many of Hannibal's soldiers and most of the elephants died in the snowy Alps.

By the time Hannibal's army reached the Italian Peninsula, it was much smaller in number than the Roman army. However, Hannibal's skill at planning strategies made up for the size of his army. He won battle after battle against the Romans. But he could not completely defeat them.

One strategy Hannibal used was to arrange his soldiers so they formed a bulge in the center of the front lines. When the Romans attacked the bulge, the Carthaginian soldiers in the bulge

Hannibal started out from Spain with about forty thousand men and a herd of war elephants. The cold weather made travel difficult for the elephants and the Carthaginian soldiers. In the mountains lived fierce tribes. A **tribe** is a group of people who share common ancestors and a common culture. The mountain tribes

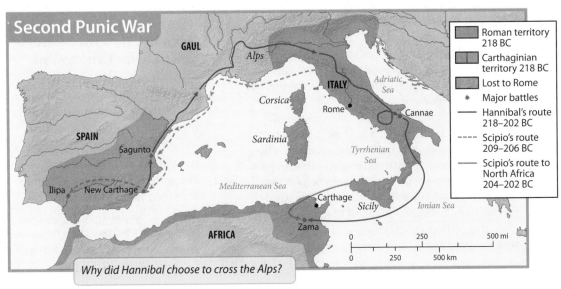

Second Punic War

GAUL
Alps
ITALY
Adriatic Sea
Corsica
Rome
Cannae
SPAIN
Sardinia
Tyrrhenian Sea
Sagunto
Ilipa   New Carthage
Mediterranean Sea
Carthage
Sicily
Ionian Sea
Zama
AFRICA

Roman territory 218 BC
Carthaginian territory 218 BC
Lost to Rome
* Major battles
— Hannibal's route 218–202 BC
--- Scipio's route 209–206 BC
— Scipio's route to North Africa 204–202 BC

0   250   500 mi
0   250   500 km

Why did Hannibal choose to cross the Alps?

238

Who: Hannibal

What: general of Carthage

When: 248–183 or 182 BC

Where: Carthage

General Hannibal was a brilliant soldier who, during the Second Punic War, tried repeatedly to conquer Rome. He is considered one of the greatest generals in ancient history.

retreated, forming a U-shaped trap around the Romans. Using this method, Hannibal's army almost completely wiped out the Roman army.

The turning point of the war came when Rome sent an army to attack Carthage. The army was led by the Roman commander Scipio (SIP ee oh). Hannibal immediately rushed home to protect his city. At the Battle of Zama, Scipio gained the victory. Carthage was forced to give up the territories outside Africa and pay for war damages.

The Third Punic War (149–146 BC)

Approximately fifty years after the Second Punic War, Carthage decided to fight one of Rome's allies. This action angered the Romans. As a result Rome declared war on Carthage.

After a three-year siege, Rome captured and destroyed Carthage. The Romans sold the survivors into slavery and plowed salt into Carthage's soil to keep crops from growing.

While fighting Carthage, Rome conquered other lands. It marched eastward and conquered what was left of Alexander the Great's empire. Then it conquered Greece itself, made an alliance with Egypt, and gained control over the eastern Mediterranean Sea. Rome was now in control of the Mediterranean world.

Ruins of Carthage

Things People Did

The Roman Roads

Milestone along a Roman road to mark the distance to the next town as well as the distance to the Forum in Rome

Have you ever heard the saying "All roads lead to Rome"? Rome is famous for the system of roads it built. The roads connected the lands Rome had conquered. In a span of five hundred years, Rome constructed over fifty thousand miles of roads. The main purpose for these roads was for the armies to travel to all of Rome's provinces. Traveling to and from Rome became fast and easy. The Romans had cut through mountains to keep the roads straight. The roads were durable. They were built in layers of sand, gravel, and concrete. The word *street* comes from the Latin word *strata*, which means "layers."

The Roman roads played a key part in Rome's trade and influence. Many goods were taken along the Roman roads to other lands. Slaves, money, grain, and precious metals traveled back into Rome as tribute paid to a ruler by conquered peoples. Visitors to Rome exchanged philosophies and religious ideas with the Romans. Rome used and improved the inventions and discoveries of other peoples. Cultures from the East and the West blended and changed.

In 312 BC construction began for the first and most famous Roman road, the Appian Way. This long road began in Rome and ended in the southern part of the Italian Peninsula. The apostle Paul traveled the Appian Way on his journey to Rome (Acts 28:14–15). Early Christians used the Roman roads to carry the gospel throughout the empire.

A section along the Appian Way near Rome

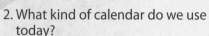

1. What were some of the problems that the Romans faced as their borders expanded?

2. What kind of calendar do we use today?

The Collapse of the Republic

Rome organized their conquered peoples into provinces. The Roman Senate appointed governors to the provinces to serve as chief military and civil rulers. The provinces had to pay Rome tribute of money or grain. In return Rome provided order and protection.

Problems arose from Rome's expansion. Farmers who had left their farms to be soldiers came home to find their property ruined from neglect. Many sold their farms and moved to the city to find work. They found that most jobs had already been filled by slaves taken from conquered territories.

The wealthy profited from the wars. They bought the farms of the conquered lands, and they had slaves run those farms. The wealthy also took advantage of the poorer plebeians by buying their votes in the Tribal Assembly. This allowed the plebeians to earn money, but it also filled the government with more rich men.

The Senate increased in power and dominated the republic. Although Rome's social and economic problems were growing, the Senate was unwilling to address them. The corruption of the government soon spread throughout the Roman provinces.

Each of Rome's newly acquired provinces was required to pay taxes to Rome. Men called publicans collected these taxes. Many of the publicans and the governmental officials they worked for became greedy. They would collect a higher amount of taxes than needed. Then they kept the extra money for themselves. Publicans became the most despised people in the Roman provinces.

In Rome the plebeians became less concerned about how the government was run. They no longer studied the governmental issues so that they could vote wisely. The plebeians cared only for what benefits they could gain by selling their votes.

Tiberius and Gaius Gracchus proposed changes that would have helped the poor, but they were killed before the changes could take effect.

241

Rivalry Between Commanders

The Senate's failure to deal with the poor weakened the republic. The common people found a new champion who tried to help their cause. **Marius**, a military hero, reorganized the Roman army. He allowed the poor citizens to enlist for long terms of service. In exchange they received a share of land, money, and the spoils of war. This created a professional army that fought for financial gain rather than for patriotic causes. Generals began to use their armies for their own gain. Soldiers were more devoted to their commanders than they were to Rome.

War broke out in Asia Minor. The Senate appointed the general **Sulla** to command the Roman army. The Tribal Assembly did not like the Senate's choice

Crassus

Pompey

and appointed Marius instead. Rivalry between the two commanders developed into civil war. After many years of battles, Sulla and the Senate emerged victorious.

Sulla declared himself the dictator and reorganized the Roman government. After restoring stability to the Senate, he stepped down as dictator. But the Senate was not able to keep control of the government.

The Triumvirate

Ambitious men tried to gain control of the Senate. Three men competed with one another for fame and power. Crassus was a wealthy military commander. He defeated a slave revolt. **Pompey** was popular with the Senate for his accomplishments. He turned Asia Minor, Syria, and Palestine into Roman provinces. He also

Gaius Julius Caesar

As a member of a patrician family in Rome, Julius Caesar received an excellent education in his youth. He married a patrician and was quick to make his voice heard in government. He had an eloquence and determination that made him popular with the common people of Rome. Caesar rose early to high positions in government and eventually became dictator of Rome. He accomplished many reforms in the government.

Caesar was also an outstanding military general. Leading a mighty army of fifty thousand men, he began conquering the land northwest of the Italian Peninsula called Gaul. For nine years his soldiers defeated tribes in what is today Switzerland, France, Spain, Holland, Belgium, and parts of Germany. Caesar even attacked Britain, which until then had been a land unknown to the Romans. He wrote of his military accomplishments in *Commentaries on the Gallic Wars*.

rid the Mediterranean Sea of pirates. **Julius Caesar** (SEE zer) was a wise politician who could sway the common people to accomplish his goals.

In 60 BC the three men formed an alliance called the **Triumvirate** (try UHM vuhr it) to rule Rome together against the Senate. Caesar was appointed governor of Gaul. There he trained a loyal army and led many campaigns. Crassus died in a war in Asia. Pompey became jealous of Caesar's growing strength and popularity. Pompey eventually sided with the Senate against Caesar.

Caesar's popularity as a conqueror threatened the power of the government leaders. They ordered him to disband his army. Instead Caesar marched to Rome and plunged into a second civil war against Pompey and the Senate. Caesar's army fought Pompey's army for four years before defeating it. Caesar was proclaimed the dictator of Rome. At first his term was to last only ten years, but he soon changed it so that he would be dictator for life. He made many changes in the government, hoping to solve the problems of the republic.

Death of a Dictator

Caesar limited the power of the corrupt Senate. He granted citizenship to people from territories on the Italian Peninsula and even allowed them to be represented in the Senate. He promoted colonization, schools, libraries, and public works throughout Rome and its surrounding territories. He improved the Roman calendar. His actions helped to unify Rome and strengthen its bonds with its conquered peoples.

Although many Romans liked Caesar and respected his accomplishments, others were angry with him. They knew that as long as Caesar insisted on having absolute power, the government of Rome could no longer be a true republic.

As Caesar's reign continued, angry Romans grew more and more desperate. They wanted the government of Rome to once again belong to the people. Brutus and Cassius, two senators whom Caesar considered his friends, met with a group of other Senate members. Secretly they plotted to kill Caesar.

In 44 BC, on the fifteenth day of March (called the **Ides of March**), the two men hid in the Senate chamber. When Caesar entered the room, they assassinated him.

Men eager to take Caesar's place as ruler led Rome into a third civil war. Eventually Caesar's nephew, **Octavian**, formed an alliance with one of Caesar's generals, **Mark Antony**. They divided the empire so Antony ruled the east and Octavian ruled the west. Both men, however, were too ambitious to share the power of ruling Rome. In 31 BC, at the Battle of Actium, Antony and Octavian clashed in a naval battle off the coast of Greece. Octavian defeated Antony and became the ruler of Rome and the Roman world.

Julius Caesar stabbed by Brutus in a scene from Shakespeare's *Julius Caesar* (Bob Jones University Classic Players)

Julius Caesar's Calendar

Early Roman calendars did not recognize that the solar year is not exactly 365 days, but almost six hours longer. By the time of Julius Caesar's reign, the calendar was so inaccurate that none of the seasons fell in the right place. Caesar decided to add an extra day every four years to balance out the calendar. The fourth year is called a *leap year*. Since the Roman calendar started with March, the extra day was added to the last month, February.

Before putting his new idea into practice, Caesar had to bring the calendar up to date. So he made the year 46 BC last 445 days! This extra-long year was often called the "year of confusion."

Caesar's calendar, known as the *Julian calendar*, was used by Europeans for centuries. Today the United States as well as most countries use a reformed version of this calendar, called the **Gregorian calendar**. It is based on the birth of Christ. But echoes of Caesar's calendar can still be heard in the names of our months. Many of the months were named after Roman gods or rulers. Julius Caesar was born in the month that he named for himself—July.

Mars, the god of war

Roman Origins of the Names of Months			
January	named after Janus, the Roman god of gates and doors	July	named by Julius Caesar after himself; his birth month
February	from the Latin word that means "to purify"	August	named by Caesar Augustus (Octavian) after himself
March	named after Mars, the Roman god of war	September	from the Latin word for "seven"
April	from the Latin word that means "to open"	October	from the Latin word for "eight"
May	named after Maia, the Roman goddess of spring	November	from the Latin word for "nine"
June	named after Juno, the Roman goddess of marriage	December	from the Latin word for "ten"

Designing a Travel Brochure for Ancient Rome

The roots of modern Rome can be traced back to the founding of Rome on Palatine Hill. Rome is a wonderful place to visit. There are many historical sites to explore, activities to experience, and festivals to attend.

1. Work with a partner. Choose a topic for your brochure about an ancient place found in Italy today. You may choose a site, an activity, or a festival to promote.

2. Research your choice. Write a brief paragraph that encourages people to visit your choice.

3. List five significant facts about your choice.

4. Include other information such as an itinerary, a list of available transportation, important places, major cities, landmarks, historical sites, museums, activities, or festivals and other events.

5. Illustrate the brochure with pictures, drawings, and maps.

FOCUS

1. Under whose reign did a period of peace and prosperity begin?

2. What civilization greatly influenced Rome?

The Roman Empire
(31 BC–AD 476)

Caesar's death paved the way for the beginning of Rome's history as an empire. Octavian worked to restore honesty, diligence, and respect to the government of Rome. He restored power to the Senate and the Tribal Assembly, reserving the office of tribune for himself. He could propose or veto new laws. He also reorganized the army and the governments of Rome's territories. He continued to promote trade and industry and to build roads throughout the empire.

Octavian had complete control of Rome, but he did not call himself a dictator as Caesar had done. He used several different titles. One of these was *princeps*, meaning "first citizen." He was also commonly called Augustus, which meant "revered one." The name of Octavian found in Luke 2:1 is **Caesar Augustus**.

The reign of Augustus began a period of peace and prosperity that Rome enjoyed for the next two hundred years. This period is called the **Pax Romana**, which means "Roman peace." It ended in AD 180 with the death of Emperor Marcus Aurelius, who is often referred to as the last good emperor of Rome.

During the Pax Romana, the culture of Rome was similar to Greek culture. Like the Greeks, the Romans placed importance on education, architecture, and religion.

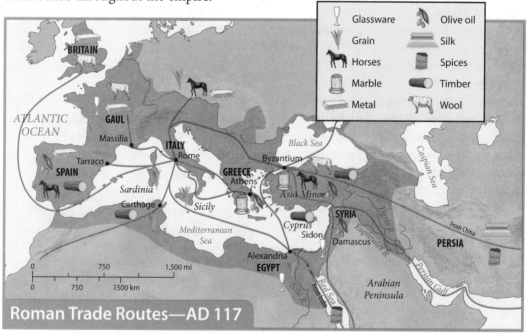

Roman Trade Routes—AD 117

A Roman school

Education

During the Pax Romana, fathers were responsible for the education of their children. Many wealthy families hired tutors or servants to educate their children. Some boys and girls received an education by attending school. They studied reading, writing, and mathematics. They wrote on wax tablets that could be smoothed and reused. An abacus was used for math. After mastering these basics, most girls stayed home to learn the art of homemaking from their mothers. Some studied further with a private tutor.

Some boys continued their education by studying Greek, Latin, history, geography, astronomy, and literature. At sixteen a boy became a citizen, and a special citizenship ceremony was held at the Forum, the Roman marketplace. The boy was given an official citizen's garment—a loose, one-piece robe called a **toga**. After becoming citizens, young men continued their studies or entered business or the army.

Many Romans loved to read. The greatest Latin literature was written during the Pax Romana. **Cicero** was a master of Latin prose who influenced other writers and students. He was known as the greatest orator of his day. An orator is an eloquent and skilled public speaker. **Virgil** is considered the greatest Roman poet. He wrote the *Aeneid*, an epic about Rome's glory. Another major writer, Livy, wrote a detailed history of Rome. He also wrote of events from the day in which he lived.

BIOGRAPHY

Who: Marcus Tullius Cicero

What: politician, scholar, author, lawyer, orator, and philosopher

When: 106–43 BC

Where: ancient Rome

Cicero was a philosopher, a lawyer, and a member of the Senate. He introduced Romans to Greek philosophy. He was also an excellent orator who wrote many speeches to persuade the Senate. Many of his writings have survived and are still studied by historians.

Culture and Achievements

Rome came in contact with a variety of different cultures while it was expanding. As a result, many elements from these cultures were integrated into Roman culture. Roman life was especially influenced by Greek culture. The Greeks were artists and philosophers. They studied to learn about the world around them. The Romans strove to improve their lives. They learned much from Greek ideas and improved many of them. The Romans also made contributions in law and politics.

Architecture in the Pax Romana

Rome's greatest artistic achievements were in architecture. Although the Romans built for practical purposes rather than for beauty as the Greeks did, Roman works were impressive. Augustus claimed that he had found Rome as a city of brick and left it as a city of marble.

The Romans obtained ideas from craftsmen and artists they captured during conquests. Romans used their own building techniques and improved on techniques borrowed from other civilizations. Some of the borrowed architectural ideas enhanced and strengthened Roman structures.

Romans were the first to use concrete, a mixture of gravel, sand, and mortar. Rather than using solid marble, Romans often built with concrete and covered the structure with a thin layer of marble. Not only did concrete help lower building costs, but it also made Roman structures durable.

One architectural feature the Romans improved on was the dome. Since a dome requires no pillars or other supports, the room under a dome is large and open. The largest dome in Rome was atop a temple called the **Pantheon**. Its concrete

A painting by Giovanni Paolo Panini of the interior of the Pantheon in the 1700s
What kinds of Roman architecture were used in the Pantheon?

dome reaches fourteen stories above the ground.

Arches were used in many public buildings, houses, and other structures such as bridges and aqueducts (raised troughs that carried water). Arches are a main feature in the large arena known as the **Colosseum**.

Both the Pantheon and the Colosseum are still standing today. With the development of concrete and arches, the Romans were able to construct other massive structures. Many structures were so well built that they, too, are still standing.

THE COLOSSEUM

The Roman Colosseum was a feat of engineering and design that still marvels architects and engineers today. Construction took place between AD 70 and 72. This massive arena was over 160 feet high and covered six acres of land. It was designed to hold nearly fifty thousand people.

The arena floor was made of wood and covered with sand. It had many sections that could be raised and lowered. Elevators brought animals, props, and other items to the arena from the rooms and tunnels beneath. The floor could even be flooded to reenact naval scenes.

Roman emperors staged events to win public favor and to keep the unemployed entertained. Admission was free. People were seated according to their social classes. Chariot races, gladiator contests, and wild animal fights were some of the events that spectators watched in the arena. Criminals and war captives were also brought to fight in the arena.

Inside of the Roman Colosseum

FOCUS

1. What Greek philosophies became religions for the Romans?

2. Who began His ministry during the Pax Romana?

Religion

The ancient Romans adopted gods from many of the people they conquered. As a result, the Romans had a polytheistic religion. Some Roman gods were the same as those worshiped by the Greeks,

Some Roman gods and goddesses had several roles. Diana, Apollo's twin, was the goddess of the moon, hunting, and childbirth.

but with Roman names. The Romans honored their gods by building them temples and naming the planets after them. Festivals, offerings, and prayers were part of worship. The entrance of each household had a shrine. The people worshiped their gods daily.

The Romans accepted other religions from different parts of their empire. Religions from the Far East became popular. Two Greek philosophies were also practiced as religions in Rome—Epicureanism and Stoicism. The followers of **Epicureanism** (EP ih KYOOR ee uh NIZ um) believed that everything—including gods, man, and the earth—was only matter. Epicureans believed that man was free from fear of the gods and what would happen after death. They believed that if people are free from fear, they can find true happiness in this life. Epicureans lived for pleasure alone and tried to keep their lives happy and free from pain.

EPICUREAN BELIEFS

Epicureans used knowledge to help rid them of their fears of the gods and death. They believed that there is no life after death. The Bible teaches that there is everlasting life for those who put their trust in Christ (John 3:16). Those who love God have nothing to fear (1 John 4:16–19).

Epicureans believed that happiness is achieved through simple pleasures and peace of mind. The Bible teaches that anyone who hopes to find happiness in this life will be disappointed (Eccles. 2:1–11). All who trust God will find joy in this life and in the life to come (Ps. 16:11).

Another Greek philosophy was **Stoicism** (STO ih sɪz um). The Stoics believed that doing one's duty led to happiness. They emphasized virtues such as courage, justice, and obedience. Stoicism was popular among the Roman soldiers.

Christianity in the Roman World

God chose the Pax Romana as His perfect time for Jesus Christ to live on the earth. Caesar Augustus decreed that everyone in the Roman Empire return to his birthplace to be taxed. So Joseph and Mary traveled to Bethlehem, a small city of Judea, to pay their taxes. It was there in Bethlehem that Jesus, the promised Messiah, was born.

> Blessed are ye, when men shall revile you, and persecute you, and shall say all manner of evil against you falsely, for my sake. Rejoice, and be exceeding glad: for great is your reward in heaven: for so persecuted they the prophets which were before you.
>
> **Matthew 5:11–12**

Jesus Christ began His earthly ministry at the age of thirty. Many Jews and religious leaders rejected Him as their Messiah and did not agree with His teachings. They plotted to have Him killed. After Christ's death and resurrection, His followers, called **Christians**, were hated by both the Romans and the Jews.

One Roman emperor, **Nero**, blamed the Christians for starting a fire that destroyed nearly two-thirds of the city of Rome. Even though he did not have enough evidence to convict them, Nero ordered that many Christians be put to death by crucifixion or burning. Christians often faced this

Roman Christians buried their dead in underground tombs called catacombs.

Christ in the Roman World

"But when the fulness of the time was come, God sent forth his Son, made of a woman, made under the law." Galatians 4:4

God used the decree of Caesar Augustus to fulfill the prophecy in Micah 5:2 that the Messiah would be born in Bethlehem. Jesus Christ, the Son of God, was born into the world around 4 BC. He lived, died for the sins of all mankind, and rose again. During His life, Jesus submitted to the Roman government by paying the required tax to Caesar. Jesus encouraged the other Jews to do the same (Matt. 22:21).

After His trials, Christ was condemned to death by crucifixion. This method of death was painful, humiliating, and reserved for the worst of criminals. In this way God fulfilled Christ's words that the Messiah would be "lifted up" in death (John 12:32).

Procession to Calvary; Giovanni Antonio Bazzi, called Il Sodoma; From the Bob Jones University Collection

type of persecution and torture under Rome until about AD 312.

One form of persecution took place in large arenas, such as the Colosseum. These arenas were places for entertainment such as theater, circuses, and combat. Citizens would watch armed men called **gladiators**, who fought other men or animals to the death. At times, some emperors would send faithful Christians, rather than gladiators, into the arena, where they were killed by lions, bears, tigers, bulls, or other wild animals.

Do you think these persecutions caused Christians to give up their faith? Many surviving Christians became even more determined to follow Christ when they saw the courage of others.

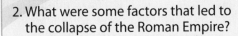

1. What were some ways that Diocletian persecuted Christians?

2. What were some factors that led to the collapse of the Roman Empire?

The Spread of Christianity

In Matthew 28:18–20, Christ charged His disciples to teach all nations, or civilizations, how to be forgiven of sin and to live God's way. The Roman roads enabled Christians to carry the gospel to many parts of the world.

The spread of Christianity was greatly aided by the conversion of Paul, a Roman citizen. Paul was a well-educated Pharisee who persecuted Christians. Acts 9:1–6 tells the story of Paul's conversion.

After his conversion, Paul became the first missionary to the Roman world. He traveled thousands of miles on Roman roads preaching the gospel.

Collapse of the Roman Empire

The emperor Diocletian (DY uh KLEE shun) reigned from AD 284 to 305. He thought that the Roman Empire was too large to be ruled by one man. He divided the empire in half, keeping the eastern part under his own control and appointing another ruler for the western part. He eventually appointed assistant rulers for each half, further dividing his power.

During the reign of Diocletian, the persecution of Christians was widespread. The Romans hoped that persecution

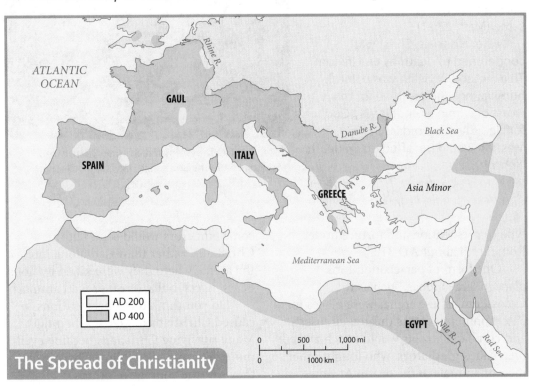

ATLANTIC OCEAN

Rhine R.

GAUL

SPAIN

ITALY

Danube R.

Black Sea

GREECE

Asia Minor

Mediterranean Sea

☐ AD 200
☐ AD 400

EGYPT

Nile R.

Red Sea

0   500   1,000 mi
0   1000 km

The Spread of Christianity

would cause Christians to reject their faith in God and discourage others from converting. Diocletian ordered the destruction of Christian places of worship, the burning of the Scriptures, and the imprisonment of the religious leaders. In spite of the persecution, the Christian church grew.

After Diocletian retired, a struggle for power began. The struggle turned into civil war. When Constantine became the ruler, he unified the empire. In 313 Constantine issued a decree to legalize Christianity. As a result, many citizens converted to Christianity because it was the law rather than because of their belief in Jesus Christ as Savior.

Corruption from nonbelievers soon became part of religious teachings in Christian churches. Churches struggled against false teachers. One false teacher named Arius taught that Jesus was not God. This error divided the churches. The church leaders met at a council in the city of Nicaea. In this meeting the leaders rejected the false teachings of

Who: Constantine

What: emperor of Rome

When: ruled 306–337

Where: Rome

Constantine ended the persecution of Christians by issuing the Edict of Milan. He made Sunday a legal holiday. He restored property and rebuilt many churches that had been destroyed.

Arius and affirmed the Bible's teaching that Jesus is God.

In the fourth century AD, the Roman Empire continued to decline. Ambitious generals tried to gain control of the government but did not succeed. The high costs of keeping a large army and employing a large number of governmental officials drained the empire's treasury. As a result, the government raised taxes to pay costs. Constantine further strained the economy by building a new capital called Constantinople.

Ancient map of Constantinople

Moral decay was another factor in the decline of Rome. Instead of working to provide for their families, many Romans looked to the government to supply free food. In addition, leaders continued to provide amusements at the arenas to distract the crowds of unemployed people.

In 395 Emperor Theodosius I divided the Roman Empire between his two sons. The western part soon fell to barbarian invasions. The Huns moved across Asia and into Europe. Led by Attila, the Huns invaded the west. The Vandals, a Germanic tribe that had established a kingdom in northern Africa, raided Rome. In 378 another Germanic tribe, the Visigoths, defeated the Roman army at the Battle of Adrianople.

The assault of these barbarian tribes along with the decline of Rome's government, economy, and society caused the collapse of the Western Roman Empire. Historians give the date **476** for the **fall of the Roman Empire**. The Eastern Roman Empire endured for another thousand years and became known as the Byzantine Empire.

We remember Greece for its glory—its beautiful artwork, its elegant poetry, its athletic grace. But how do we remember the civilization of Rome? We uphold Rome for its practicality and its power. Massive domes, arched aqueducts, grand road systems, brave legionaries, and fiery patriots who lived and died for the republic—these are the things we think of when we remember Rome.

The Pont du Gard, a Roman aqueduct in southern France

Chapter 10

The Byzantine Empire

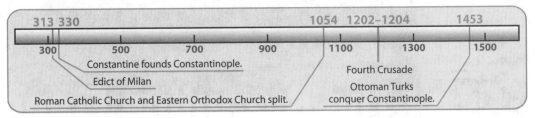

FOCUS

1. What was the importance of the location of Byzantium?

2. What two decisions did Constantine make that led to the development of the Byzantine Empire?

The history of the Byzantine (BIZ uhn TEEN) Empire tells of cultural advances and the rise and fall of leaders. A division of world powers took shape between the East and the West. This division influenced future world events up to modern times.

The Village by the Sea

The beginning of the Byzantine Empire can be traced back to a village in southeastern Europe. The village was known as **Byzantium**, from which the name Byzantine is taken.

Byzantium was founded by Greek colonists. The site they had chosen for the village was on a peninsula. Water on both sides of the land served as protection for the colonists.

The location of the village was ideal for trading. The nearby Bosporus Strait, which lies between Europe and Asia Minor, was a popular trading route. Merchants from India and China passed through Byzantium, selling silks and spices. A harbor to the north of the village was another advantage. Villagers could travel around the Black Sea to trade with Asian merchants for furs and amber. The villagers could also sail west into the Aegean Sea and the Mediterranean

The ancient walls of the Rumeli Hisari, a fortress on the Bosporus Strait

Sea. They traded with the Greeks, the Romans, and the North Africans for grain, gold, ivory, and other goods. Eventually Byzantium grew into a city and a center for world trade.

313 330				1054	1202–1204		1453
300	500	700	900	1100	1300		1500

Constantine founds Constantinople.

Edict of Milan

Roman Catholic Church and Eastern Orthodox Church split.

Fourth Crusade

Ottoman Turks conquer Constantinople.

258

Turkey

Location—Turkey is located on two continents. Most of Turkey is a large peninsula in Asia Minor. Turkey is bordered by the Black Sea and the Mediterranean Sea. The smaller part of the country is bordered by Greece in southeastern Europe.

Climate—Turkey's topography causes the climate to vary in different regions of the country. The climate is temperate along the coast. Inland the climate is harsh and dry, and in the mountains it is snowy or icy in the winters. Average temperatures in Turkey range from 13°F to 80°F (−11°C to 27°C).

Topography—The portion of Turkey in Asia Minor is a plateau between the Taurus and the Pontic mountain ranges. In eastern Turkey, where these two ranges meet, is Mount Ararat.

Natural Resources—Turkey's natural resources include oil, coal, chromium, mercury, copper, boron, and gold.

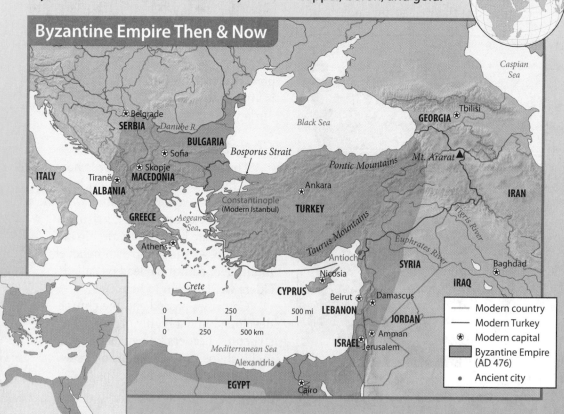

Byzantine Empire Then & Now

Belgrade · SERBIA · Danube R. · Black Sea · GEORGIA · Tbilisi · Caspian Sea · BULGARIA · Sofia · Bosporus Strait · Pontic Mountains · Mt. Ararat · ITALY · Tiranë · Skopje · MACEDONIA · Ankara · IRAN · ALBANIA · Constantinople (Modern Istanbul) · TURKEY · GREECE · Aegean Sea · Taurus Mountains · Euphrates River · Tigris River · Athens · Antioch · SYRIA · Baghdad · Nicosia · IRAQ · Crete · CYPRUS · Beirut · Damascus · 0 250 500 mi · LEBANON · JORDAN · 0 250 500 km · Amman · Mediterranean Sea · ISRAEL · Jerusalem · Alexandria · EGYPT · Cairo

Modern country
Modern Turkey
Modern capital
Byzantine Empire (AD 476)
Ancient city

The Birth of Eastern Power

A New City

In the west, Rome was suffering from threats of invasion and a weakening economy. The Roman emperor **Constantine** decided to move the capital to another location. He saw that Byzantium would be a good site. For several years he rebuilt and expanded Byzantium. He adorned it with many new structures. He also built strong walls to protect the city.

In 330 the city became the Roman Empire's new capital. Constantine called it the "New Rome." It was more widely known as **Constantinople** or Constantine's city. Constantinople became one of the richest and most

Mosaic of Constantine

powerful cities in Europe. Today this city is known as Istanbul and is located in Turkey.

Christianity Spreads

The New Testament records how the early church began. The earliest leaders of the church were the **apostles** who were chosen directly by Christ. Christians met in private homes for worship and fellowship. As the number of believers multiplied, additional leaders called elders were chosen to help.

Centuries passed and the church developed into a highly organized structure. Leaders known as bishops, archbishops, and patriarchs oversaw individual churches or groups of churches.

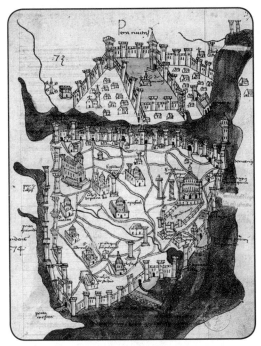

This 1422 map of Constantinople is the oldest known map of the city.

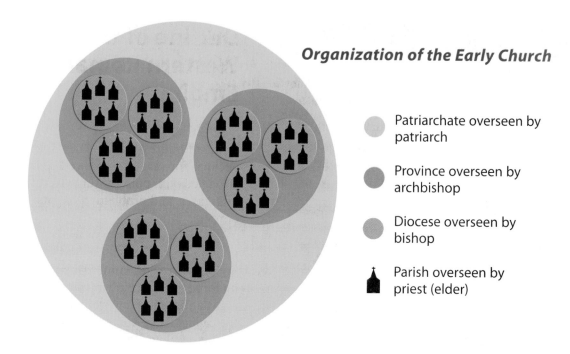

Organization of the Early Church

- Patriarchate overseen by patriarch
- Province overseen by archbishop
- Diocese overseen by bishop
- Parish overseen by priest (elder)

The patriarchs lived in the most important cities of the empire. These five cities were Jerusalem, Alexandria, Rome, Antioch, and Constantinople. At first, each patriarch had equal authority. However, the patriarch of Rome eventually came to be regarded as the "first among equals." He was later called the pope.

It was at this point in the development of the church that Constantine made a decree. The decree, called the **Edict of Milan**, was issued in 313. It legalized Christianity. The Roman government's persecution of Christians became illegal. Under Constantine's rule, the government protected and helped the church.

The Rise of the Roman Church

The early Christians faced many challenges. Two of these challenges were persecution and false teachers. After the Edict of Milan was passed, the church grew rapidly. However, not all who claimed to be Christians stayed true to Scripture and the teachings of Christ and the apostles. False teachers wrote their own gospels and changed parts of the New Testament to fit their beliefs. Other false teachers accepted the truths of Scripture, but they also taught falsehoods such as not accepting Christ's **deity**, the fact that Christ is God.

Nevertheless there were still true believers in the church who defended the truth. They were called **orthodox**, which means "right belief." In 325 Constantine called the bishops of the church to a meeting that came to be known as the **Council of Nicaea**. At this meeting and other meetings that followed, the bishops carefully tried to define what true Christians should believe about each person of the Trinity.

The church in the Byzantine Empire became known as the Eastern Orthodox Church. Today, conservative Protestant Christians (Christians who are not Catholic or Orthodox) and members of the Eastern Orthodox Church agree on two truths: (1) God is a Trinity, three equal persons (the Father, the Son, and the Holy Spirit) Who are one God, and (2) the Son is both fully God and fully man (not partly God, not partly man, and not a combination of the two). These are very important truths to agree on.

But Protestants and the Eastern Orthodox disagree about some very important issues. Protestants argue that the Scripture is the only authority for what Christians believe and practice (2 Tim. 3:16). However, the Eastern Orthodox believe that their church's tradition is an equal authority to Scripture. The Eastern Orthodox Church also emphasizes that Jesus' death was a victory over Satan. Protestants agree with this, but they point out that the emphasis in Scripture is on Jesus' dying in place of sinners so they can be saved (Rom. 3:21–26). The Eastern Orthodox Church teaches that salvation is obtained through the sacraments of the church. These sacraments include baptism, communion, and confession. Protestants argue that salvation can be received only by faith alone in what Christ has done (Eph. 2:8–10).

Decline of the Western Roman Empire

As Christianity grew, the Roman Empire continued to decline. For years the empire had struggled with political turmoil, high taxes, and problems along its borders.

In the west the city of Rome grew weaker. Constantine had hoped to strengthen the empire by building a new capital in the east, Constantinople. However, moving the capital from Rome to the east further weakened the western part of the empire.

In 395 the Roman emperor Theodosius I permanently divided the empire into two separate parts: the Western Roman Empire and the Eastern Roman Empire. Several years after this division, the city of Rome was plundered by barbarians. Romans gave the name **barbarian** to nomadic peoples who had not adopted Roman culture and who did not speak Latin or Greek.

The Western Roman Empire was an easy prey for barbarian invasions. However, the Eastern Roman Empire was stronger and more secure. Unlike the empire in the west, it was to last for many more years.

Sadly, errors continued to creep into the church. This happened even among those who were fighting to keep the purity of the church's beliefs, or **doctrine**. Some even claimed that certain traditions not in the Bible were from the apostles. The same people claimed that these traditions had the same authority as the Bible. This way of thinking became a way for more and more errors to enter the church.

Theodosius I

FOCUS

1. What general led Justinian's troops in conquering lands for the empire?

2. What was a hippodrome?

Early Years of the Byzantine Empire

Eventually the Eastern Roman Empire became known as the **Byzantine Empire**.

Constantinople

Constantinople, the capital city of the Byzantine Empire, was well protected. Being on a peninsula, the city was surrounded by water and high cliffs on three sides. Constantine built strong, high walls around the entire city. The walls were about fifteen feet thick with nearly one hundred towers. For a thousand years the city remained protected from foreign invaders.

The standard of living in Constantinople was extremely high. The structure and the economics of the city could support a population of a million people. In addition to the fortified walls, craftsmen constructed sewage and water systems throughout the city. Literacy and education among men and women far exceeded any other city at that time. Constantinople was a stronghold that attracted both invaders and merchants.

The walls of Constantinople today

Justinian I

Justinian I, also known as Justinian the Great, reigned over the Byzantine Empire from 527 to 565. Justinian had been taught from his youth that just as there was one God in heaven, there was only one empire here on earth. Justinian claimed that he, as the sole Christian emperor, had absolute authority. He made it his duty to fulfill this heavenly order.

By now, former Roman territory in the west was controlled by barbarians. Justinian wanted to restore the greatness of the former Roman Empire. He believed the time had come to deliver the west from these barbarians.

Justinian sent his best general, **Belisarius**, to conquer the regions of the former Roman Empire. These regions were known as provinces. Belisarius first conquered Egypt, an important province that produced grain. Then he marched his army across North Africa to the city of Carthage. A people called the Vandals ruled there. They were fierce fighters, but Belisarius's army defeated them and destroyed their kingdom.

Next, Belisarius and his men built ships so that they could cross the Mediterranean Sea and invade the island of Sicily. Before long, Belisarius led his army through the Italian Peninsula and claimed it for Justinian. As a result of Belisarius's amazing victories, he became very popular in Constantinople.

Justinian did not conquer all the former Roman Empire. But he did conquer every part he fought for. Justinian controlled land on three continents.

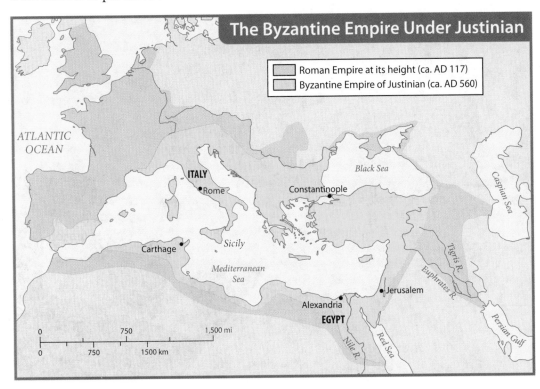

The Byzantine Empire Under Justinian

- Roman Empire at its height (ca. AD 117)
- Byzantine Empire of Justinian (ca. AD 560)

ATLANTIC OCEAN

ITALY
Rome
Black Sea
Constantinople
Caspian Sea
Carthage
Sicily
Mediterranean Sea
Tigris R.
Euphrates R.
Jerusalem
Alexandria
EGYPT
Nile R.
Red Sea
Persian Gulf

0   750   1,500 mi
0   750   1500 km

Corpus Juris Civilis

Justinian believed that a well-governed empire needed a good system of law. He adopted all the laws of the former Roman Empire. Roman laws had been made over a span of five hundred years. Imagine how many laws there were! There were so many that no one could learn all of them.

Tribonia, a member of the court, was chosen to simplify the laws so they would be easier to understand. In just four years, he and his committee finished their work. The new and much shorter law code was called the *Corpus Juris Civilis*, or the *Body of Civil Law*. In some modern European countries, such as France and Italy, this law code still "echoes" in their legal systems.

Political Groups

In the city of Constantinople, almost all the people, even the emperor, supported political groups. The two most popular groups were the Blues and the Greens. They represented different social and political views but also competed as teams in sporting events.

The people of both the former Roman Empire and the Byzantine Empire enjoyed participating in and watching sports. At sporting events, especially chariot racing, the people cheered their favorite teams to victory. Sporting and social events took place in open-air stadiums called **hippodromes**. During these games, supporters often shouted out political views. Hostility among the supporters and between the groups was often hard for the authorities to control.

The Nika Revolt

Not everyone in the Byzantine Empire was pleased with Justinian's rule. Justinian taxed all the citizens heavily to finance huge building projects. He ignored the positions people held in society and the privileges many had. Tension grew as the citizens became increasingly unhappy and angry.

Justinian's efforts to prevent an uprising failed. Early in January of 532, games took place in the Hippodrome in Constantinople. During the games the spectators exploded in thunderous shouting to ridicule Justinian. The anger flowed to people outside the Hippodrome. An enormous riot soon broke out. Seven leaders were arrested and sentenced to death. Two men, one from the Blue team and one from the Green team, were taken to safety by several monks. However, the imperial guard surrounded the monastery. The crowd that followed demanded that the two be pardoned.

Justinian tried to calm the situation by announcing new games, but tempers grew even worse. The Blues and the Greens were now united against the emperor. Justinian retreated to the imperial palace. The crowd moved into the streets again, burning and looting buildings.

BIOGRAPHY

Who: Justinian I (the Great)

What: Byzantine emperor (527–565)

When: ca. 482–565

Where: ancient Turkey

Justinian was born to Slavic parents in what is modern-day Macedonia. He was later adopted by his uncle Justin I. Justinian was made co-emperor with Justin and given the title Augustus ("revered one"). When Justin died, Justinian became the only emperor. He is most remembered for having the magnificent Hagia Sophia built and creating a simplified code of Roman laws.

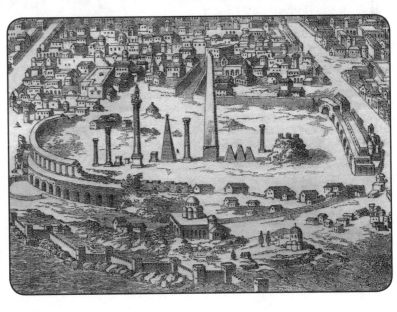

The Hippodrome

Theodora

Theodora was the wife of Emperor Justinian. She had been a circus performer before she married him. Theodora had a great influence on Justinian. She advised Justinian in the building projects he undertook. She also offered him good advice in running the government.

During the Nika Revolt, Justinian would have run for his life had it not been for his wife. She told Justinian that she preferred to die an empress and that royal purple made a fine shroud to be buried in. Justinian found enough courage to stay but sent Belisarius out to fight the rioters. The power Theodora had over Justinian was evident after she died in 548. After that time it seemed that Justinian lost his ability to rule effectively.

As the rioting continued, the nobles did not rally behind Justinian. They saw the uprising as an opportunity to take over the throne. They had already selected a successor for Justinian. The nobles decided to storm the palace and kill the emperor. Justinian was about to take a ship into exile when his wife, Theodora, convinced him to stay and fight. He called upon Belisarius to end the rebellion.

Belisarius and his men slew over thirty thousand people in the Hippodrome. Nineteen senators who plotted a takeover were executed. Their palaces were destroyed, and their bodies were thrown into the sea.

The events in Constantinople during that week in January became known as the **Nika Revolt** because the people shouted "Nika!" ("Conquer!") as they rioted.

Rebuilding the City

During the Nika Revolt much of Constantinople was looted and burned. Taxes went up even more to pay for the damage. Justinian took advantage of the opportunity to make the city more beautiful than it had ever been before. The emperor set his architects to work planning and building new public baths, governmental buildings, churches, and aqueducts and cisterns for carrying and storing water.

The most famous of all these structures was a church called the **Hagia Sophia** (HAH-jee-uh so-FEE-uh), which means "holy wisdom." The Hagia Sophia was the most important and most beautiful church in the empire. The church was built in the shape of a cross. Over the center of the church, the builders erected a magnificent dome that reached 184 feet above the floor.

The inside of the Hagia Sophia was brilliantly decorated. An image of God the Father surrounded by angels and archangels looked down from the highest part of the dome. Images of saints covered the walls of the church. Many of these images were in the form of mosaics made of thousands of pieces of colored glass, stone, or other materials.

The Hagia Sophia as it looks today. The four minaret towers were constructed when the Ottoman Turks used the building as a mosque.

Making a Paper Mosaic

Mosaics have been an art form since the early Mesopotamian civilizations. The Romans made mosaics of colored stones to cover floors and walkways. Artists in the Byzantine Empire expanded the use of mosaics to decorate walls as well. Many of the mosaics were made of colored Italian glass. Some of the glass was backed with a thin layer of gold.

Mosaic of Christ from inside the Hagia Sophia

1. Get several sheets of colored construction paper, two sheets of black construction paper, scissors, and glue.

2. Cut the colored construction paper into small pieces of different shapes.

3. Arrange the colored pieces to form a picture on one sheet of black paper. Lay the pieces close together without letting them touch so that some of the black paper can be seen.

4. Apply a thin layer of glue to a small portion of the second sheet of black paper. Transfer the colored pieces onto the glued area.

5. Continue applying glue and transferring pieces until the entire sheet of paper is covered.

1. What were the successes and failures of Justinian's reign?

2. What positive changes took place under Heraclius?

The Final Years and Legacy

Under the command of Belisarius, the Byzantine army conquered surrounding lands. The Italian Peninsula, parts of northern Africa, and other regions were now part of the Byzantine Empire. Some believe that Justinian may have become jealous of the success Belisarius had in the Italian Peninsula. This may

Justinian (with crown) and Belisarius (left)

have been the reason that the general was stripped of power and imprisoned. Without Belisarius, Justinian could not hold the peninsula. A new general led the army in conquering Spain and eventually conquered the Italian Peninsula once again.

During Justinian's thirty-eight years on the throne, the Byzantine Empire experienced vast improvements in the government, the law, and the economy. He conquered every country his armies attempted to take. Leaders of surrounding nations recognized his power.

Even so, Justinian left his successors with many problems. He had neglected the defense of the empire's eastern and northern borders. He also left the empire financially drained. His military campaigns and massive building program were extremely costly. Justinian took the Byzantine Empire to the height of glory but left it on the brink of ruin.

The Struggle for Existence

Despite all of Justinian's accomplishments and efforts to restore the old Roman Empire, Rome's glory was gone and would not return. Byzantine rulers after Justinian had difficulty holding lands that had been conquered. The weak leaders and loss of life from disease contributed to the decline in both the west and the east. In the west, education, commerce, and maintenance of the public buildings came to a grinding halt. In the east, merchants, industrialists, and small land owners struggled as wars and uprisings disrupted trade.

Since Justinian had left the government bankrupt, there was no more money for lavish buildings. The growth of arts and sciences slowed. The central government was forced to take severe measures to collect taxes.

The emperors who ruled after Justinian found it impossible to keep the loyalty of conquered people in distant provinces. Each province was very different from the others in its culture and religious beliefs.

By this time the Byzantine army was much weaker. The army was made up of **mercenaries**, foreigners hired by the government to fight in the army.

Persian emperors had been attacking the Byzantine Empire for several hundred years. After Justinian's death, the Persians renewed their attack to take the province of Syria. The Persian emperor wanted Syria because it was rich from trade and could afford high taxes. The Byzantine government was not able to pay for strong mercenaries to defend Syria. As a result the Persians seized the territory with little difficulty.

The Byzantine Empire also faced trouble on the **Balkan Peninsula**. Two barbarian tribes, the Avars and the Bulgars, migrated into the area. They were strong enough to take the land and settle in it.

Another tribe of barbarians called the Lombards successfully invaded the Italian Peninsula. In just one hundred years, the Byzantine Empire lost nearly all the land conquered by Justinian. The Byzantine Empire seemed to be disappearing from the map.

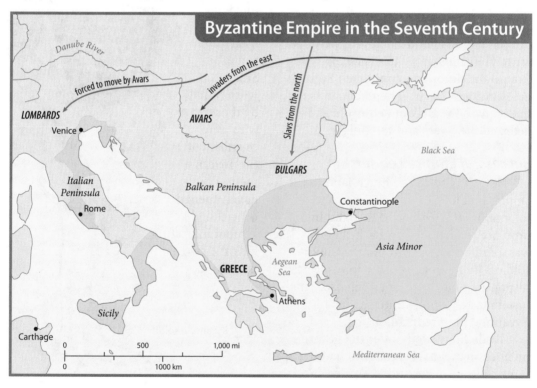

Byzantine Empire in the Seventh Century

Heraclius

Military Success

The emperor **Heraclius** (hih RAK lee us) began his reign in 610. Without him the Byzantine Empire might have disappeared. He reformed the army, reconquered the land taken by Persia and the barbarians, and made the roads safe for commerce.

Because of the empire's desperate situation, the Byzantine people often did whatever Heraclius demanded of them. He convinced the church to provide the necessary money to fund the war against the Persians and the barbarians.

To strengthen the army, Heraclius fired the mercenary soldiers and trained Byzantine peasants for the army. It took him ten years to prepare his new citizen soldiers. He promised to pay them by giving each one enough land to support himself and his family. With his new army, Heraclius drove the Persians from Asia Minor and conquered Syria, Palestine, and Egypt. Then he marched the army to the Balkan Peninsula and defeated the Avars and the Bulgars.

Successful Empire Leadership

Heraclius added so much land to the empire that he had to find a new way to organize it. He divided the land into provinces called *themes*. Each theme was a military zone with many peasant soldiers living in it. These soldiers were responsible for the theme's defense. This system lasted almost until the fall of the Byzantine Empire in **1453**.

Trade flourished under the government of Heraclius. People who had the same skills or occupations formed special groups called *guilds*. There were many kinds of guilds. For example, there were guilds for moneychangers, goldsmiths, and notaries (officials who oversaw the writing of legal documents). In the cities, other guilds supplied meat, fish, and bread to the people. Foreign merchants traveled throughout the Byzantine Empire selling grain, wax, leather, furs, spices, and ointments. They also sold slaves.

One of the most important items of trade was silk. Silk was extremely expensive because it came all the way from China. Persians controlled much of the silk trade route. Silk was worn only by those who were members of the government. Each governmental official had a symbol indicating his office woven into the fabric.

Byzantine soldier

272

Byzantine spies discovered how the Chinese made silk. The spies stole some silkworms and smuggled them out of China. Silk production became one of the most important industries in the Byzantine Empire, especially in the cities of Constantinople, Antioch, Tyre, and Beirut.

Heraclius also changed the language of the empire. Although the Byzantine people believed their empire was a continuation of the old Roman Empire, very few of them spoke Latin in the 600s. Since almost everyone spoke Greek, Heraclius decreed that the language of the empire would be Greek. He even used the Greek title *Basilius* rather than a Roman title.

A New Enemy and a New Idea

World Conditions

Persians and Byzantines continued to fight for the same land. Their fighting, however, only made both empires weaker. Many people living in the region were not loyal to either empire.

During this time a powerful movement was gaining strength in a remote region far away on the **Arabian Peninsula**. This new movement was about to dramatically change history for the Persians, the Byzantines, and eventually the world.

Muhammad

Wars and pirates on the Red Sea caused merchants to open routes along the western edge of the Arabian Peninsula. The trading brought great wealth to cities there, such as Mecca. The trade routes also became a means for the rapid spread of ideas.

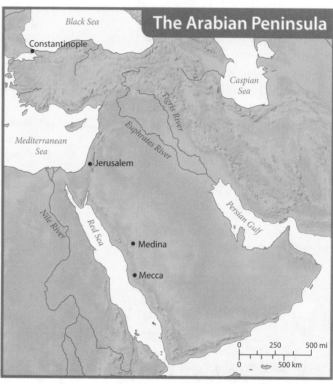

A man named **Muhammad**, who lived in Mecca, made many commercial trips along the trade routes with his uncle. Muhammad's travels brought him into contact with many religions. He particularly took notice of Christianity and Judaism. These faiths were different from the polytheistic religions in the Arabian Peninsula. Muhammad used his knowledge of Christianity and Judaism to form a new belief.

At the age of forty, Muhammad claimed that he had a vision of the angel Gabriel. In this vision the angel gave Muhammad a revelation. This was one of many visions Muhammad claimed to have throughout his life. According to some historians, Muhammad's followers later wrote down the revelations from these visions. The revelations were compiled in a work known as the **Qur'an** (or Koran). Muhammad taught that there was only one god. The Arabic word for his god is *Allah*. Even though the Bible teaches there is only one God, Muhammad's beliefs were very different from the Bible's teachings about the true God.

The Kaaba in Mecca

THE FIVE PILLARS OF ISLAM

Islam requires every Muslim to perform certain religious duties to reach heaven.

1. Sincerely believe and recite "There is no god but Allah, and Muhammad is his prophet."
2. Pray five times a day while facing Mecca.
3. Give to the poor.
4. Fast from sunrise to sunset during the sacred month of Ramadan.
5. If able, make at least one **pilgrimage**, or sacred journey, to Mecca.

Muhammad began to speak out against the evils practiced by the people of Mecca. One thing he rebuked them for was their practice of polytheism. In Mecca there was a cube-shaped building called the Kaaba. It was used for pagan rituals and held many idols. Having the idols in Mecca brought some unity between the Arabian tribes and great prosperity to the city. However, Muhammad's message threatened this unity and the prosperity of Mecca. Muhammad gained a small following but was forced to flee from Mecca in 622.

Muhammad and his followers traveled to a small oasis called Medina. The groups of Arabian tribal warriors there accepted his teachings and submitted to his leadership. During this time Muhammad's beliefs developed into the religion known as **Islam**. Muhammad expanded his influence and increased a following among Arabian tribes. Together they raided passing caravans that were on their way to trade in Mecca. The attacks increased Muhammad's wealth and served as his punishment to the merchants of Mecca.

By 630 Muhammad's army took control of Mecca with little fighting. He removed the idols from the Kaaba and forced many of the people to accept Islam. Everyone who followed Islam was called a **Muslim**. Not everyone in Mecca accepted the leadership of Muhammad and his religion. Those who did not submit to him and Islam were called *infidels*.

ISLAM

Like Christianity and Judaism, Islam teaches there is only one god. But the god of Islam is not a triune god like the God of Christianity. Christians worship the Father, the Son, and the Holy Spirit. These are the different persons of the one true God. This truth is important. The Father sent the Son to provide salvation for mankind (John 3:17). The Son became a man (while remaining God) to die in our place for sin (Rom. 3:21–26). And the Holy Spirit convicts people of sin and draws them to come to Christ for salvation (John 16:8). Each member of the Trinity has an important role to play in providing salvation.

In Islam, people are not guaranteed eternity in heaven simply because they are Muslim. Their eternity depends on whether Allah will be merciful to them or not. The Bible teaches that people can have assurance of God's mercy and salvation. Jesus fully satisfied God's rightful wrath against sin when He died on the cross. All those who are united with Him in salvation have nothing to fear. Jesus has saved them from sin and judgment (Eph. 2:1–10).

Researching the Bible

The Bible tells us that Jesus is the Son of God, but Muslims do not believe this. They believe He was just another prophet, less important than their prophet Muhammad.

1. Get your Bible and your Activity Manual.

2. Complete the page using your Bible.

3. Discuss the questions, Bible verses, and your answers.

The baptism of Jesus

FOCUS

1. Why was Jerusalem important to the Muslims?

2. What caused the division between the West and the East branches of the church?

The Conquests of the Muslims

Muhammad died in 632. One of his followers took his place to lead the Muslims. The man in this position of leadership was called a caliph (KAY lif). The first caliph was Abu-Bakr. He was a fine general, as were many of the caliphs that followed. Abu-Bakr led a war to conquer the entire Arabian Peninsula. His goal was to convert the people there to Islam. Muslims call a war such as this a **jihad** (ji HAHD), a holy war fought for the cause of Islam. Within two years Abu-Bakr and his army reached their goal.

The word *jihad* is an Arabic word that means "to strive hard." Some Muslims think of a jihad, not as an actual physical war, but as a mental struggle to become a good Muslim. However, the Qur'an describes a jihad as a holy war against non-Muslims. From the beginning, Muhammad commanded his followers to conquer or kill people who were not followers of Islam.

Muslim Victories

The next caliph was a man named Umar. He led the Muslims to conquer Persia. After defeating one of the Persian armies, Umar sent his army to Syria and Egypt. The Muslims captured both regions. They faced Heraclius, the first Byzantine emperor to fight Muslims.

The Muslim army had an advantage when attacking the Persian and the Byzantine empires. Although both empires were powerful, they were weakened from years of battling each other. The Byzantine army also had been fighting the Avars and the Bulgars. It simply was not large enough to fight the Arabs at the same time.

The Dome of the Rock is built on the spot that is believed to be the site of Muhammad's ascension to heaven.

The Muslims considered three cities to be sacred: **Jerusalem**, **Medina**, and **Mecca**. In Jerusalem there was a rock that the Muslims believed was sacred. Umar went on to conquer Jerusalem. The Muslims built a shrine on the rock. The shrine, which still stands today, is called the Dome of the Rock.

Empire in Turmoil

After Heraclius died, the Byzantine Empire again faced crises. To provide soldiers for all their wars, the Byzantine emperors gave more and more land to peasants who joined the army. The nobility disliked this practice. They thought only noblemen should own land. The wars also brought a rise in taxes, which angered the Byzantines. For twenty years, civil war further weakened the empire. Seven emperors tried to rule during that time. Most of them were assassinated only a few months after coming to power.

A New Hero

In the early 700s a man named Leo served as an administrator and a general in the Byzantine government. Soon he grew in power and seized the opportunity to be emperor. With his army, Leo captured the emperor and his entire household. He named himself Emperor **Leo III**. He was also known as Leo the Syrian.

Leo had much experience that was a benefit to his rule. He was familiar with the empire's enemies. As a boy he had lived among the Arabs and learned their language. When he was older, he and his family moved to the Balkan Peninsula. There he became familiar with the barbarians and their way of life.

Muslim Invasion

Just six months after Leo III became emperor, Muslim armies camped outside the walls of Constantinople. Their navy closed off the city by sea to stop goods from coming into the port. The Muslims hoped to starve the citizens into surrendering. Leo III sent his ships out against the Muslims. The Byzantines had only a few ships, but they also had a powerful weapon. This weapon was Greek fire, an explosive mixture that burst into flames whenever it touched water. When the Muslim ships drew close, the defenders of Constantinople threw Greek fire toward them. After the enemy ships

Greek fire

Iconoclasm

In the Byzantine Empire the use of icons became popular in churches. **Icons** are sacred images representing Christ, Mary, saints, or other sacred subjects. Most of the icons were paintings, mosaics, or frescoes.

Icon of Mary and Jesus

The emperor Leo III considered icons a type of idol. When an earthquake shook Constantinople in 726, he believed it was a judgment from God against the use of icons. Leo then ordered the destruction of all the icons in the churches to prevent further judgment.

The destruction of religious icons is called *iconoclasm* (eye KON uh KLAZ um). People who think icons are sinful and destroy them are called iconoclasts.

Throughout the empire iconoclasts painted over or destroyed many of the icons. This action led to a division within the Eastern Orthodox Church. Leo imprisoned those who tried to protect the icons.

The controversy over icons lasted until 843. In that year the ruler officially recognized icons and allowed them back in the churches. This event is still celebrated each year in the Eastern Orthodox Church as the Feast of Orthodoxy.

burned, the ships with supplies for the citizens could enter the port.

The following winter was so cold that many of the Muslim soldiers who were encamped around Constantinople froze to death. The next summer a large number of the citizens and many Muslims died of a plague. Eventually, the remaining Muslims withdrew.

Leo led his army into Asia Minor and took the peninsula back from the Muslims. Although the Muslim threat had not ended, Leo proved his ability to lead the empire.

Height of the Byzantine Empire

The Byzantine Empire had its best and most powerful years between 850 and 1050. It was strongly influenced by Hellenistic culture. Some historians refer to this time as a golden age in the history of the Byzantine Empire.

During this time, the emperors successfully fought their enemies on the Balkan Peninsula and in the Middle East. Some rulers helped develop the empire's government and culture. Emperor Michael III reorganized the University of Constantinople. Basil I oversaw the revision of the law. The empire also became wealthier from its trade throughout Asia, Europe, and Africa.

Christian missionaries from Constantinople traveled throughout eastern Europe in the 860s. In the process of trying to make converts, the missionaries helped standardize the language, ethics, laws, and political patterns of the people, including the Bulgarians and the Slavs.

Two missionaries, Cyril and Methodius,

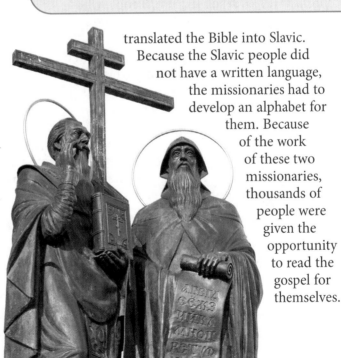

translated the Bible into Slavic. Because the Slavic people did not have a written language, the missionaries had to develop an alphabet for them. Because of the work of these two missionaries, thousands of people were given the opportunity to read the gospel for themselves.

Cyril and Methodius

280

FOCUS

1. Why was Basil II called the Bulgar Slayer?

2. What was the pope's reaction when he found out what the crusaders did to Constantinople?

The Bulgar Slayer

Basil II became emperor in 976. He never married, and he devoted his life to making the empire stronger. His army was well trained, and he made the nobles pay their taxes. He kept the church from taking land from the peasants. Basil II was serious by nature and a fair ruler. He was one of the best emperors the Byzantine Empire ever had.

Basil II was a great warrior. When the Bulgars attacked the empire, Basil led an army in defeating them. He captured fourteen thousand Bulgarian soldiers. Because of this victory and his harsh treatment of the captives, Basil II was often called the Bulgar Slayer.

Coin showing co-emperors Basil II and Constantine VIII

Another Muslim Advance

After Basil II's death in 1025, no other emperor was able to run the government the way he had. For two hundred years the empire had experienced victories and expansion. Now the empire faced new obstacles. Venice, an Italian city, took over much of the trade that used to come through Constantinople. New enemies appeared and attacked the empire. These invaders included the Normans from northern Europe, the Patzinaks from Russia, and the Muslim Seljuk (sel JOOK) Turks from central Asia. The Byzantines especially hated the Turks because of their earlier capture of the holy city of Jerusalem.

BIOGRAPHY

Who: Basil II (the Bulgar Slayer)

What: Byzantine emperor (976–1025)

When: ca. 958–1025

Where: ancient Turkey

Basil was crowned co-emperor with his brother Constantine in 960. At the time both were too young to rule. After their father's death in 963, their stepfather, a great-uncle, and two generals tried to rule the empire. Later, with the help of the Russians, Basil became sole emperor. He was as ruthless in his rule of the empire as he was in his military command. Basil was a short, stocky man and twirled his beard in his fingers when deep in thought or angry.

The Crusades

The Crusades Begin

In 1095 Pope Urban II issued a call to the knights of France. He wanted them to free the city of Jerusalem in Palestine from Islamic rule. These religious campaigns of the Roman Church became known as the **Crusades**. The warriors were called crusaders.

The First Three Crusades

In the first Crusade the crusaders were able to capture Jerusalem in the summer of 1099. However, the Muslim Turks continued to invade the land. The second and the third Crusades did not end successfully. In July of 1187, Muslims regained Jerusalem for Islam.

The Fourth Crusade

When Innocent III became the pope in 1198, he made it his primary goal to reclaim Jerusalem. Within a few years he organized another crusade. However, the crusaders made their own alliances and began attacking cities that the pope did not intend.

By 1200 the Muslim Turks controlled the Middle East from Egypt to Syria. The crusaders' plan was to gain control of Egypt, which was under Muslim rule. They believed that their success in this wealthy center of trade would divide the Muslim power. Crusaders made an agreement with the navy of Venice. The Venetians were to supply ships, and the crusaders would supply the army and money.

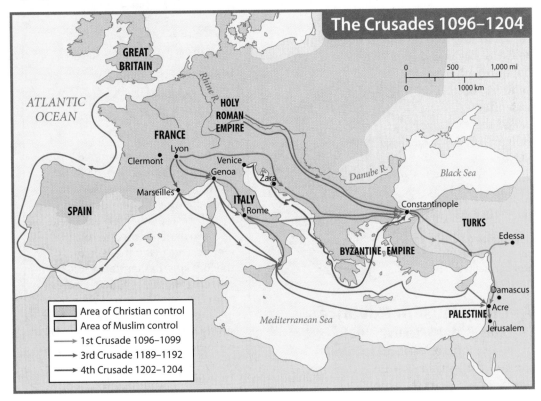

The Crusades 1096–1204

GREAT BRITAIN

ATLANTIC OCEAN

Rhine R.

HOLY ROMAN EMPIRE

FRANCE
Lyon
Clermont

Venice
Genoa

Zara

Danube R.

Black Sea

Marseilles

ITALY
Rome

Constantinople

TURKS

SPAIN

BYZANTINE EMPIRE

Edessa

Mediterranean Sea

Damascus
Acre
PALESTINE
Jerusalem

0   500   1,000 mi
0   1000 km

Area of Christian control
Area of Muslim control
1st Crusade 1096–1099
3rd Crusade 1189–1192
4th Crusade 1202–1204

The Venetians kept their part of the agreement. However, as time wore on, it became apparent that the crusaders would be unable to supply the huge army and necessary money for success.

A new plan was made to invade other cities to provide the money and the resources needed. The Venetians convinced the crusaders to attack Zara, even though it was a Christian city.

While the crusaders were in Zara, a prince made a request of them. The prince claimed to be the rightful heir to the throne of the Byzantine Empire. He offered money and men for the Crusade if, in return, the crusaders would help put him on the throne. The prince wanted to take the place of the Byzantine emperor Alexius III. The crusaders accepted the offer and with the Venetians headed for Constantinople.

Emperor Alexius III learned about the treachery. He rallied support to oppose the prince. When the Venetians and the crusaders arrived at Constantinople, the Byzantine army resisted them for several days. However, the crusaders were eventually able to take the city. Alexius slipped out and fled into exile.

A group of Byzantine churchmen and senior nobles offered their submission to the crusaders. These Byzantines were hoping for a peaceful takeover. Their hopes were in vain. Over the next three days, the crusaders plundered the city, including the churches. They divided the Byzantine lands and goods amongst themselves and their Venetian allies.

Pope Innocent III condemned the actions of the crusaders, but it was already too late. He was unable to control them. What had started out as a noble effort to reclaim Jerusalem had turned into a serious problem.

LASTING CONSEQUENCES

For many centuries, including current times, the actions taken by the crusaders in Constantinople have not been forgotten.

The late Pope John Paul II tried to mend the lasting bitterness held by the Eastern Orthodox Church. In June of 2004, he apologized to Patriarch Bartholomew I of the Eastern Orthodox Church. "In particular, we cannot forget what happened in the month of April 1204," the pope said in reference to the sacking of Constantinople by crusaders. "How can we not share, at a distance of eight centuries, the pain and disgust."

Patriarch Bartholomew I (left) and Pope John Paul II (right)

So often we think that things we do and say that hurt others will heal with time. Time does not always heal. Many times bitterness festers and grows. Only forgiveness and love can heal emotional wounds.

The Recovery of the Byzantine Empire

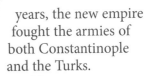

The crusaders never did go on to Egypt to fight. From 1204 to 1261, the Venetians and the crusaders ruled Constantinople. It looked as if the Byzantine Empire had come to an end. But the empire had not been completely destroyed. Some Byzantines fled to Asia Minor where they organized a new empire. Its capital was Nicaea. For over fifty-seven years, the new empire fought the armies of both Constantinople and the Turks.

The emperors at Nicaea worked hard to strengthen their revived empire. One emperor, John III, banned evil practices in government and the courts. He helped the poor by founding hospitals and charitable institutions. His government built churches and gave land to its citizen-soldiers.

The government also encouraged the improvement of agricultural methods and raising livestock. To protect his people, John III had a system of fortifications and frontier defenses built.

By 1261 the Byzantine emperor Michael VIII had strengthened his army enough to attack and recapture Constantinople. He entered the city on August 15, 1261, and within weeks was crowned emperor in the Hagia Sophia. Michael VIII spent vast sums of money to rebuild and beautify the capital.

Byzantine artifacts: (top to bottom) gold earrings, painted pitcher, and silver basket

Analyzing Political Cartoons

Have you ever read a cartoon on the editorial page in your daily newspaper? Political cartoons can be found in newspapers, magazines, books, and on the Internet. The focus of a *political cartoon* is usually on an important person or an important political or social event. A political cartoon gives a summary of an event in a quick and entertaining way. Political cartoons are primary sources that present insights into the public mood and attitudes toward key events of the time.

The cartoonist expresses his own political opinion through his art. He uses emotional techniques trying to persuade the reader to accept his opinions. Often the cartoon characters are drawn with exaggerated features. The artist may use symbols to stand for something in the news. For example, a dollar sign may represent the economy.

1. Get your Activity Manual page and the political cartoon from your teacher.

2. With your partner study the political cartoon.

3. Complete the cartoon analysis on the Activity Manual page.

4. Discuss your analysis with the class.

FOCUS

1. What weakened much of Europe during the 1300s?

2. Who conquered Constantinople?

The Fall of the Byzantine Empire

Emperor Michael VIII attempted to win back the land once held by the Byzantine Empire. But he faced a new enemy. A group of Turks called the **Ottomans** had invaded the Middle East. The Ottomans conquered the Seljuk Turks, adopted Islam as their religion, and moved north to attack the Byzantine Empire.

The Ottomans threatened the empire in Asia Minor. Since Michael VIII did not have enough money to go to war, he divided the empire among his family members. His hope was that each relative would protect his share, but his relatives all wanted to make their parts of the empire independent countries. They each hired mercenaries and were soon fighting each other instead of protecting the empire.

Meanwhile, Venetian merchants gained control of Constantinople's trade. They collected the profits and taxes that had once belonged to the emperor. The emperors from that time on became very poor. To pay their bills, they sold their gold and silver dishes and even their palace decorations.

By 1371 the Ottomans had conquered all the Byzantine Empire except the city of Constantinople. As the conquests took place, different Byzantine emperors tried to save the empire by visiting Europe. Each time an emperor went, he hoped to find a European king who would send an army to help fight the Ottomans. Meanwhile, the leaders of the Eastern Orthodox Church begged the pope in Rome to help the empire.

However, conditions in Europe prevented the Europeans from helping the Byzantines. England and

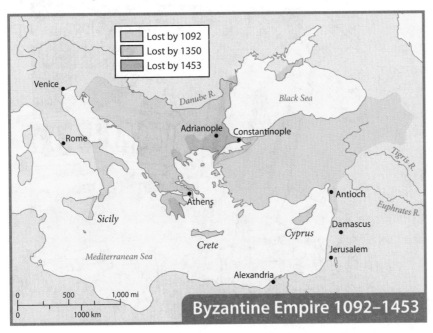

Byzantine Empire 1092–1453

Lost by 1092
Lost by 1350
Lost by 1453

France had been at war with each other for over one hundred years. Neither had an army nor the money to help. Additionally, in the 1300s all Europe was weakened from the **Black Death**, a fatal disease also known as the bubonic plague. The disease killed at least one-third of all the people in Europe.

After the Ottomans completed their conquest of Asia Minor, they crossed into the Balkan Peninsula. The city of Adrianople and the country of Bulgaria fell to them. The Ottomans went on to conquer Greece.

By March of 1453, the Ottomans surrounded Constantinople. The Byzantine emperor Constantine XI had spent more than half his life fighting the Ottomans. He did not want to give in easily.

The Ottomans used cannons to fire on the walls of Constantinople. Constantine did not have many cannons for his army. The Byzantines defended their positions but spent time each night repairing the damages the Ottoman cannons had made. After a few days the Turks entered the city. Constantine died fighting the Turks. He chose death over surrender.

During the invasion of Constantinople, the Ottomans destroyed or stole priceless works of art, icons, and precious

THE BLACK DEATH

The Black Death, or bubonic plague, was a terrible disease. Fleas bit rats and other rodents infected with bacteria. Then the fleas bit humans, passing on bacteria that caused the plague. Symptoms of the disease were a high fever and aching limbs. The most characteristic symptom was the swelling of spots on the neck, armpits, and legs. These spots turned blackish in color, which gives the disease its name, the Black Death. The swellings continued to expand until they burst. It usually took only three or four days for the patient to die.

The Black Death began in the Gobi Desert in China in the late 1320s and spread west along the Silk Road and other trade routes. The disease also traveled by merchant ships. In two years, one in every three people in Europe died from the disease. Some cities suffered very little. Others suffered greatly.

Giovanni Boccaccio was a writer who lived in Florence, Italy, during the time of the Black Death. He lost family members and many friends to the plague. In his famous collection of stories, *The Decameron*, he begins with a description of the Black Death:

> As consecrated ground there was not in extent sufficient to provide tombs for the vast multitude of corpses which day and night, and almost every hour, were brought in eager haste to the churches for interment, least of all, if ancient custom were to be observed and a separate resting-place assigned to each, they dug, for each graveyard, as soon as it was full, a huge trench, in which they laid the corpses as they arrived by hundreds at a time, piling them up as merchandise is stowed in the hold of a ship, tier upon tier, each covered with a little earth, until the trench would hold no more. (J. M. Rigg, trans.)

The Ottomans achieved victory as they used large bombard cannons in their attack on land.

The Importance of the Byzantine Empire

manuscripts. The **sultan** (the ruler of the Ottomans) entered the city and made it the capital of the Ottoman Empire. The beautiful Hagia Sophia became an Islamic mosque. The Byzantine Empire had come to an end.

Like all empires before it, the Byzantine Empire rose and fell. In fact, it expanded and declined several times. But while it existed, the Byzantines made many important achievements. They kept Roman law from disappearing. The scholars of the empire preserved Greek literature, learning, and philosophy. Without the Byzantine Empire, much of what we study today about the ancient world would have been lost.

The Ottomans attacked the city on all sides.

Chapter 11

Mesoamerica

FOCUS

1. Why is it difficult to know where the early Americans came from?

2. What was probably the oldest Mesoamerican civilization?

world. Consider the boat technology needed to make such a voyage between continents.

A number of questions surround the beginnings of people in the Americas. Where did these civilizations originate?

The Other Side of the World

Thousands of miles from Rome and Greece, people lived in what is now part of Mexico and Central America. They were accomplished artists, mathematicians, and builders. Their huge civilizations were a secret from the outside world until Christopher Columbus met one of their sailors on his voyage to the Americas. Even then, it was years before a European saw their cities.

Notice on the globe the vast oceans that separate the continents of North and South America from the other continents. These oceans isolated the ancient American civilizations from the rest of the

How did the ancients get to the Americas? Why did they migrate? These questions still mystify scholars today.

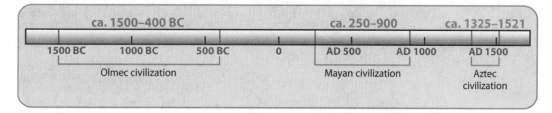

ca. 1500–400 BC				ca. 250–900		ca. 1325–1521
1500 BC	1000 BC	500 BC	0	AD 500	AD 1000	AD 1500
Olmec civilization				Mayan civilization		Aztec civilization

290

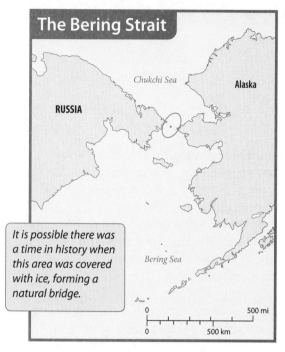

The Bering Strait

Chukchi Sea

Alaska

RUSSIA

It is possible there was a time in history when this area was covered with ice, forming a natural bridge.

Bering Sea

0   500 mi

0   500 km

So far, archaeological findings vary on where these people migrated from. Some **anthropologists** (scientists who study the origins of man) think that they migrated from Africa. Others link together evidence that early Americans may have come from Asia, particularly India or China. The most popular theory suggests that migration to North America started as people crossed over the Bering Strait into what is now Alaska. Migration then continued southward to an ancient region researchers call **Mesoamerica** (MEZ oh uh MEHR ih kuh). *Meso-* comes from the Greek word for "middle." Mesoamerica includes lands from central Mexico to Costa Rica in Central America.

From studying the Bible we know that God created Adam and Eve, the first man and woman. All people descended from them. We know the whole world was covered with a flood and Noah and his family were the only survivors. But how did some of their descendants finally arrive in the Americas? There is much about the past that is not known. Archaeologists continue to study, trying to piece together possible answers.

An archaeologist at work

Mesoamerica

Location—Mesoamerica extends from near the middle of Mexico to the central part of Central America. It includes the **Yucatán** (yoo kuh TAN) **Peninsula**, which is the landmass extending into the Gulf of Mexico in present-day southern Mexico.

Climate—The northern part of the Yucatán Peninsula is dry, receiving only 20–40 inches (51–102 cm) of rain per year. The southern part receives more. The temperatures in the peninsula range from 68°F to over 86°F (20°C–30°C). Lands south of the peninsula have temperatures averaging around 80°F (27°C) and receive almost daily rain. The mountains in the southernmost region of Mesoamerica have a mild climate and receive 20–30 inches (51–76 cm) of rain per year.

Topography—The peninsula is a lowland with thin soil. The central lands are mainly rainforest. The southernmost land rises into mountains and plateaus.

Natural Resources—The rainforest and highlands offer rich sources of lumber and good places to grow coffee, cotton, rubber trees, spices, and bananas. The northern region provides the right conditions for growing cocoa and sugar cane. Many minerals, natural lakes, and rivers can be found throughout the region.

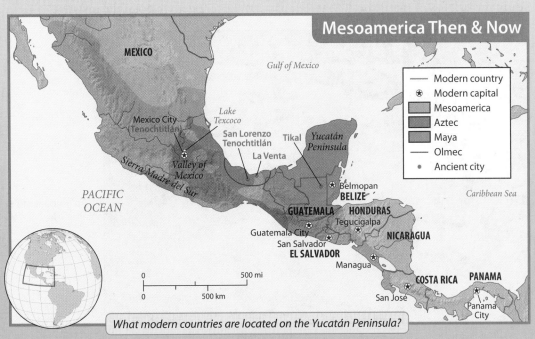

Mesoamerica Then & Now

Legend:
— Modern country
⊛ Modern capital
Mesoamerica
Aztec
Maya
— Olmec
• Ancient city

What modern countries are located on the Yucatán Peninsula?

Olmec head in Villahermosa, Mexico

Olmecs

The ancient **Olmec civilization** is considered one of the earliest great civilizations in Mesoamerica. Its culture developed around 1500 BC. Historians believe the Olmecs lived along the southern Gulf Coast of Mexico. The Olmec civilization declined by about 400 BC.

The major center of the Olmec civilization included the cities of Tenochtitlán (teh NOHCH tee TLAHN), San Lorenzo, and Potrero Nuevo. Historians call this urban center **San Lorenzo Tenochtitlán**. San Lorenzo Tenochtitlán had water and drainage systems. Houses were constructed of wood, clay, and palm leaves. Another city, **La Venta**, was one of the largest and most famous Olmec cities. La Venta was located in Mexico on the northeastern coast of Mesoamerica.

Very few written records exist about the Olmec culture and its everyday life. Historians do know from archaeological evidence that the Olmecs lived near rivers and were hunters and fishermen as well as farmers.

The most famous findings from the Olmec civilization are gigantic stone heads. The Olmecs carved these heads from stone, jade, and a volcanic rock called **basalt**. Some of the stones were from as far away as sixty miles and weighed over forty tons. It is astonishing to people today that the Olmecs could accomplish the seemingly impossible feat of transporting these huge stones. Some archaeologists suggest that the Olmecs floated the stone heads down rivers on rafts.

Olmec ceramic fish container

MAKING RUBBER

The Olmecs are believed to have been among the first people to use rubber. The name Olmec means "rubber people." The Olmecs and the people of later Mesoamerican civilizations developed a method to collect sap from trees. The people called these trees *cahuchu* ("weeping trees"). The cahuchu sap is a milky white liquid. Today it is known as latex. Early Mesoamericans used it to make waterproof items such as containers and foot coverings. It also was used to make balls that bounced.

By the 1700s, cahuchu sap had been taken to Europe. Scientists experimented and developed new uses for it. In 1770 Joseph Priestley found that pieces of the hardened sap could be used to rub away pencil marks. This use led to the substance being called "rubber."

Today latex and rubber products are used every day. The tires of cars, the soles of shoes, and the gloves used by surgeons are just a few of the items made of rubber.

Latex being collected

Many of the Olmec beliefs and customs were passed on to other Meso-american civilizations. The calendar used for centuries in Mexico may have originated with the Olmecs. Astronomy was important to them, and later peoples continued studying the heavenly bodies. Some historians believe that the Olmecs were the first to play a ritual ball game that became popular in later Mesoamerican civilizations.

Drawing Conclusions as an Archaeologist

What do you think of when you hear the word *archaeologist*? Do you think of a person exploring dark caves or dusty ruins? Do you picture a person sitting with a magnifying glass studying an artifact? The job of an archaeologist includes these tasks and many others. An important part of an archaeologist's job is to use artifacts and other evidence to determine characteristics of the people he is studying.

1. Collect ten items at home that tell about you. Place them in an unlabeled paper bag and staple it closed. Give the closed bag to your teacher. Take care not to let anyone see the items.

2. Work with a partner. Get two stapled bags from your teacher. Open one bag and examine the items inside.

3. Use the questions on the Activity Manual page to help determine the habits and activities of the items' owner. Discuss your ideas with your partner and record your conclusions.

4. Repeat this process with the second bag.

5. Share your results. Try to identify the owner of each bag.

Mayas

Another great civilization in Meso-america was the **Mayan civilization**. Archaeologists have found early traces of Mayan-speaking villages dating as far back as the time of the Olmecs. These villages contained groups of houses surrounded by fields. Some villages had public buildings, possibly for religious and governmental uses.

Archaeologists have uncovered more than three thousand buildings of the ancient city of Tikal in the Guatemalan rainforest.

For about 2,500 years the Mayas built farms and homes in the rainforests and high plateaus. The Mayas also settled in the lowlands. There they could get fresh water from deep sinkholes called **cenotes** (suh NO teez).

As the Mayas prospered, their population increased and their villages grew larger. By AD 250, Mayas dominated the region and built city-states. One of the largest and most magnificent city-states was **Tikal**. Archaeologists believe this city-state's population was at least sixty thousand. Tikal's buildings and people covered more than forty-seven square miles.

Mayan Achievements

Art, Architecture, and Literature

Between 250 and 900 the Mayas made advances in art, architecture, and literature. The Mayas wrote hundreds of books. They made thousands of sculptures and constructed huge palaces and pyramid-shaped temples. The Mayas built irrigation systems for their fields. They studied the stars, composed music and songs, and played games. They traded regularly within the network of their own cities and with other peoples.

The plaza of Tikal

In the mid-1500s, a Spanish priest named **Diego de Landa** tried to make the Mayas accept Roman Catholicism. When the Mayas refused to accept the new religion, de Landa had some of them stretched on pulleys, burned with candles, or tortured in other ways. De Landa had an entire library of Mayan books burned in 1562 "since they contained nothing but superstitions and falsehoods of the devil."

Afterward, de Landa realized that converting the Mayas would be easier if he knew more about them. He became a careful student of the Mayas and tried to translate their symbolic writing into Spanish. Much of the information known today about the Mayas of the 1500s and their ancient ancestors comes from de Landa's writings. The rest of the information has been carefully gathered from the stones and artifacts in Mayan lands.

Today some Mayan descendants still play the music of their ancestors. Some of the ball courts, irrigation systems, and roads the traders used can still be seen.

But many of the buildings and statues lie in ruins. Almost all the Mayan books are gone and with them, much information about how the Mayas lived and thought.

Math and Astronomy

Is there a zero in your telephone number or your street address? The ancient Mayas were one of the early civilizations that developed the idea of zero. With their zero, the Mayas were able to do difficult calculations and keep detailed records. Their math system was based on the number 20, unlike our decimal system now, which is based on 10.

The Mayas also made calendars similar to the calendar developed by the Olmecs. The Mayan calendar was based on the cycles of the moon and the sun. Their solar year had the same number of days that ours does. The calendar was made after years of careful observations of the sky. These observations were so accurate that the Mayas were able to figure out the orbits of the planets and could predict an eclipse of the sun.

Mayan Numbers 0–24				
0	1	2	3	4
5	6	7	8	9
10	11	12	13	14
15	16	17	18	19
20	21	22	23	24

Writing and Books

It was not until the 1970s that the Mayan hieroglyphs were understood. Today, 85 percent of known Mayan texts have been translated. Mayan writing was a combination of words and units of sound. Thus, anything that could be spoken could also be written.

Furthermore, the Mayas made books of their writings. They wrote on long strips of "paper" made of fig-tree bark. To make this paper, the Mayas pulled bark off the fig trees and soaked it in water to remove the sap. Then they beat the bark with wooden hammers and stretched it out to make a wide, flat surface. The material was then cut into strips.

Each strip was coated with a thin layer of a gummy substance for strength. Then the strip was painted over with lime to make its surface white. Scribes wrote and drew on the paper with paints made from vegetables and minerals. When the strips were dry, they were folded in an accordion fashion and bound between wooden covers. The type of book that the Mayas made is called a **codex**. A Mayan codex was usually about eight inches high and several yards long when unfolded.

Today only three Mayan books are known to exist. One contains observations about the planet Venus and charts used to predict solar eclipses. It does not tell anything about Mayan customs or history, nor does it give any clues to the fate of the Mayan civilization.

A portion of the Dresden Codex
What numbers do you see?

Mayan People

Physical Appearance

Historians today can see how the ancient Mayas looked from the sculptures and paintings they left behind.

According to Diego de Landa, the Mayan people were about five feet tall. They had thick, dark hair. The men wore their long hair in braids around the tops of their heads with one braid down the back. Women also wore braids, usually coiled around their heads and held in place with ribbons.

The Mayas appeared to have preferred long noses and sloping foreheads. Some used clay to create a ridge from the top of the forehead to the bridge of the nose. A true sign of beauty, the sloping head, had to be formed early in life. Parents bound newborns' heads between boards until the soft bones grew into a slanted, almost cone shape.

Historical evidence indicates that Mayas also preferred crossed eyes, perhaps because one of their gods was cross-eyed. To achieve this look, parents hung a bead between the baby's eyes. After the baby looked at the bead for months, his eyes grew permanently crossed.

When older, the Mayas made other changes to their appearances. Most young men shaved the hair above their foreheads to show off their slanting foreheads and brows. They also tattooed symbols on their arms, legs, and faces. Many had their ears pierced. The men wore earplugs in holes sliced into their lobes. They kept adding bigger and bigger plugs until the holes were several inches across. In these holes they placed disks of jade or shell. Both men and women would often file their teeth to points and inlay them with jade.

Mayas took frequent baths, a practice shunned and feared in Europe at the time. They liked perfume, which they made from flowers and herbs. Most of the men carried mirrors to check their appearance from time to time.

Discovering How

Sculpting a Maya

The Mayan people had distinctive facial features and hairstyles. Research to find details of what they looked like. Make a model of a Mayan person to display.

1. Get a lump of clay about the size of your fist, a plastic knife, and a toothpick.

2. Set aside about 1/3 of the clay.

3. Mold the remaining clay into an egg-shaped head with a neck and shoulders.

4. Use clay from the smaller lump to add ears, a nose, and hair. Include braids, earplugs, and other details. Refer to descriptions and photos from your research as you work.

5. Display your model.

Clay figure of a Mayan official

FOCUS

1. What were the levels in Mayan society?

2. How did the houses that the Mayas lived in show their social class?

Social Classes

Classes of Mayan society had several levels. At the top was the ruler, the absolute king. Like the Egyptians, the Mayas believed that their kings were descended from the gods and that they should be obeyed without question. The kings, in return, claimed to speak to the gods on behalf of the people. Most kings took advantage of this absolute authority and cruelly mistreated the people.

Each city-state had a unique hieroglyph to represent it and its king. Through these hieroglyphs, scholars have been able to identify thirty-three rulers of the city-state Tikal. At least one ruler was a queen. One notable king of Tikal was Jasaw Chan K'awiil I. Tikal had been weak and struggling when Jasaw came to power. Under his leadership it became strong once again. Many steles and other carvings tell of this king.

Just below the kings in power were the priests. There were at least four classes of priests. The highest-ranking priests were in charge of all the others. They taught writing, astronomy, mathematics, and religious rituals. Lower ranks included priests who treated sickness. Sometimes their cure was more dangerous than the illness. Imagine going to the doctor with a nosebleed only to have your foot cut off! This was done to the sufferer to let him bleed freely. Other priests were fortunetellers. The priests also offered sacrifices to the gods.

In the same social class as the priests were the nobles. All the priests came from the nobility. The nobles, both men and women, were educated, and they held important positions in the government.

Lesser nobles included the artists and architects, traders and scribes, and advisors and engineers. Although they did not have the high positions of the first class of nobles, they had many of the same privileges. No nobleman or noblewoman had to do manual work, such as planting crops, grinding corn, or cleaning. Such labor was left to the common people.

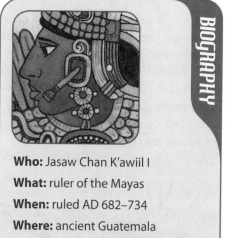

BIOGRAPHY

Who: Jasaw Chan K'awiil I

What: ruler of the Mayas

When: ruled AD 682–734

Where: ancient Guatemala

Jasaw Chan K'awiil I ruled the Mayas from the city-state of Tikal. When Jasaw defeated a rival city-state, Tikal began to prosper. He began rebuilding Tikal. Unlike other rulers who were harsh to their people, Jasaw tried to help his people make their civilization strong.

The peasants did the hard manual work of the Mayan society. They grew, harvested, and processed the food. The peasants grew cotton and produced fabrics. They tended the buildings. Some were soldiers in the armies and laborers for the construction of monuments and temples.

At the bottom of Mayan society were the slaves. Anyone who was in debt or who had committed a crime was considered a slave, the property of another. Sometimes prisoners of war were kept as slaves as well. Important prisoners were used for sacrifices. Lesser ones were made to work.

Mayan Dress

Most Mayas wore simple cotton clothes. The men wore tunics and loincloths, sometimes with a short cape. The women wore straight, plain dresses or wraparound skirts and long blouses. The Mayas either went barefoot or wore sandals made of straw and rope. Both men and women wore a lot of jewelry: earrings, rings, armbands, and necklaces. They made jewelry from jade, shells, volcanic rock, or animal teeth and bones.

Mayan priest

Wealthy people wore the same things as the common people, only with more embellishments, such as feathers woven into the fabric. They wore shoes made of deerskin.

The kings wore jaguar skins and jade breastplates. The three-foot plumes in their headdresses and on their clothes came from the quetzal, a beautiful bird of the rainforest. Kings also wore jade bands on their wrists and ankles as well as gold rings on their toes. To the common Maya, a king's appearance must have been dazzling indeed.

The Mayas obtained feathers of many brilliant colors from native birds to use in their clothing.

The Desire for Chocolate

Do you like hot chocolate? Many people do. It is a tasty "echo" from the tables of Mayan kings and nobles. The Mayas invented the drink that, with some variations, has been popular for centuries. The Mayas made their hot drink from powdered cacao beans.

Chocolate was so special to the Mayas that the cacao beans were also used for money. In the Mayan society, a slave was worth one hundred cacao beans. Because cacao beans were so valuable, counterfeiters sometimes filled empty bean pods with dirt or sand and passed them off as real beans. If caught, the counterfeiter was made a slave. Poor people could rarely afford the luxury of grinding up their money to make a hot drink.

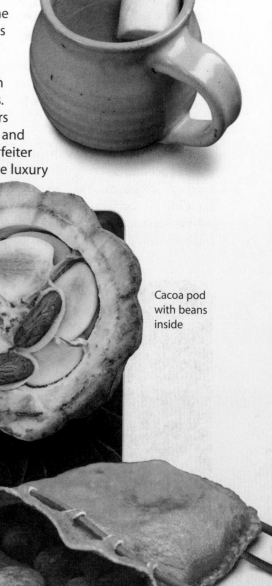

Cacoa pod with beans inside

Dried cacao beans used as money

Mayan Homes

The classes of Mayan society were reflected not only in people's jobs and dress but also in the places they lived. Kings lived in palaces that covered many acres. Nobles lived in large houses near the center of the cities—the closer to the center, the more impressive. These houses had many airy rooms and walls covered with decorative plaster called **stucco**. Embroidered cotton draperies divided large rooms. Some houses had fireplaces, ovens, and possibly plumbing. Most peasant families lived in small wooden houses with grass-thatched roofs.

Daily Life

While the kings, priests, and nobility practiced their ceremonies, waged wars on neighbors, and planned huge building projects, the average Maya led a far quieter and simpler life. Before four o'clock in the morning, women were awake and building fires to prepare breakfast. By five o'clock the men and boys had eaten breakfast and were tending to the crops. Family life was a very important part of the Mayan civilization.

Farmers

Farmers grew many crops. Their crops included beans, squash, avocados, and **maize** (corn). When planting corn in swampy places or on riverbanks, farmers made ridges in the soil and poked holes into the ridges with a planting stick. Another person came behind, dropping in corn kernels and covering the holes.

In the dry seasons, farmers went into the rainforests and cut down trees. They burned the stumps and the underbrush. In the ashes they planted corn. The corn grew well for a year or two, but such soil wore out quickly. The only remedy was to move to a new place to cut and burn again. Farmers gave part of all they grew to the upper classes.

A modern Mayan home
What social class would this house represent in the Mayan civilization?

FOCUS

1. Why did the Mayas talk to objects?

2. How did the Mayas view the shape of the world?

Women

Mayan women worked all day grinding grain in stone bowls or making cotton thread for use on looms. They also wove cloth and made clothing, kept house, and tended the children. Even the little girls helped make *tortillas* and other food. The big meal of the day, which usually included beans, fruit, *tamales,* and, occasionally, meat, came in the late afternoon. A favorite drink, *pozole,* was made from corn paste and water, sometimes mixed with honey. Women and girls made the meal, served it to the men and boys, and ate afterward.

Traders

Mayan cities in the highlands traded with those in the lowlands. In this way people were able to get what they needed. The lowlands produced cotton, rubber, and cacao beans. The highlands had valuable stones such as jade and obsidian. **Obsidian** is a sharp glasslike volcanic rock that Mayas used to make the blades of tools and weapons.

People came to the cities for festivals and games and to buy and sell goods. The markets were busy places where people came to trade salt, vegetables, animals, jewelry, jade, pottery, honey, fabrics, and, of course, cacao beans.

A Mayan woman weaving cloth

305

Mayan Religion

The whole Mayan society, even their popular ball game, was dominated by religion. Everything the Mayas did, whether cooking beans or attending ceremonies for a solar eclipse, had to be done according to a ritual. A man about to kill a deer had to stop the hunt to first ask the deer to forgive him by saying, "I have need."

Everything, even pottery, was believed to have a spirit. Mayas talked to the objects around them and were always in fear of imaginary evil dwarfs who they believed would cause sickness and crop failure. To **appease**, or satisfy, the dwarfs, Mayas put out food for them.

If illness came or crops failed, a priest might prescribe a homemade medicine or perform a ritual. Some of the medicines, made from herbs and other plants, were helpful and often cured the illnesses. Other "cures," however, had results that were worse than the illnesses.

The Mayas thought that the world was a flat square that was atop a giant crocodile god in a pond with water lilies. When a person died, he left the square and went to one of nine underworlds or thirteen heavens, each under the control of a separate god.

Mayas believed that almost everything had its own god—the sea, the moon, the sun, bees, medicine, corn, life, death, days of the calendar, and so on. Since there were so many gods and so many rules on how to please each god, the Mayas had to depend on the priests to keep everything in order.

Of all the rituals of the Mayan religion, the one most often written about is human sacrifice. Like other ancient religions, such as the one practiced by the priests of Baal in Bible times, the Mayan religion taught that the gods must be satisfied with human blood.

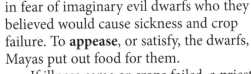

An altar near the Jaguar Temple at Tikal

A GAME OF LIFE AND DEATH

A ball game was played throughout the ancient Mayan civilization. Every Mayan city had at least one ball court—one city had seven. The I-shaped courts measured 100–150 feet long and 25–50 feet wide. The players' goal was to hit a small rubber ball through a vertical hoop or onto a marker on the side of the wall. However, the players were allowed to use only their padded wrists, elbows, and hips.

Only the nobles could play the ball game, but everyone in the city watched. Many nobles placed bets on the outcome, losing much property or many slaves when their wagers were wrong.

The ball game was more than just a sport like soccer or basketball played in America today. The Mayan game had serious religious meaning. Crowds cheered the winners as heroes as we do today. Most likely, though, the losers did not just hang their heads and return to the locker room. Some scholars believe that some members of the losing team may have been sacrificed to the gods in a ceremony after the game.

I-shaped ball court (below) and goal hoop (above)

In all their care to obey the priests and please the gods, the Mayas also feared death greatly. The only people sure of entering Mayan paradise included priests, warriors who had died in battle, and people who had been sacrificed by the priests. All others, no matter how well they had kept the rules, might—by the whim of some god—be condemned to the underworld.

When someone died, he was mourned for days. He was buried according to his social class. The common people were often buried under their houses, which were then abandoned by the others who lived there. The rich could afford tombs with heavy stone coverings that were elaborately engraved. Almost everyone, regardless of his class, had a piece of valuable jade placed in his mouth so that he would have it for money in the next life.

Kings were buried with great ceremony and wealth. One king, Pacal, was buried in a large room under a Mayan pyramid. Buried with him were six other people and a huge supply of jade jewelry and other treasures. This king had a jade mask over his face, perhaps to show his power in the afterlife.

Decline of the Mayan Civilization

Archaeologists have found a stele in the city of Tikal dated at 869. This appears to have been the last record of the Mayas in that location. The Mayas seem to have fled their major cities after that time. No one knows what happened. In many places the Mayas seem to have left suddenly. The belongings left behind suggest that the people meant to return, but they never did—at least not to rebuild. For the next six hundred years, they lived in other cities and parts of Mesoamerica, never regaining their former power.

Some archaeologists believe that the people moved away because of famine. Others think that war may have ended the great civilization. Still others think that the way of life in Mayan cities—full of rituals and religious superstitions—may have caused the people to rebel. Perhaps a combination of all these reasons ended the society. Forms of the Mayan civilization continued in smaller towns and in the cultures of other peoples.

Relief of Mayan nobleman

Making a Codex

The pages of a Mayan book were folded and attached to covers to form a codex. You will make your own codex to use as an organizer for this chapter.

1. Gather two cardboard squares, wrapping paper, scissors, glue, and your Activity Manual.

2. Decorate the pieces of cardboard with wrapping paper or your own design. These are the covers for your book.

3. Cut the codex organizer strips from the Activity Manual. Connect the strips as indicated on the tabs. Fold the long strip accordion style.

4. Glue a cover to each end of the long strip as indicated on the end tabs.

5. Fold the book and use a rubber band or a piece of string to hold it closed.

309

FOCUS

1. What was unique about the city of Tenochtitlán?

2. Why were the Aztecs feared by surrounding neighbors?

Aztecs

Many historians believe that some ancient Americans in the north migrated southward to settle in the area known today as Mexico. By the 1400s people in that region had developed into an advanced society known as the **Aztec civilization**. In spite of some shocking and primitive customs, they developed a complete language along with some amazing technology.

The Aztecs held to a superstitious legend that claimed their sun god would lead them to a place where they were to settle and build a city. The place that the Aztecs eventually settled in was a swampy lake. Rather than be discouraged by this location, the Aztecs accepted this as the ideal location for them. On **Lake Texcoco** (tay SKOH кон), the Aztecs built one of the largest cities in the world at that time.

The Aztecs began building their unusual city on two small islands on the lake. The city was called **Tenochtitlán**. Part of modern Mexico City has been built on the land where Tenochtitlán had been. (This Aztec city of Tenochtitlán is different from the Olmec city of San Lorenzo Tenochtitlán.)

The resourceful Aztecs created additional garden islands called **chinampas** (chin AHM puhz). The gardens were made by bunching twigs, limbs, and sticks together and piling silt on top. Plants grew easily in the fertile soil. The Aztecs made strategic **causeways** (land bridges) to connect the islands to the mainland. Specially designed canals separated fresh water from salt water. Canoes could easily travel in these canals.

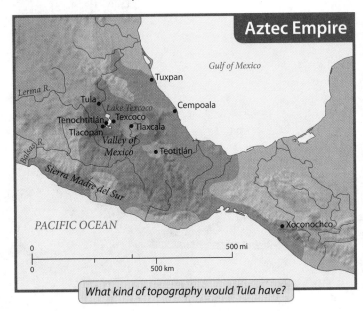

Aztec Empire

What kind of topography would Tula have?

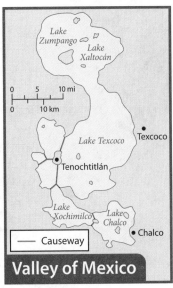

Valley of Mexico

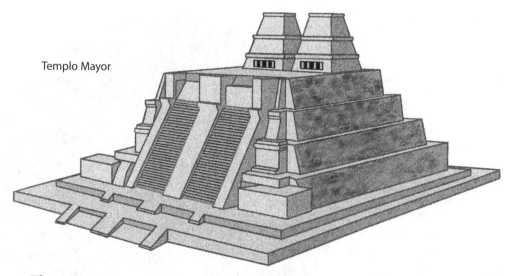

Templo Mayor

The Aztecs were a united people. As their population grew, they formed alliances with neighboring city-states. As their military power grew, they began to conquer peoples in the surrounding areas.

As early as the beginning of the 1500s, Tenochtitlán dominated all other cities. Its power and splendor were well-known and feared. At one point, this city had a population of about two hundred thousand people as well as an abundance of religious buildings and activities. The **Templo Mayor**, or Great Pyramid, was the primary location for religious ceremonies and rituals.

Aztec Religion

The religion of the Aztecs ruled every aspect of their lives. While the Olmecs and the Mayas also followed religious beliefs,

the Aztecs raised their duty to the gods to a new level. The Aztecs believed their sun god had a tremendous appetite for blood and human hearts. He had to be constantly appeased or the very existence of their world was at risk.

HOW DO THEY KNOW?

The question is often asked, What happens to people who never hear the gospel message from a believer? Ancient Mesoamericans were thousands of miles from any other civilization. Did they have an excuse for following false beliefs? How could they have heard the truth about God and Jesus? The Bible explains how these people had an opportunity to accept the truth. Romans 2:15 states that the "law [is] written in their hearts." This statement means that their conscience lets them know when they violate God's law.

God has provided all peoples with enough revelation for them to know that He exists and to know how to worship Him. However, every culture in the world has chosen instead to reject God's truth. The gospel message is the power of God to bring people salvation (Rom. 1:19–23). Missionaries seek to take the gospel to every culture on earth (Rom. 10:14–17).

311

The Aztecs are believed to have sacrificed thousands of people each year. In war, their objective was not to gain territory or kill the enemy but to capture prisoners to sacrifice to their gods.

When **Hernando Cortés**, the Spanish **conquistador** (kahn KEE stuh DOOR), or conqueror, arrived with his army in Tenochtitlán in 1519, they were horrified when they saw the vast scale of ritual sacrifices made by the Aztecs. Even today historians are appalled at such slaughter in the name of religious sacrifice. It is a demonstration of how greatly the sinful heart of man can distort the truth into unimaginable wickedness.

Aztec Sun Stone

Hernando Cortés with Montezuma II

MESOAMERICAN BELIEFS

Mesoamericans believed in many gods. They believed that the sun god was superior. The Bible teaches that there is only one true God and no other gods (1 Cor. 8:6).

Mesoamericans chose to worship nature rather than the Creator of nature. The Bible teaches that man is created in God's image. God commands mankind to have dominion over nature and to be a good steward of it (Gen. 1:28).

Mesoamericans believed a blood sacrifice was necessary and sacrificed humans. It is out of the wicked heart that man creates wicked imaginations (Prov. 6:18). The Old Testament taught animal sacrifice, and the New Testament teaches the only sacrifice necessary is the Son of God (Heb. 7:26–28).

A Warrior's Pride

Aztec warriors began training at an early age. By going to war, they believed they were showing service and respect to the gods. Men were expected to prove their worth on the battlefield. As warriors, they were to be brave and noble.

The bravest Aztec warriors achieved the rank of jaguar warrior or eagle warrior. They were the most feared of all the Aztec warriors.

Most Aztec weapons were designed to stun and capture enemies rather than to kill them. This way the captured enemy could walk and not have to be carried to the temple for sacrifice.

Eagle and jaguar warriors on an ancient codex

Social Classes

The social classes of the Aztecs were similar to other Mesoamerican civilizations. The nobility lived in brick or stone homes while the common people lived in homes made of interwoven twigs and mud.

Tenochtitlán and the Aztec Empire had the same ruler. All other governing officials were expected to pay tribute to this supreme ruler. As in the Mayan society, he was considered to be a descendant of the gods. Also in keeping with the Mayan society, Aztec nobility, warriors, and priests were responsible for supporting the ruler.

The common men, which included artisans, soldiers, laborers, farmers, and merchants, were expected to support the nobles. The women worked hard at home, where they were expected to take care of their families. A commoner had little opportunity to change his life and leave his social class.

FOCUS

1. How did a written language help the Aztecs?

2. Why were the Aztecs defeated by the Spanish conquistadors?

Economy

The Aztec culture was built on hard work from people of all ages and both genders. Citizens were expected to help in the building of **dikes** (walls that prevent flooding), temples, roads, and aqueducts.

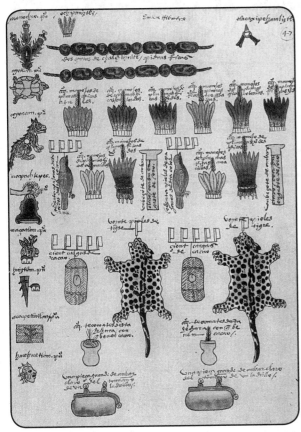

This page of an Aztec codex shows the kinds of tribute that towns were required to pay.

The Aztec economy was very specialized and highly structured. A variety of goods were produced within the Aztec empire. These included tools, pottery, figurines, jewelry, cloth, and baskets. The goods were either made specifically for the ruler or sold in the local markets. As in other Mesoamerican civilizations, farming was an important business for the Aztec people.

Trade took place along the lowlands of the Gulf Coast. The Aztecs sought goods such as gold ornaments, salt, and garments made of fine cloth. In return the Aztecs offered coveted goods, such as jaguar skins, tropical-bird feathers, rubber, cotton, and cacao beans.

Language and Technology

The development of a written language played an important role in the Aztec civilization. Like the Mayas, the Aztecs used hieroglyphs to represent their spoken language. This written language was used while conducting business and trade. They also recorded their customs and beliefs to be passed on to future generations. This unified their culture for many years.

The Aztecs developed their technology based on the knowledge they gained from contact with the Mayas. The Aztec number system and knowledge of the solar system were very advanced compared to other cultures of the time. They developed many forms of helpful medicines, such as ointments, tonics, and salves. The Aztecs did not have access to iron or bronze but still made excellent practical tools and weapons. These included drills made of reed or bone.

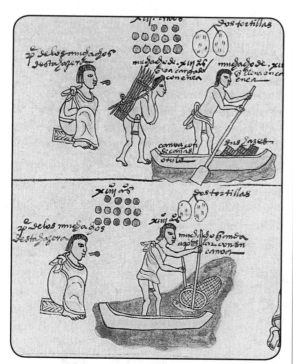

This page from the Mendoza Codex shows the use of canoes.

The Aztecs did not have horses, mules, or other beasts of burden for transporting trade goods. They made dugout canoes for travel through the many canals, lakes, and waterways found in the Valley of Mexico.

Spanish Invasion

Montezuma (mon tuh ZOO mah) was the emperor of the Aztecs when the Spanish conquistadors began landing on the shores of Mesoamerica in 1519. In less than a year, Hernando Cortés and the Spanish conquistadors entered Tenochtitlán. Montezuma was not certain of how to respond to the Spanish force. Some historians believe Montezuma thought Cortés might be the Aztec god-king who was supposed to return that year from the east. The white skin of Cortés fit the description the Aztecs had of the god-king.

Montezuma eventually welcomed Cortés with elaborate gold and silver gifts. Cortés, on the other hand, seized control of the city and took Montezuma hostage. The Aztec people revolted under Spanish control. Cortés brought Montezuma before the people, expecting them to back down. Instead the Aztec ruler was struck by a stone while addressing his subjects. He died three days later. The Spanish gained control of all Tenochtitlán and many surrounding territories.

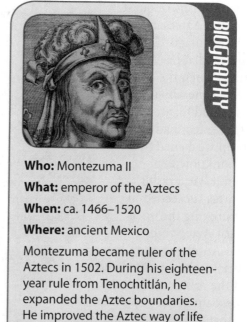

BIOGRAPHY

Who: Montezuma II

What: emperor of the Aztecs

When: ca. 1466–1520

Where: ancient Mexico

Montezuma became ruler of the Aztecs in 1502. During his eighteen-year rule from Tenochtitlán, he expanded the Aztec boundaries. He improved the Aztec way of life by building many temples, canals, and hospitals. His people did not like paying the taxes he imposed on them. After his death the empire fell to the Spanish.

The Fate of the Mesoamericans

Why was the well-trained Aztec army defeated so quickly? There were several possible reasons for the sudden downfall. Some of their superstitions led the Aztecs to believe that the enemy was a tool of the gods. Under these circumstances, making peace without fighting may have seemed the best strategy. Even though the Aztecs by far outnumbered the enemy, fear of the gods stripped them of their power. Also, the timing of the Spanish conquest put the Aztecs at a disadvantage. Cortés attacked at harvest time, when the Aztecs were generally not prepared for war. The Aztecs had also been weakened by an unknown epidemic. As a result, Cortés succeeded in destroying the once-great Aztec empire.

Another reason historians give for the defeat of the Aztecs and other Mesoamerican populations is that these people simply lost the will to survive. Not only were the Mesoamerican peoples defeated in battle with Europeans, but they also lost their culture. As a result of the European conquests, the Mesoamericans could no longer practice many of their traditions or any form of native religion.

Like every other civilization you have studied in this book, the Mesoamericans accomplished many great things, but they rejected the true God. God will only strive with man and his pride for a time. There will come a day when all nations will bow before Him in humility (Rom. 14:11).

This map of the Atlantic Ocean was drawn in 1513 and shows the coast of Africa on the right and the Americas on the left.

Chapter 12

Ancient Africa

FOCUS

1. What is one way that geographers study the continent of Africa?

2. What land features make Africa a land of great variety?

Voices called from the rainforest—not human voices, but voices of birds and monkeys and insects. The sun blazed down on Namasha, warming her face and arms. It turned the distant river to gold. She glanced around her at the faces of the other village children. Their eyes were fixed on the storyteller.

"This is a tale of how the mountains came to be," said the old man seated before them. "Long, long ago, before any of us were born, the earth was smooth and flat like this river stone I hold in my hand. But one day, the earth decided to have a conversation with the sky. She rose up high, higher than birds fly, until she touched the sky. The earth and the sky told one another their secrets. When they finished talking, the earth said good-bye to the sky and started to return to her place. But on the way down, she became very tired. Parts of her became so tired that they stopped right where they were before reaching the ground. Now we call these parts mountains and hills."

Namasha looked at the other children and smiled. She loved the old man's stories. Stories about mountains and rivers and lakes and animals. Stories about the ancient people who had lived here before. The old stories were fascinating, but sometimes Namasha longed to hear new ones. She squinted beyond the old man toward the river. Namasha remembered the old Congolese proverb her father often quoted: "No matter how full the river, it still wants to grow."

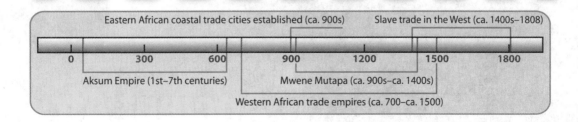

Eastern African coastal trade cities established (ca. 900s)   Slave trade in the West (ca. 1400s–1808)

| 0 | 300 | 600 | 900 | 1200 | 1500 | 1800 |

Aksum Empire (1st–7th centuries)   Mwene Mutapa (ca. 900s–ca. 1400s)

Western African trade empires (ca. 700–ca. 1500)

318

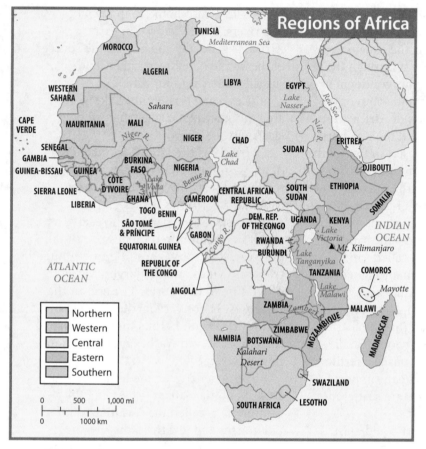

Regions of Africa

Map labels: TUNISIA, MOROCCO, ALGERIA, LIBYA, EGYPT, Mediterranean Sea, Lake Nasser, Red Sea, Nile R., Sahara, WESTERN SAHARA, CAPE VERDE, MAURITANIA, MALI, NIGER, CHAD, SUDAN, ERITREA, Niger R., SENEGAL, GAMBIA, GUINEA-BISSAU, GUINEA, BURKINA FASO, NIGERIA, Lake Chad, Benue R., DJIBOUTI, SIERRA LEONE, CÔTE D'IVOIRE, Lake Volta, GHANA, CAMEROON, CENTRAL AFRICAN REPUBLIC, SOUTH SUDAN, ETHIOPIA, SOMALIA, LIBERIA, TOGO, BENIN, SÃO TOMÉ & PRÍNCIPE, DEM. REP. OF THE CONGO, UGANDA, KENYA, INDIAN OCEAN, EQUATORIAL GUINEA, GABON, RWANDA, BURUNDI, Lake Victoria, Mt. Kilimanjaro, REPUBLIC OF THE CONGO, Congo R., Lake Tanganyika, TANZANIA, COMOROS, Mayotte, ATLANTIC OCEAN, ANGOLA, Lake Malawi, ZAMBIA, MALAWI, MOZAMBIQUE, MADAGASCAR, Zambezi R., ZIMBABWE, NAMIBIA, BOTSWANA, Kalahari Desert, SWAZILAND, SOUTH AFRICA, LESOTHO

Legend:
- Northern
- Western
- Central
- Eastern
- Southern

0   500   1,000 mi
0   1000 km

The Continent of Africa

Africa is a large continent. It has large lakes, grand mountain ranges, mighty rivers, vast deserts, and lush rainforests. In ancient times Africa was also a land of many thriving civilizations. Many of Africa's great empires rose and fell in isolation from the other empires you have read about. For hundreds of years, the people of Europe, Asia, and the Americas knew little about the interior of Africa. You have already read about the people of Egypt, Kush, and Carthage in earlier chapters. This chapter introduces several other civilizations that developed in ancient Africa.

Africa's Regions

There are different ways to organize a study of Africa's land and peoples. One of the easiest ways is to divide the continent into regions. Geographers often divide Africa into its northern, western, central, eastern, and southern regions.

Northern Africa includes the modern countries of Algeria, Egypt, Libya, Morocco, Sudan, South Sudan, Tunisia, and Western Sahara. Western Africa includes Niger and Nigeria and all the countries west of them. Central Africa extends from Chad in the north down to Angola in the south. It also includes the small islands of São Tomé and Príncipe. Eastern Africa includes more countries than any other region in Africa. It extends from Eritrea in the north to Mozambique in the south. It includes the large island of Madagascar with the smaller islands that surround it. Southern Africa includes the remaining countries of Namibia, Botswana, Swaziland, Lesotho, and South Africa.

Africa's Geography

Africa is both a dry and a wet land. If you were to walk along the equator, you would be walking right through the heart of Africa. It is the only continent to have **deserts** both north and south of the equator. The main deserts of Africa are the Sahara in the north and the Kalahari Desert and the Namib Desert in the south.

The Sahara is the largest desert in Africa. It covers most of the northern half of Africa. The Sahara is made up of vast seas of sand, rocky plains, and stony plateaus. Winds blow the sands and create ridges or hills called sand dunes. The dunes continually change in shape and size. Some dunes rise to over four hundred feet high. Most of the Sahara receives less than three inches of rainfall a year. However, people can live there if they live near an **oasis**, a fertile area with water. An oasis can support animals and crops. Oases are scattered throughout the desert.

Do you think a desert could exist on a peninsula surrounded by water? Somalia in eastern Africa is part of a peninsula known as the **Horn of Africa**. The land of Somalia is a kind of desert called a rain shadow desert. A **rain shadow desert** forms when the wind blows the water vapor high into nearby mountains without allowing rain to fall on the lowlands.

Africa is also home to many lakes and rivers. Lake Victoria, in eastern Africa, is generally considered the source of the White Nile River. Lake Chad supplies water for four different African countries. Lake Nasser and Lake Volta are both man-made lakes that supply electricity.

Africa has the largest tropical area of any continent. The tropics are just north and just south of the equator. Much of the tropics is made up of **rainforests**. Some parts of it receive as much as one hundred inches of rainfall per year. Rainforests are filled with huge trees and vines and the largest variety of wildlife in the world. The soil in the rainforest is not very fertile. Farmers cannot raise good crops there because the constant rain washes many nutrients out of the soil.

The area between the Kalahari Desert and the Sahara (excluding the rainforest) is called the **savanna**. With tall grasses and few trees, the savanna is where the people raise crops and cattle. Wild antelope, giraffes, zebras, elephants, leopards, and lions also live on the savanna.

Africa has many mountain ranges. Mount Kilimanjaro, in Tanzania, is over nineteen thousand feet high. This mountain and others, such as those in the Sahara, were formed by volcanic activity.

Africa

Location—Africa, the second largest continent, lies to the southwest of Asia. It includes the islands of Madagascar, Comoros, Réunion, Mauritius, Mayotte, and Seychelles in the Indian Ocean. Africa is divided almost in half by the equator.

Climate—Much of the land has a tropical climate, with warm temperatures during the day and cool temperatures at night. Other parts have a dry desert climate. Temperatures in the Sahara range from 50°F (10°C) in the winter to 100°F (38°C) in the summer. In northern Somalia, summer temperatures of 115°F (46°C) or higher are common.

Topography—Deserts cover about two-fifths of Africa's land. Africa also has mountain ranges, rivers, rainforests, large lakes, and savannas.

Natural Resources—Rich in mineral resources, Africa has deposits of gold, petroleum, oil, copper, diamonds, and natural gas.

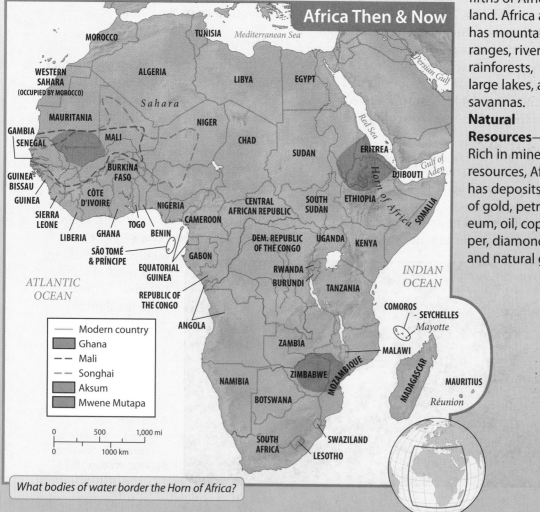

Africa Then & Now

Legend:
- Modern country
- Ghana
- Mali
- Songhai
- Aksum
- Mwene Mutapa

0   500   1,000 mi
0   1000 km

What bodies of water border the Horn of Africa?

321

FOCUS

1. What methods were used to track the migration routes of African peoples?

2. How do historians evaluate the truth of a story that has been passed down orally?

Keys to Africa's Past

We often learn about people and their history from what we read in books. We know that the Egyptians left written records on both stone and papyri. But most of the people of ancient Africa did not have a written language. How then can we know anything about them? There are many ways of learning about people other than by reading written records.

Linguistics

One way is to study the spread of languages. Long ago the **Bantu**, an early African people, left their homes on the Benue River and migrated into central and eventually eastern and southern Africa. This migration took place over hundreds of years. When the Bantu migrated, they took their language with them. After settling in a new area, they learned to speak with the people already living there. Both groups shared and borrowed bits of language. Slowly, each language changed.

The study of the structure and changes of languages is known as **linguistics**. By studying the words and grammar that people lent and borrowed, linguists can learn of people's migration routes. Linguists helped trace the migration route of the Bantu.

Botany

While linguists follow people through changes in their language, **botanists**, scientists who study plants, can trace the movements of people by their crops. Botanists can also make assumptions about why people moved or spread out and how their methods of food gathering and production changed.

When the Bantu farmers moved to new homes, they took seeds with them so that they could plant crops to feed their families. By tracking the spread of crops, botanists helped trace the Bantu migration routes.

An African farmer plowing fields with oxen
How does this farmer compare with the farmer pictured on page 4?

322

Bushman paintings found on caves in the Namib Desert in southern Africa *What kind of information do these paintings give an archaeologist?*

Archaeology

Another important source of information comes from archaeology. Discoveries of ancient city ruins show exactly where people lived and sometimes reveal their manner of life. Burial sites are also an important means of learning about the past. Jewelry, pottery, and other artifacts at these sites are often clues to social structure and religious beliefs.

In some areas of Africa, archaeologists have found caves with paintings on the walls. From these drawings they know about the weapons that the early African people used for fighting and hunting, as well as what animals they hunted. Some of the paintings are accompanied by symbols that may have been part of a written language. Unfortunately, no one has discovered what these symbols mean.

Oral History

Do you have an older friend or relative who tells stories about the times when he or she was a child? Such stories are called **oral history** because they are spoken and not written.

Most African villages had at least one official storyteller, or **griot** (gree OH). It was his job to learn the village's history. He did not write it down; instead he kept it in his mind and passed it on by word of mouth. The griot taught the children and reminded the adults of their past. He described the journeys of their ancestors when they looked for new farmland. He told of the deeds of past leaders and heroes, and he reminded the villagers about their ancient traditions.

The village griot told his stories at every opportunity. He wanted to keep the village's history from being forgotten. Modern historians know that oral history is important in learning about the past. They often try to evaluate the truth of a story by comparing it with stories from different areas. If many different parts of Africa have stories of the same past event, modern historians can assume that the event really happened.

Discovering How

Preserving History Orally

1. Think of an important event in the history of your family, such as an adventure or a meaningful accomplishment. It should be something you could tell about in less than three minutes.

2. In your group, tell your own story and listen to the stories of the other group members. Try to remember the details of each story.

3. Now find a student from another group. Tell him your own story and the stories of your group members. Listen as he tells you his story and the other stories from his group. Do you think you could remember all these stories to tell someone else?

FOCUS

1. What people in northern Africa was known for its use of camels?

2. Which peoples settled in southern Africa?

Africa's People

Ancient Africa was home to many different peoples. Historians divide Africa's early peoples into groups by common language. These language groups migrated, spread out, and eventually settled in various regions. Distinct tribes formed, and many different dialects came into use.

Northern Africa

More than in other African regions, the people of northern Africa were influenced by the rest of the world. The presence of gold, copper, and ivory drew traders from Europe and Asia. Some cities on Africa's northern coast, such as Carthage, were established for trading by outside civilizations. As part of the Roman Empire after the Punic Wars, the northern coast was strongly influenced by western culture. Christianity entered northern Africa in the first century.

In the north there also lived the nomads of the Sahara. Most of these nomads belonged to a language group called the Berbers. The greatest of these nomadic people were the **Tuareg** (TWAH reg).

The Tuareg dressed in loose, flowing garments and rode swift camels. The men wrapped their heads with a long piece of dark blue cotton that acted as both a turban and a veil. It hid the man's face except for a narrow slit for his eyes. Sometimes it stained his skin, earning the Tuareg the name "blue people."

The Tuareg were farmers and herders. They were also traders. They knew the best ways for caravans to cross the desert and often acted as guides. But they were also feared for their skill as warriors. Bands of Tuareg frequently attacked caravans. They even attacked towns built on the edges of the desert.

A Tuareg woman with her baby

Tuareg traveling through the desert
Why would this man be part of the "blue people"?

The camel was one of the most valuable possessions of the Tuareg. Camels had been introduced into northern Africa shortly after the birth of Christ. Though ill-tempered and stubborn, the camel was a necessity because of its ability to live and work in the desert. Horses and cattle often could not survive the long distances between oases. Camels could travel much longer without water. With camels, the Tuareg could move freely across the Sahara. They also used camel hides to make tents, and from camel milk they made butter and cheese.

Tuareg people still live in the countries of Algeria, Mali, Niger, Mauritania, Burkina Faso, and Libya.

Central Africa

In the grassy savanna and the forests south of the Sahara lived many prosperous peoples. Some farmed the fertile soil. Others built cities and sent their goods across the Sahara to the Mediterranean coast. These peoples formed great empires to protect themselves and their trade routes. Some of these empires are covered later in this chapter. It was also to this area of Africa that European missionaries first traveled with the gospel.

The Nilotic (ny LOT ik) language group originally lived in the area that is the modern country of South Sudan. Then they migrated to the shores of Lake Victoria and into what are now the countries of Kenya, Tanzania, and Uganda. Perhaps the best known of these peoples are the tall and slender **Maasai** (MAH sy). The Maasai were herders. They measured their wealth and social standing by the number of cattle they owned.

A young Maasai herder
How do your chores compare with his?

Even today Maasai brides wear these bright-colored bead necklaces at their weddings.

Young Maasai warriors had to go through certain ceremonies to prove their manhood. They would paint their skin red and go live in the wilderness to learn about survival. The young men were required to build a village and live in it together for a period of time. They also had to kill a lion using only a spear.

Maasai men could buy a bride in exchange for cattle. Many had more than one wife. Maasai women learned to care for their homes, husbands, and children. The women built the family huts from tree branches and grass. They milked cows and fetched water.

The Maasai still live in Kenya today. Their government has ended the practice of killing lions, but many of their traditions remain the same.

Southern Africa

Much of the rest of Africa was settled by the Bantu, who migrated from the Benue River. They wandered east and south and finally settled in the Congo basin. For perhaps two hundred years or more, the Bantu prospered and their numbers grew. Finally, the land could support no more villages. Some of the Bantu packed their belongings and moved southeast once more, all the way to the southern tip of Africa.

The Bantu were not the only ones living in the area south of the Sahara. **Pygmies**, a people of very small stature, lived deep in the rainforest of the Congo basin. The **Bushmen** and Khoikhoi lived there too. When these two groups lost their land to the Bantu, they moved to the south and the west, where they formed small family groups of hunters and gatherers.

Both the Bushmen and the Khoikhoi spoke unusual click languages. Think of all the noises that can be made with the tongue, teeth, and lips that are not words at all. In a click language, these sounds have meaning. Try talking to a friend and adding a few clicks and pops as you speak. It is not easy!

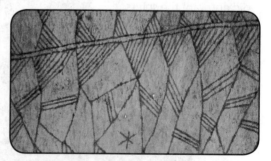

Today the Pygmy people make beautiful cloth from hand-beaten tree bark and paint it with various designs.

In the middle of the 1600s, large groups of Europeans came to live in Africa. The Dutch found a beautiful place on the southern tip of Africa. They set up a station there to provide water and food for ships that were on their way to India.

The Dutch also thought the land would be a good place to live. People from England joined them about 150 years later. Descendants of both the Dutch and the English have lived in South Africa ever since.

TRADITIONAL AFRICAN BELIEFS

Until Christianity and Islam were introduced to Africa from other nations, Africa's people had certain traditional beliefs that varied slightly from tribe to tribe. Their religious beliefs influenced every area of their lives. Many Africans still hold these beliefs today.

Most Africans had a concept of a god as a supreme being, but they relied on their tradition to explain what this god was like. They believed he could be reached through sacrifices and offerings. But only Christ's sacrifice is sufficient to reconcile people to God. God's Word tells us that people come into a personal relationship with God only through repenting of their sins and trusting Jesus Christ (Eph. 2:8–9).

The belief in spirits who control natural forces for good or for evil was very common. Africans worshiped these spirits and tried to make them happy. They did not want the spirits to use their powers to harm them and their surround-

ings. Many African religions taught that spirits lived in animals or things in nature such as trees and rivers. This belief is known as *animism*. The Bible teaches that there is only one God Who controls all the forces of nature for His own glory. He is the only One Who deserves to be worshiped (Rev. 4:11).

Africans often relied on a person thought to have magical powers, such as a medicine man or a rainmaker, to connect them with the supernatural world. The Bible teaches that God may be approached only through Jesus Christ (1 Tim. 2:5).

Africans believed that the spirits of their departed relatives visited them and influenced their lives. The people gave offerings to these spirits and tried to stay in favor with them. However, the Bible warns people not to try to contact the dead. It also implies that once people go to heaven or hell, they do not return to earth (Lev. 20:27; Luke 16:26–31).

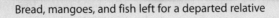

Bread, mangoes, and fish left for a departed relative

African Empires

Aksum

On the eastern side of Africa lies the modern nation of Ethiopia. Long before the birth of Christ, farmers settled in this area and eventually built the empire of **Aksum**. Aksum was a wealthy and powerful kingdom. It supplied precious stones, incense, gold, ivory, ebony, myrrh, and elephants to the Egyptian pharaohs, and it traded with Arabs and Europeans as well. It is the kingdom that eventually conquered Kush in AD 330.

Archaeologists who have studied the ruins of Aksum say that walled castles dominated the capital city. Stone inscriptions found among the ruins indicate that Aksum's educated people spoke Greek. Linguists believe that the Aksumites visited the Greek city of Byzantium often, perhaps to trade. Eventually Aksum developed a written language of its own called Ge'ez (gee EZ).

A system of social classes developed in Aksum. The king and the nobles were the highest class, followed by merchants, then artisans and tradesmen, and then servants.

King **Ezana** ruled the empire of Aksum in the AD 300s. He had great wealth and built many beautiful palaces, temples, and monuments. At least one of his steles, or upright stone pillars, has survived until today. Under Ezana, Aksum became the strongest empire in eastern Africa, conquering neighboring kingdoms.

Byzantine traders may have introduced Christianity into eastern Africa in the 300s. After Ezana conquered the people of Kush, he is recorded as giving thanks to the Lord for the victory. A Syrian Christian named Frumentius had become a servant to King Ezana. It was probably through his influence that Ezana became a Christian. With Ezana's conversion, Christianity became Aksum's official religion.

BIOGRAPHY

Who: Ezana

What: king of Aksum

When: ruled AD 300s

Where: eastern Africa

Ezana became a Christian, likely through the influence of Frumentius, and made Christianity the official religion of Aksum. He was the first to issue coins with a Christian symbol, the cross, on them.

King Ezana's stele in Aksum is seventy feet tall.

The Queen of Sheba and King Solomon

First Kings 10 tells how a wealthy queen from the kingdom of Sheba visited King Solomon during his reign over Israel. Many scholars believe that the kingdom of Sheba was located in what is now Ethiopia. The descriptions of the gifts the queen brought to Solomon indicate that Sheba was a wealthy kingdom.

The queen of Sheba had heard of Solomon's great wealth and about the wisdom he had gained from the Lord. She wanted to see Solomon's wealth and hear his wisdom firsthand. She devised difficult questions to ask Solomon, and he answered all of them, revealing his vast knowledge. After he showed her his treasures and the richness of his lifestyle, she admitted that the reports she had heard were true. She told Solomon that his riches and wisdom were even greater than the stories claimed.

Solomon gave the queen gifts in return for those she had brought him. Anything that she requested he gave her. Many believe that the queen of Sheba came to personal faith in Israel's God and brought the religion of Judaism back to her own people.

In the New Testament, Jesus used the queen of Sheba as an example of the eager faith with which the Jews should have welcomed Him, their Messiah. The queen had come from "the uttermost parts of the earth" to hear Solomon's wisdom and had seen the glory of Solomon's God. Someone much greater than Solomon, Christ Himself, had brought the glory of God to the Jewish people, but they did not receive Him in faith (Matt. 12:42).

After the fall of Rome, Aksum's trade dwindled. Then in the 600s, Muslim armies conquered Egypt and cut Aksum off from its trade with the Mediterranean world. The power of the kings declined as the kingdom grew poorer. Yet even after the kingdom disappeared, the civilization continued. It formed the basis for the modern state of Ethiopia.

Trade in Western Africa

What was the main center of trade in Ghana?

In the grassy savanna of central and western Africa, three great empires flourished: Ghana, Mali, and Songhai. You can see the outlines of these empires on the map on page 321.

Ghana

The ancient empire of **Ghana** was located along the Niger River. It was not in present-day Ghana but in what is now Mauritania. No one knows who founded ancient Ghana, but the kingdom probably appeared about three hundred years after the birth of Christ. By 700 Ghana was an empire. It was governed by African kings; in fact, the word *ghana* was the title these rulers used for themselves.

Many Arabian merchants traveled back and forth to Ghana, and some lived there. They introduced the use of camels on trade routes across the Sahara. Much of what historians know about this empire is from the merchants' accounts.

Ghana became a wealthy center of trade. Its location was ideal. Ghana was situated at the edge of the Sahara and was near the only source of water for miles around. To the south of Ghana, there was a land that had gold mines. Gold was traded for goods from merchants from all over the world. The main item traded for was salt. Ghana controlled all the trade of salt and gold.

Trade for gold and salt was done in a unique way—the traders never saw one another. This system was called silent trade. Merchants placed their slabs of rock salt in a special place and left. Then the traders brought their gold and left it beside the salt before retreating. The merchants then returned to take the gold. If either side was not satisfied with the amount that had been left, the deal was not complete. The merchants and the traders continued to come and go, adjusting their amounts until the deal was acceptable to both. This method of trade kept both sides happy and the location of the gold mines a secret.

A mosque in modern Mauritania (former Ghana)

named al-Bakri wrote a work called the *Book of Highways and Kingdoms.* In it he described the king of Ghana's court as reported to him by traders. Gold was lavishly displayed everywhere. The precious metal decorated everything from clothing to swords and shields. Even dog collars and saddles had gold in them.

Arabian merchants brought the religion of Islam to Ghana. The king of Ghana continued to practice traditional beliefs, but many of the traders converted to Islam. As the ancient capital city of Koumbi Saleh grew, a separate Islamic community developed there.

Ghana had a huge army that helped protect its trade. But eventually wars with the Arabs began to interrupt trade and weaken Ghana's kings. The empire's military power declined. When the army of Mali attacked, Ghana could not fight back. The empire of Ghana ended in the thirteenth century.

The merchants of Ghana brought the gold back to the city and traded it with Arabian and European merchants who traveled across the Sahara. Along with gold, the Ghanians traded cola nuts, honey, textiles, and slaves. One of the main necessities exchanged for gold was salt. There were no sources for salt in Ghana, so salt from the Saharan mines was very valuable. The Ghanians also traded for copper, dried fruit, cowry shells, horses, cloth, swords, and books from North Africa and Europe.

The king of Ghana charged taxes on all trade with his kingdom. The king was fabulously rich. An Arabian geographer

Gold

Cloth

What item did Ghana not have any source for?

Salt

Cowry shells

Making Tie-Dyed African Cloth

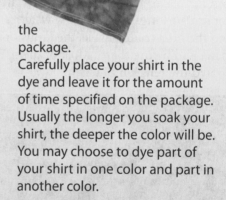

One of the items Africans traded was cloth. Many tribes had their own special styles of cloth. The designs and colors in the fabric had special meaning for them. The Tuareg dyed their cloth in indigo to produce a dark blue color. The Ashanti people of Ghana were known for the intricate designs they wove into their fabrics using looms and brightly colored threads. Some African tribes used tie-dyeing to create designs in their cloth.

1. You will need a white prewashed cotton T-shirt. Label it with your name or initials in permanent ink on the tag. You will also need rubber or latex gloves, rubber bands, prepared dye, and buckets of cool water. Plan to work outside. Cover your work area with plastic to avoid staining it with dye.

2. Fold or twist your shirt and fasten the folds in place with rubber bands. The way you fold and tie your shirt will determine the look of your design. Any part of the fabric that is not "tied" with the rubber bands will be colored when you dip your shirt in the dye.

3. Your teacher will prepare the dye according to the instructions on the package. Carefully place your shirt in the dye and leave it for the amount of time specified on the package. Usually the longer you soak your shirt, the deeper the color will be. You may choose to dye part of your shirt in one color and part in another color.

4. When you have finished soaking the shirt in dye, rinse it in cool water until the water runs clear. This part of the process sets the color.

5. Remove the rubber bands and hang your shirt to dry.

FOCUS

1. Who were the two greatest rulers of Mali?

2. Under whose leadership did Songhai become a great empire?

Mali

The empire of **Mali** included all of Ghana and much more land as well. In the 1200s Mali had a strong ruler named **Sundiata** (suhn JAHT ah). After taking the throne of Mali, Sundiata and his army conquered Ghana. In just a few years, Sundiata gained control of the gold and salt trade and built his capital on the main trade route across the Sahara. Legends grew that were based on Sundiata's life. He became the hero of an epic that was popular with West Africans.

Sundiata and his successors were called by the title mansa. *Mansa* is the word for "ruler" in the language of Mali's people. The kings of Mali grew wealthy from the gold trade, just as the kings of Ghana had before them. Most of them adopted the religion of Islam.

Materials used in an Islamic school

Ibn Battuta, a traveler from Tangier, visited Mali in the 1300s. He described the people as loving justice and honesty.

> They are seldom unjust, and have a greater abhorrence of injustice than any other people. Their sultan shows no mercy to anyone who is guilty of the least act of it. There is complete security in their country. Neither traveller nor inhabitant in it has anything to fear from robbers or men of violence. (Trans. and ed. H. A. R. Gibb, *Travels in Asia and Africa, 1325–1354* [London: Broadway House, 1929])

Although the people of Mali did many good deeds, they did not follow Christ. Islam and traditional beliefs dominated the kingdom.

BIOGRAPHY

Who: Sundiata

What: king of Mali

When: ruled AD 1200s

Where: western Africa

Sundiata was the first mansa of Mali. The famous *Epic of Sundiata,* a legend handed down through oral history, tells about his life. He became known as the Lion King. The story credits him with overcoming a disability and miraculously beginning to walk after seven years of paralysis.

Mansa Musa

The most famous of all the Malian kings was **Mansa Musa**. Musa ruled from AD 1312 to 1337. He was famous for his immense wealth and his devotion to Islam.

In 1324 Mansa Musa made a pilgrimage to Mecca, as faithful Muslims are required to do. People who witnessed his procession wrote descriptions of the scene. Hundreds of slaves marched along with him, many of them carrying golden staffs. Camels loaded down with gold also traveled in the grand parade. The stories claim that he carried more than a ton of gold.

In spite of his love of pomp and extravagance, Mansa Musa was very generous. During his pilgrimage, he gave away so much gold that the price of gold went down in that region for the next several years. Upon his return to Mali, he used his wealth to build many mosques, schools, and even a university in the city of Timbuktu. The university became a great center of Islamic learning.

After Mansa Musa's death, there were no more strong kings in Mali. Men fought over who had the right to the throne, and the great empire slowly weakened. The fighting inside the empire encouraged enemies on the outside to attack. Parts of the empire gradually broke away. After four hundred years, Mali was once again a small village on the banks of the Niger River.

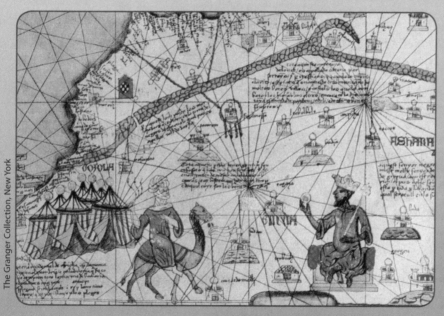

The Granger Collection, New York

A 1375 map of Africa showing Mansa Musa with a gold nugget and a scepter at his capital of Timbuktu
Why would Mansa Musa be drawn with a gold nugget in his hand?

Songhai

Songhai (SONG HY) was an important town in the empire of Mali. Like Mali, it depended on trade and sent merchants to other parts of Africa, Europe, and Asia.

In the 1400s, under the leadership of a ruler named **Sunni Ali**, Songhai won its independence from Mali. Sunni Ali conquered the cities around him to establish the large empire called **Songhai**.

Sunni Ali was a man of war, and he was never defeated. Some people believed that he was a magician who could change himself, his horses, and his soldiers into other creatures or even make them invisible. Sunni Ali fought Mali for twenty-eight years. Eventually he controlled all the trade routes and the best farmland. Sunni Ali built a fleet of canoes to patrol the Niger River. He also built several capital cities to rule his empire better. The ancient city of **Timbuktu** became Songhai's center of Islamic faith and learning.

After Sunni Ali's death, another ruler, Askia Muhammad, took control. He fought more wars and conquered even more territory. Songhai became larger than either Ghana or Mali had been. It looked as though no one would ever be able to defeat Songhai.

The empire of Songhai continued for more than a hundred years. Finally Morocco, one of its neighbors to the north, attacked. The Moroccan army had muskets, and its soldiers were better trained than Songhai's. The army of Songhai was defeated, and its government was destroyed.

Other enemies attacked Songhai, and soon the empire disappeared. In its place appeared many smaller kingdoms that frequently fought each other over land and trade.

These merchants are conducting trade in different goods in front of a famous mud-brick mosque. It was the largest and most elaborate structure of its kind. *What religion would have been practiced in this mosque?*

Making Economic Predictions

Most of the empires in ancient Africa rose to power because of the wealth they gained through trade. Each of these empires had a healthy economy. A country's economy is the way that country handles its money and products.

An economy is based on a country's production of goods, its selling of goods, and its buying of goods. Most economies depend on the *law of supply and demand*.

People who buy products are called consumers. What and how much consumers are willing to buy at a given price is called *demand*. In ancient African economies, Arabian and European traders were consumers of gold and ivory. They wanted to buy these items from Africans.

The items available for consumers to purchase are the *supply*. The Africans tried to produce only as much gold, ivory, and other items as the traders and the Africans themselves wanted. If there was a greater supply of gold or ivory than people wanted, the prices would go down.

When Mansa Musa gave away gold on his journey to Mecca, he created a change in the economy. The demand for gold decreased because people had received the gold they wanted for free. This caused the price of gold to go down.

Law of Supply and Demand			
	Supply goes up.	Supply goes down.	Supply stays the same.
Demand goes up.	Prices do not change.	Prices rise.	Prices rise.
Demand goes down.	Prices fall.	Prices do not change.	Prices fall.
Demand stays the same.	Prices fall.	Prices rise.	Prices do not change.

Pretend you are a citizen of an imaginary African country called Tanzimar. You are located near some gold mines, and you also have elephant herds in the surrounding area. Predict what will happen to your economy in each of the following situations.

1. A band of Tuareg brings news that new gold mines have been discovered farther north. Merchants traveling across the Sahara have been stopping to trade there rather than coming south to your country.

2. Merchants from Arabia inform you that more and more people in the Byzantine Empire need ivory. Ivory is in great demand there for carvings, furniture, and mosaics to be used in churches.

3. Elephant hunters return from an expedition. They report that a drought in the savanna has caused most of the elephant population to migrate hundreds of miles to the south to look for food and water. Even if hunters from your country could find these elephants, transporting their tusks back to your area would take more time and expense than ever before.

4. Your army fought with a growing country to the west and conquered its people. Your country now owns its gold mines in addition to your own.

1. What was a zimbabwe?

2. What did the coastal cities in eastern Africa have in common?

FOCUS

Mwene Mutapa

Far to the south of ancient Ghana, Mali, and Songhai is the land that is present-day Zimbabwe. Today many ruins of stone walls and buildings lie there. These are the ruins of the Mwene Mutapa kingdom.

The **Mwene Mutapa** were the first settlers in ancient Zimbabwe. They were the ancestors of a people that historians call the Shona. Some Shona still live in Zimbabwe today. The ancient Shona settled near the Zambezi River to have more room to live and plant crops. They organized themselves into **clans** and built big stone houses that they called **zimbabwes**.

One city was known as **Great Zimbabwe**. Historians believe this city could have been home to as many as twenty thousand people. All the buildings were built of stone without any mortar. Stone slabs were tightly stacked on top of one another to create a smooth surface. In some places, the remaining walls are more than fifteen feet wide and up to thirty-two feet tall.

In the city was a large zimbabwe that historians believe may have been the king's palace. They call it the Great Enclosure. A huge outer wall surrounds the Great Enclosure. This wall is over eight hundred feet long.

The ancient Shona were farmers and raised cattle. The Shona found gold along the rivers and streams and traded it for textiles, glass beads, and porcelain. Why the Shona moved away during the 1400s remains a mystery. The empire may have grown too big for the land to support them or the center of trade may have moved farther north.

The Great Enclosure, part of the Great Zimbabwe ruins

Eastern Africa's Coastal Cities

The Shona traded their gold on the eastern coast of Africa in cities built especially for trade. By the 900s these cities were controlled by Arabian and Persian merchants who traded with far-away ports in Asia and India. Mogadishu (мон guh DEE shoo) was the northern-most city, and Sofala (soh FAHL uh) was the southernmost city.

These coastal cities were not part of any empire. They were independent. However, they still had certain things in common. Almost all the cities were Muslim. They also used the same language when conducting trade. This language was Swahili. Swahili includes many words from Arabic. In fact, the name Swahili comes from the Arabic word that means "coast." This language is still spoken in parts of eastern Africa today.

As the cities grew, more items became available for trade. In addition to gold, other popular products included ivory, rhinoceros horns, tortoise shells, and animal skins. A Chinese admiral, Cheng Ho, visited eastern Africa's coastal cities. He reportedly brought back live exotic animals to China, such as giraffes, ostriches, and zebras.

Trading was not the only occupation along Africa's eastern coast. Fishermen, farmers, masons, and builders also lived there. Because so many traders needed boats, boat building was a profitable business. In some of the cities, masons made a living by building houses out of coral. Coral could easily be found in reefs all along the coast. When it was brought out of the ocean and exposed to air, it hardened into a sturdy building material. Only the wealthy merchant families could afford to have coral houses.

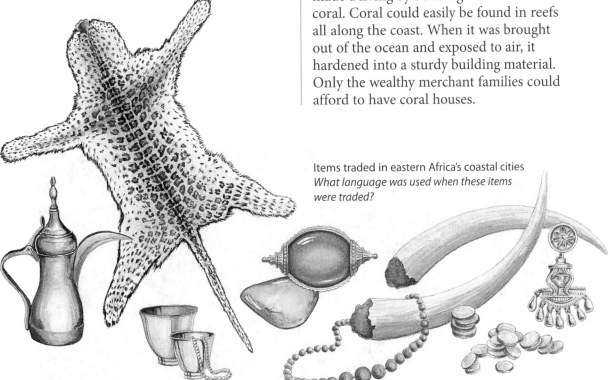

Items traded in eastern Africa's coastal cities
What language was used when these items were traded?

340

The Cape Coast Castle in Ghana was built for the trade of timber and gold and later used for the slave trade.
Look at both pictures. What else was the castle used for?

New Influences in Africa

The culture and customs of Africa remained unchanged for centuries. But as trade and exploration increased, new practices and new influences traveled into the continent.

One new practice that harmed Africa was the slave trade. Slaves became one of the most prominent exports from Africa. Slavery had long been practiced within Africa itself, and Africans had sometimes traded slaves to Europe and Asia. But the international trade of African slaves did not become widespread until the 1600s. As Europeans settled and formed colonies on the continents of North and South America, their demand for slaves increased.

The slave trade had many negative effects on Africa. The African population declined. More than ten million Africans were sold into slavery from the 1400s to the 1800s. Because a popular item of trade was guns, wars and violence increased. Families were torn apart, and fear reigned. Because the Africans often fled from their cities to avoid capture, civilization and culture in many parts of Africa were hindered from growing.

Trade with the outside world brought new religions into Africa. Often these religions were mixed with traditional African beliefs. Many African peoples who conducted business with Muslim traders adopted Islam. Christianity also began to spread in Africa as European missionaries came to preach the gospel.

Fishermen outside the Cape Coast Castle, where cannons look out onto the Gulf of Guinea

Namasha watched the face of this new storyteller. His eyes were kind. His stories came from the thick book that he carried everywhere.

"In the beginning, God created the world—the sky, the trees, the mountains, the hills, the rivers. And then He created man and woman. He walked on the earth and talked with them and loved them. But then they disobeyed Him. He still loved them, even after they had sinned, so He gave them a gift—His only Son. Jesus Christ came to earth to walk and talk with men and women. He came to die for them because He loved them just as His Father did. Now people who believe in Him can be forgiven and spend eternity with God."

A Ghanian national missionary

Ever since this new storyteller had come to the village, something had changed. Monkeys and parrots still called from the forest. Light still slanted through the bamboo trees and made crisscrossed shadows on the village paths. The river still rippled in the distance. But something was different.

Namasha leaned closer as the missionary held up a picture of a man, torn and bleeding, hanging on a wooden cross. She wanted to hear more of these new stories about Jesus.

> And this gospel of the kingdom shall be preached in all the world for a witness unto all nations; and then shall the end come.
>
> **Matthew 24:14**

342

Chapter 13

Ancient Japan

Located off the northeastern coast of Asia, an ancient tribal people were slowly rising to power. The civilization of Japan would become a world power that would help shape modern history. The name Japan comes from the Chinese words *jih pen*, meaning "origin of the sun." Japan is an **archipelago** (AR kuh PEL uh GO), or a large group of scattered islands. The four main islands of Japan are **Hokkaido** (hah KY doh), **Honshu** (HAHN shoo), **Shikoku** (shee KO koo), and **Kyushu** (kee OO shoo). For centuries Japan was isolated from the rest of the world by the Sea of Japan and the North Pacific Ocean.

Early History

Little is known of Japan's early history. Like other nations, the Japanese people did not keep records during the early development of their civilization. Like the ancient Romans and Greeks, the Japanese passed down their early history through legends and myths. For centuries these stories greatly shaped Japan's culture.

One myth tells of how the Japanese believe life began. A god and a goddess dipped a jeweled spear into the ocean. The drops that fell from the spear formed the islands of Japan, where the god and the goddess lived. Their children were the Japanese people. Even today some of the Japanese believe that they are descendants of gods.

Early Settlers

The earliest settlers in Japan likely migrated from northeastern Asia. Pieces of pottery have been found that might have been made by these early settlers. Most of this pottery has a cord or rope design. Some archaeologists have named these people the Jomon (JAW mawn), which means "cord pattern." They were probably hunters, fishermen, and gatherers of plants for food.

Pottery made by the Jomon people for storing food
What was unique about Jomon pottery?

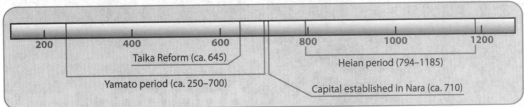

200   400   600   800   1000   1200

Taika Reform (ca. 645)

Heian period (794–1185)

Yamato period (ca. 250–700)

Capital established in Nara (ca. 710)

Bronze bell crafted in the late Yayoi period

Another group of immigrants also came to Japan. They mingled with the Jomon. Archaeologists named these immigrants the Yayoi (yah YOI). Some historians believe they are the ancestors of the Japanese people today.

Villages in Japan developed along freshwater sources. The Yayoi are credited for introducing farming to Japan. They used a form of irrigation to grow rice.

Among the artifacts of the Yayoi people are a pottery wheel and some metalwork. These objects show advanced craftsmanship.

Clans

By 200 BC the people of Japan were organized into clans. Each clan had its own warrior chieftain who protected his people from other clans. In return for protection, the people had to give part of their rice harvest to the chieftain. Each clan also had its own land and god.

Yamato Period

Around AD 250 the **Yamato** clan rose to power over rival clans and formed strong military states. The Yamato ruled these states. They also developed organized cities, a government, social classes, and a written language. The Yamato were influenced by the Chinese and the Koreans. As the peoples traded, Japan borrowed Chinese and Korean concepts.

Part of the Yamato period was also known as the Kofun (ko FOON) period, named after giant tomb mounds called **kofuns**. The aristocracy during this period built these magnificent kofuns to show their wealth and power. These tombs were circular, square, or keyhole-shaped. The keyhole-shaped kofun in the city of Nintoku was longer than five football fields. From the excavation of the kofuns, much can be learned about the ancient Japanese culture.

Aerial view of a kofun

Monuments on a mountain trail in the Nara Prefecture, a small area in southern Japan

The Imperial Rule

The Yamato chose one man to be their emperor. They claimed that their emperor was a descendant of **Jimmu Tenno**, the mythical ancestor of Japanese emperors. According to legend, he was the first emperor and a descendant of the sun goddess, Amaterasu. For this reason he was to be worshiped. By claiming a relationship to Jimmu, the Yamato gained the loyalty of other clans.

The imperial, or ruling, family of Japan came from the Yamato clan. It remained the only imperial family throughout Japan's history. All the emperors continued to claim that Jimmu Tenno was their ancestor.

The Japanese admired Chinese achievements. One of these achievements was a strong system of government. The Japanese wanted such progress in their own land. **Prince Shotoku** developed a constitution that became the basis of the imperial government of Japan. He also encouraged his people to accept the Chinese religion and way of life.

BIOGRAPHY

Who: Prince Shotoku

What: prince of Japan

When: AD 574–622

Where: Japan

At an early age Shotoku was schooled in Buddhism and Confucianism. Both influenced him greatly when he served as prince of Japan. Shotoku sent representatives to China to learn from the Chinese civilization. He is most noted for developing the Seventeen Article Constitution, which established rules for Japan's officials.

346

Japan

Location—Japan is an archipelago of over 6,800 islands in the Pacific Ocean. It is to the east of China and Korea.

Climate—Northern and southern Japan vary in climate. Southern Japan is generally warmer. Average temperatures range from winter lows of 21°F (−6°C) in the north to summer highs of 79°F (26°C) in the south. Annual precipitation is an average of 50 inches (127 cm).

Topography—Japan is made up of four main islands and a large number of smaller islands that are the peaks of submerged mountains. The Japanese Alps on the island of Honshu include Mount Fuji, Japan's highest mountain (12,388 ft [3776 m]). Many of Japan's mountains are volcanoes.

Natural Resources—Japan has few natural resources. The mountainous terrain leaves less than 15 percent of land that can be farmed. Small deposits of coal, zinc, copper, lead, and gold can be found. Several short, swift rivers are used to provide electricity and to irrigate rice paddies.

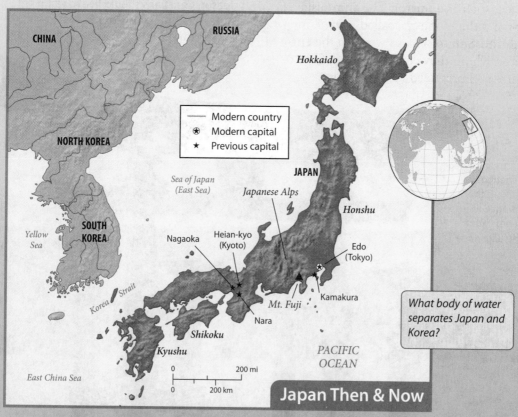

Japan Then & Now

What body of water separates Japan and Korea?

FOCUS

1. What religion did Prince Shotoku help spread in Japan?

2. What changes did the Taika Reform bring to Japan?

Religion

The main religion of Japan was **Shintoism**. *Shinto* means "the way of the gods." This religion is a form of nature worship. It teaches that every object or creature in nature has a spirit that should be worshiped as a god. These gods, or nature spirits, are called **kami**. The most important kami is the sun goddess, Amaterasu. A kami can also reside in an object such as a mirror. The Shintoists worship these objects, called *shintai*, in a shrine. Shintoists also worship the emperor, whom they consider a god. Shintoism is still practiced in Japan today.

SHINTO BELIEFS

Shintoism teaches that the kami are spirits of animals, natural objects like mountains or streams, and even ideas like growth. Shintoists worship these spirits either at home or in shrines. The Bible teaches that there is only one God and that He alone should be worshiped. God's Word also warns people against worshiping His creation instead of Him (Rom. 1:18–25).

Shintoism teaches that the main purpose of existence is to lead a moral life. The Bible teaches that a person should live a moral life by the power of the Holy Spirit (Rom. 8:1–17). The reason Christians should live moral lives is to bring glory to God and to serve Him (1 Cor. 6:20).

A floating torii marking the entrance to a Shinto shrine in Itsukushima

348

In addition to Shintoism, Buddhism is practiced in Japan. Prince Shotoku is credited for spreading this second religion. He sent students to China to learn about Buddhism and encouraged the Japanese to practice it. Several Buddhist temples were built throughout Japan. Many Japanese practice a mixture of both Shintoism and Buddhism.

Built by Prince Shotoku, this Buddhist temple is one of the oldest wooden structures in the world and one of Japan's national treasures.
What is the five-story tower called?

Buddhist missionaries from China were sent to Japan. They had a significant influence there. Many Buddhist missionaries were scholars and teachers. They taught the Japanese how to read and write Chinese, study Chinese literature, and create art in the Chinese style. The missionaries also brought new customs and new styles of clothing. Later, many Japanese traveled to China to study in the Buddhist schools.

Government

The Yamato emperor controlled the government. He chose people from the most powerful families to help him govern the many clans. An official passed his position to his son. The government paid an official by giving him control over land and farmers.

About **645**, a time of political and economic changes came to Japan. This was known as the "Great Change" or **Taika** (tie EE kuh) **Reform**. The leaders of Japan wanted to weaken the influence of the clan chieftains. They modeled their changes in the Japanese government after the strong centralized Chinese government. The Japanese established a civil service examination. Governmental positions were given to men of ability. New laws were established and a tax system was put into place. Clan chieftains no longer collected the taxes. Instead governmental officials gathered the taxes for the emperor.

Japanese artist's rendition of a woman weaving
How did Chinese art influence Japanese art?

Writing in Calligraphy

Calligraphy is the art of fine hand-writing. Chinese calligrapher **Wang Xizhi** (WAHNG shih-zhi) is credited for being the father of this art form. Calligraphy was introduced to the Japanese by Buddhist missionaries from China. The Japanese adapted the Chinese characters to the Japanese language.

Japanese calligraphy is called *shodo*. One style of shodo is called *kaisho*, which means "correct writing." This is a formal block style used in most publications in Japan, such as newspapers and magazines. Another style is called *gyosho*, which means "traveling writing." Students use this semicursive style to write notes. A third style, *sosho*, means "grass writing." This is a flowing cursive style used in formal Japanese calligraphy.

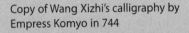

Copy of Wang Xizhi's calligraphy by Empress Komyo in 744

The handle of the brush is held in the middle with three fingers. The hand does not touch the paper. The student sits straight with his back away from the chair.

Making a Japanese Windsock

Every year on May 5, the Japanese celebrate a holiday called Children's Day. This day celebrates the health and happiness of all children. The people fly *koinobori,* windsocks shaped like carp. *Koi* means "carp" and *nobori* means "streamer" or "flag." The Japanese consider the carp a strong and determined fish. Carp can swim upstream against the swift flow of water. Families display a koinobori for each member of the family.

1. Get a paper lunch bag, a pencil, crayons or paints, chenille wire, paper clips, yarn or ribbon, and a hole punch.

2. Cut the bottom out of the bag. Flatten the bag and sketch a fish so the bottom of the fish is along the fold. Cut out the fish.

3. Sketch eyes, scales, and other details onto the fish. Decorate it with crayons or paints. (Allow it to dry if paint is used.)

4. Glue a chenille wire inside the edge of the mouth. Fold the paper over the wire.

5. Put glue along the inside of the top edge of the fish and press the top edges together. Leave the tail and mouth edges open.

6. Punch holes on either side of the mouth and thread a strand of yarn or a ribbon through each hole and knot. Tie the ends of the yarn together for hanging. Hang the fish and watch it swim in the breeze.

FOCUS

1. What was the official language of the Japanese imperial court?

2. What role did the Fujiwara family assume during the Heian period?

Heian Period

The Japanese government established its first permanent capital at **Nara** in 710. Nara had broad streets, governmental offices, and large public squares. Later, the capital was moved to **Heian-kyo**. Today Heian-kyo is the city of Kyoto (kee OH toh).

After the capital was moved to Heian-kyo, a period called the Heian (HAY AHN) followed. It was named after the capital city and was a time of peace and security. Japan began to develop a culture independent of the Chinese during this time.

Life at the Court

The nobles who followed the emperor to Heian-kyo lived near him to win his favor. This group of nobles, known as the **imperial court**, served or advised the emperor. Life at the imperial court demanded strict rules of behavior. Court **etiquette**, or manners, included proper actions and responses for all activities, whether accepting a piece of food or meeting the emperor. Above all, a person at the court was supposed to have composure and not show his emotions at any time. If someone did not follow these rules, he was not welcome at court.

The nobles of the court loved beauty and elegance. Many nobles supported

An artist's rendition of court culture during the Heian period
What design elements are seen in each lady's clothing?

the arts. The court became the center of culture and learning. The Heian period was the golden age of the arts in Japan.

The love of beauty by the nobles began with their own appearance. The nobles loved elaborate outfits. For example, the women wore long gowns of twelve layers of colored silk. As the wind blew, the various colors showed in shifting patterns. Both men and women wore makeup. They blackened their teeth because white teeth were considered ugly.

Nobles often carried decorative fans. The fans were painted with flowers, trees, and birds. Some fans had flowers and long silk cords attached to them.

Language

During the Heian period the Japanese nobles took care in how they spoke and wrote. Chinese was the official language used by the men of the imperial court. Japanese scholars spent many years learning Chinese.

Although the Japanese had a common spoken language, they had no written language of their own. The Japanese language differed greatly from Chinese.

In the Heian period the Japanese began to include phonetic alphabets in their own writing system. Japanese is still a difficult language to master today.

Literature

Writing was very popular among the nobles, especially the women. Since the women were not trained in Chinese writing as the men were, women wrote in the common Japanese language. They spent their leisure time writing about their experiences in the imperial court. Most of the literature that has survived the Heian period are writings by women.

One of the greatest writers in early Japan was **Lady Murasaki Shikibu** (MOO-rah-SAH-kee SHEE-kee-BOO). As a lady at the court, she wrote what has been called the world's first true novel. Her six-volume *The Tale of Genji* tells the story of Prince Genji, his life at court, and his countless loves. A modern edition of the novel fills over four thousand pages.

Poetry was an important part of Japanese culture. To be accepted in Heian society, a person had to write poetry. One type of Japanese poem that is still popular today is the haiku. **Haiku** (HY koo) is a verse form with seventeen syllables and a *kigo*. A kigo is a word that hints in what season the poem takes place. The words in a haiku are chosen according to meaning and syllables. The poet tries to develop a mood and a picture with his words.

Statue of Lady Murasaki Shikibu, author of *The Tale of Genji*

Arts and Architecture

Even today, one can see how Japanese art and architecture reflect Chinese art. However, the Japanese also developed their own artistic patterns. One characteristic of Japanese art was its use of brilliant colors. Bright colors made paintings full of life and activity. In architecture, colors were used to decorate houses and temples. A second characteristic of Japanese art was its use of everyday objects. Artists made and painted objects such as fans, combs, boxes, baskets, and carved furniture. These objects were beautiful as well as useful.

The Japanese also liked to arrange flowers. *Ikebana* was a special art form that involved flower arranging. Colors and types of flowers were chosen carefully to match the occasion and the season. For example, chrysanthemums were used in the month of May. Every year a Chrysanthemum Festival was held. At that time the emperor inspected the palace flower gardens. One emperor adopted the chrysanthemum for his official seal and crest. This seal and crest are still used today.

The nobles of Heian-kyo worked to make their city beautiful. They admired Chinese architecture and modeled Heian-kyo after the Chinese city, Changan. They copied Chinese building styles, especially those of temples. For other buildings, the nobles liked simple, airy designs. To add beauty to these buildings, the nobles surrounded them with elegant gardens and ponds.

Religion

During the Heian period, religion was a part of everyday life. The Japanese blended Shintoism with Buddhism. They worshiped at Shinto shrines to obtain help for their daily lives. They worshiped in Buddhist temples to prepare for the

The Japanese flag and imperial crest

life to come. Religion shaped Japanese culture and affected art, architecture, and education.

Government

During the Heian period, Japan's central government was strong. However, it would soon be challenged. Instead of the emperor being in authority, the key posts in government came to rest in the hands of powerful families. One family, the **Fujiwara**, had their daughters marry the sons of the imperial family. Whenever an imperial heir was born to one of these daughters, the reigning emperor was forced to give up his throne. A Fujiwara court official then ruled as regent for the infant emperor. A **regent** is a person who rules in place of a rightful ruler who is unable to fulfill his duties because of age, illness, or other reasons.

As regents, the Fujiwara family controlled the Japanese government during much of the Heian period, which was from 794 to 1185. They became wealthy and powerful. However, they also brought corruption to the government. By 1156 the country was in a civil war. After almost thirty years of fighting, the power struggle ended with the rule of Japan shifting to military officials. Although the line of the imperial family continued, the emperor did not have any power. Thus began the feudal age of Japan.

Reconstruction of the Heian Palace

Discovering How

Writing a Haiku

The poet Matsuo Basho is credited for making haiku a popular form of poetry. Since haiku is usually focused on nature, Basho traveled the Japanese countryside to gain inspiration for his writings.

1. You will need paper and a pencil.

2. Go outside and look at your surroundings. What do you see? Select an object or a scene to describe in your haiku.

3. Write your haiku with 5 syllables in the first line, 7 syllables in the second line, and 5 syllables in the last line. The lines do not need to rhyme. Remember to include a word or an idea that lets the reader know what season the haiku is taking place in.

4. Illustrate your haiku.

Celebration
Leaves sprinkle the grass
Confetti tangled in hair
Fall hosts a party

Playground
Sloping string of grass
Droplets quiver at the top
To ride the green slide

FOCUS

1. What were the four levels of social classes in Japan's feudal system?

2. What name was given to the typhoon that caused the Mongol's defeat?

Feudal Japan

During the late Heian period, a feudal system of social classes developed. **Feudalism** (FYOO duhl IH zuhm) is a system for organizing and governing society based on land and service. The ruler divided the land among the nobles, who then subdivided it among the peasants, all in exchange for loyalty and allegiance.

At the top of the Japanese feudal system were the emperor, his family, and the military leader. The emperor was the religious leader but had little political power. The military leader, called the

The first shogun was Minamoto Yoritomo. (In Japan a person's family name comes first, followed by his first name.)

Feudal Society	
Emperor and shogun	The emperor had no governmental power. The shogun ruled in the emperor's name.
Daimyo	The daimyo were powerful warlords or chief nobles.
Samurai	The samurai were warriors who served the shogun and the daimyo.
Peasants	There were several subclasses of peasants. The farmers were the highest ranking. The artisans came next, and the merchants were last.

shogun, was chosen by the emperor and given supreme political power.

In 1192 **Yoritomo** (yoh ree toh moh), the leader of the Minamoto clan, was appointed as the first shogun for winning the war amongst the clans. He became the supreme military leader of Japan and set up his government from the city of Kamakura. This military government was known as a *shogunate*. Shoguns continued to rule for the next seven hundred years while the imperial emperor had no power but was still the official ruler.

Next in the feudal system were the **daimyo** (DY mee OH), who were the chief nobles or powerful warlords. The daimyo had military and economic power to rule over their lands. They also had armies to protect their lands and the workers on

them. The most powerful daimyo often became shoguns.

The daimyo's armies were made up of **samurai** (SAM uh ʀʏ), the next feudal class. The samurai warrior mastered the skills of horsemanship, fencing, archery, and *jujitsu* (a form of self-defense that uses no weapons). The samurai worked under the daimyo. It was a samurai's duty to protect the daimyo. A samurai had additional privileges that included being able to have a surname, a family crest, and the right to carry two swords. The samurai lived by a strict code of conduct called the "way of the warrior," which demanded loyalty, honor, duty, justice, courage, sincerity, and politeness.

The last class of the Japanese feudal system was the peasants. The peasants were divided into several subclasses. The highest-ranking peasants were the farmers. If a farmer owned his own land, he had a higher position than a farmer who did not own land. Farmers were highly valued because they produced the food. They paid their taxes by giving a percentage of their crops to the government or to the daimyo.

The artisans were in the next peasant subclass. They made products from metal and wood for the other classes. These products included tools for the

farmers, fish hooks and anchors for the fishermen, and swords and other weapons for the samurai.

The last peasant subclass was made up of merchants. They were the lowest ranking because they relied on others for their livelihood. Traders and shopkeepers were part of this subclass.

The early Japanese people had been mainly fishermen and hunters. Other

A samurai's helmet was often carefully decorated.

A samurai usually carried two swords. The shorter one was called the *wakizashi,* and the longer one was the *katana.*

His armor was made from layers of metal or leather. It was brightly painted and laced together with silk or leather.

A samurai carried a *naginata,* a blade mounted on a long handle. It was used against cavalry. *Why do you think the long handle was necessary?*

Samurai

358

The Granger Collection, New York

A late-1500s painting of farmers paying taxes in rice to their local daimyo

jobs and trades developed as the needs in society increased.

The Mongols

In the late 1200s a people from China called the Mongols tried to attack Japan twice. The shoguns were strong enough to turn back both invasions. In the second invasion the Japanese samurai fought the Mongols for fifty-three days. Suddenly, the sky darkened and a typhoon swept across the Sea of Japan. Much of the Mongol fleet was destroyed, and many Mongols drowned. Others were slain by the samurai. As a result, the Mongol invasion failed. The Japanese

A Mongol Buddhist monk trying to calm a typhoon

named the strong storm **kamikaze** (KAH mih KAH zee), meaning "divine wind." The Japanese believed that spirits had sent the kamikaze.

The Japanese victory over the Mongols drained Japan's treasury. The loyal samurai resented the government when they were not paid. The shoguns began to lose their power. Over the next five hundred years, power struggles continued and the country once again isolated itself from the rest of the world.

KAMIKAZE

Kamikaze pilot in World War II
What was the highest gift a person could give the emperor?

During World War II, Allied sailors came to fear a new type of Japanese attack. This attack was done by kamikazes, Japanese pilots who deliberately tried to crash their planes into an enemy ship. Such attacks were the product of the Japanese belief that the highest gift one could give the emperor was one's life. Japan had already lost its first-rate pilots and its best planes. In kamikaze warfare, the Japanese could load out-of-date or poorly built planes with explosives and let inexperienced pilots fly them. The planes had only to dive into a ship. The results were devastating. Although many of the kamikaze missions were stopped, too many got through. The emperor's kamikazes sank or crippled three hundred U.S. warships in the final ten months of the war and inflicted fifteen thousand casualties.

Chapter 14

The Middle Ages in Europe

FOCUS

1. What was the period in Europe from AD 476 to 1400 known as?

2. From what region were the tribes who invaded the western portion of the Roman Empire?

The Medieval Period

On a hill in France stands a deserted castle with massive stone towers lifting to the sky. It seems to be listening for sounds of the past. The rustle of a lady's silk dress. The clank of a shield against a breastplate. Distant echoes of horses' hooves cantering off to battle. The gruff voice of a serf, humming as he works out in the lord's field. Sounds that belong to a different world.

Defense tower of Haut-Kœnigsbourg castle in Alsace, France

The Roman Empire had fallen. After being the greatest power on earth for several hundred years, it began to weaken around AD 400. Northern tribes that had often challenged the empire finally prevailed. They swept through the empire and conquered its cities. By **476**, the great empire had been gradually replaced by small kingdoms governed by military heroes. In that year the first non-Roman took over as emperor of Italy.

After the fall of the Roman Empire, Europe entered an era known as the **medieval** period. The word *medieval* comes from two Latin words: *medius*, meaning "middle," and *aevum*, meaning "age." Many people also call the period between the fall of Rome and the Renaissance the **Middle Ages**.

THE RENAISSANCE

During the Middle Ages there was little opportunity for education. The arts were a luxury to people who did not have much money. The Renaissance was a period that began in Italy around **AD 1400**. The word *renaissance* means "rebirth" and refers to the rebirth of learning. This cultural revival spread north and into other parts of Europe over the next two hundred years. It greatly changed European life and culture. Classical Greek and Roman literature were rediscovered, and universities developed. As a result of this revival of education, the arts and original thinking flourished as they had not since the days of the Roman Empire.

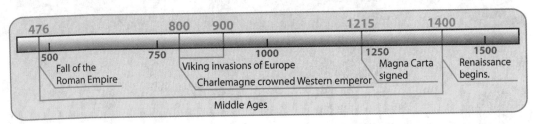

476		800	900		1215	1400
500	750		1000		1250	1500
Fall of the Roman Empire		Viking invasions of Europe			Magna Carta signed	Renaissance begins.
		Charlemagne crowned Western emperor				

Middle Ages

Roman Lands in Other Hands

What happened to the lands that had been part of the Roman Empire? In an earlier chapter, you read that the eastern part of the fallen empire eventually became the Byzantine Empire. The western part was taken over by Germanic peoples from Scandinavia. A tribe called the Visigoths fought their way into Spain. The Ostrogoths set up a kingdom in Italy. The Franks conquered Gaul (present-day France), and the Angles, the Saxons, and the Jutes invaded the British Isles.

Even before Rome fell completely, the Roman Church began to grow more powerful in the West. It even helped negotiate the safety of Rome with the invaders. In many parts of Rome, the only source of law and authority among Roman citizens was the local bishop.

Many of the invading Germanic rulers had already converted to a form of Christianity. But they followed a teaching called Arianism, a belief that God the Son is separate from and lesser than God the Father. The church condemned Arianism as heresy.

Once the Germanic warriors had conquered Roman lands, their rulers quickly adopted the beliefs of the Roman Church. In this way the rulers could gain support from the local Roman people and from the church leaders. The conquering rulers gradually added Roman law into their culture.

As Rome fell apart, civilized life in most of Europe disappeared. Roads became overgrown with weeds, trade stopped, and cities stood in ruins. People built isolated villages and worked hard to grow enough food to feed their families. Disorder and destruction by invaders were constant threats. No one had much time or money for education.

The people of the former Roman Empire needed a place to turn for leadership. Without an emperor to guide them, many turned to local leaders and the church.

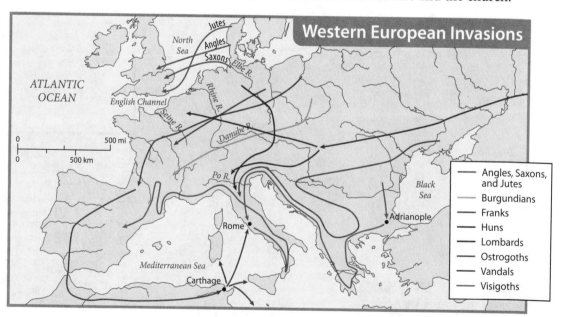

Western European Invasions

Legend:
- Angles, Saxons, and Jutes
- Burgundians
- Franks
- Huns
- Lombards
- Ostrogoths
- Vandals
- Visigoths

363

The Region Today

Europe

Location—Europe is bordered by the Arctic Ocean to the north, the Atlantic Ocean to the west, the Mediterranean Sea to the south, and the Ural Mountains to the east.

Climate—Europe's climate has great variety, which is influenced by the Gulf Stream. Most of Europe has cool summers and cold winters. The average annual rainfall is 20–60 inches (51–152 cm). Average temperatures range from 2°F (17°C) to 95°F (35°C).

Topography—Europe includes icy tundra in the north, mountainous regions in the south, and lush farmland in the east and the west. Europe's islands include Great Britain, Ireland, Iceland, Cyprus, Crete, and Sicily. Bodies of water include the Caspian Sea, Baltic Sea, North Sea, Black Sea, and Mediterranean Sea. Mount Elbrus is Europe's highest point. The Caspian Sea is Europe's lowest elevation.

Natural Resources—Europe has large oil, coal, and natural gas reserves. Other resources include uranium deposits, timber, peat, potash, zinc, and copper. Europe also has a well-developed fishing industry.

Europe Then & Now

FOCUS

1. What was the highest leader of the Roman Church called?

2. How did the teachings of the church begin to change during the Middle Ages?

The Roman Church

Church Leadership

The patriarch of the church of Rome was called the pope, a title that comes from the Latin word for "father." He gradually extended his leadership over the Roman Church in all of Europe, not just the church in Rome. Most Europeans followed his teachings. The pope directed the activities of the **clergy**, or religious leaders, during the Middle Ages.

Some clergymen lived among the people. They ministered as priests in the churches. They led the services and instructed the people in how to live and worship. The priests preserved and developed many of the doctrines that the Protestant Christians hold even today. However, over time, the priests taught that the church and its leaders had a role in salvation. Many of them began to teach that people could not receive God's grace without the help of a priest. They also taught that, to be saved, people had to participate in certain religious ceremonies called **sacraments**. Although true believers were part of the church, many people began to trust the church, rather than the Savior, Jesus Christ, for salvation.

Other clergymen called **monks** rarely had contact with the outside world. They lived together in large secluded buildings called **monasteries**. Many monks vowed never to marry but instead devoted their lives to serving the Roman Church.

During the early Middle Ages, monasteries were the primary places where education and art were valued. Literature, science, mathematics, and medicine were not often taught to the common people. But some monks learned to read and write. These monks spent hours copying the Scriptures and the writings of the early churchmen. They bent over their desks, scratching with quill pens for hours at a time. The word *clerical*, describing office work, can be traced back to this duty of clergymen in the Middle Ages.

A monk copying the Scriptures

365

Another group of clergymen was the **friars**. *Friar* comes from a Latin word for "brother." Like the monks, friars dedicated their lives to service. Neither monks nor friars owned property. However, friars were different from monks in several ways. Friars did not live together in monasteries. Instead, they lived among the people and were traveling preachers. They lived simply and often begged for food. Friars wore plain robes, and some did not wear shoes. A friar's main goal was to teach people how to live good lives.

Some women also devoted their lives to the church. These women who took religious vows were called **nuns**. Monks, nuns, priests, and popes still exist today. The Roman Catholic Church carries on traditions and teachings from the Middle Ages.

The Roman Church Today

The word *catholic* means "universal." When the word was first applied to the church, it referred to all true believers in Jesus Christ all over the world. Gradually the word came to apply to the organization that the Roman Church

became. Roman Catholicism took centuries to develop and settle into its current form. When people use the term *Roman Catholic Church* today, they refer to a specific organization whose members hold certain beliefs.

Title page of the Sacramentary of Gellone from the end of the 700s

THE SACRAMENTS

By the 1200s the Roman Catholic Church had developed seven sacraments that it believed would earn grace for salvation.

1. Baptism (to remove original sin)
2. Confirmation (to receive the Holy Spirit)
3. Confession/penance (to receive forgiveness from a priest)
4. Communion/Eucharist (This is the primary sacrament to receive redemption from sin.)
5. Matrimony (Marriage is controlled by the church, and children are to be educated by the church.)
6. Holy orders (The priest is considered another Christ; the nun is considered the bride of Christ.)
7. Last rites (Anointing of the sick brings forgiveness of sin and prepares one for death.)

Benedict

A boy named Benedict grew up in a wealthy Roman family and was well educated. As a young man he saw the moral corruption in Roman society and decided to withdraw from it. He cut off almost all contact with other people and lived as a hermit. As he concentrated on prayer and holy living, a friend who lived nearby supplied him with food and clothing.

After about three years, **Benedict** founded the Monte Cassino monastery in the mountains near Rome, Italy. He produced a set of instructions for living as a monk that came to be known as the Benedictine Rule.

The Benedictine Rule became the model for nearly all other monasteries in Western Europe. Benedict's rule encouraged monks to vary their daily routine between prayer, manual labor, and study of the Scriptures and other writings. Although some monks of Benedict's day abused their bodies in an attempt to rid themselves of sin, Benedict ordered his monks to get sufficient food and sleep to live healthy lives. Although his rule encouraged strict obedience and did not allow monks to own private possessions, it also made allowances for physical and spiritual weaknesses.

ROMAN CATHOLIC BELIEFS

The Roman Catholic Church teaches that salvation comes at baptism and is maintained through good works and doing penance, an act that shows devotion to God and repentance for sin. The Bible teaches that salvation is the gift of God (Rom. 6:23). God's grace and salvation are received by faith alone; they can never be earned (Eph 2:8–9). God gives the Holy Spirit to believers at the time of their salvation.

The Roman Catholic Church teaches that people cannot pray directly to God for forgiveness. They must go to the priest, whom they believe is a mediator between God and man. However, 1 Timothy 2:5 teaches that Christ is the mediator between God and man. Because of His death for our sins and His resurrection, believers can go directly to God for forgiveness and other needs.

The Roman Catholic Church teaches that the Eucharist, or Communion, must be taken to maintain salvation and that the elements taken are changed into Jesus' body and blood. The Bible teaches that observing Communion, also called the Lord's Supper, is a means to remember what Christ has done for believers in making atonement for their sin on the cross. The bread and the cup are symbols of Jesus' body and blood. These symbols remind us of the cost of His sacrifice and encourage us to examine our hearts for any sin that we need to confess to Him. Observing the Lord's Supper is a matter of obedience, but it does not cause believers to earn any merit with God (1 Cor. 11:23–31).

The Roman Catholic Church teaches that a person needs to perform special rituals and prayers to prepare for death. The Bible teaches that anyone who has received salvation is already prepared for death because of Christ's resurrection from the dead. Christ conquered death's power (1 Cor. 15:53–57).

Medieval priests of the Roman Church

FOCUS

1. What name was given to the lands that Pepin gave to the Roman Church?

2. What two modern European countries formed from Charlemagne's divided empire?

The Franks

Clovis

After the fall of Rome, a people called the Franks invaded Europe. They were a Germanic tribe that came from the northeast of the Rhine River. The Franks inhabited the wealthy Roman provinces of Gaul and gained the support of the Roman Church. They became the most powerful of the Germanic tribes. Over the next several centuries, the Franks formed a kingdom. Their first king was **Clovis**, who conquered the last of the Romans in Gaul. In 507 the Franks successfully drove out the Visigoths from southern Gaul. The conquests of Clovis shaped what would eventually become the French nation.

Clovis divided his kingdom among his four sons just before his death. His sons and their descendants were called the Merovingian kings. They struggled and plotted against one another, each wanting greater control. The authority of the Merovingians weakened until most of the governmental work was done by their palace officials.

Charles Martel

In the 700s a new leader named Charles rose up to unite the Franks. Charles was not a king but a high official in a Frankish palace. He became famous for leading an army against Muslim invaders and defeating them at Tours in what is now France. This victory kept the rest of Europe free from Muslim rule. Charles was given the name Martel, which means "the Hammer." **Charles Martel**, powerful both as a soldier and a leader, lived up to his name. The empire which Charles and his descendants ruled became known as the **Carolingian Empire**.

A Merovingian fibula, or brooch, decorated with gold, garnets, and precious stones

369

Pepin the Short

After Charles Martel died, his son **Pepin the Short** ruled for ten years before becoming the new king of the Franks. Pepin is best known for making an alliance with the church of Rome.

Before Pepin became king, Pope Stephen II asked him to help defend Rome against invaders, the **Lombards**. In exchange for Pepin's help, the pope officially approved Pepin's taking the Frankish crown away from the Merovingians. In a public ceremony, Frankish bishops anointed Pepin with oil, and he received the pope's blessing as king of the Franks.

Pepin went on to defeat the Lombards and to give part of their conquered lands to the church leaders. The church called these lands the **Papal States**, and they belonged to the Roman Church until the 1800s. Pepin's alliance with the church played a major role in both politics and religion for the next several centuries.

Charlemagne

The Carolingian Empire Grows

Pepin's son, **Charlemagne** (SHAR luh MAYN) was the greatest of the Carolingian kings. The Latin word *magnus* means "great." The name

Charlemagne comes from the Latin words *Carolus Magnus*, meaning "Charles the Great." He reigned for about forty-five years.

Charlemagne defeated many tribes in Europe. Among them were the Saxons and the Lombards, who had again invaded Rome. His military aid to Rome earned him favor with the pope. According to tradition, on Christmas Day in **800**, Charlemagne was praying beside Pope Leo III at a church service. There the pope turned and placed a crown on Charlemagne's head, proclaiming him emperor of the Western Roman Empire.

What was Pepin anointed with as he became king?

Charlemagne had extended the Frankish kingdom to be greater in size than ever before. It was now an empire that included most of Western Europe. Charlemagne divided his lands into small districts, each having several **manors**, or large farming communities. Each of these was controlled by a lord and farmed by peasants. Each manor sent Charlemagne a yearly report on its workers, production, and resources. Charlemagne regularly checked on local officials to make sure that their methods of rule were just.

A Love for Learning

Under Charlemagne's rule, the importance of learning expanded throughout the empire. Believing in the value of education, Charlemagne invited scholars to his royal court to study and train others. With the help of these scholars, Charlemagne began schools for boys from both noble and poor families. The students studied reading, writing, mathematics, and astronomy.

Although he enjoyed studying, Charlemagne struggled to read and write. He kept a tablet and a pen beneath his pillow and practiced often. He also learned how to make mathematical calculations. Charlemagne never mastered these subjects, but he was an excellent speaker, even in the Latin language.

Charlemagne also reformed handwriting in his empire. During the Middle Ages, books were rare and those that were available were made by hand in monasteries. Scholars had difficulty reading the handwriting in the books. When Charlemagne found out, he ordered a church scholar named Alcuin to develop a new style of writing. Alcuin's writing style, which used both small and capital letters, is the basis for our handwriting today.

> Study to shew thyself approved unto God, a workman that needeth not to be ashamed, rightly dividing the word of truth.

The text of 2 Timothy 2:15, written in the style Alcuin developed

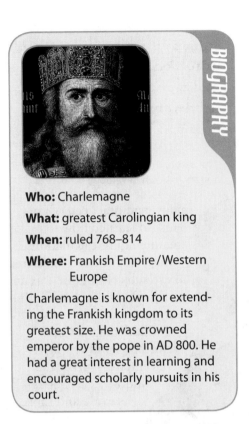

Who: Charlemagne

What: greatest Carolingian king

When: ruled 768–814

Where: Frankish Empire/Western Europe

Charlemagne is known for extending the Frankish kingdom to its greatest size. He was crowned emperor by the pope in AD 800. He had a great interest in learning and encouraged scholarly pursuits in his court.

Charlemagne's conduct as a ruler was not always ideal. He dealt harshly with those he captured in his military conquests. He married and divorced many wives. In spite of his faults, Charlemagne was greatly revered by his people. Although the empire did not last beyond his death, Charlemagne's accomplishments made him the most memorable of the Frankish kings.

Division of the Frankish Empire

After Charlemagne's death, his son, Louis the Pious, inherited the empire. But it was too large for one man to rule successfully, so it weakened. Wars took place among Louis's three sons—Lothair, Charles the Bald, and Louis the German.

The conflicts led to a division of the empire into three parts after the death of Louis the Pious. Each of Louis's sons received a share. Two of these parts formed the basis for two of our modern European countries: France and Germany. Lothair's part of the empire, located between the territories of his brothers, would be a source of strife between France and Germany for centuries.

At the time of the division, the languages of the Franks in the western and eastern parts of the empire began to change. Western Frankish was changing into French, and eastern Frankish was developing into German.

The weakened remains of Charlemagne's empire had become prey for invaders. Many of them were from modern Scandinavia, which includes Sweden, Denmark, and Norway. These invaders were called Norsemen, Northmen, or **Vikings**. The Vikings raided different parts of Europe.

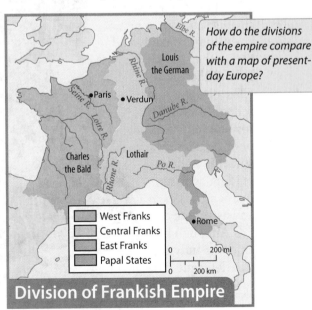

How do the divisions of the empire compare with a map of present-day Europe?

Division of Frankish Empire

Vikings

The bells in the church at Tours began to ring wildly, a shrill warning to villagers. "I've seen their ships!" cried one of the monks. "Coming down the Loire River! It's the Northmen—the Vikings! May God help us!"

Long wooden boats with curved ends sailed toward the village. Some villagers caught glimpses of the boatmen's faces. Beneath their thick, blond hair, their expressions were fierce. Even when seated, they looked tall. Strong hands gripped long oars. Fifty warriors must have been in each boat.

The attack was swift. Armed with spears, the Vikings invaded the village. They killed people, stole gold and expensive jewelry, and destroyed homes and buildings. Then, as quickly as they had come, they shoved offshore and were gone. Behind them the village lay in ruins.

This scene was a common one in Europe in the 800s. Viking raiders attacked England and then struck at the Franks in Western Europe. They often attacked small villages, one at a time. Their attacks were always sudden and merciless, and they were feared by all.

The Vikings attacked the modern-day countries of Britain, Germany, France, and Spain. Their uniquely shaped boats and expert sailing skills allowed them to sail up inland rivers to attack small, defenseless towns.

One of the later Carolingian kings made a treaty with a Viking chieftain in 911. The king gave the Vikings the territory of Normandy. They became known as Normans. Their descendants were warriors and conquerors and also great administrators and explorers.

During the 900s, the Vikings also established powerful lines of kings in both Britain and Germany. Vikings were also the first to discover Iceland, Greenland, and the North American Atlantic coast.

A reproduction of a Viking longship

Echoes from the Past

Names of the Days

Like the Greeks and the Romans, Norsemen worshiped many gods. The Norsemen's chief god was named Odin, or Wodan. He was the god of war, creation, and the dead. His appearance was that of an old man with a beard and only one eye. Odin's wife was Frigg, the goddess of marriage. Under Odin was Thor, the god of thunder. Thor controlled the wind and rain and was the champion of the gods.

Almost every day, we echo the names of these gods from the Norse myths. Think about the names of the days in our week. Wednesday comes from the name for the chief god, Odin (Wodan's Day). Thursday is named for Thor (Thor's Day). Can you guess the origin of the name Friday?

Odin, or Wodan
Which day of the week was named after this god?

Feudalism

The people of Europe no longer had a central government after Charlemagne's kingdom was divided. They passed into a period of feudalism. This political system provided a form of order and security to all people. Under this system wealthy landowners promised protection to others in exchange for their services. People in Europe were in constant danger of attacks from invaders, such as the Vikings, the Muslims, and Asiatic nomads.

Lords and Vassals

Under the system of feudalism, kings granted estates called **fiefs** to nobles who had performed a service to the king. These nobles were known as **lords**.

A lord would then choose nobles who did not own land to manage portions of the fief. These nobles were called **vassals**. In a special ceremony, the vassal knelt before the lord and took an oath of faithfulness, promising his loyal service to the lord. Being asked to become a vassal was considered a great honor.

In exchange for the vassal's service, the lord gave the vassal a piece of land. Although the fief still belonged to the lord, the vassal could use it freely. A vassal could also divide up the land and become a lord over lesser vassals. Divisions of land and loyalties often continued until the fief was the size of an average manor.

Knights

You have probably seen pictures of or read stories about knights. A **knight** was a mounted soldier who defended the manor for the lord during the Middle Ages. He wore metal armor from head to foot, and his horse was also heavily armored. He carried a sword, a lance, and sometimes a battle-ax. He wielded a heavy shield to protect himself in battle.

Nearly any nobleman could become a knight if he proved himself worthy. He had to be faithful and skilled in warfare. A young boy who wanted to be a knight could take the first step at the age of seven by becoming a **page**. As a page, a boy went to live in the castle of another noble to learn horsemanship and fighting skills. He also did chores for the lord and the lady of the castle. At fourteen, a page became a **squire**. His responsibilities then included helping his master dress, accompanying him on hunts or in battles, and caring for his master's warhorse. A squire continued his lessons in bow, sword, and lance fighting. When he was twenty-one, he could become a knight.

An elaborate ceremony was necessary for a man to become a knight. Before this ceremony, the man spent the entire night in church, praying that he would be worthy of the honor. The next morning, other knights solemnly dressed him in his armor. The knight knelt before his lord, who touched him on the shoulder with a sword and said, "I dub you knight."

What preparations did a knight go through before his ceremony?

Sometimes new knights went immediately into battle. When there were no battles going on, groups of knights might plan mock battles called **tournaments**. At other times pairs of rival knights met to compete in jousts. The goal of a joust was for one knight to knock the other off his horse with a blunt lance. Great honor went to the winning jouster.

While a knight was fighting, the only way to identify him was by his coat of arms. The **coat of arms** was the emblem painted on his shield, and each knight had a different coat of arms.

What kind of person do you imagine when you think of a knight? Knights of the Middle Ages were supposed to live by a code of behavior called **chivalry**. This code taught a knight to be generous, loyal to his lord, skillful and brave in battle, faithful to the Roman Church, and protective of women.

Life on the Manor

The manor was the center of daily life during the Middle Ages. The manor system allowed wealthy nobles to defend their lands and the people living on them. In the early Middle Ages, the lord who owned the manor lived in the manor house, usually a large house made of logs. From about the ninth century on, lords lived in castles. The lord's home was safe and strong and offered a place of protection during attacks.

The manor was like a large farm. It had woods, fishing ponds, and fields where grain was grown. It also had little villages where the peasants lived. Every manor had a church building. The people living on each manor attended the church. No one worked on Sundays. People were released from work on some of the special *holy days* celebrated by the church. Our word *holiday* comes from this medieval term.

A jousting match
Can you locate the coat of arms for each knight?

homes of serfs · church · manor house

Most serfs shared their homes with their sheep, cows, or pigs. The animals usually stayed in a separate room, partitioned off from the living area.

Serfs were bound to the same land all their lives. They could leave only if they paid the lord. However, some peasants on manors were more privileged. They were the **freemen**, skilled craftsmen such as blacksmiths and carpenters. They paid less rent and worked fewer hours for the lord. They were allowed to move from the manor if they wanted to.

The peasants who lived on the lord's land were called **serfs.** They paid rent to the lord and worked part-time for him. They farmed his land, cleared new lands, built and repaired buildings, dug ditches, and fixed roads. Some lords expected extra gifts from their serfs at Christmas and Easter.

The serfs did not have many possessions of their own. They had to use the lord's mill to grind their grain into flour. They had to bake their bread in the lord's oven. Often the lord made them pay to use these items.

The homes of the serfs were very small. Some were only about fifteen feet long and six feet wide. Entire families ate, slept, and lived in the same room.

Great Chalfield Manor in Wiltshire, England

Discovering How

Designing a Coat of Arms

A knight's coat of arms was his own distinct emblem that identified him in battle. Knights had their coats of arms painted on their shields. Each knight's coat of arms represented him or the family he served. Its symbols and colors had special meanings.

In this activity you will design a coat of arms. The Internet is a good source for finding examples of various coats of arms. You may research your family coat of arms and copy it if you choose, or you may design one of your own.

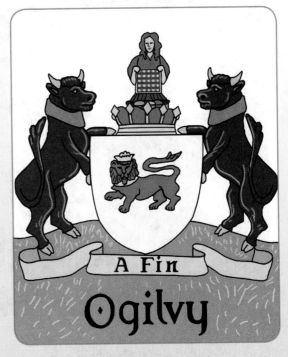

1. Gather the following materials: blank shield page, markers, paper, a ruler, glue, and other materials for decorating your coat of arms.

Color	Meaning
gold	generosity
white	peace, sincerity
red	military strength
blue	truth, loyalty
green	hope, loyal love
black	constancy, grief
purple	justice, royalty
orange	worthy ambition
maroon	patience, victory

2. Decide what color you want your shield to be and color it. Some shields are a solid color; others are divided into four parts or checkered. The table lists some common colors in heraldry and their meanings.

3. Choose symbols or a design to include in your coat of arms and draw or glue them in place.

4. Choose a motto for your coat of arms. Design a banner over the top or at the bottom of the shield that displays this motto.

1. What were some results of the Battle of Hastings?

2. Why is the Magna Carta a significant document?

Medieval England

The Battle of Hastings

As more and more nobles obtained land, their social class became more and more powerful. People looked to them for protection rather than to the king. In 1066 the king of England died without an heir. Two powerful nobles, Harold Godwinson and Duke William of Normandy, both claimed the throne. When Harold set himself up as the next king of England, William called upon his vassals to provide him with men and supplies to form an army. William and

One of many scenes on the Bayeux Tapestry (reproduction) depicting the Battle of Hastings
What military strategy are the foot soldiers using?

his army then met Harold's forces on a field near the town of Hastings.

Harold, wanting to force William to attack first, placed his men along the top of a hill. Standing side by side with their shields raised, Harold's men formed a **shield wall**. William knew his men would have to break through this wall to win the battle.

William and the Norman army surged up the hill toward Harold's men. Shouts rang out and metal clanged as the two armies clashed. William's army attacked the shield wall again and again. Late in the afternoon, the Norman army finally broke through. Harold was killed in the fierce struggle, and soon afterward, his army fled. This conflict became known as the **Battle of Hastings**.

William was now the king of England. He chose some of his own men to be lords, replacing the ones who were not loyal to him. All England became a feudal kingdom. William was called William the Conqueror. The new royal line that he began was called the Normans.

Henry's Legal System

The line of Norman kings in England lasted through only two generations. William's great-grandson, **Henry II**, came to power in 1154 after many years of civil war. Henry II's family, called the Plantagenets (plan TAJ uh nets), ruled England until the end of the 1400s. Henry developed England's legal system, extending the king's power into new areas.

Who: Henry II

What: first Plantagenet king

When: ruled 1154–1189

Where: England

A Frenchman, Henry possessed more wealth and territory outside England than within. Through inheritance and marriage, he had gained landholdings in France that exceeded those ruled directly by his feudal lord, the French king.

During King Henry's time, the legal courts practiced what was called **trial by ordeal**. A common method of trial by ordeal was to tie an accused person's hands and feet with rope and throw him into deep water. The people believed that if he floated, the pure water had "rejected" him because of his sin, and he was considered guilty. If he sank, he was innocent. Sadly, many innocent people lost their lives under this system.

After the civil wars, many land claims had to be settled to determine rightful landowners. Henry II developed procedures to handle these issues. He issued royal orders called **writs** to the local sheriffs. A writ instructed the sheriff to decide who actually held each piece of disputed land. Even though someone else may have owned the land, the person who actually lived on it usually got to keep it. The sheriff's decision required a **trial by jury**. Jury members were local people who came to the court. They told what they knew about the people who had claims to the land.

The sheriff made his decision with the help of the jury. He then gave the writ to whom he determined was the landowner. When there was a disagreement over the sheriff's decision, the case could be retried in court. When a particularly difficult case came up, it was sent directly to Henry II for his decision. Over time, such decisions were written down and enforced throughout England, becoming England's common law.

What would the trial by jury be deciding?

Signing the Magna Carta

In 1199 Henry II's youngest son, John, became the king of England. **King John** was not popular with the people. He imposed heavy taxes to cover his military losses, and he used his power to gain money and land for himself. He was often at odds with the church. The pope in Rome even excommunicated him for a time after a dispute about who would be the archbishop of Canterbury.

As dissatisfaction with King John's reign increased, a group of nobles examined English laws and determined that King John's abuses of power were violating their rights. The nobles agreed that the king's power needed to be limited.

In **1215** the nobles led a revolt against King John. They captured the city of London, and John began negotiating with them to try to end the conflict. One of their demands was that John sign a document called the **Magna Carta**, or "Great Charter."

The Magna Carta was based on English laws from the time of the Norman kings. The document was designed by the nobles to ensure that their own rights were protected. However, in time, the English people viewed the Magna Carta as a statement of the rights of all citizens. Under the Magna Carta, the king had to submit to the law. If he did not, the Magna Carta gave the nobles power to compel him to obey. This greatly limited the king's power to tax and control his subjects.

THE MAGNA CARTA

The Magna Carta was written as if the king were addressing his subjects. It was addressed to "all free men of our kingdom." Although much of it concerned only matters in feudal times, some of it applied to later times as well. Here are a few of the rights granted to free citizens by the king in the Magna Carta.

(9) Neither we nor our officials will seize any land or rent in payment of a debt, so long as the debtor has movable goods sufficient to discharge the debt. . . .

(12) No 'scutage' or 'aid' [types of taxes] may be levied in our kingdom without its general consent. . . .

(30) No sheriff, royal official, or other person shall take horses or carts for transport from any free man, without his consent.

(31) Neither we nor any royal official will take wood for our castle, or for any other purpose, without the consent of the owner. . . .

(38) In future no official shall place a man on trial upon his own unsupported statement, without producing credible witnesses to the truth of it. (Magna Carta, Revised Edition, trans. G. R. C. Davis [England: British Library, 1989])

King John signed the Magna Carta. It is doubtful that he seriously intended to abide by it. But the following year, he died suddenly, and his nine-year-old son became king. At that time, the Magna Carta was confirmed by the king's council and approved by the pope.

When the Magna Carta was signed, the people did not know the significance that it would have in the future. The document continues to be a statement of rights for free citizens. Its influence has spanned several centuries of history and even reached other countries. American colonists used the rights granted in the Magna Carta as the basis for their resisting unfair taxation by the king of England. The Magna Carta's legacy can be seen in the United States Constitution and the Bill of Rights.

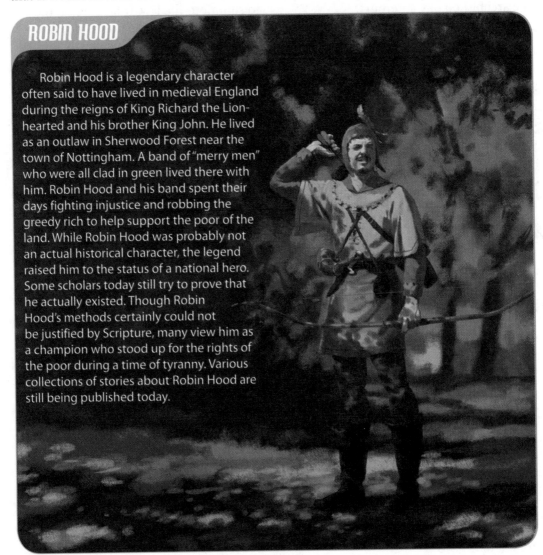

ROBIN HOOD

Robin Hood is a legendary character often said to have lived in medieval England during the reigns of King Richard the Lion-hearted and his brother King John. He lived as an outlaw in Sherwood Forest near the town of Nottingham. A band of "merry men" who were all clad in green lived there with him. Robin Hood and his band spent their days fighting injustice and robbing the greedy rich to help support the poor of the land. While Robin Hood was probably not an actual historical character, the legend raised him to the status of a national hero. Some scholars today still try to prove that he actually existed. Though Robin Hood's methods certainly could not be justified by Scripture, many view him as a champion who stood up for the rights of the poor during a time of tyranny. Various collections of stories about Robin Hood are still being published today.

Participating in a Mock Trial

After the Magna Carta became official, the system of trial by jury became the common practice. This was not only for cases of land disputes but for serious crimes as well. The concept of trial by jury has been adopted by many modern civilizations. In the United States, juries are made up of randomly selected citizens who hear evidence, confer with one another, and reach a decision in a trial. The jury is an important part of our legal system, helping to ensure that a fair decision is reached in any trial.

1. Listen as your teacher tells you which role you will play in the mock trial.

2. Follow your teacher's instructions as the trial proceeds.

3. Discuss the trial with your classmates. Was enough evidence given? Was the jury fair in its decision? How is this kind of trial superior to a trial by ordeal?

PROSECUTING ATTORNEY

DEFENSE ATTORNEY

SUSPECT

JURORS

383

1. What function did the castle have in addition to being the home of a lord and his family?

2. What were some reasons for the decline of feudalism?

The Castle

Castles gradually began to replace large log houses as homes of medieval lords. Castles had become common in Europe by the eleventh century. The castle in the Middle Ages was both a home and a military fortress.

Castles were surrounded by strong walls. Some castles in the late Middle Ages had stone walls over thirty feet thick. Inside the walls were towers, a courtyard, living areas, kitchens, and a great hall, where meetings and banquets were held.

Some castles had a strong central tower, called the **keep**, where the lord and his family lived. It was the safest place in the castle. Often the keep stood on a hill. Inside the keep were several rooms. They included the family's bedrooms and sitting rooms and a few other rooms, such as offices or a chapel. Most servants slept in the rooms where they worked, rather than having private bedrooms.

Harlech Castle was built on the rocky west coast of Wales in the 1200s.

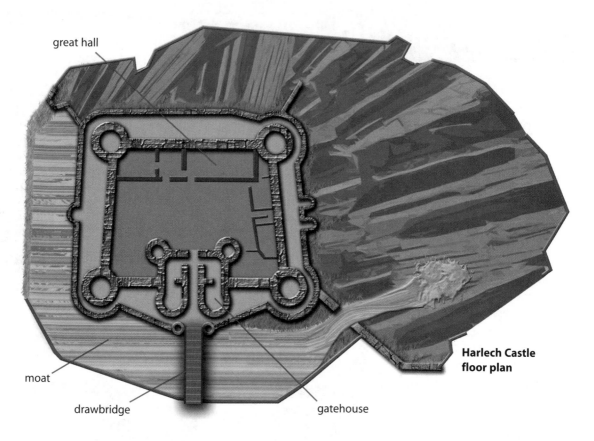

great hall

moat

drawbridge

gatehouse

Harlech Castle floor plan

Castles were cold and dark inside. Lords tried to brighten them by painting the walls and the ceilings with bright colors and placing burning torches in the rooms. They also put mats on the floors and hung large woven tapestries on the walls to keep out the cold.

Early castles were made of wood. By the twelfth century most castles were made of thick stone. Builders dug a **moat**, a wide trench filled with water, around the castle to keep attackers from reaching it easily. A **drawbridge** crossed the moat to the castle gate. During an attack, the guards raised the drawbridge to cover the gate, cutting off the entrance to the castle.

If attackers got safely across the moat, they had to face the gatehouse. The **gatehouse** was a large stronghold in the castle wall. If the attackers entered the gatehouse, castle defenders could lower a large screen to trap them inside.

Soldiers attacked castles in different ways. Sometimes they used a battering ram, a long log tipped with iron. This weapon could knock down the gate or part of the castle wall. Some soldiers might have rolled tall siege towers up against a wall and then climbed over into the castle. Sometimes the attacking army threw rocks and burning rags over the walls. The soldiers also dug tunnels under the castle and started fires there. They hoped to burn away the castle's foundation to make the structure collapse.

Medieval Banquets

During the Middle Ages wealthy people liked to give large banquets. Lords would invite many guests, and they would eat at long tables in the great hall of the castle. Pages waited on tables. Squires were often responsible to carve the meat for the guests. Court jesters provided live entertainment, such as music, juggling, and acrobatics, for the lord and his guests.

Many different foods were served at these banquets. One meal might have included soup, cheese made from a pig's head, puddings, baked fish, pork, venison, pheasants, larks, and other birds. Dessert was usually a pie filled with fish or fowl. Have you ever heard the nursery rhyme that tells of four and twenty blackbirds baked in a pie? One medieval custom was to insert live birds into a pie and release them in front of the guests when dessert was served.

Banquet guests used large, flat pieces of bread as plates. Forks were not used until the 1600s, so the guests used their fingers to eat most foods. But they still observed certain rules about table manners. No one was supposed to gnaw on the bones, and it was considered rude to dip food into the common salt bowl.

Page from a calendar showing Jean, Duc de Berry's household exchanging New Year's gifts. The duke is seated and is dressed in blue.
What are small dogs doing on the table?

The Decline of Feudalism

While the Plantagenet kings were ruling England, a family called the Capets ruled France. Germany and most of Italy made up the Holy Roman Empire, an empire under the joint control of an emperor and the pope of the Roman Catholic Church. You have already studied about the Byzantine Empire, which thrived in Eastern Europe during the early Middle Ages.

By the late 1000s most of the Byzantine Empire had fallen into the hands of Muslim invaders. The pope called for Western Europeans to join the Byzantines in a crusade to recapture the Holy Land from the Turks. As you have read, this crusade was the first in a series of unsuccessful wars between the Christians and the Muslim Turks.

The Crusades did much to weaken the system of feudalism. Fighting in them was expensive. Most of the money for them was provided by individual lords. Some lords had to sell or mortgage their properties to pay for their Crusade expenses. Many serfs left their manors to fight in the Crusades. Most who left, having tasted freedom, never returned.

By the year 1500, central governments all over Europe were run by kings. England and France were well on their way to becoming strong nations. More and more people were living in towns and cities rather than on manors. Most of the medieval world was no more.

Changes were taking place that would usher in a new era in Europe. Scholars and thinkers were beginning to question the teachings of the Roman Catholic Church. Their efforts to uncover the true teachings of Scripture regarding the Christian faith would eventually lead to the Protestant Reformation. In addition, universities began to form in cities where prominent teachers lived. Scholars were no longer confined to monasteries and church-sponsored schools. A revival of learning was beginning that would sweep Europe and result in new discoveries and accomplishments. The modern era of history was about to begin.

Sidon Sea Castle, built by crusaders, off the coast of Sidon in southern Lebanon

Identifying Simple Machines

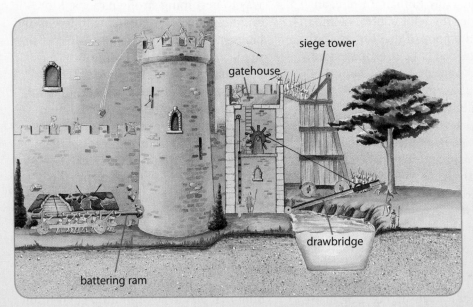

siege tower

gatehouse

battering ram

drawbridge

People who lived in the Middle Ages used simple machines to make their work easier. These simple machines can be seen in the castle architecture defenses and in the weapons they used.

In this activity you will identify the following types of simple machines. A *lever* is any bar that turns on a point, such as a seesaw, a wheelbarrow, or a broom. We use a *wheel and axle* everyday. It is a wheel with an axle, or rod, running through the wheel. A *pulley* is a simple machine that has a grooved wheel with a rope that fits in the groove.

A ramp is a simple machine called an *inclined plane*, a flat, sloped surface. A screw is related to an inclined plane.

A *screw* is an inclined plane wound around an axle. A simple machine made up of one or more inclined planes used to force materials apart is called a *wedge*. The inclined planes in the wedge form a point at the end.

1. Get your Activity Manual page.

2. Identify the simple machines in the pictures.

3. Choose one of the castle defenses or weapons and write a paragraph describing how the simple machines gives it a military advantage.

Chapter 15

A Kingdom from Shore to Shore

1. What is the source of the greatness of the civilizations you have studied?

2. How is a person placed into Christ's kingdom?

Your Worldview

When you think back over the chapters in this book, what comes to your mind? You may think of mighty empires that once spread over vast portions of the earth. You may picture interesting details from each culture, such as its language, architecture, or styles of dress. You may recall world-changing events—important battles or new inventions. You may think with sadness of the false religions that have led many people along different paths to hell.

But when you look deeper than the surface of these civilizations, what do you see? Do you see a world of chaos that has no purpose? Do you see a world guided by an impersonal, unknown power? Or do you see a God with a master plan Who controls the affairs of men to accomplish His purposes?

Your answers to these questions reflect your **worldview**. The people who study and write about history have many different viewpoints. Some historians and archaeologists look at past civilizations and reject the account of history in the Bible. However, Christians look at the past and see how the plan of God has unfolded. The Bible teaches a Christian not only what happened in history but also how to think about what happened.

Creation

You have learned that the perfect world God created fell into sin. Man's sinfulness is seen in the record of history. The Fall damaged the abilities that God gave men and women when He created them in His image. But these abilities were not completely destroyed. By God's grace, history also records many wonderful events because people still do what God created them to do, even if they do it imperfectly.

Adam and Eve in the Garden of Eden

Egyptian pyramids

God's first words to mankind were, "Be fruitful, and multiply, and replenish the earth, and subdue it: and have dominion over the fish of the sea, and over the fowl of the air, and over every living thing that moveth upon the earth" (Gen. 1:28). In many ways God's first words to humanity have been marvelously fulfilled. Think of all the civilizations that you have read about—civilizations in Egypt, Persia, Japan, Mesoamerica, Africa, Europe, and other places. People truly have filled the earth.

Mankind has also exercised **dominion** over the earth. The Egyptians harnessed the Nile. They built pyramids that still awe people today. The Romans built a vast empire that filled Europe and the Middle East with roads, new cities, and

systems of government that still exist. The Greeks and the Persians developed philosophies that lived on even when their countries were conquered.

Although the people may not have realized it, the greatness of each civilization had a single source—the image of God in man. Intelligence was one feature of every ancient civilization that causes historians to marvel. Ancient peoples designed impressive structures, developed languages, and wrote beautiful poetry. People can do creative, intelligent things because an intelligent God created them to be like Him. In early civilizations, people also had a sense of right and wrong. They organized

A scene from the handscroll of *The Tale of Genji*

GOD'S MERCY ON DISPLAY

After the fall of man, God told Eve He would put hatred between her offspring and Satan's offspring. We can look at all history as a struggle between Eve's seed (God's people) and the serpent's seed (Satan's people). The book of Genesis records that the descendants of Adam and Eve's son Cain rebelled against God. The godly descendants of Seth, Cain's brother, worshiped God for a while but soon also turned to wickedness. God had to destroy the world's first civilization with a universal flood. Only Noah and his family received grace from God and survived the destruction.

In the rise and fall of civilizations, we have seen God's mercy in keeping the human race from complete self-destruction. God has kept His promise to never again send another universal flood. At the tower of Babel, God divided the people into different language groups that forced them to scatter over the earth. As civilizations formed around the world, He brought down their power as their wickedness increased. God also preserved the Israelites as His chosen people through whom the Messiah would come. Throughout ancient history, God was gradually preparing the world for the Redeemer.

governments to protect people and to establish rules of conduct. People desire a justice system because they are made in the image of God, Who is a God of justice and is the perfect Lawgiver. God deserves praise and glory for the greatness and contributions of civilizations.

The Fall

Each civilization you have studied this year also had a dark side. The Egyptians built their magnificent buildings on the backs of slaves.

The Japanese developed fine literature, including the first novel, but some of their stories praised behavior that God condemns. Mesoamericans developed advanced civilizations, but these civilizations were drenched in the blood of human sacrifices.

People used the very abilities God gave them as bearers of His image to rebel against Him. This is most clearly seen in the religions of each culture.

If you look at the world's religions, you might see elements of worth in them. Religious myths often contain creative stories. Religious structures such as pyramids or cathedrals are some of the most impressive ever built.

Philosophies may also contain some elements of worth. Philosophers have tackled difficult problems and beliefs. Sometimes their thoughts have been studied for hundreds of years by people from many other cultures.

Yet every one of the world's religions and philosophies formed because people rejected God's truth. Often people had a concept of God, but they accepted only the features of His character that they liked or feared. They then used this flawed knowledge to create their own religious systems. Many beliefs came from people's sinful imaginations.

Noah and the ark

Redemption

God's plan has always been to redeem mankind from sin and its effects in the world. History is very important to God's plan of redemption.

From the beginning God intended for man to rule the world wisely. But by giving in to temptation, Adam failed to rule wisely, and all his descendants were unable to perfectly exercise righteous dominion over the earth. Even the Israelites, whom God had chosen to be His special people, were unable to rule their small nation according to God's law.

Yet God's plan of redemption was underway in the Israelites' history. God had given them His law, and He continued to give them promises of a Savior and King. This King would rule over Israel and over the entire world. He would save Israel as well as people from every nation in the world.

That King is Jesus, the Son of God. Jesus came as both a man and a king to redeem the world. Jesus lived a perfect life as a man. When He died He paid the penalty for sinful people in all times and in all places. Those who turn from their sin to trust Christ for salvation receive His righteousness. Another way of saying this is that they are brought out of the kingdom of darkness and placed into the kingdom of His light (Col. 1:12–14).

When Jesus rose from the dead and ascended to heaven, He rose as a king. All authority was given to Him in heaven and on earth. His kingdom is not like the empires of Persia or Rome. Today, as in the past, Jesus' kingdom spreads as more and more people enter it by placing their faith in Him.

The Ascension by Gustave Doré, From the Bob Jones University Collection

Making Inferences

An *inference* is a conclusion drawn from the facts given about a topic. An inference is not something that has been directly stated. It is an idea that seems reasonable based on the facts.

1. Read the paragraphs indicated on the Activity Manual page.

2. Identify the stated facts and ideas from each paragraph and record them. Write a summary of the information you identified.

3. Apply any other information you already know about the topic. Make inferences based on all the information you have, including the summary you wrote.

4. Discuss the inferences you made.

Making Inferences

1. What topic is the writer describing?

2. What facts are given?

3. What can you infer from the information?

4. What conclusions can you draw?

1. What warning and what promise did Jesus give about His kingdom?

2. What is one reason that Persians have persecuted Christians?

The Spread of Christ's Kingdom

For each nation or culture in this book, you have learned about its religious beliefs. During the first three hundred years after Christ lived, His followers carried the gospel to many parts of the world. Often the early Christians faced persecution, but this difficulty did not stop Christianity from spreading. Sometimes persecution had the opposite effect. As believers fled to other parts of the world to escape imprisonment, torture, or death, they carried the gospel along with them. By the Middle Ages, forms of Christianity had been embraced in nations such as Egypt, Israel, Greece, Rome, and Byzantium.

After the period of history covered in this book, the world continued to change. Christianity is rapidly growing today in many regions that used to have little Christian influence. Some of these regions include Mesoamerica, China, and Africa. However, there are also regions that were once strongly Christian that are no longer so. Such countries include Egypt, Turkey, and parts of Europe.

The spread of Christ's kingdom is not always consistent in all places and at all times. In the book of Revelation, Jesus warned believers that if they were not faithful, their churches would be removed. Yet He also promised that His kingdom would continue to grow, just as yeast gradually spreads through every part of a piece of dough (Matt. 13:33).

Egypt

Think about what the ancient civilization of Egypt was like. They believed that Ra, the sun god, created and ruled the world. They believed that, after burial, a dead person traveled by boat to Osiris, the god of the underworld, for judgment. The Egyptians treated their pharaohs as gods and counted on priests to tell them how to worship. The pharaohs often ruled harshly and took the people's wealth to support their own lavish living. They also cruelly enslaved the Israelites

The Christian Martyrs' Last Prayer by Jean-Léon Gérôme

A page of the Egyptian Oxyrhynchus Papyri with the text of Romans 1:1–7

for four hundred years until God delivered His people.

In spite of all that was wrong in ancient Egypt, the prophet Isaiah made a surprising prediction. He foretold that one day Egyptians would be considered God's people, just as Israel was in Old Testament times.

The **gospel**, the message of God's redemption for man, may have been taken to Egypt shortly after Christ's resurrection. Some historians believe that Mark, who wrote the book of Mark, was the first missionary to that land. The Egyptian city of Alexandria grew to be one of the most important places for early Christianity. Some of the church's most influential teachers came from Egypt.

Over time the church in Egypt developed errors. Some followers of Christianity embraced false views held by the Eastern Orthodox Church and the

ATHANASIUS

Athanasius was an important Christian leader in the early church in Egypt. He defended the deity of Christ against false teachers who believed that Jesus was not equal with God the Father. Sometimes the Roman emperors sided with these false teachers. Persecuted for his beliefs, Athanasius had to hide in the Egyptian desert, sometimes for years on end, to carry on his fight for truth.

Athanasius probably felt as if he were the only one standing for truth with the whole world opposed to him. But in the end, true Christians embraced the right teaching that he had spent his life defending.

Roman Catholic Church. Later, Muslims conquered Egypt and placed great restrictions on the Christians. Muslim leaders seized church property and threatened death to Christians who did not convert to Islam.

Today Christianity does not have the same strength in Egypt as it once had. However, we can be sure that Isaiah's prophecy will still come to pass. One day the Lord will say, "Blessed be Egypt my people" (Isa. 19:25).

Mesopotamia and Persia

What do you remember about Mesopotamia? Did it seem like a likely place for Christ's kingdom to spread? Both the Assyrian Empire and the Chaldean Empire rose out of the region of Mesopotamia. The Assyrians were known for their fierceness and cruelty. God used them to judge many sinful nations, including His own people. Even though the Assyrian people repented and turned to God for a while in the days of Jonah,

they later returned to their evil ways. The Chaldean Empire, which conquered the Assyrians, was also used as God's tool of judgment on His people. One Chaldean king, Nebuchadnezzar, humbled himself and acknowledged God, but later rulers continued living wickedly.

The mighty Persian Empire rose to power after the fall of the Chaldean Empire. The Persians introduced the false religion of Zoroastrianism to the world, and their rulers tolerated many other religions. However, God used several pagan Persian kings to protect and provide for His people. These rulers were an important part in God's plan for the Israelites to return to their land and rebuild their nation.

As early Christians traveled east of the Roman Empire, they established churches. Christ's kingdom spread into the regions of Mesopotamia and Persia and beyond. Archaeologists have discovered an ancient Christian hymnal in the Mesopotamian city of Edessa,

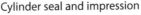

Cylinder seal and impression

located in modern Turkey. A few other works of Christian writers have also been found.

Christians profited from the tolerance of Persian rulers at the time of the early church. Some Christians fled to Persia to escape Roman persecution. Later, after the Roman emperor Constantine converted to Christianity, the Persians feared that the Christians would side with Rome and fight against them. Since that time, Persian Christians have suffered persecution during various periods of history. Many Persian Christians today have connected themselves with the Roman Catholic Church. There are some independent churches in Iran, but their numbers are quite small.

CONSTANTINE AND THE CHURCH

In AD 313 Constantine declared that Christianity would be tolerated in the Roman Empire. This decision had both disadvantages and benefits. The new freedom for Christians encouraged a decline in the purity of the church. Many people claimed to be Christians even though they had never been truly saved and transformed by Christ. The seeds of errors that the Protestant Reformation would deal with much later were already being planted.

On the other hand, the freedoms and privileges resulted in rapid growth for the church in the Roman Empire. It increased both in members and in material prosperity. Although some members were not genuine Christians, there were still true believers who defended the truth. Many scholars believe Constantine's protection of the church at a crucial time in its history kept it from being stamped out by persecution.

Ephrem the Syrian lived during the fourth century. The lack of persecution gave him the freedom to write sermons, poetry, and a hymnal, which have been found by archaeologists. The following is one of his hymns.

A portion of a sermon by Ephrem the Syrian

The One who said that by light
darkness was defeated, and death by
  life,
taught that envy is conquered by love,
and by his scripture deceit is transformed into wisdom.
Blessed is the one who arms the tongue
  with Your word,
who quotes from what is Yours to Your
  adversary.
Our Lord, let us gaze upon You,
Who from Moses quoted to the evil one
  in Your temptation.

(tr. by Kathleen E. McVey, *Ephrem the Syrian: Hymns*, Hymn 14)

FOCUS

1. What missionary was influential in bringing the true gospel to India?

2. Who first brought the gospel to South Africa?

Greece, Rome, and Europe

You have read that both Greece and Rome were cultures that worshiped many different gods. They were also cultures that brought many new ideas and philosophies to the world. Yet these religions and ideas were unsatisfying to the people. The gods they worshiped were unholy and spiteful, and human philosophies could not deal with the problem of man's sin.

It was during the period of the Roman Empire that the apostle Paul traveled throughout Asia Minor and Greece, sharing the gospel and planting churches. He led many people to Christ. Eventually the Romans arrested him and sent him to Rome to await trial. There, as a prisoner, he continued to write letters and encourage churches. Many of his letters are part of the New Testament.

Emperors and officials in the Roman Empire persecuted Christians for hundreds of years. But the persecutions were unable to stop the church. Christians multiplied, and as the empire spread north, Christianity also spread. Under Constantine's protection in the fourth century, the number of those who called themselves Christians grew tremendously.

As you have read, many errors in doctrine and practice had crept into the church by the Middle Ages. Neverthe-less, the Bible and Christian books were copied in monasteries. By the beginning of the 1500s, many priests and monks studied and taught the Bible and theology. Some of these men understood Scripture better than others. It was in one of these monasteries in Germany that the monk **Martin Luther** grasped the truth of how a person can be right with God—a truth that had not been clearly expressed for many years. Luther realized that a person is justified, or declared righteous, simply by putting his faith in Jesus' life and His death on the cross.

Luther and many others wanted the Roman Catholic Church to reform its teachings. The movement known as the **Protestant Reformation** resulted from their efforts. During the Reformation many citizens of European nations separated from the Roman Catholic Church and placed their trust in Christ alone

Martin Luther Discovering Justification by Faith, Edward Matthew Ward, From the Bob Jones University Collection

Martin Luther
What does this painting tell about life in a monastery?

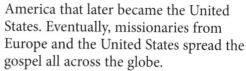
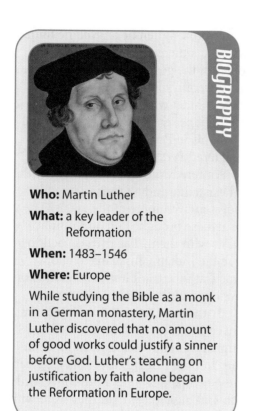

Who: Martin Luther

What: a key leader of the Reformation

When: 1483–1546

Where: Europe

While studying the Bible as a monk in a German monastery, Martin Luther discovered that no amount of good works could justify a sinner before God. Luther's teaching on justification by faith alone began the Reformation in Europe.

for the forgiveness of their sins. One of these European nations was England. The English planted colonies in North

America that later became the United States. Eventually, missionaries from Europe and the United States spread the gospel all across the globe.

The Reformation is still viewed today as one of the most important events in history for spreading Christ's kingdom in this world. Sadly, many Europeans today have rejected Christ. There are still some faithful churches in Europe, but not as many as there were one hundred years ago. Many old church buildings where believers once gathered stand empty. Some have even been turned into apartments, bars, or mosques. Because many European churches did not remain faithful to Christ, God removed them just as He had warned.

India

Ancient India was the birthplace of two major world religions. Hinduism, India's earliest major religion, held people captive in the caste system. A person's behavior, relationships, and practices were carefully controlled by this religion. One young Indian man, Siddhartha Gautama, saw his people suffering under the Hindu caste system. He responded by forming a new religion called Buddhism. This religion gave people the false

Today France has the largest Muslim population of any Western European country. The Grand Mosque in Paris is one of more than one thousand Islamic centers of worship in France.

401

hope that they could end their suffering by following a path of good works. These works would lead to a state called nirvana.

For centuries Indians lived under these religious beliefs with no knowledge of the true and living God. Even though Buddhism never became the dominant religion of India, it has spread throughout Asia by Buddhist missionary efforts.

According to tradition, the apostle Thomas first brought the gospel to India. Travel between the Roman Empire and India was common in the first century. The church historian Eusebius (yoo SEE bee us) recorded that an early believer named Pantaenus traveled as a missionary to India. When he arrived he found Christians there already, and they had copies of the gospel of Matthew. By the fourth century Persian Christians had made contact with Christians in India. The Indians sent their church leaders to schools in Persia until the Muslims conquered Persia.

Scattered communities of Christians still existed in India when Portuguese traders arrived there in the 1600s. The Portuguese brought Roman Catholic priests with them. The priests tried to force the Indian Christians to adopt some Catholic traditions, and confusion developed in the church in India.

By the end of the 1700s, Protestants arrived in India through two trading companies, the Dutch East India Company and the British East India Company. These companies were more concerned with making money than they were with the eternal future of the Indians. The Dutch and the English forbade evangelism of the Indians for fear of upsetting the Hindus and hindering trade.

Despite the opposition from the trading companies, missionaries still came to India. **William Carey**, a Baptist from England, went to India in 1792. He and his coworkers knew that they needed Indian evangelists if the gospel were ever to spread throughout the vast region. However, it took many years for them to lead only a handful of Indians to Christ.

In 1813, England passed a law that required the British East India Company to permit missionary work in the areas the company controlled. This opened the way for more missionaries. More and more Indians became Christians. Eventually Carey and the other missionaries

William Carey
What event in American and English history occurred about a decade before Carey went to India?

were able to train Indian pastors and evangelists to serve their own people.

By the mid-1850s, England had gained complete governmental control of India. This changed in 1947 when India gained its independence from the British. Hinduism remained the dominant religion of India. Today Christians in some parts of India are persecuted. Despite this, the number of Christians there has grown from a handful to millions. Although this is a large number, it represents only a small percentage of India's vast population.

Africa

The continent of Africa contains many different countries and geographic regions. Much of ancient Africa was dominated by traditional beliefs involving the spirit world. Christianity entered different parts of the continent at different times.

One of Africa's neighboring countries is Israel. After Christ's time on earth, the gospel quickly spread from Israel to Egypt and other parts of northern Africa. At the time of the apostles, northern Africa was part of the Roman Empire. Some of Africa's greatest Christian teachers, such as Tertullian and Augustine, greatly influenced European Christianity. Christianity in northern Africa continued strongly until the Muslim conquest in the seventh century.

Before the Muslims arrived, Christianity had spread south into Nubia, which is now Sudan and Ethiopia. In ancient times this area was home to the official that the apostle Philip evangelized in Acts 8. No doubt the official shared the gospel with others in Nubia. But it was not until Byzantine missionaries came in the sixth century that Christianity really took hold in Nubia. The Nubians fought the Muslims, and their victory stopped the spread of Islam in Nubia and Aksum for several centuries.

You have already read how the gospel came to Aksum, present-day Ethiopia, in the fourth century. After the young Aksum king converted to Christianity, his kingdom followed. Aksum was never conquered by the Muslims, but its influence of Christianity was weakened through false teaching.

Portuguese explorers attempted missionary work among the people of Africa's interior. The king of the Congo was their first significant convert. He asked that priests come to teach his people. However, the priest who came did

Illuminated Augustine manuscript

not care for the people's souls. Instead, the priests played a part in enslaving the people of the Congo and sending them off to work in foreign lands.

Great Britain and Germany established trade and built colonies in Africa. Their presence in Africa opened the way for Protestant missionaries to come. In the nineteenth century the missionary **Robert Moffat** arrived in the country of South Africa. He provided an example that many later missionaries followed. He set up a mission station, translated the Bible into the local language, and began

a church. Throughout the 1800s and early 1900s, many mission stations were established and churches were formed.

By the mid-1900s many Africans were seeking independence from their European colonial rulers. African Christians wished to provide the leadership of their churches rather than have foreign missionaries lead them. Today foreign missionaries still come to Africa, but many churches there are now led by African Christians. Christianity is now growing faster in Africa than it is in Europe and in North America.

ROBERT AND MARY MOFFAT

In 1817 the Scottish missionary Robert Moffat arrived in Cape Town, South Africa. He had left Mary Smith, the woman he hoped to marry, behind in England. Her parents refused to allow her to go away to a foreign land.

Robert Moffat worked in Africa alone for nearly three years before Mary's parents changed their minds. During this time he shared the gospel with a chief named Afrikaner, who eventually trusted Christ along with many of his people.

Robert and Mary were married in Cape Town. They set up mission stations, first in the village of Lattakoo, and later in the town of Kuruman. Progress in both stations was slow. Years went by with the African people showing little interest in the gospel. Mary became very sick and nearly died before the birth of their first child. A time of drought came, and the water supply ran low. In addition the mission station they lived at was threatened by tribal warfare.

A friend in England wrote to Mary and asked her if there was anything she needed. "Please send us a communion set," Mary wrote back, knowing that goods shipped from England could take months to arrive. "Some day we will need it."

The Lord rewarded Mary's faith. A few years later, the Moffats held a baptism for the first six African converts. Afterward they had a communion service, using the communion set that had arrived from England only the day before.

Persian
Immortal

Writing a Compare-Contrast Essay

A compare-contrast essay tells how two things are alike and how they are different. Compare-contrast essays can be organized in various ways. Two common ways to organize this type of essay are by subject or by similarities and differences. You will write an essay that compares and contrasts the same topic from two different civilizations that you have studied in this book.

1. Choose a topic from two civilizations to compare and contrast. Gather information by reviewing the appropriate chapters in this book and taking notes. Use the Venn diagram in the Activity Manual to help you organize the information you have collected.

2. Write a brief outline to put your ideas in order. Remember that your essay should have an introduction and a conclusion.

3. Follow the writing process to draft, revise, and proofread your essay.

4. Share your completed essay.

Japanese
samurai

FOCUS

1. What countries sent missionaries throughout Latin America?

2. What missionary translated the entire Bible into Chinese?

Latin America

At the same time that Martin Luther was launching the Reformation in Europe, Hernando Cortés was subduing the Aztec people in Mesoamerica. The Spaniards brought with them the Latin languages of Spanish and Portuguese. They also brought Roman Catholicism. This religion soon had a strong grip on all Mesoamerica. Spanish and Portuguese exploration and colonization reached from Mexico through South America. These lands became known as Latin America. As leaders of the Roman Catholic Church saw many in Europe turning to Protestant Christianity, they were determined that Latin America remain Catholic.

In the 1500s, missionaries from Geneva, Switzerland, were some of the first Protestant missionaries to come to a French colony in Brazil. They hoped to preach the gospel to the people of that area. But the French colonists drove them away. Three hundred years later, Spanish and Portuguese rule in Latin America ended. After this Latin American nations became more open to Protestant missionaries and invited them to their lands.

Immigrants sometimes helped with the missionary efforts to Latin America. African Americans from the United States immigrated to Haiti and the Dominican Republic in the early 1800s. Many of them worked diligently to spread the gospel. Some immigrants from Europe and the United States started churches in Latin America. At first they used their own languages with little success. After living in the Latin American culture for a time, they learned to speak Spanish and Portuguese and were better able to minister to those around them.

Jesuit mission ruins in Argentina

The British Bible Society and the American Bible Society also sent missionaries to Latin America. Bibles in Portuguese, Spanish, and many national languages were distributed all over the continent. Church planters founded many churches that shaped Christianity in Latin America for much of the twentieth century.

Gethsemane Independent Baptist Church in Mexico

Just as in Africa, the leadership of these churches today has gradually shifted from missionaries to the Latin Americans themselves. Although some churches mix the gospel with false teaching, many preach the truth and continue the spread of Christ's kingdom.

China

China's isolation seemed to have kept Christianity outside its borders for centuries. The earliest known instance of Christianity in China was in the 600s, during the Tang dynasty. This dynasty began almost four hundred years after the Han dynasty. One of the Tang emperors loved books and had a library with thousands of volumes. When Christian missionaries from Persia arrived with a religion that centered on a holy book, the emperor was very interested. He asked them to translate the Bible into Chinese. Evidence found in 1908 shows that parts of the Bible were translated during that period.

By the 900s the Tang dynasty had ended. Foreign religions in China came under attack, and Christianity there was eliminated.

Under the Mongol rule in the thirteenth century, Persian Christians again brought the gospel into China for a time. But once again, with the rise of the Ming dynasty, foreign religions were no longer welcome.

After the Reformation, Protestant missionaries began to arrive in China. In 1642 Dutch Reformed missionaries arrived in Taiwan, an island off the coast of China. They lived in the villages among the people, learned their languages, taught them, and began to translate the Bible. Many were converted to Christ. However, after more than twenty years of missionary work, the Chinese drove them away.

Robert Morrison working on the Chinese Bible
What job title would you give to the Chinese men helping Morrison?

break through the barriers. In 1807 he sailed to China. Once there, he dressed like the Chinese and sought to avoid attention. He did not openly evangelize, knowing if caught he would be forced to leave China. Instead he spent his time learning Chinese and translating the entire Bible. His Chinese Bible had a tremendous impact on the evangelization of China that would follow.

Morrison counseled other missionaries to go to Chinese-speaking areas just outside China. There, on the borders of the country, they could learn Chinese, evangelize, and prepare Chinese evangelists to travel through their own country with the gospel. Missionaries followed this strategy until 1858, when China

China remained closed to missionaries, but an English missionary named **Robert Morrison** was determined to

HUDSON TAYLOR

A young English missionary named **Hudson Taylor** earnestly desired to take the gospel to the interior of China. He began to pray for laborers. At first he prayed for twenty-four, then for seventy more, then for a hundred more, then for a thousand more. God answered his prayers.

God also answered prayer in saving multitudes of Chinese people. Many of the new converts worked closely with Hudson Taylor's China Inland Mission. He insisted, however, that the workers support themselves rather than be paid with foreign funds. This way, the Chinese church could still stand on its own even if the foreigners were driven out.

Who: Robert Morrison

What: English missionary

When: 1782–1834

Where: China

As one of the first English missionaries to China, Robert Morrison was careful and discreet in the way he worked. He avoided attention from the Chinese government by dressing and living like the Chinese. He remained in China for twenty-seven years, long enough to learn Chinese and publish a translation of the Bible.

began opening certain port cities to the Europeans for trade. Missionaries moved to these port cities to establish missionary work in them.

As a result of the Boxer Rebellion (1899–1900), many foreigners were driven from the Chinese empire. Some missionaries as well as Chinese Christians were attacked and even killed. When the Communists took over China after World War II, all the missionaries were forced to leave. But because the Chinese church had long been self-supporting, it was able to stand on its own. Believers continued worshiping Christ and spreading the gospel.

Although Christians in China have experienced much persecution and often have to meet in secret, Christianity has not been stamped out. Researchers estimate that there are between twenty-five and eighty million Christians in China today.

Japan

Like China, Japan was closed to outside influences for many centuries. Shintoism and Buddhism held sway over its people. But in 1853 four American naval ships sailed into Tokyo Bay. The Americans asked for permission to use certain Japanese ports on a regular basis, and the Japanese government agreed. An American diplomat worked to negotiate

Gospel of Grace Christ Church in Japan

a trade agreement with Japan, and he also helped open up Japan to missionary work. Christianity's spread in Japan has been slow, and today, Christians are still a very small part of the population. But God is still calling missionaries to spread His kingdom in Japan.

Christ's Kingdom and You

In Matthew 13 Jesus described His kingdom as a tiny mustard seed that grows into a large plant. His kingdom started out small—only a handful of people in the Roman provinces on the eastern shore of the Mediterranean Sea. But this kingdom has now spread over the entire globe. The book of Revelation tells us that the kingdom of Christ will one day include people from every tribe and nation who will sing His praises continually before His throne.

Christ's kingdom spreads one person at a time. Each person who places his faith in Christ becomes a member of His kingdom. Are you a part of that kingdom?

Part of God's plan for Christians is to carry the message of salvation to all the world. Christians can accomplish this through the power of the Holy Spirit, in any walk of life. How will you participate in the spread of Christ's kingdom while you live your life on this earth?

(Top to bottom) Present-day believers in Papua New Guinea, the Philippines, and Cambodia

RESOURCE TREASURY

Epic of Gilgamesh

The following excerpts are from Tablet 11 of the Epic of Gilgamesh *and give an account of a great flood.*

[14] The hearts of the Great Gods moved them to inflict the Flood.

O man of Šuruppak, son of Ubar-Tutu [i.e., Ut-napištim]
Tear down the house and build a boat!
Abandon wealth and seek living beings!
Spurn possessions and keep alive living beings!
Make [the seed of] all living beings go up into the boat.
The boat which you are to build, its dimensions must measure equal to each other:
its length must correspond to its width.
Roof it over like the Apsu. [i.e., the firmament in the primordial waters]

[75] I set my hand to the finishing of the ship.
The boat was finished by sunset.
The launching was very difficult:
They had to keep carrying a runway of poles front to back,
until two-thirds of it had gone under water.
[80] Whatever I had I loaded on it:
whatever silver I had I loaded on it,
whatever gold I had I loaded on it.
All the living beings that I had I loaded on it,
I had all my kith and kin go up into the boat,
all the beasts and animals of the field and the craftsmen I had go up.

[93] I went into the boat and sealed the entry.
For the caulking of the boat, to Puzur-Amurri, the boatman,
I gave the palace together with its contents.

[96] Just as dawn began to glow there arose from the horizon a black cloud.
[the storm god] Adad rumbled inside of it,
before him went Šhullat and Haniš [Sack and Suppression],
heralds going over mountain and land.

[108] All day long the South Wind blew, blowing fast - and then the Flood came,
overwhelming the people like an attack.

[111] No one could see his fellow, they could not recognize each other in the torrent.

[113] Even the gods were frightened by the Flood,
and retreated, ascending to the heaven of Anu.
The gods were cowering like dogs, crouching by the outer wall.

"*Epic of Gilgamesh*—Sumerian Flood Story 2750–2500 BCE." HistoryWiz. http://www.historywiz.com/primarysources/sumerianflood.html (accessed May, 5, 2011).

Pyramid Texts

The Pyramid Texts are inscribed on the interior walls of certain pyramids. The texts include prayers, hymns, and spells for the dead pharaoh for his passage to his new celestial abode.

Thy two wings are spread out like a falcon with thick plumage, like the hawk seen in the evening traversing the sky (Pyr. 1048).

He flies who flies; this king Pepi flies away from you, ye mortals. He is not of the earth, he is of the sky. . . . Thou ascendest to the sky as a falcon, thy feathers are (those of) geese (Pyr. 913).

King Unis goes to the sky, king Unis goes to the sky! On the wind! On the wind! (Pyr. 309)

[S]tairs to the sky are laid for him that he may ascend thereon to the sky (Pyr. 365).

King Unis ascends upon the ladder which his father Re (the Sun-god) made for him (Pyr. 390).

Atum has done that which he said he would do for this king Pepi II, binding for him the rope-ladder, joining together the (wooden) ladder for this king Pepi II; (thus) this king is far from the abomination of men (Pyr. 2083).

"How beautiful to see, how satisfying to behold," say the gods, "when this god (meaning the king) ascends to the sky. His fearfulness is on his head, his terror is at his side, his magical charms are before him." Geb has done for him as was done for himself (Geb). The gods and souls of Buto, the gods and souls of Hierakonpolis, the gods in the sky and the gods on earth come to him. They make supports for king Unis on their arm(s). Thou ascendest, O King Unis, to the sky. Ascend upon it in this its name "Ladder" (Pyr. 476–9).

Opened are the double doors of the horizon; unlocked are its bolts (Pyr. 194).

Thy messengers go, thy swift messengers run, thy heralds make haste. They announce to Re that thou hast come, (even) this king Pepi (Pyr. 1539–40).

This king Pepi found the gods standing, wrapped in their garments, their white sandals on their feet. They cast off their white sandals to the earth, they throw off their garments. "Our heart was not glad until thy coming," say they (Pyr. 1197).

O Re-Atum! This king Unis comes to thee, an imperishable glorious-one, lord of the affairs of the place of the four pillars (the sky). Thy son comes to thee. This king Unis comes to thee (Pyr. 217).

The king ascends to the sky among the gods dwelling in the sky. He stands on the great [dais], he hears (in judicial session) the (legal) affairs of men. . . . become thou a spirit dwelling in Dewat. Live thou this pleasant life which the lord of the horizon lives (Pyr. 1169–72).

Development of Religion and Thought in Ancient Egypt, trans. by James Henry Breasted (Chicago, 1912), pp. 109–15, 118–20, 122, 136.

The Second Book of Maccabees

The following verses are excerpts from the second book of Macca-bees. The first number is the chapter and the second number is the verse.

[2 Maccabees 8]

{8:16} But Maccabeus, calling together seven thousand who were with him, asked them not to be reconciled to the enemies. . . .

{8:19} Moreover, he reminded them also of the assistance of God which their parents had received; and how, under Sennacherib, one hundred and eighty-five thousand had perished;

{8:21} By these words, they were brought to constancy and were prepared to die for the laws and their nation.

{8:24} And, with the Almighty as their helper, they slew over nine thousand men. Furthermore, having wounded and disabled the greater part of the army of Nicanor, they forced them to take flight.

{8:29} And so, when these things were done, and supplication was made by all in common, they asked the merciful Lord to be reconciled to his servants unto the end.

{8:36} And he who had promised to pay a tribute to the Romans from the captives of Jerusalem, now professed that the Jews had God as their protector, and, for this reason, they were invulnerable, because they followed the laws established by him.

[2 Maccabees 10]

{10:2} Then he demolished the altars, which the foreigners had constructed in the streets, and likewise the shrines.

{10:3} And, having purged the temple, they made another altar. And, taking glowing stones from the fire, they began to offer sacrifices again after two years, and they set out incense, and lamps, and the bread of the Presence.

{10:5} Then, on the day that the temple had been polluted by the foreigners, it happened on the same day that the purification was accomplished, on the twenty-fifth day of the month, which was Kislev.

{10:6} And they celebrated for eight days with joy, . . .

{10:7} Because of this, they now preferred to carry boughs and green branches and palms, for him who had prospered the cleansing of his place.

{10:8} And they decreed a common pre-cept and decree, that all the people of the Jews should keep those days every year.

The Sacred Bible: The Second Book of Maccabees, Catholic Public Domain Version, Original Edition. trans. and ed. Ronald L. Conte Jr.

The Laws of Manu

Manu was a mythical character. Because of his ability to protect the people, the god Brahma transformed him into a king. The ancient Indians credited the beginnings of kings and social classes to Manu, who they believed was the first man. These ancient laws discuss the Indian social structure.

I.3. . . . The brahmin is the lord of all castes.

I.31. But for the sake of the prosperity of the worlds, [the Creator] caused the brahmin, the kshatriya, the vaisya, and the sudra to proceed from his mouth, his arms, his thighs, and his feet.

I.87. But in order to protect this universe He, the most resplendent one, assigned separate duties and occupations to those who sprang from his mouth, arms, thighs, and feet.

Duties of a Brahmin

X.75. Teaching, studying, sacrificing for himself, sacrificing for others, making gifts and receiving them are the six acts prescribed for a brahmin.

X.76 But among the six acts ordained for him three are his means of subsistence, sacrificing for others, teaching, and accepting gifts from pure men.

Duties of a Kshatriya

VII.2. A kshatriya . . . must duly protect this whole world.

VII.3. . . . The Lord created a king for the protection of this whole creation.

VII.20. If the king did not, without tiring, inflict punishment on those worthy to be punished, the stronger would roast the weaker, like fish on a spit.

VII.35. The king has been created to be the protector of the castes and orders, who, all according to their rank, discharge their several duties.

Duties of a Vaisya

IX.326. After a vaisya has received the sacraments and has taken a wife he shall be always attentive to the business whereby he may subsist and to that of tending cattle.

IX.327. For when the Lord of creatures created cattle, he made them over to the vaisya; to the brahmins and the king he entrusted all created beings.

IX.332. He must be acquainted with the proper wages of servants, with the various languages of men, with the manner of keeping goods, and the rule of purchase and sale.

Duties of a Sudra

IX.334. [T]o serve brahmins who are learned in the Vedas, householders, and famous for virtue, is the highest duty of a sudra, which leads to beatitude.

IX.335. A sudra who is pure, the servant of his betters, gentle in his speech, and free from pride, and always seeks a refuge with brahmins, attains a higher caste.

IX.413. But a sudra . . . may [be compelled] to do servile work; for he was created by the Self-existent [Lord] to be the slave of a brahmin.

A Sourcebook in Indian Philosophy, ed. Sarvepalli Radhakrishnan and Charles A. Moore (Princeton: Princeton University Press, 1957).

The Analects by Confucius

The following excerpts are from Section 1 of The Analects. *The Analects are sayings of Confucius that were written by his disciples after his death.*

Book I—Concerning Fundamental Principles

The Master said; "Is it not indeed a pleasure to acquire knowledge and constantly to exercise oneself therein?"

***

The Master said; "A Scholar who is not grave will not inspire respect, and his learning will therefore lack stability. His chief principles should be conscientiousness and sincerity. Let him have no friends unequal to himself. And when in the wrong let him not hesitate to amend."

***

The Master said: "While a man's father lives mark his tendencies; when his father is dead mark his conduct."

Book II—Concerning Government

The Master said: "Observe what he does; look into his motives; find out in what he rests. Can a man hide himself! Can a man hide himself!"

***

The Master said: "Learning without thought is useless. Thought without learning is dangerous."

***

"To see the right and not do it is cowardice."

Book IV—Concerning Virtue

The Master said: "Only the Virtuous are competent to love or to hate men."

***

The Master said: "Wealth and rank are what men desire, but unless they be obtained in the right way they are not to be possessed. Poverty and obscurity are what men detest; but unless it can be brought about in the right way, they are not to be abandoned."

***

The Master said: "The man of honour thinks of his character, the inferior man of his position. The man of honour desires justice, the inferior man favour."

***

The Master said: "The self-restrained seldom err."
The Master said: "The wise man desires to be slow to speak but quick to act."
The Master said: "Virtue never dwells alone; it always has neighbours."

Book V—Concerning Certain Disciples and Others

Tzŭ Kung said: "What I do not wish others to do to me, that also I wish not to do to them."

The Analects of Confucius, trans. William Edward Soothill (Fleming H. Revell, 1910).

The Histories, Book III

The following is an excerpt from a history book about Persian judges. It is written by the historian Herodotus.

Now the royal judges are certain picked men among the Persians, who hold their office for life, or until they are found guilty of some misconduct. By them justice is administered in Persia, and they are the interpreters of the old laws, all disputes being referred to their decision. When Cambyses, therefore, put his question to these judges, they gave him an answer which was at once true and safe—"they did not find any law," they said, "allowing a brother to take his sister to wife, but they found a law, that the king of the Persians might do whatever he pleased." And so they neither warped the law through fear of Cambyses, nor ruined themselves by over stiffly maintaining the law; but they brought another quite distinct law to the king's help, which allowed him to have his wish. Cambyses, therefore, married the object of his love.

The History of Herodotus, trans. George Rawlinson (New York: Dutton & Co., 1862).

The King Dethrones Queen Vashti

The book of Esther was written to explain the origin of the Feast of Purim. This excerpt tells of the first step in moving Esther into a position of power before the threat of Haman emerges.

In the third year of his [Ahasuerus] reign, he made a feast unto all his princes and his servants; the power of Persia and Media, . . . On the seventh day, when the heart of the king was merry with wine, he commanded . . . To bring Vashti the queen before the king with the crown royal, to shew the people and the princes her beauty: for she was fair to look on. But the queen Vashti refused to come at the king's commandment by his chamberlains: therefore was the king very wroth, and his anger burned in him. Then the king said to the wise men . . . What shall we do unto the queen Vashti according to law . . . ? And Memucan answered before the king and princes, Vashti the queen hath not done wrong to the king only, but also to all the princes, and to all the people that are in all the provinces of the king Ahasuerus. For this deed of the queen shall come abroad unto all women, so that they shall despise their husbands . . . . If it please the king, let there go a royal commandment from him, and let it be written among the laws of the Persians and the Medes, that it be not altered, That Vashti come no more before king Ahasuerus; and let the king give her royal estate unto another that is better than she.

Esther 1:3, 10–13, 15–17, 19; King James Version.

Pericles' Funeral Oration

*Pericles gave this speech at a funeral after the beginning of the
Peloponnesian War. He used this public occasion to state the values
of democracy.*

I shall begin with our ancestors: it is
both just and proper that they should
have the honour of the first mention
on an occasion like the present. They
dwelt in the country without break in the
succession from generation to generation,
and handed it down free to the present
time by their valour. . . .

Our constitution does not copy the
laws of neighbouring states; we are
rather a pattern to others than imitators
ourselves. Its administration favours
the many instead of the few; this is why
it is called a democracy. If we look to
the laws, they afford equal justice to all
in their private differences; if no social
standing, advancement in public life
falls to reputation for capacity, class
considerations not being allowed to
interfere with merit; nor again does
poverty bar the way, if a man is able to
serve the state, he is not hindered by the
obscurity of his condition. The freedom
which we enjoy in our government
extends also to our ordinary life. . . . But
all this ease in our private relations does
not make us lawless as citizens. . . .

. . . We throw open our city to the
world, and never by alien acts exclude
foreigners from any opportunity of
learning or observing, although the eyes
of an enemy may occasionally profit by
our liberality. . . .

. . . And it is only the Athenians,
who, fearless of consequences, confer
their benefits not from calculations of
expediency, but in the confidence of
liberality. . . .

. . . Such is the Athens for which these
men, in the assertion of their resolve not
to lose her, nobly fought and died; and
well may every one of their survivors be
ready to suffer in her cause.

. . . You must yourselves realize the
power of Athens, and feed your eyes
upon her from day to day, till love of
her fills your hearts; and then, when all
her greatness shall break upon you, you
must reflect that it was by courage, sense
of duty, and a keen feeling of honour in
action that men were enabled to win all
this. . . .

Comfort, therefore, not condolence,
is what I have to offer to the parents of
the dead who may be here. . . . Fortunate
indeed are they who draw for their lot
a death so glorious as that which has
caused your mourning. . . . Still I know
that this is a hard saying, especially when
those are in question of whom you will
constantly be reminded by seeing in the
homes of others blessings of which once
you also boasted: for grief is felt not so
much for the want of what we have never
known, as for the loss of that to which we
have been long accustomed.

. . . The state thus offers a valuable
prize, as the garland of victory in this
race of valour, for the reward both of
those who have fallen and their survivors.
And where the rewards for merit are
greatest, there are found the best citizens.

Thucydides' Peloponnesian War, Book 2.34–46, trans. Richard
Crawley (London: J.M. Dent and Co.,1903).

"Pallanteum—the Site of Rome"

Ancient Roman Poem

Then they all returned to the city, the sacred rites complete.
The king walked clothed with years, and kept Aeneas and his son
near him for company, lightening the road with various talk.
Aeneas marvelled, and scanned his eyes about
eagerly, captivated by the place, and delighted
to enquire about and learn each tale of the men of old.
So King Evander, founder of Rome's citadel, said:
'The local Nymphs and Fauns once lived in these groves,
and a race of men born of trees with tough timber,
who had no laws or culture, and didn't know how
to yoke oxen or gather wealth, or lay aside a store,
but the branches fed them, and the hunter's wild fare.
Saturn was the first to come down from heavenly Olympus,
fleeing Jove's weapons, and exiled from his lost realm.
He gathered together the untaught race, scattered among
the hills, and gave them laws, and chose to call it Latium,
from *latere*, 'to hide', since he had hidden in safety on these shores.
Under his reign was the Golden Age men speak of:
in such tranquil peace did he rule the nations,
until little by little an inferior, tarnished age succeeded,
with war's madness, and desire for possessions.
Then the Ausonian bands came, and the Siconian tribes,
while Saturn's land of Latium often laid aside her name:
then the kings, and savage Thybris, of vast bulk,
after whom we Italians call our river by the name
of Tiber: the ancient Albula has lost her true name.
As for me, exiled from my country and seeking
the limits of the ocean, all-powerful Chance,
and inescapable fate, settled me in this place,
driven on by my mother the Nymph Carmentis's
dire warnings, and my guardian god Apollo.'
He had scarcely spoken when advancing he pointed out
the altar and what the Romans call the Carmental Gate,
in ancient tribute to the Nymph Carmentis,
the far-seeing prophetess, who first foretold
the greatness of Aeneas's sons, the glory of Pallanteum.

Reprinted with permission from Toni Kline, "Pallanteum—the Site of Rome," *The Aeneid*, Book VIII, trans. A. S. Kline. http://www
.poetryintranslation.com/PITBR/Latin/VirgilAeneidVIII.htm#_Toc3637703 (accessed May 17, 2011).

The Edict of Milan

In 313 the Roman emperors Constantine I and Licinius proclaimed the Edict of Milan, which established a policy of religious freedom. This ended the persecution of Christians in the Roman Empire. The following is an English translation of an excerpt from the edict.

When I, Constantine Augustus, as well as I Licinius Augustus, fortunately met near Mediolanurn (Milan), and were considering everything that pertained to the public welfare and security, we thought, among other things which we saw would be for the good of many, those regulations pertaining to the reverence of the Divinity ought certainly to be made first, so that we might grant to the Christians and others full authority to observe that religion which each preferred; whence any Divinity whatsoever in the seat of the heavens may be propitious and kindly disposed to us and all who are placed under our rule. And thus by this wholesome counsel and most upright provision we thought to arrange that no one whatsoever should be denied the opportunity to give his heart to the observance of the Christian religion, of that religion which he should think best for himself, so that the Supreme Deity, to whose worship we freely yield our hearts, may show in all things His usual favor and benevolence.

Therefore, your Worship should know that it has pleased us to remove all conditions whatsoever, which were in the rescripts formerly given to you officially, concerning the Christians and now any one of these who wishes to observe Christian religion may do so freely and openly, without molestation. We thought it fit to commend these things most fully to your care that you may know that we have given to those Christians free and unrestricted opportunity of religious worship. When you see that this has been granted to them by us, your Worship will know that we have also conceded to other religions the right of open and free observance of their worship for the sake of the peace of our times, that each one may have the free opportunity to worship as he pleases; this regulation is made that we may not seem to detract from any dignity or any religion.

"Galerius and Constantine: Edicts of Toleration 311/313," Medieval Sourcebook, made available online by Fordham University at http://www.fordham.edu/halsall/source/edict-milan.html.

Excerpts from the Qur'an

These excerpts are translations from the Qur'an (Koran).

Selections on Good Works

101.001 The (Day) of Noise and Clamour:

101.002 What is the (Day) of Noise and Clamour?

101.003 And what will explain to thee what the (Day) Of Noise and Clamour is?

101.004 (It is) a Day whereon men will be like moths scattered about,

101.005 And the mountains will be like carded wool.

101.006 Then, he whose balance (of good deeds) will be (found) heavy,

101.007 Will be in a life of good pleasure and satisfaction.

101.008 But he whose balance (of good deeds) will be (found) light,—

101.009 Will have his home in a (bottomless) Pit.

101.010 And what will explain to thee what this is?

101.011 (It is) a Fire Blazing fiercely!

Selections on Jihad

002.190–191 Fight in the cause of Allah those who fight you . . . And slay them wherever ye catch them, and turn them out from where they have Turned you out; for tumult and oppression are worse than slaughter; but fight them not at the Sacred Mosque, unless they (first) fight you there; but if they fight you, slay them. Such is the reward of those who suppress faith.

003.169 Think not of those who are slain in Allah's way as dead. Nay, they live, finding their sustenance in the presence of their Lord.

005.082 Strongest among men in enmity to the believers wilt thou find the Jews and Pagans; and nearest among them in love to the believers wilt thou find those who say, "We are Christians": because amongst these are men devoted to learning and men who have renounced the world, and they are not arrogant.

009.029 Fight those who believe not in Allah . . . nor acknowledge the religion of Truth, (even if they are) of the People of the Book, until they pay the Jizya [a tax] with willing submission, and feel themselves subdued.

Qur'an Yusufali translation; selections on good works from Sura 101; selections on jihad from Sura 2, 3, 5, and 9. www.usc.edu/schools/college/crcc/engagement/resources/texts/muslim/quran/.

Offensive and Defensive Arms

The following narrative contains firsthand accounts of the offensive and defensive weapons used in ancient Mesoamerican cities.

Their weapons of offense are bows and arrows, and darts which they throw with a machine made of another stick. . . . They use slings which carry very far, and ordinarily carry all these weapons. It is one of the finest things in the world to see them in war in their squadrons, because they move with perfect order, and are splendidly attired, and make such a fine appearance that nothing could be better. Among them are very resolute men who affront death with determination. I saw one of them defending himself most valiantly against two light-horsemen, and another against three or four. The Spaniards seeing that they could not kill him, one of them lost patience, and darted his lance at him, but the Indian, before it reached him, caught it in the air, and with it fought for more than an hour until two foot-soldiers arrived who wounded him with one or two successful arrows. One of them got in front of him, and the other grabbed him from behind and stabbed him. While they are fighting they sing and dance, and from time to time utter the most frightful whoopings and whistlings in the world, especially when they see that they are gaining the advantage, and it is a certain fact that, to any one who had never seen them fight before, their yells and manly appearance would be intimidating. . . . They are not permitted to kill Lords, but they made them their prisoners, and carried them off well guarded. Soon afterwards they prepared a festival, in anticipation of which there are in the middle of the squares of the cities certain massive platforms of masonry, . . . and in the middle of this place is fixed a round stone, having a hole in the center. The Lord prisoner mounted, and was tied to the stone by the narrow part of the foot with a long thin cord. They gave him one of their swords and a buckler, and soon the same man who took him prisoner came to fight with him. If he again succeeded in the combat he was esteemed a most valiant man, and was given some insignia of feats of arms, and the Lord in whose service he was gave him other rewards. But if the prisoner conquered him and six others, making in all seven vanquished, he was restored to liberty, and every one who had taken anything from him was compelled to restore it.

Saville, Marshall, trans. *Narrative of Some Things of New Spain and of the Great City of Temestitan, México.* 1917. http://www.famsi.org/research/christensen/anon_con/section05.htm (accessed May 16, 2011).

The Story of Liongo Fumo

Liongo Fumo was of the ruling family in the tribe of Shaka, near what is now Mombasa, Kenya. His descendants are thought to live in the area to this day, and many there can tell his story. Shaka was founded by Persians, and its rulers took the Persian title "shah." Shaka was conquered by Sultan Omar of Pate.

Liongo, as we have seen, was of the house of the Shaka Mashah, but, though the eldest son, could not succeed his father, his mother having been one of the inferior wives. He seems, however, to have been in every way more able than his brother, the lawful Shah Mringwari. His extraordinary stature and strength, his courage, his skill with the bow, and his poetical talents have been celebrated over and over again in song and story.

***

Liongo and his brother were not on good terms. . . . It would seem as if Liongo had been living for some time at Pate . . . no doubt as a result of the quarrel with his brother. But now some one . . . stirred up trouble; "enmity arose against him," and, finding that the sultan had determined on his death, he left Pate for the mainland. There he took refuge with the forest-folk, the Wasanye and Wadahalo. These soon received a message from Pate, offering them a hundred *reals* (silver dollars) if they would bring in Liongo's head. They were not proof against the temptation, and, unable to face him in a fight, planned a treacherous scheme for his destruction. . . . They were to dine off *makoma*, (the fruit of the *Hyphaene* palm), each man taking his turn at climbing a tree and gathering for the party, the intention being to shoot Liongo when they had him at a disadvantage. However, when it came to his turn, having chosen the tallest palm, he defeated them by shooting down the nuts, one by one, where he stood.

***

The Wasani now gave up in despair, and sent word to the sultan that Liongo was not to be overcome either by force or guile. He, unwilling to trust them any further, left them and went to Shaka, where he met his mother and his son. . . . Here, at last, he was captured by his brother's men, seized while asleep . . . then secured in the prison in the usual way, his feet chained together with a post between them, and fetters on his hands. He was guarded night and day by warriors. There was much debating as to what should be done with him. There was a general desire to get rid of him, but some of Mringwari's councillors were of opinion that he was too dangerous to be dealt with directly. . . .

Meanwhile Liongo's mother sent her slave-girl Saada every day to the prison with food for her son, which the guards invariably seized, only tossing him the scraps.

Mringwari, when at last he had come to a decision, sent a slave-lad to the captive, to tell him that he must die in three days' time, but if he had a last wish it should be granted. . . . Liongo sent word that he wished to have a *gungu*

dance performed where he could see and hear it, and this was granted.

He then fell to composing a song, which is known and sung to this day:

O thou handmaid Saada, list my
    words to-day!
Haste thee to my mother, tell her
    what I say.
Bid her bake for me a cake of chaff
    and bran, I pray,
And hide therein an iron file to cut
    my bonds away,
File to free my fettered feet, swiftly
    as I may;
Forth I'll glide like serpent's child,
    silently to slay.

When Saada came again he sang this over to her several times, till she knew it by heart—the guards either did not understand the words or were too much occupied with the dinner of which they had robbed him to pay any attention to his music. Saada went home and repeated the song to her mistress, who lost no time, but went out at once and bought some files. Next morning she prepared a better meal than usual, and also baked such a loaf as her son asked for, into which she inserted the files, wrapped in a rag.

When Saada arrived at the prison the guards took the food as usual, and, after a glance at the bran loaf, threw it contemptuously to Liongo, who appeared to take it with a look of sullen resignation to his fate.

When the dance was arranged he called the chief performers together and taught them a new song—perhaps one of the "Gungu Dance Songs" which have been handed down under his name. There was an unusually full orchestra: horns, trumpets, cymbals (*matoazi*), gongs (*tasa*), and the complete set of drums, while Liongo himself led the singing. When the band was playing its loudest he began filing at his fetters, the sound being quite inaudible amid the din; when the performers paused he stopped filing and lifted up his voice again. So he gradually cut through his foot-shackles and his handcuffs, and, rising up in his might, like Samson, burst the door, seized two of the guards, knocked their heads together, and threw them down dead. The musicians dropped their instruments and fled, the crowd scattered like a flock of sheep, and Liongo took to the woods, after going outside the town to take leave of his mother, none daring to stay him.

Excerpted from Chapter 10 of *Myths and Legends of the Bantu* by Alice Werner (1933).

Songs of Japan

The emperor entertained the Imperial army with banquets. The common soldiers then sang this song. It is called a Kume song. Today, when the Department of Music in Japan performs this song, the musicians still beat out the great and small rhythms by hand, accompanying the coarse and fine notes of distinct voices.

> In the high castle of Uda
> I set a snare for woodcock,
> And waited,
> But no woodcock came to it;
> A valiant whale came to it.

After eating, the emperor and his troops set forth on their march. They attacked the eighty bandits at Mount Kunimi and killed them. During this campaign, the emperor made these verses. The great rock refers to the Hill of Kunimi.

> Like the Shitadami
> Which creep around
> The great rock
> Of the Sea of Ise
> Where blows the divine wind
> Like the Shitadami,
> My boys! my boys!
> We will creep around,
> And smite them utterly,
> And smite them utterly.

Michi no Omi no Mikoto did as the emperor commanded. He dug a pit at the village of Osaka and prepared a banquet. He hid his bravest soldiers in the pit. He then invited the enemy to come to the banquet. When Michi no Omi no Mikoto sang a song, the soldiers in the pit would know that the time was right to spring out of the pit and strike the enemy. This is the song he sang:

> At Osaka
> In the great muro-house,
> Though men in plenty
> Enter and stay,
> We the glorious
> Sons of warriors,
> Wielding our mallet-heads.
> Wielding our stone-mallets,
> Will smite them utterly.

The plan worked and all the enemy were killed. The Imperial army was delighted. They laughed after Michi no Omi no Mikoto sang this song. When the song is sung today, the singers laugh out loud after the song is done.

> Though folk say
> That one Yemishi
> Is a match for one hundred men
> They do not so much as resist.

Then Michi sang this verse.

> Ho! now is the time;
> Ho! now is the time;
> Ha! Ha! Psha!
> Even now
> My boys!
> Even now
> My boys!

Nihongi: Chronicles of Japan from the Earliest Times to A.D. 697, trans. W. G. Aston, 1896.

Christopher Columbus:
Extracts from Journal

The following is a translation of entries from the 1492 journal kept by Christopher Columbus on his voyage to the New World.

Whereas, Most Christian, High, Excellent, and Powerful Princes, King and Queen of Spain and of the Islands of the Sea, our Sovereigns, this present year 1492, . . . Your Highnesses, as Catholic Christians, and princes who love and promote the holy Christian faith, . . . determined to send me, Christopher Columbus, to the above-mentioned countries of India . . . and furthermore directed that I should not proceed by land to the East, as is customary, but by a Westerly route, in which direction we have hitherto no certain evidence that any one has gone. . . . Hereupon I left the city of Granada, on Saturday, the twelfth day of May, 1492, and proceeded to Palos, a seaport, where I armed three vessels, very fit for such an enterprise, and having provided myself with abundance of stores and seamen, I set sail from the port, on Friday, the third of August, half an hour before sunrise, and steered for the Canary Islands of your Highnesses which are in the said ocean, thence to take my departure and proceed till I arrived at the Indies, and perform the embassy of your Highnesses to the Princes there, and discharge the orders given me. For this purpose I determined to keep an account of the voyage, and to write down punctually every thing we performed or saw from day to day, as will hereafter appear.

Wednesday, 10 October

Steered west-southwest and sailed at times ten miles an hour, at others twelve, and at others, seven; day and night made fifty-nine leagues' progress; reckoned to the crew but forty-four. Here the men lost all patience, and complained of the length of the voyage, but the Admiral encouraged them in the best manner he could, representing the profits they were about to acquire, and adding that it was to no purpose to complain, having come so far, they had nothing to do but continue on to the Indies, till with the help of our Lord, they should arrive there. . . .

Thursday, 11 October

Steered west-southwest; and encountered a heavier sea than they had met with before in the whole voyage. Saw pardelas and a green rush near the vessel. The crew of the Pinta saw a cane and a log; they also picked up a stick which appeared to have been carved with an iron tool, a piece of cane, a plant which grows on land, and a board. The crew of the Nina saw other signs of land, and a stalk loaded with rose berries. These signs encouraged them, and they all grew cheerful. . . .

At two o'clock in the morning the land was discovered, at two leagues' distance. . . . The Admiral bore the royal standard,

and the two captains each a banner of the Green Cross, which all ships had carried; this contained the initials of the names of the King and Queen each side of the cross, and a crown over each letter. Arrived on shore, they saw trees very green many streams of water, and diverse sorts of fruits. . . . Numbers of the people of the island straightway collected together. Here follow the precise words of the Admiral: "As I saw that they were very friendly to us, . . . I presented them with some red caps, and strings of beads to wear upon the neck, and many other trifles of small value. . . ."

Wednesday, 17 October

. . . I strayed about among the groves, which present the most enchanting sight ever witnessed, a degree of verdure prevailing like that of May in Andalusia, the trees as different from those of our country as day is from night, and the same may be said of the fruit, the weeds, the stones and everything else. . . .

Thursday, 18 October

As soon as the sky grew clear, we set sail and went as far round the island as we could. . . .

Friday, 19 October

. . . The wind being favorable, I came to the Cape, which I named Hermoso, where I anchored today. This is so beautiful a place, as well as the neighboring regions, that I know not in which course to proceed first; my eyes are never tired with viewing such delightful verdure, and of a species so new and dissimilar to that of our country, and I have no doubt there are trees and herbs here which would be of great value in Spain, as dyeing materials, medicine, spicery, etc. . . .

Sunday, 21 October

. . . This island even exceeds the others in beauty and fertility. Groves of lofty and flourishing trees are abundant, as also large lakes, surrounded and overhung by the foliage, in a most enchanting manner. Everything looked as green as in April in Andalusia. The melody of the birds was so exquisite that one was never willing to part from the spot, and the flocks of parrots obscured the heavens. The diversity in the appearance of the feathered tribe from those of our country is extremely curious. A thousand different sorts of trees, with their fruit were to be met with, and of a wonderfully delicious odor. . . . It is my wish to fill all the water casks of the ships at this place, which being executed, I shall depart immediately, if the weather serve, and sail round the island, till I succeed in meeting with the king, in order to see if I can acquire any of the gold, which I hear he possesses. . . . And according as I find gold or spices in abundance, I shall determine what to do; at all events I am determined to proceed on to the continent, and visit the city of Guisay, where I shall deliver the letters of your Highnesses to the Great Can, and demand an answer, with which I shall return.

"Christopher Columbus: Extracts from Journal," *Medieval Sourcebook*, made available online by Fordham University at http://www.fordham.edu/halsall/source/columbus1.html.

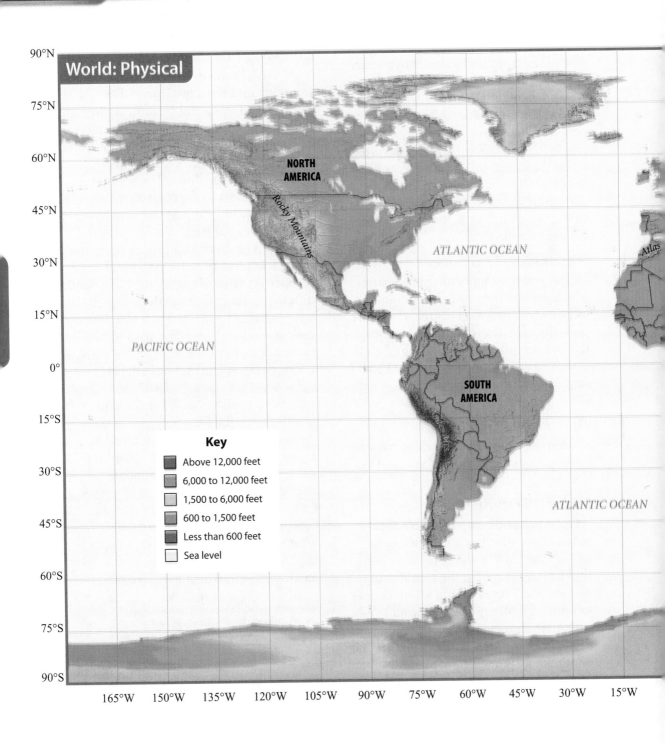

World: Physical

90°N

75°N

60°N

NORTH
AMERICA

45°N

Rocky Mountains

ATLANTIC OCEAN

30°N

Atlas

15°N

PACIFIC OCEAN

0°

SOUTH
AMERICA

15°S

Key

30°S

Above 12,000 feet

6,000 to 12,000 feet

1,500 to 6,000 feet

600 to 1,500 feet

45°S

Less than 600 feet

ATLANTIC OCEAN

Sea level

60°S

75°S

90°S

165°W   150°W   135°W   120°W   105°W   90°W   75°W   60°W   45°W   30°W   15°W

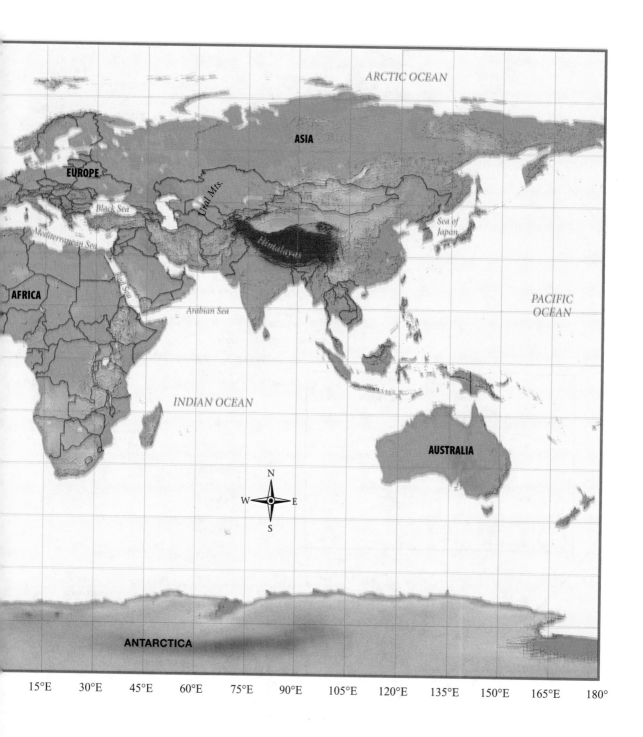

ARCTIC OCEAN

ASIA

EUROPE

Ural Mts.

Black Sea

Mediterranean Sea

Himalayas

Sea of Japan

AFRICA

Red Sea

Arabian Sea

PACIFIC OCEAN

INDIAN OCEAN

AUSTRALIA

N
W E
S

ANTARCTICA

15°E   30°E   45°E   60°E   75°E   90°E   105°E   120°E   135°E   150°E   165°E   180°

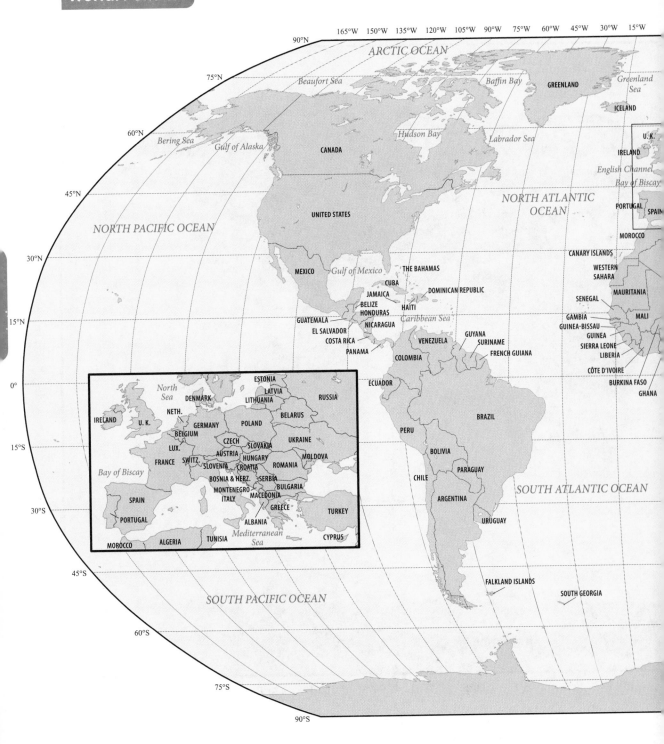

ARCTIC OCEAN

90°N
75°N
60°N
45°N
30°N
15°N
0°
15°S
30°S
45°S
60°S
75°S
90°S

165°W 150°W 135°W 120°W 105°W 90°W 75°W 60°W 45°W 30°W 15°W

Beaufort Sea

Baffin Bay

GREENLAND

Greenland Sea

ICELAND

Hudson Bay

Labrador Sea

U. K.

IRELAND

English Channel

Bay of Biscay

CANADA

NORTH ATLANTIC OCEAN

PORTUGAL SPAIN

MOROCCO

Bering Sea

Gulf of Alaska

NORTH PACIFIC OCEAN

UNITED STATES

CANARY ISLANDS

WESTERN SAHARA

MEXICO Gulf of Mexico

THE BAHAMAS

CUBA

JAMAICA

DOMINICAN REPUBLIC

BELIZE
HONDURAS

HAITI

Caribbean Sea

GUATEMALA
EL SALVADOR
COSTA RICA
PANAMA

NICARAGUA

VENEZUELA

GUYANA
SURINAME
FRENCH GUIANA

COLOMBIA

ECUADOR

MAURITANIA

SENEGAL

GAMBIA
GUINEA-BISSAU

MALI

GUINEA
SIERRA LEONE
LIBERIA

CÔTE D'IVOIRE

BURKINA FASO

GHANA

PERU

BRAZIL

BOLIVIA

ESTONIA
LATVIA
LITHUANIA

North
Sea DENMARK

IRELAND

U.K.

NETH.

BELGIUM

LUX.

FRANCE SWITZ.

Bay of Biscay

SPAIN

PORTUGAL

MOROCCO

GERMANY

CZECH

AUSTRIA

SLOVENIA CROATIA

BOSNIA & HERZ.

MONTENEGRO

ITALY

ALGERIA

POLAND

SLOVAKIA

HUNGARY

SERBIA

MACEDONIA

ALBANIA

TUNISIA

RUSSIA

BELARUS

UKRAINE

MOLDOVA

ROMANIA

BULGARIA

GREECE

Mediterranean
Sea

TURKEY

CYPRUS

PARAGUAY

CHILE

ARGENTINA

URUGUAY

SOUTH ATLANTIC OCEAN

SOUTH PACIFIC OCEAN

FALKLAND ISLANDS

SOUTH GEORGIA

430

15°E 30°E 45°E 60°E 75°E 90°E 105°E 120°E 135°E 150°E 165°E 180°

Norwegian Sea

NORWAY
SWEDEN
FINLAND

RUSSIA

North Sea
NETH.
DENMARK
ESTONIA
LATVIA
LITHUANIA
BELARUS

GERMANY POLAND
BELGIUM
LUX.
FRANCE
CZECH
SLOVAKIA
UKRAINE
AUSTRIA HUNGARY
SWITZ.
SLOVENIA CROATIA ROMANIA MOLDOVA
ITALY
BOSNIA & HERZ. SERBIA
MONTENEGRO BULGARIA
MACEDONIA
ALBANIA GREECE

KAZAKHSTAN

MONGOLIA

Sea of Okhotsk

Caspian Sea *Aral Sea*
UZBEKISTAN
KYRGYZSTAN

Black Sea
GEORGIA
ARMENIA AZERBAIJAN
TURKMENISTAN
TAJIKISTAN

Sea of Japan
NORTH KOREA
SOUTH KOREA JAPAN

TUNISIA
CYPRUS
Mediterranean Sea
SYRIA
LEBANON
ISRAEL
JORDAN
IRAQ IRAN AFGHANISTAN

CHINA

East China Sea

NORTH PACIFIC OCEAN

ALGERIA LIBYA EGYPT
KUWAIT
QATAR
U.A.E.
Gulf of Oman
PAKISTAN
NEPAL BHUTAN

TAIWAN

NIGER CHAD SUDAN
SAUDI ARABIA
Red Sea
OMAN *Arabian Sea*
ERITREA YEMEN
INDIA
MYANMAR LAOS
BANGLADESH
Bay of Bengal
THAILAND

South China Sea

Philippine Sea

NIGERIA
DJIBOUTI
SOMALIA
Gulf of Aden
Andaman Sea
CAMBODIA
VIETNAM

PHILIPPINES

BENIN
TOGO
CAMEROON
CENTRAL AFRICAN REPUBLIC
SOUTH SUDAN
ETHIOPIA
SRI LANKA
Gulf of Thailand
BRUNEI
MALAYSIA

SAO TOME
& PRINCIPE
EQUATORIAL GUINEA
GABON
REPUBLIC OF THE CONGO
UGANDA KENYA
RWANDA
DEM. REPUBLIC OF THE CONGO
BURUNDI
TANZANIA
SINGAPORE

Java Sea
INDONESIA
PAPUA NEW GUINEA

ANGOLA
ZAMBIA
Timor Sea
Arafura Sea
Gulf of Carpentaria
Coral Sea
FIJI

INDIAN OCEAN

ZIMBABWE
MALAWI
MADAGASCAR
NEW CALEDONIA

NAMIBIA
BOTSWANA
MOZAMBIQUE

AUSTRALIA

SWAZILAND
LESOTHO
SOUTH AFRICA

Great Australian Bight

Tasman Sea

NEW ZEALAND

N
W E
S

ANTARCTICA

431

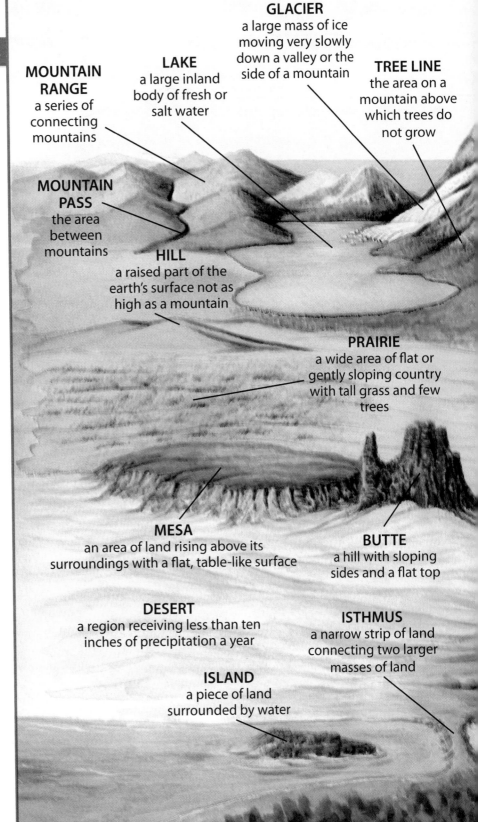

GLACIER
a large mass of ice moving very slowly down a valley or the side of a mountain

LAKE
a large inland body of fresh or salt water

TREE LINE
the area on a mountain above which trees do not grow

MOUNTAIN RANGE
a series of connecting mountains

MOUNTAIN PASS
the area between mountains

HILL
a raised part of the earth's surface not as high as a mountain

PRAIRIE
a wide area of flat or gently sloping country with tall grass and few trees

MESA
an area of land rising above its surroundings with a flat, table-like surface

BUTTE
a hill with sloping sides and a flat top

DESERT
a region receiving less than ten inches of precipitation a year

ISTHMUS
a narrow strip of land connecting two larger masses of land

ISLAND
a piece of land surrounded by water

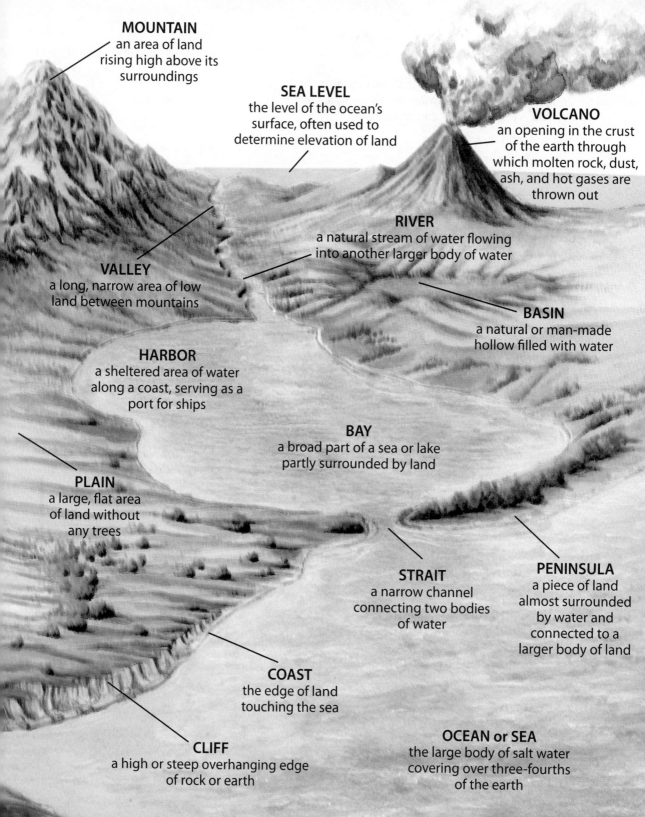

MOUNTAIN
an area of land rising high above its surroundings

SEA LEVEL
the level of the ocean's surface, often used to determine elevation of land

VOLCANO
an opening in the crust of the earth through which molten rock, dust, ash, and hot gases are thrown out

RIVER
a natural stream of water flowing into another larger body of water

VALLEY
a long, narrow area of low land between mountains

BASIN
a natural or man-made hollow filled with water

HARBOR
a sheltered area of water along a coast, serving as a port for ships

BAY
a broad part of a sea or lake partly surrounded by land

PLAIN
a large, flat area of land without any trees

STRAIT
a narrow channel connecting two bodies of water

PENINSULA
a piece of land almost surrounded by water and connected to a larger body of land

COAST
the edge of land touching the sea

CLIFF
a high or steep overhanging edge of rock or earth

OCEAN or SEA
the large body of salt water covering over three-fourths of the earth

433

Gazetteer

A gazetteer is a geographical dictionary or index. In this gazetteer, important places from this book are listed. Most descriptions are followed by the page number of a map on which that place can be located.

A

Acropolis A hill overlooking the city of Athens; the center of religious life in Athens.

Aegean Sea A sea east of Greece. (m. 199)

Aksum An ancient civilization in eastern Africa; a town in present-day Ethiopia. (m. 321)

Arabian Peninsula A peninsula in southwestern Asia between the Red Sea and the Persian Gulf. (m. 273)

Asia Minor The peninsula between the Black Sea and the Mediterranean Sea in what is present-day Turkey. (m. 42)

Aswan High Dam The man-made dam across the Nile River that formed Lake Nasser. (m. 85)

Athens A powerful city-state in ancient Greece, where the world's first democracy developed; capital of present-day Greece. (m. 199)

Atlantic Ocean A large body of water bordered by North America and South America to the west and by Europe and Africa to the east. (m. 231)

B

Babylon One of the greatest cities of the ancient world, located on the Euphrates River near present-day Baghdad. (m. 48)

Balkan Peninsula A peninsula in southeastern Europe bordered by the Adriatic, Black, Aegean, and Mediterranean Seas. (m. 271)

Black Sea A sea between Asia and southeastern Europe, located north of Asia Minor. (m. 173)

Bosporus Strait A strip of water uniting the Black Sea and the Sea of Marmara and separating Asian Turkey from European Turkey. The village of Byzantium began along this strait. (m. 259)

Byzantine Empire The Eastern Roman Empire. Its capital city was Constantinople. (m. 259)

C

Carthage A city that served as a key trade center on the North African coast of the Mediterranean Sea. (m. 237)

Caspian Sea A salt lake between Asia and southeastern Europe. (m. 173)

China A country in East Asia and the third-largest country in the world; called the Middle Kingdom by the ancient Chinese. (m. 143)

Constantinople The capital city of the Byzantine Empire; present-day Istanbul in Turkey. (m. 259)

Crete An island in the Mediterranean Sea off the coast of Greece. (m. 199)

E

Egypt An ancient kingdom and later a modern country in northeastern Africa. (m. 58)

Euphrates River A river that flows from the Taurus Mountains through Turkey, Syria, and Iraq to the Persian Gulf; a border of Mesopotamia. (m. 20)

Europe A continent to the north of Africa, separated from Asia by the Ural Mountains. (m. 364)

F

Fertile Crescent A curved area from the Persian Gulf to the Mediterranean Sea. (m. 20)

G

Ganges River A river that waters the northern plain of India. (m. 120)

Ghana 1. An ancient African empire located along the Niger River, present-day Mauritania. 2. A modern nation in western Africa. (m. 321)

Gobi Desert A desert covering most of northern China; one of the natural boundaries that protected ancient China from foreign invaders. (m. 143)

Great Wall A series of fortified barriers over 1,500 miles (2414 km) long built across northern China to keep out invaders. (m. 161)

Greece A country in southern Europe, a land of mountains, valleys, natural harbors, and hundreds of tiny islands. (m. 199)

Gulf of Mexico A body of water surrounded by Mexico, the United States, and Cuba. (m. 292)

H

Harappa A city of one of the first civilizations in the Indus Valley, the sister city of Mohenjo-Daro. (m. 120)

Hastings A town in England near the site of the battle between Harold Godwinson and William of Normandy for rule of England.

Heian-kyo The capital city of Japan after Nara; present-day Kyoto. (m. 347)

Hellespont The strait between Asia Minor and ancient Greece, the present-day Dardanelles. (m. 184)

Himalaya Mountains A mountain range in south-central Asia between Tibet and India that includes the highest mountains in the world. (m. 120)

Hokkaido One of the four main islands of Japan. (m. 347)

Honshu One of the four main islands of Japan. (m. 347)

Horn of Africa A peninsula in northeastern Africa containing present-day Somalia and adjacent countries. (m. 321)

Huang He (Yellow River) A river that begins in northern China and flows to the Pacific Ocean; sometimes called "China's Sorrow." (m. 143)

I

India A country in southern Asia, home to several ancient civilizations or empires that began in the Indus valley. (m. 120)

Indian Ocean A body of water bordered by southern Asia, eastern Africa, and western Australia. (m. 319)

Indian subcontinent A peninsula in southern Asia that extends into the Indian Ocean, separated from neighboring countries by the Himalaya Mountains. (m. 120)

Indus River A river that waters the northern plain of India; its surrounding valley was the location of the first civilization of India. (m. 120)

Ionian Sea A sea west of Greece. (m. 199)

Israel 1. The nation God made from the descendants of Jacob; named after God's special name for Jacob. 2. The name of the Northern Kingdom after Israel split into two kingdoms. (m. 97, 102)

Italian Peninsula A boot-shaped peninsula in the Mediterranean Sea, present-day Italy. (m. 231)

J

Japan An archipelago and empire in east Asia (m. 347)

Jerusalem The capital city of ancient and present-day Israel; remained the capital of Judah, or the Southern Kingdom, when ancient Israel split; sacred to Jews, Muslims, and Christians. (m. 97)

Jordan River A river east of Israel that flows through the Sea of Galilee to the Dead Sea. (m. 97)

Judah The Southern Kingdom of ancient Israel, formed when Israel split into two kingdoms after Solomon's death. Its capital city was Jerusalem. (m. 102)

K

Kalahari Desert A desert in southwestern Africa (m. 319)

Kush An ancient land along the Nile stretching from just south of Egypt to Khartoum in present-day Sudan. (m. 85)

Kyushu One of the four main islands of Japan. (m. 347)

L

La Venta One of the largest and most famous Olmec cities, located on the northeastern coast of Mexico. (m. 292)

Lake Nasser The man-made lake formed by the Aswan High Dam. (m. 85)

Lake Texcoco The lake on which the Aztec city of Tenochtitlán was built. (m. 310)

M

Madagascar An island nation in the Indian Ocean about 240 miles (386 km) off the southeast coast of Africa. (m. 321)

Mali 1. An ancient empire located in northwestern Africa. 2. A modern nation in western Africa. (m. 321)

Marathon An ancient plain in Greece; the site of the battle in which the Athenian rebel army defeated the Persian army. (m. 184)

Mecca A sacred Muslim city in present-day Saudi Arabia (m. 273)

Medina A sacred Muslim city in present-day Saudi Arabia. (m. 273)

Mediterranean Sea The sea surrounded by Europe, Asia, Asia Minor, the Near East, and Africa. (m. 18)

Mesoamerica The region that includes lands from central Mexico to Costa Rica in Central America. (m. 292)

Mesopotamia The ancient region between the Euphrates River and the Tigris River. (m. 20)

Mogadishu A trade city on the eastern coast of Africa.

Mohenjo-Daro A city of one of the first civilizations in the Indus Valley, the sister city of Harappa. (m. 120)

Mount Olympus The highest mountain in Greece, believed by the ancient Greeks to be the dwelling place of the gods.

N

Nara Japan's first capital city. (m. 347)

Nile River The river that flows from central Africa through Egypt, the longest river in the world. (m. 58)

Nineveh The capital city of the Assyrian Empire, located on the Tigris River. (m. 51)

P

Pasargadae The capital city of the Persian Empire under the rule of Cyrus the Great. (m. 173)

Pataliputra The city chosen by Chandragupta to be the capital of the Mauryan Empire. (m. 137)

Peloponnesus A peninsula that forms the southern portion of Greece; site of the Peloponnesian War. (m. 199)

Persepolis The capital city of Persia after Susa, built by Darius. (m. 170)

Persia An ancient empire in southwestern Asia in what is now Iran. (m. 173)

R

Rome The capital city of the Roman Empire and of present-day Italy. (m. 231)

Royal Road The longest stone road in the Persian Empire, stretching over 1,600 miles (2575 km) from Susa to Sardis. (m. 175)

S

Sahara The world's second-largest desert, located in northern Africa. (m. 58)

Salamis An island off the coast of Greece where the Greeks defeated the Persians in a naval battle. (m. 184)

Samaria The capital city of the Northern Kingdom of ancient Israel. The Northern Kingdom formed after Israel split into two kingdoms. (m. 97)

San Lorenzo Tenochtitlán An urban center of the Olmec civilization, which included the cities of Tenochtitlán, San Lorenzo, and Potrero Nuevo. (m. 292)

Shikoku One of the four main islands of Japan. (m. 347)

Sicily The largest island in the Mediterranean Sea; a part of Italy. (m. 231)

Sierra Madre del Sur A mountain range in southern Mexico. (m. 292)

Silk Road The trade route that stretched about 4,000 miles (6427 km) from China to the Mediterranean Sea, linking China to the nations in the West. (m. 166)

Sofala A trade city on the eastern coast of Africa.

Songhai An important town in the Malian Empire that won its independence and became its own empire near the Niger River in Africa. (m. 321)

Sparta A powerful city-state in ancient Greece. (m. 199)

Sumer One of the first civilizations in Mesopotamia. (m. 20)

Susa The capital city of ancient Persia after Darius I came to power. (m. 173)

T

Tenochtitlán An ancient Aztec city built on Lake Texcoco, one of the largest cities of its time. Part of present-day Mexico City is built on this site. (m. 310)

Thermopylae A narrow mountain pass in Greece; the site where the Greeks were defeated by the Persians. (m. 184)

Tigris River A river that flows from the Taurus Mountains through Turkey, Syria, and Iraq to the Persian Gulf; a border of Mesopotamia. (m. 20)

Tikal One of the largest and most magnificent Mayan city-states, located in modern Guatemala. (m. 292)

Timbuktu An African city in the Malian Empire that became a center of Islamic faith and learning. (m. 331)

U

Ur A powerful city-state in Sumer. (m. 42)

V

Valley of Mexico A highlands plateau in central Mexico. (m. 292, 310)

Y

Yangtze River The longest river in Asia, which flows from the highlands of Tibet through eastern China and to the East China Sea. (m. 143)

Yucatán Peninsula A peninsula extending into the Gulf of Mexico; mostly in present-day southeastern Mexico; location of several Mayan cities. (m. 292)

Biographical Dictionary

A

Abraham Man whom God revealed Himself to around 2091 BC and whose descendants became the nation of Israel.

Aesop Greek author who wrote fables.

Ahasuerus *See* Xerxes.

Akhenaton Pharaoh during the New Kingdom; tried to change the Egyptians' beliefs about many gods and believed there was only one god, Aton.

Alexander the Great Became ruler of Macedonia at the age of twenty-two; led the Greek army in conquering many lands and spreading Greek culture.

Antiochus IV Seleucid king who became ruler of Judea in 176 BC.

Archimedes Greek mathematician who advanced the lever and compound pulleys.

Aristophanes Playwright of the only surviving Greek comedies.

Aristotle Greek philosopher who devoted himself to the study of science.

Artaxerxes King of Persia and son of Xerxes; allowed the Israelites Ezra and Nehemiah to return to Jerusalem to rebuild its walls.

Asoka Ruler of the Mauryan Empire in ancient India; promoted Buddhism.

B

Basil II Byzantine emperor from 976–1025; a great warrior; also known as the Bulgar Slayer.

Belisarius Byzantine general under Justinian I.

C

Caesar, Gaius Julius Military general who became dictator of Rome; member of the triumvirate; also known as Julius Caesar.

Caesar Augustus *See* Octavian.

Carey, William British Baptist missionary to India; began missionary work there in 1793. He and other missionaries trained Indian pastors and evangelists to serve their own people.

Champollion, Jean-François Egyptologist and translator of the hieroglyphics on the Rosetta stone in 1822.

Chandragupta Maurya Indian warrior who conquered a large part of India and began the Mauryan dynasty.

Chang Heng Chinese inventor of the seismoscope.

Charlemagne King of the Franks; greatest of the Carolingian kings; extended the Frankish kingdom to its greatest size; crowned by the pope as emperor of the Western Roman Empire.

Cicero, Marcus Tullius Philosopher, lawyer, and member of the Senate who introduced Romans to Greek philosophy; an excellent orator who wrote many speeches to persuade the Senate.

Clovis First king of the Franks whose conquests shaped what would eventually become the French nation.

Confucius Chinese philosopher whose teachings greatly influenced China's classical age.

Constantine I Roman emperor who moved Rome's capital to Byzantium; legalized Christianity; also known as "Constantine the Great."

Cortés, Hernando Commander of the Spanish conquistadors who entered the Aztec city of Tenochtitlán in 1519.

Cyrus II A Persian leader who led a successful revolt against the Medes.

D

Darius I (the Great) Persian noble who helped put down a rebellion; third ruler of the Persian Empire.

David Second king of Israel; loved and obeyed God.

E

Eratosthenes Greek scholar; the first to draw lines of latitude and longitude on a map.

Esther Hebrew who was chosen to be queen by King Xerxes (Ahasuerus) of Persia and whom God used to save the Israelites in Babylon from destruction.

Euclid Greek mathematician; wrote the first geometry book.

Ezana King of Aksum in ancient eastern Africa; made Christianity the official religion of Aksum; the first to issue coins with a Christian symbol, a cross.

G

Gautama, Siddhartha Founder of Buddhism.

H

Ham A son of Noah; received a curse for his wickedness. Ham's descendants founded nations in the Far East, in Africa, and along the eastern coast of the Mediterranean Sea.

Hammurabi King of the Amorites and ruler of the Babylonian Empire.

Hannibal General of Carthage; tried repeatedly to conquer Rome during the Second Punic War; is considered one of the greatest generals in ancient history.

Hatshepsut Queen of Egypt; first woman to be pharaoh; ruled during the New Kingdom.

Henry II Last of the Norman kings of England; came to the throne in 1154; developed England's legal system.

Heraclius Emperor of the Byzantine Empire; reconquered land taken by the Persians and the barbarians; made roads in his empire safe for commerce.

Herodotus Greek historian; known as the Father of History.

Hippocrates Greek physician; famous for his contributions to the study of medicine; called the Father of Medicine.

Homer Greek poet and storyteller; author of the *Iliad* and the *Odyssey*.

J

Japheth A son of Noah. Japeth's descendants moved to what is now Turkey and eastern Europe.

Jasaw Chan K'awiil I Mayan ruler in the city-state of Tikal.

Jesus Christ God's Son; second Person of the Trinity; the promised Messiah; came to earth as a man and died on the cross to pay the penalty for the sins of mankind.

Jimmu Tenno Mythical Japanese ancestor who was believed to be the first of the Japanese emperors.

John King of England after Henry II; was forced to sign the Magna Carta because of his abuse of power.

Jonah Prophet whom God sent to Nineveh to tell the Assyrians to turn from their evil ways and follow Him.

Joseph Hebrew who was sold into slavery in Egypt during the Middle Kingdom; used by God to help the Egyptians through a famine and preserve the Hebrew people.

Josephus Jewish historian; sided with the Romans during the destruction of the Jewish temple in AD 70.

Justinian I Emperor of the Byzantine Empire; created a simplified code of Roman laws; also known as Justinian the Great.

L

Landa, Diego de Spanish priest who tried to make the Mayas accept Roman Catholicism. Much information about the Mayans is found in his writings.

Luther, Martin German monk who separated from the Roman Catholic Church and helped start the Protestant Reformation.

M

Maccabeus, Judas Leader of the Jewish revolt against the Seleucids (Syrians) in the second century BC.

Mansa Musa Malian king in ancient western Africa; known for his immense wealth and devotion to Islam; most famous of the Malian kings.

Marius Military hero who reorganized the Roman army and allowed poor citizens to enlist for long terms of service.

Mark Antony Roman general who ruled the eastern part of the Roman Empire after forming an alliance with Octavian.

Marshall, John Hubert British archaeologist who discovered and helped excavate the ancient cities of Harappa and Mohenjo-Daro in the Indus Valley in the early 1920s.

Martel, Charles High official of the Franks who led their army to many great military victories. He and his descendants ruled the Carolingian Empire.

Moffat, Robert Scottish missionary to Africa; began missionary work there in 1817; set up mission stations and translated the Bible into the local language.

Montezuma II Aztec emperor who expanded the Aztec boundaries; built many temples, canals, and hospitals.

Morrison, Robert British missionary to China; began missionary work there in 1807; the first to dress like the national people to tell them about Jesus; translated the entire Bible into Chinese.

Moses Hebrew whom God used to lead the Israelites out of slavery in Egypt; wrote the first five books of the Bible.

Muhammad Founding prophet of Islam.

Murasaki Shikibu Japanese author who wrote what is considered to be the world's first novel; a lady of the Japanese court.

N

Nebuchadnezzar II King of Babylon around 612 BC.

Nero Roman emperor who ordered many Christians to be put to death by crucifixion or burning.

Noah Man whom God saved from the Flood with his wife, three sons, and his sons' wives; directed by God to build an ark and put every kind of animal and insect in it.

O

Octavian Ruler of the western part of the Roman Empire and eventually the Roman world; also called Caesar Augustus.

P

Pepin the Short King of the Franks; son of Charles Martel; gave conquered Lombard lands to leaders of the Roman Church.

Pericles One of the leaders of the democracy in Athens; considered one of the best orators of all time.

Plato Greek philosopher who wrote books about government in the form of conversations (dialogues).

Pompey General who was popular with the Senate for his accomplishments of turning Asia Minor, Syria, and Palestine into Roman provinces and ridding the Mediterranean Sea of pirates.

Pythagoras Greek mathematician who studied geometry and came up with an important theorem about the area of triangles.

Q

Qin Shi Huang Ti Chinese emperor who began the Qin dynasty; name means "First Emperor."

R

Rameses II One of the last pharaohs of Egypt; also called Rameses the Great.

S

Samuel Last judge in Israel; anointed Saul to be king.

Sargon I Ruler of the Sumerian city-state Kish around 2270 BC; established the first empire.

Saul First king of Israel.

Shem A son of Noah; Shem's descendants were the future nation of Israel.

Shotoku Japanese prince who developed a constitution that later became the basis for laws in Japan.

Socrates Greek philosopher who encouraged his students to seek truth through human reason.

Solon Greek nobleman from Athens who wrote new laws allowing men of the lower classes to participate in government.

Sophocles Playwright of Greek tragedies.

Sulla General appointed by the Senate to command the Roman army; declared himself dictator after winning a civil war.

Sundiata King of Mali in ancient western Africa; known as the first mansa (ruler) of Mali and as the Lion King.

Sunni Ali African ruler who established the large empire of Songhai.

T

Taylor, Hudson British missionary to the interior land of China; began missionary work there in 1854; founded the China Inland Mission.

Theodora Wife of Byzantine emperor Justinian I.

Thucydides Athenian historian who recorded the events of the Peloponnesian War.

Thutmose III Became pharaoh of Egypt after Queen Hatshepsut.

Tutankhamen Pharaoh of Egypt at the age of nine; died around age nineteen; also called King Tut; known for his tomb of treasures.

V

Virgil Roman poet who wrote the *Aeneid*; considered the greatest Roman poet.

W

Wang Xizhi Chinese calligrapher; credited by some as the Father of Calligraphy.

Woolley, Leonard Archaeologist who, in the 1920s, uncovered many treasures from Ur and the land of Sumer.

Wu Ti A Chinese emperor in the Han dynasty who greatly expanded China.

X

Xerxes King of Persia; also called Ahasuerus; son of Darius.

Y

Yahweh Hebrew name for the one true God.

Yoritomo Leader of the Minamoto clan; the first shogun, the supreme military leader of Japan; set up a military government called the shogunate.

Z

Zoroaster Founder of Zoroastrianism in ancient Persia.

Glossary

A

abacus An instrument used to teach math. An abacus has a wooden frame with rows of moveable beads on it.

Abrahamic Covenant The agreement in which God promised Abraham that his descendants would become a great nation and that through them all the nations of the world would be blessed.

Achaemenid The name of the Persian dynasty that began with Cyrus II.

acupuncture A medical procedure of poking needles into the skin at certain points on the body to relieve pain or cure sickness; originated in ancient China.

agora A busy marketplace and meeting place in ancient Greece.

amphitheater A large outdoor theater.

amulet A large ornament worn on a necklace and thought to protect the wearer from evil spirits.

ancestor worship A belief that the spirits of ancestors live on in the afterworld and have powers to help or punish people who are still alive.

Angles A Germanic tribe who invaded the British Isles in the Middle Ages.

anthropologist A scientist who studies the origins of man.

apostle One of the twelve disciples of Christ; one of the early church leaders chosen by Christ.

appease To satisfy or make calm.

archipelago A large group of islands.

artisan A skilled craftsman.

Aryans Nomads who moved into the Indus Valley around 1500 and conquered the people of northwestern India. *Arya* means "noble" in Sanskrit.

Asia Minor The peninsula between the Black Sea and the Mediterranean Sea; present-day Turkey.

Assembly A group of citizens who met together to make laws in ancient Greece.

Assembly of Centuries A powerful group of patricians in early Rome.

assimilate To absorb.

atonement The restoration of the broken relationship between God and man.

Avesta The sacred writings of Zoroastrianism.

Aztec civilization A Mesoamerican society; around 1325–1521.

B

Bantu An early African people.

barbarian The name given by Romans to nomadic people who did not speak Greek or Latin and who did not adopt Roman culture.

basalt A type of volcanic rock from which the Olmecs carved giant heads.

Battle of Hastings The English battle in 1066 in which William of Normandy was victorious over Harold Godwinson; resulted in Harold's death and the ascension of William to the throne.

Black Death A fatal disease known as the bubonic plague that killed one-third of the people in Europe.

bodhisattva A Buddhist who has reached enlightenment but delays nirvana to help others reach enlightenment.

botanist A scientist who studies plants.

Brahman The great god of Hinduism; also called the "world soul."

Buddhism A religion founded by Siddartha Gautama. Buddists follow the Eightfold Path and the Four Noble Truths.

bureaucracy The managing of government through bureaus, or departments, with appointed officials.

Bushmen An African people living south of the Sahara.

Byzantine Empire The eastern part of the Roman Empire, also known as the Eastern Roman Empire; ruled first by Constantine.

C

ca. Abbreviation for *circa*, meaning "around."

calligraphy The art of fine handwriting.

canopic jar A special container for an organ of a dead body.

Carolingian Empire The Frankish empire under the rule of Charles Martel and his descendants.

cartouche An oval shape containing hieroglyphs of a name written inside.

caste A strict social class a person is born into in India.

causeway A land bridge.

cenote The name given to a deep sinkhole that the Mayans got water from.

chinampa A floating garden island made of twigs, limbs, sticks, and silt; created by the Aztecs.

chivalry A special code of behavior that taught a knight to be generous, loyal to his lord, skillful and brave in battle, faithful to the Roman Catholic Church, and protective of women.

Chou The dynasty that began ruling China around 1000 BC.

Christians Followers of Christ.

city-state A city and the surrounding land and villages it controls.

civilization A group of people who establish cities, government, social classes, specialized jobs, arts, science, written language, and religion.

clan A group of families descended from a common ancestor.

classical age A time in a civilization's history that is thought to be its high point of cultural development and achievement.

clergy Religious leaders during the Middle Ages.

coat of arms A distinctive emblem that identified a knight in battle.

codex A type of book the Mayans made.

Colosseum A large arena where events were held to entertain the Roman people.

conquistador A Spanish conqueror.

Council of Nicaea A meeting of Byzantine bishops; it defined what Christians should believe about each person of the Trinity.

covenant A binding agreement.

Crusades Religious campaigns of the Roman Church to free Jerusalem from Islamic rule.

cuneiform Wedge-shaped writing.

currency Money; any material of value that is exchanged for goods or services.

cylinder seal A clay cylinder used to imprint one's signature.

Cyrus Cylinder A cylinder seal found at an ancient Babylonian temple; contains a message about King Cyrus's respect for Marduk, the false god of Babylon.

D

daimyo Chief Japanese nobles or powerful warlords who had military and economic power to rule over their lands.

daric The coin used in the Persian empire; named after Darius I.

Davidic Covenant The agreement in which God promised to establish David's throne forever. Jesus is the fulfillment of this promise.

deity Having the nature of a god.

delta A fan-shaped area of fertile land at the mouth of a river.

democracy A form of government in which the people of the country have the power.

descendant A person whose family line can be traced to a certain person or group.

desert A region receiving less than 10 inches (25 cm) of rain a year.

dharma The duty a Hindu believer must follow to become part of Brahman.

Diaspora The scattering of the Israelites to many other nations at the time of the Babylonian captivity.

dike A wall that prevents flooding.

doctrine What a certain group believes and teaches; a belief or principle.

dominion The authority to rule.

drawbridge A bridge that can be raised or lowered to prevent or allow passage.

dynasty A line of kings or rulers who belong to the same family.

E

Edict of Milan The decree by Constantine in AD 313 that legalized Christianity.

enlightenment The act of giving someone knowledge or understanding.

epic A long poem about the actions of a hero.

Epic of Gilgamesh A Mesopotamian poem describing the adventures and eternal life of Gilgamesh, a legendary hero.

Epicureanism The belief that everything, including men, gods, and the world, is only matter and that people do not have to fear gods or what may happen after death.

etiquette Proper actions and responses that are expected in society; manners.

Etruscans An advanced ancient civilization with a Hellenistic culture on the Italian Peninsula.

Exodus The Israelites' departure from Egypt.

F

fable A story designed to teach a lesson.

Fall (of man) The breaking of God's law by Adam and Eve with the consequence of sin for them and all people.

fall of the Roman Empire The collapse of the Roman government in AD 476.

Fertile Crescent A curved region from the Persian Gulf to the Mediterranean Sea.

feudalism A system of organizing and governing society based on land and service.

fief A tract of land given by a lord to a vassal.

Franks A tribe of people who conquered Gaul.

freeman Skilled craftsman on a manor.

friar A Catholic clergyman who lived among the people, lived simply, owned no property, and taught people how to live good lives.

Fujiwara A Japanese ruling family who gained power by marrying into Japan's imperial family.

G

gatehouse A stronghold for the gatekeeper at the gate in the wall of a castle.

Gentiles A name given to Greeks and other people who are not Jews.

gladiator An armed Roman who fought animals or other men in an arena such as the Colosseum.

gospel The message of God's redemption of man through Jesus Christ.

Gregorian calendar The reformed version of Julius Caesar's calendar; now used by most countries.

griot An African oral storyteller.

H

Hagia Sophia An important and beautiful church in Constantinople.

haiku A type of Japanese poem that has a verse form with seventeen syllables and an aspect of nature or seasons.

Hammurabi's Code A collection of Mesopotamian laws written by Hammurabi.

Han The dynasty that began ruling China around 202 BC.

Hanukkah The yearly celebration by the Jews of the rededication of the temple after their victory over the Syrians.

Harappan civilization People from the ancient cities of Harappa and Mohenjo-Daro.

Hellenistic A term describing Greek culture as it spread into other lands through Alexander the Great's conquests.

hieroglyphics A system of writing made of picture symbols.

Hinduism A religion developed in India by the Aryans.

hippodrome An open-air stadium.

holy day A special day during the Middle Ages for which people were often released from work. The word *holiday* comes from this term.

Hyksos A people who invaded Egypt at the beginning of the New Kingdom; their technology included bronze and iron weapons and horse-drawn chariots.

I

icon A sacred image representing Christ, Mary, the saints, or other sacred objects.

Ides of March The fifteenth day of March on the Roman calendar; the day on which Julius Caesar was assassinated.

Iliad An epic poem of ancient Greece written by Homer.

Immortal A special soldier for the king in ancient Persia.

imperial court A group of nobles who live near, serve, and advise the ruler.

inspiration (of Scripture) God's breathing out the Scriptures, using holy men to record them.

irrigation A way of supplying water to land or crops.

Islam The religion started by Muhammad.

J

jihad A holy war fought for the cause of Islam.

Judaism The monotheistic religion of the Jews.

jury A group of local people who give a verdict on a matter in court.

Jutes A Germanic tribe that invaded the British Isles.

K

kami The gods or nature spirits of Shintoism.

kamikaze The name given by the Japanese to the typhoon that helped them defeat the Mongols; a name for a Japanese suicide pilot during World War II.

karma The Hindu belief that the result of a person's deeds, good or bad, determines a person's state in reincarnation.

knight A mounted soldier who defended a manor during the Middle Ages.

kofun A giant circular, square, or keyhole-shaped burial mound built by the Japanese aristocracy during the Yamato dynasty.

L

Latins A group of settlers from central Europe who were the first people to live in Italy.

Law of the Twelve Tables The Roman law written on twelve bronze tablets.

Legalism The belief that people are evil by nature and so must be controlled by strict laws.

legend A story that has been passed down for generations.

legion Three to six thousand military men.

linguist A scholar who studies languages.

linguistics The study of the structure and changes of languages.

lintel The beam above a door.

lord A noble.

Lord's Supper A church ordinance by which Christians remember Christ's sacrifice on the cross; the last meal Jesus had with His disciples; Communion.

lyre A type of harp.

M

Maasai African people of the Nilotic language group from present-day Sudan and South Sudan who were known for herding cattle.

magi The name for priests in ancient Persia.

Magna Carta An important document that nobles forced King John of England to sign. It limited the king's powers and guaranteed certain rights to the people.

Mahayana Buddhism The branch of Buddhism that came to China.

maize Corn.

Mandate of Heaven The Chou belief that heaven gave the king his right to rule but required him to rule righteously.

manor A large farming community during the Middle Ages.

marathon A race that is 26.2 miles long; named after a city in ancient Greece.

Mayan civilization A Mesoamerican civilization; around AD 250–900.

medieval Of or relating to the Middle Ages. The term comes from the Latin words *medius* (middle) and *aevum* (age).

mercenary A foreign soldier hired to fight for a country.

Meroitic A script language developed by the people of Kush.

Messiah The Old Testament name for the promised Redeemer, Jesus Christ.

Middle Ages A period in Europe after the fall of the Roman Empire; AD 476–1400.

Middle Kingdom The name the ancient Chinese gave their civilization because they thought it was the center of the earth.

migrate To move from one country or region to settle in another.

Minoan civilization The earliest known civilization in Greece.

moat A wide trench filled with water surrounding a castle; meant to keep out attackers.

monarchy A form of government with one ruler.

monastery A large secluded dwelling where monks live and work.

monk A clergyman who lives a secluded life of devotion and service to the Roman Catholic Church.

monotheism The belief in one god.

monsoon A wind that reverses direction with the change of season.

Mosaic Covenant The agreement in which God gave the nation of Israel His law through Moses. Through obedience to the law, Israel would be blessed and other nations would see the greatness of God.

mummy A dead body that has been preserved from decaying.

Muses The goddesses whom the Greeks believed presided over the arts.

Muslim A person who follows Islam.

Mycenaean civilization An early civilization in Greece.

myth A legend or traditional story that explains a part of nature; often about gods and goddesses.

N

New Covenant The agreement in which God promised to give His Holy Spirit and to transform the hearts of His people to love and obey Him.

Nika Revolt The Byzantine revolt under Justinian, put down by Belisarius.

nilometer A device used to measure the Nile's water levels.

nirvana The Buddist belief of a state of complete enlightenment where a person has peace and freedom from desires and wants.

nun A woman who takes religious vows of service to the Roman Catholic Church.

O

oasis A fertile area in the desert with water.

obsidian A sharp, glass-like volcanic rock that the Mayans used to make blades of tools and weapons.

Odyssey An epic poem of ancient Greece written by Homer.

oligarchy A form of government in which a few people rule.

Olmec civilization One of the earliest known Meso-american civilizations.

Olympic Games Special festivals held in the city of Olympia in Greece to honor the gods. The Olympic Games had many athletic contests, and the winners received crowns of laurel leaves.

oracle bones Animal bones or turtle shells used by the Shang in ancient China to predict the future.

oral history Stories about the past that are spoken instead of written down.

orthodox Meaning "right belief"; refers to true believers in the church who defend the truth.

Ostrogoths A Germanic tribe who set up a kingdom in Italy during the Middle Ages.

Ottomans The group of Turks who conquered the Byzantine Empire.

P

page A young boy about the age of seven in his first stage of becoming a knight. He lived in a noble's castle to learn horsemanship and fighting skills and did chores for the lord and lady of the castle.

pantheism The belief that everything in the universe is part of a supreme being.

Pantheon A temple in Rome with the largest dome in the city.

Papal States Conquered Lombard lands given to the Roman Catholic Church by Pepin the Short.

papyrus Paper made from the stems of the papyrus plant.

Parthenon The ancient Greek temple on the Acropolis; known for its many columns and optical illusions in its design.

Parthians A nomadic people from northern Persia that began retaking part of the Persian Empire around 171 BC.

Passover A Jewish celebration that commemorates the Lord's deliverance of the Jews from death and slavery in Egypt.

patrician A member of the wealthy ruling class in ancient Rome.

Pax Romana The period of peace in the Roman Empire that began with the reign of Caesar Augustus.

pedagogue A servant in ancient Greece who accompanied a boy to school to make sure he behaved well.

Peloponnesian War The war between Athens and Sparta that lasted over twenty-seven years.

Persian Wars The wars between the Persians and the Greeks.

pharaoh A ruler of Egypt.

philosopher A scholar who devotes himself to the pursuit of earthly wisdom.

pilgrimage A sacred journey.

plebeian A member of the working class in ancient Rome.

polytheism The worship of many gods.

prehistory The period when humans supposedly evolved and when there were no written records.

Protestant Reformation The religious movement that led to the forming of Protestant churches; when people separated from the Roman Catholic Church and trusted in Christ alone for salvation.

proverb A wise saying that expresses a simple truth.

Punic Wars The three major wars between Rome and Carthage.

Pygmies An African people of small stature who live in the rainforest of the Congo basin.

pyramid A large tomb constructed on a rectangular base with four sloping triangular sides.

Q

Qin The dynasty that began ruling China around 221 BC.

Qur'an (Koran) The Islamic book of Muhammad's visions, written down by his followers.

R

rabbi A Jewish religious teacher.

rainforest A tropical forest filled with huge trees and vines and a large variety of wildlife; receives annual rains of 100 inches (254 cm) or more.

rain shadow desert A lowland area that receives little rain; formed when wind blows water vapor high into nearby mountains.

redemption Christ's act of rescuing a person and freeing him from sin; salvation.

regent A person who rules in place of a rightful ruler who is unable to fulfill his duties because of age, illness, or other reasons.

reincarnation The Hindu belief that after a person dies, he comes back in another form, such as another person, an animal, or an insect.

rendering An artist's interpretation, as in a drawing or painting, of a place or an object.

republic A government ruled by law and representatives chosen by the people.

rhyton A decorative Persian drinking vessel.

Roman Forum A public meeting place in ancient Rome.

Rosetta stone An ancient tablet carved with Egyptian hieroglyphics, Greek, and other scripts; used as a key to decipher Egyptian hieroglyphics; discovered in the Egyptian town of Rosetta in 1799.

S

sacrament A religious ceremony developed by the Roman Catholic Church and believed to provide grace for salvation.

Samaritans A people in the Northern Kingdom of Israel; descendants of conquered peoples who intermarried with Israelites.

samurai A Japanese warrior whose duty was to protect the daimyo; a master of horsemanship, fencing, archery, and jujitsu.

Sanskrit The written language of the Aryans.

sarcophagus A stone coffin.

Sassanids Rulers of the Sassanian dynasty in ancient Persia; the last of the true Persian kings.

satrap A governor in Persia who ruled a particular province. The satrap was responsible for collecting tribute for Darius and reporting to him.

satrapy A province in ancient Persia.

savanna A region with tall grass and few trees.

Saxons A Germanic tribe that invaded the British Isles during the Middle Ages.

scribe A person who records information in writing.

seismoscope A scientific instrument used to predict earthquakes.

Senate The most powerful branch of the government in the Roman Republic.

Septuagint A Greek translation of the Old Testament.

serf A peasant who lived on a lord's manor, paid rent to his lord, and worked part-time for him.

shadoof A device made from a long pole with a bucket on one end and a weight on the other; used to dip water out of the Nile River.

Shang The dynasty that began ruling China around 1500 BC.

shield wall A barrier formed when medieval soldiers stood close together and held their shields tightly together as a wall.

Shintoism A form of nature worship; the main religion of Japan.

shogun A Japanese military leader who had the most political power in the government and was chosen by the emperor.

social class A group of people in society with the same social position, often determined by economic status.

social pyramid A triangle-shaped diagram that shows the social structure of a society.

squire A boy about the age of fourteen in his second stage of becoming a knight. His responsibilities included helping his master dress, accompanying him on hunts or into battles, and caring for his warhorse.

Stoicism A Greek philosophy that taught that doing one's duty brings happiness.

stucco A decorative plaster.

stupa A dome-shaped Buddhist shrine.

sultan A ruler of the Ottomans.

surplus An amount that is more than what is needed.

synagogue A place where the Jews gather for prayer, Scripture reading, and religious instruction.

T

tabernacle The portable place of worship used by the Israelites in the wilderness; symbolized God's presence with the people.

Taika Reform A series of changes in the Japanese political and economic structure around 645; known as the "Great Change."

Taoism A false religion based on the teachings of Lao Tzu. *Tao* means "the way."

tell A mound made up of layered dirt and the remains of buildings.

Templo Mayor The primary location for the Aztecs' religious ceremonies and rituals; also called the Great Pyramid.

theorem A carefully tested idea.

ting An ornate bronze vessel used in ancient China for cooking meat for sacrifices to the ancestors.

toga A loose, one-piece robe worn by citizens of ancient Rome.

trial by jury A legal practice in which a group of local people (a jury) help decide the outcome of a court trial.

trial by ordeal A legal practice during the Middle Ages in which a person had to undergo difficult physical circumstances to determine his guilt or innocence.

Tribal Assembly The assembly in ancient Rome made up of plebeians.

tribe A group of people who share common ancestors and a common culture.

tribune A leader of the Tribal Assembly in ancient Rome. Ten tribunes made up the Tribal Assembly.

Triumvirate The alliance formed by Gaius Julius Caesar, Crassus, and Pompey to rule Rome.

Trojan War The war between the Mycenaeans and the city of Troy.

Tuareg A nomadic people of the Sahara in northern Africa.

tyrant A ruler who has absolute authority.

U

universal flood A flood in which water covers the entire earth; often used to refer to the Flood of Noah's time.

untouchable An outcast from Indian society; anyone who is not a Hindu, who works with meat, or who has been expelled from his own caste.

V

vassal A person who pledged loyalty and service to a lord and managed his land in return for protection.

Vedas The sacred books of Hinduism.

Vikings Scandinavians who raided parts of Europe during the Middle Ages; also called Norsemen and Northmen.

Visigoths A Germanic tribe that invaded the western half of the Roman Empire during the Middle Ages. After being driven out of Gaul, they continued their rule in Spain.

W

worldview How a person sees and interprets the universe and everything in it.

writ A royal order.

Y

Yamato A Japanese clan that rose to power around AD 250.

Z

ziggurat A pyramid-like temple.

zimbabwe A large stone house built by the Shona people of Africa.

Zoroastrianism The main religion of ancient Persia, founded by Zoraster.

Photograph and Map Credits

The following agencies and individuals have furnished materials to meet the photographic needs of this textbook. We wish to express our gratitude to them for their important contribution.

123RF.com
Alamy
Art Resource, NY
BiblePlaces.com
BigStockPhoto.com
BJU Photo Services
The Bob Jones University Collection
Bob Jones University Museum & Gallery
Todd Bolen
COREL Corporation
Dover Publication, Inc.
Flickr
Fotolia
Getty Images
GFA
The Granger Collection, New York

Harry S Truman Library
Images of Asia
iStockphoto.com
Kunsthistorisches Museum, Vienna
Joyce Landis
Landov
Mexican Government Tourism Office
MuseumPlanet.com
Yohane Nagata
NASA
National Archives
Craig Oesterling
The Oriental Institute of the University of Chicago
Miriam Patterson
The Penn Museum

Photo Researchers, Inc.
Reading Museum
SAWDIA
Shutterstock
Skyline Software Systems
George Stouffer
SuperStock
Thinkstock
The Trustees of the British Museum
The Tuskegee University Archives, Tuskegee University
U.S. Navy
Wikimedia Commons
Wikipedia

Cover

Craig Oesterling

Chapter 1

Getty Images/Photos.com/Thinkstock 1; © Georg Gerster / Photo Researchers, Inc. 5; U.S. Navy photo by Photographer's Mate 1st Class Arlo K. Abrahamson 6 top; From the Bob Jones University Collection / BJU Photo Services 6 bottom; John Howard/Lifesize/ Thinkstock 8; Getty Images/Hemera/Think-stock 9 top, 13 bottom right; BJU Photo Services 9 bottom, 14; The Tuskegee University Archives, Tuskegee University 10 top; Getty Images / Creatas Images / Thinkstock 10 bottom, 11 top; © vlntn/Fotolia 11 bottom left; © Rony Zmiri/Fotolia 11 bottom right; Getty Images/iStockphoto/Thinkstock 13 top right and bottom left, 17; © 2003 by Dover Publication, Inc. 15

Chapter 2

© National Geographic/SuperStock 19; Courtesy of the Penn Museum, image #141575 22 top left; Billwhittaker/Wikimedia Commons GNU 1.2, CC 3.0 22 top right; © Science and Society/SuperStock 22 bottom right; © The Trustees of the British Museum 23, 28 top, 34; © Werner Forman / Art Resource, NY 24; Courtesy of the Oriental Institute of the University of Chicago 25, 35, 37, 39 top, 41, 44 bottom left, 45 top left, 46 left, 52; © SuperStock/SuperStock 27, 49 right; Bowen Collection of Antiquities, Bob Jones University Museum & Gallery 29 both; Wendy

Levine / Saudi Aramco World / SAWDIA 30 bottom; Hulton Archive / Getty Images 31 top; The Granger Collection, New York 31 bottom, 44 top, 49 left; © age fotostock/SuperStock 32 top; © Prisma VWPics / SuperStock 32 bottom; Wade Ramsey / BJU Photo Services 33; © The Trustees of the British Museum / Art Resource, NY 36 left, 40; Photo by Mansell / Time & Life Pictures / Getty Images 36 top right; BJU Photo Services 36 bottom right, 38, 45 bottom, 54; Getty Images/Hemera/ Thinkstock 39 bottom; Wikimedia Commons/CC 2.5 45 top right; © Silvio Fiore/ SuperStock 46 right; moonb007/BigStock Photo.com 50

Chapter 3

John Feeny / Saudi Aramco World / SAWDIA 55, 66 center right and bottom right; NASA / Visible Earth 56; Getty Images/iStock-photo/Thinkstock 57 top, 66 top right, 74 bottom, 78; © janthonjackson/Fotolia 57 bottom; © Eye Ubiquitous/SuperStock 59; Kunsthis-torisches Museum, Vienna 61; Todd Bolen/ BiblePlaces.com 62; Getty Images/Able Stock.com/Thinkstock 63; Getty Images/ Hemera/Thinkstock 64; © SuperStock/ SuperStock 65; Léon Cogniet / Wikipedia / Public Domain 66 top left; Nina Aldin Thune / Wikimedia Commons / CC 2.5 67 left; The Granger Collection, New York 67 right; © Marie-Lan Nguyen / Wikimedia Commons / CC 2.5 68; Tor Eigeland / The Egyptian Antiquities Organization / Saudi

Aramco World / SAWDIA 69; © De Agostini/ SuperStock 70, 83; © iStockphoto.com/Klaas Lingbeek-van Kranen 71; Bjørn Chris-tian Tørrissen / Wikipedia / CC 3.0 73 top right; © Rue des Archives / Farell / photo by Apic / Getty Images 73 bottom left; © iStock photo.com/Denys Dolnikov 74 top; Hannes Grobe / AWI / Wikimedia Commons / CC 3.0 76; Getty Images/Photos.com/Thinkstock 79; BJU Photo Services 80, 81; © James Mor-ris / Art Resource, NY 82; NASA 86 bottom; Przemyslaw "Blueshade" Idzkiewicz / Wiki-media Commons / CC 2.0 86 top

Chapter 4

Getty Images/iStockphoto/Thinkstock 87, 99; © iStockphoto.com/SimplyRecorded 88; From the Bob Jones University Collection 89; © iStockphoto.com/DHuss 91; BJU Photo Services 93, 107; Getty Images / Thomas Northcut / Photodisc / Thinkstock 95 bottom right and top left; Getty Images/Hemera/ Thinkstock 95 top right; ChrisO / Wiki-media Commons / CC 3.0 / located at the British Museum 104; Aliganjei / Wikimedia Commons / Public Domain 105 top and bottom; UPenn Library / Wikimedia Com-mons / Public Domain 106; Wikimedia Commons / GNU 1.2 107 inset; Proesi / Wiki-media Commons / CC 2.0 108 left; Deror avi / Wikimedia Commons / CC 3.0 108 right; © iStockphoto.com/Tova Teitelbaum 109 top right; © Scott Maxwell/Fotolia 109 bottom (all); © SuperStock 110; © iStockphoto.com/

Chapter 10

© iStockphoto.com/Domenico Pellegriti 257; KeRR / Wikimedia Commons / GNU 1.2, CC 3.0 258; The Yorck Project / Wikimedia Commons / Public Domain 260 top, 266 top, 267; Cristoforo Buondelmonti / Wikimedia Commons / Public Domain 260 bottom; C. Strahlheim / Wikimedia Commons / CC 2.0 262; © iStockphoto.com / Mlenny Photography / Alexander Hafemann 263; © iStockphoto.com/Duncan Walker 266 bottom; Getty Images / iStockphoto/Thinkstock 268, 279, 284 top center; © iStockphoto.com/Erdal Bayhan 269 top; BJU Photo Services 269 bottom, 276 bottom; © De Agostini / SuperStock 270; © iStockphoto.com/ Aidar Ayazbayev 274; Getty Images / Hemera/Thinkstock 277, 280; Wikimedia Commons / Public Domain 278, 288 top; PHGCOM / Wikimedia Commons / GNU 1.2, CC 3.0 281 left; REUTERS / Patrick Hertzog / Pool / Landov 283; Marie-Lan Nguyen / Wikimedia Commons / CC 2.5 284 both; Getty Images/Photos.com/Thinkstock 287

Chapter 11

Dmitry Rukhlenko / Getty Images / iStockphoto / Thinkstock 289; NASA/ GSFC/NOAA/USGS 290; Hans Splinter / Flickr / CC BY-ND 2.0 291; Madman / Wikimedia Commons / GNU 1.2, CC 3.0 293 bottom; Glysiak / Wikimedia Commons / GNU 1.2, CC 3.0 293 top; PRA / Wikimedia Commons / CC 3.0 294; BJU Photo Services 295, 300 bottom, 303 top, 309; Jupiter Images / Getty Images / Thinkstock 296; Skyline Software Systems 296 inset; Wikimedia Commons / Public Domain 298, 300 top, 313, 314, 315 both, 316; Ilona Budzbon / Getty Images / iStockphoto / Thinkstock 303 middle; Tamorlan / Wikimedia Commons / CC 3.0 303 bottom; Mexican Government Tourism Office 304; Dave Rock/Shutterstock 306; Adalberto Hernandez Vega / Wikimedia Commons / CC 2.0 307 bottom; © iStockphoto.com/Oralleff 307 top; Michel de Leeuw / Getty Images / iStockphoto / Thinkstock 308; Getty Images/Thinkstock 312 bottom; © PB/ Fotolia 312 top

Chapter 12

© James Scully/Fotolia 317; 6786381/ 123RF 318 left and background; Getty Images/Hemera/Thinkstock 320; © Bark Fahnestock/Alamy 322; © iStockphoto.com/Jan Derksen 323; © iStockphoto.com/Steve Cole 324 middle; Jack Hollingsworth / Getty Images / Photodisc / Thinkstock 324 top; BJU Photo Services 324 bottom; © Photononstop/SuperStock 325; © iStockphoto.com/Ziva_K 326 top; Andreas Lederer / Wikimedia Commons / CC 2.0 326 bottom; © Wolfgang Kaehler/SuperStock 327 top; © Nick Greaves/Alamy 327 bottom; © iStock photo.com/narvikk 329; Wikimedia Commons / CC 1.0 332; © iStockphoto .com/Jason Lugo 333; © iStockphoto .com/David Kerkhoff 334; The Granger Collection, New York 335; Ferdinand Reus from Arnhem, Holland / Wikimedia Commons / CC 2.0 336; Jan Derk / Wikimedia Commons / Public Domain 339; Joyce Landis 341 both, 342 inset/background

Chapter 13

Getty Images/iStockphoto/Thinkstock 343; Chris 73 / Wikimedia Commons / GNU 1.2, CC 3.0 344; Getty Images/Hemera/Thinkstock 345 top; National Land Image Information (Color Aerial Photographs), Ministry of Land, Infrastructure, Transport and Tourism / Wikimedia Commons 345 bottom; PHGCOM / Wikimedia Commons / GNU 1.2, CC 3.0 346 bottom, 349 left; COREL Corporation 346 top left and top right; © iStock photo.com/chrisp0 348; Wikimedia Commons / Public Domain 349 right, 350 top, 357; Marie Dubrac / ANYONE / amana images / Getty Images 350 bottom; BJU Photo Services 351 all; © iStockphoto.com/HultonArchive 352; Francesco_G / Wikimedia Commons / CC 2.0 353; Koichi Kamoshida / Staff / Getty Images News / Getty Images 354; © iStockphoto.com/Razvan 355; The Granger Collection, New York 359 top; Getty Images/Photos.com/ Thinkstock 359 bottom; Harry S Truman Library 360

Chapter 14

© iStockphoto.com/Andrew Dernie 361; © iStockphoto.com/Nicolae Popovici 362; Wikimedia Commons / Public Domain 365, 366, 367, 374, 386; Jastrow / Wikimedia Commons / Public Domain 369; © iStockphoto.com/Duncan Walker 372; © iStockphoto.com/ TT 373; Edmund Blair Leighton / Wikimedia Commons / Public Domain 375; Neosnaps / Wikimedia Commons / CC 2.0 377; © Reading Museum (Reading Borough Council). All rights reserved. 379; BJU Photo Services 383; © iStock photo.com/Michael Owen 384; © iStockphoto.com/dia karanouh 387

Chapter 15

Mykola Velychko/Hemera/Thinkstock 389; © iStockphoto.com/Dudarev Mikhail 391; Wikimedia Commons / Public Domain 392, 396, 397, 399, 401 top, 402, 403, 408 both, 409 top; From the Bob Jones University Collection 394, 400; BJU Photo Services 395; Marie-Lan Nguyen / Wikimedia Commons / Public Domain 398; LPLT / Wikimedia Commons / GNU 1.2, CC 3.0 401 bottom; © iStockphoto.com/ Alyssa Kay 406; Miriam Patterson 407; Yohane Nagata 409 bottom; GFA 410 top; GFA/Mark Vowels 410 middle; GFA/Forrest McPhail 410 bottom

Map Credits

BJU Press files 18, 89, 102, 205; Renata 3 / Wikimedia Commons / GNU 1.2, CC 3.0 229; Madman 2001 / Wikimedia Commons / GNU 1.2, CC 3.0 310; Map Resources all others